REDEMPTION

The Life of HENRY ROTH

REDEMPTION

The Life of HENRY ROTH

STEVEN G. KELLMAN

W. W. NORTON & COMPANY

NEW YORK · LONDON

For information about permission to reproduce selections from this book, write to
Permissions, W. W. Norton & Company, Inc., 500 Fifth Avenue, New York, NY 10110

Photograph of Henry Roth on frontispiece and jacket by John Mills IV.
Courtesy of John Mills V.

Manufacturing by Quebecor Fairfield
Book design by Chris Welch
Production manager: Julia Druskin

Library of Congress Cataloging-in-Publication Data

Kellman, Steven G., 1947–
Redemption : the life of Henry Roth / Steven G. Kellman.— 1st ed.
p. cm.
Includes bibliographical references (p.   ) and index.
ISBN 0-393-05779-8
1. Roth, Henry. 2. Novelists, American—20th century—Biography. I. Title.
PS3535.O787Z75 2005
813'.52—dc22

2005011979

W. W. Norton & Company, Inc., 500 Fifth Avenue, New York, N.Y. 10110
www.wwnorton.com

W. W. Norton & Company Ltd., Castle House, 75/76 Wells Street, London W1T 3QT

1 2 3 4 5 6 7 8 9 0

For Wendy

❙❘ CONTENTS ❘❙

"O villain! thou wilt be condemned into everlasting redemption for this."

—WILLIAM SHAKESPEARE,

Much Ado About Nothing, Act IV, scene 2, l. 59

THE FAMILY OF HENRY ROTH

His Father's Family Tree

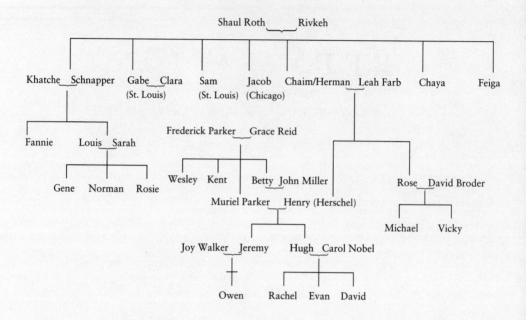

Shaul Roth___Rivkeh

Khatche___Schnapper   Gabe___Clara   Sam   Jacob   Chaim/Herman___Leah Farb   Chaya   Feiga
              (St. Louis)   (St. Louis)   (Chicago)

Fannie   Louis___Sarah   Frederick Parker___Grace Reid

Gene   Norman   Rosie   Wesley   Kent   Betty___John Miller   Rose___David Broder

Muriel Parker___Henry (Herschel)   Michael   Vicky

Joy Walker___Jeremy   Hugh___Carol Nobel

Owen   Rachel   Evan   David

His Mother's Family Tree

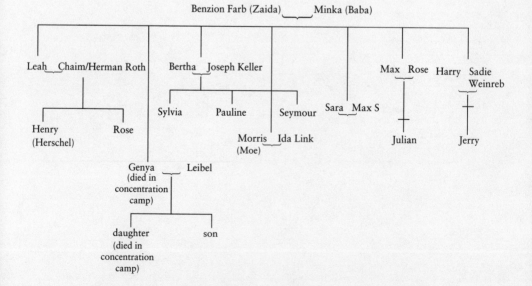

Benzion Farb (Zaida)___Minka (Baba)

Leah___Chaim/Herman Roth   Bertha___Joseph Keller   Max___Rose   Harry   Sadie Weinreb

Henry   Rose   Sylvia   Pauline   Seymour   Sara___Max S   Julian   Jerry
(Herschel)

Morris___Ida Link
(Moe)

Genya___Leibel
(died in
concentration
camp)

daughter   son
(died in
concentration
camp)

REDEMPTION

The Life of HENRY ROTH

Introduction

PILGRIMAGE

I too
Henry Roth
Call It Sleep

—VICTOR HERNANDEZ CRUZ[1]

I
T WAS CALLED Kiowa Ranch when D. H. Lawrence abandoned
Europe with his wife, Frieda, to come here in 1924. Perched at the
peak of Lobo Mountain, 8,600 feet above sea level and twenty miles
north of Taos, New Mexico, Kiowa Ranch provided the serenity that
the travel-weary Lawrence desperately craved. After fleeing his native
England at the outbreak of World War I, Lawrence had become a
celebrity vagabond, moving restlessly, ceaselessly, from one country to
the next: first to Italy, then on to Germany, Ceylon, Australia, New
Zealand, Tahiti, the French Riviera, Mexico, and finally to this
unlikely refuge. He was invited here by the proprietor, Mabel Dodge
Luhan, a much-married, gadabout socialite, patroness of the artistic
and political avant-garde of modern America. In exchange for his
gratitude, she offered Lawrence a crude pine cabin and the services of
a young caretaker named Al Bierce. It was here, on Luhan's Kiowa

3

Ranch, that Lawrence finally stopped moving, at least momentarily. It was also here that he composed numerous poems and corrected two books, *The Captain's Doll* and *Ladybird*, while accruing a volatile coterie of quarreling women whose devotion to the temperamental prophet became the stuff of literary lore.

Kiowa Ranch had been renamed the D. H. Lawrence Ranch by June 1968, when Henry Roth—famous for having written only one book more than thirty years earlier—arrived there. He was accompanied by his wife, Muriel, a composer and pianist who had relinquished her own artistic ambitions to marry and nurture a demoralized author. Owned and administered now by the University of New Mexico, the 160-acre Lawrence Ranch was offered annually as a coveted sanctuary for a visiting writer. Like the Lawrences, the Roths came to the ranch after a brief stay in Mexico. But in contrast to Lawrence, who sought to escape his fame amid the remote Sangre de Cristo Mountains, Roth was ready to embrace his. By 1968, the Lawrence Fellowship was a prestigious honor, and Roth had only recently begun to be prized as a notable novelist. Unlike the notorious author of *Sons and Lovers*, *Women in Love*, and *Lady Chatterley's Lover*, Roth came to Lobo Mountain not as an established but as a reestablished literary figure. *Call It Sleep*, Roth's only novel, had sold fewer then 2,000 copies when published in 1934 and soon fell out of print. But its reappearance in paperback in 1964 was greeted rhapsodically by Irving Howe on the front page of *The New York Times Book Review*, and suddenly Roth, an obscure waterfowl farmer in Maine, found himself the author of a best-seller written three decades earlier. New Mexico was where he would begin to write again, and where Muriel, once a student of the legendary musician Nadia Boulanger, would begin to compose again.

In 1968, a middle-aged Bierce saw to it that the Roths were cared for at the Lawrence Ranch, just as he had done for the guests who arrived in 1924. Seduced by the dry air and dramatic natural surroundings, and reluctant to endure another winter in Maine, their Spartan home for twenty-two years, the Roths stayed on in New Mexico after that summer. They moved down to Albuquerque, where both eventually ended their lengthy creative lulls.

I TOOK THE narrow, winding dirt road up to the ranch in July 2001, seventy-seven years after Lawrence arrived and thirty-three after Roth. Al Bierce, now aged and cantankerous, was still its caretaker. He had begun working for Luhan in his teens, and he continued to cherish the memory of his first employer, extolling her vitality and generosity. He remembered Lawrence well, though not fondly. "The man beat horses, children, and women," Bierce recalled.[2] He professed astonishment at the thousands of pilgrims who came to this remote spot to pay homage to Lawrence, whose ashes are buried here. Nor was he much impressed by Henry Roth, whose *Call It Sleep* he claimed he "tried to read." When I told Bierce that I intended to write Roth's biography, his response was curt. Like a Sphinx guarding the entrance to the Lawrence Ranch, Bierce challenged me with the riddle: "Why?"

The question seemed to echo like the summer thunder rumbling through the Sangre de Cristo Mountains. The challenge, as I heard it, is compounded of two other confounding questions: Why should *anyone* write about Roth? And why should I, who never even met the man, be the one to do so?

Minor figures often attract multiple biographers, yet Roth, who wrote one of the great novels of the twentieth century, still lacked a single book-length life, and the omission has been an embarrassment to American letters. "I can not think of a profile that would be as fascinating as one of Henry Roth," David Remnick wrote Roth in 1985.[3] Then a staff writer for *The Washington Post*, Remnick was attempting, without success, to coax Roth into an interview. Though profiles have appeared in many newspapers and magazines, and in editions of *Call It Sleep*, the full portrait, front and sides, remained to be painted.

Yet I sensed that defending a biography of Roth written to fill a lacuna in the ecology of publishing would not win over Bierce. And the reason left me underwhelmed as well. Any biography must itself be as compelling as the author's long, tormented life.

The task is made more daunting by a sense that all literary biography is redundant. Dante already delivers himself, more vividly than anyone else could, in his *Commedia*. Federico Fellini observed that "All art is autobiographical; the pearl is the oyster's autobiography."[4] But Roth's fictional pearls, featuring characters whose initials—and sometimes entire names—are identical to those of the author's own relatives and acquaintances, are even more overtly autobiographical than most other novelists'. While editing the last manuscripts, Robert Weil once asked Roth the real name of the louche character called Ida Link. "Why, Ida Link!" came the reply.[5] Formal disclaimers on the copyright pages of his final books—*A Diving Rock on the Hudson*, *From Bondage*, and *Requiem for Harlem*—attempt to distance the author from his fiction; but Roth might more plausibly have echoed Gabriel García Márquez's insistence about his own improbably extravagant tales: "*No hay en mis novelas una línea que no esté basada en la realidad* (There is not a single line in my novels that is not based on reality)."[6] What is left for biography to say about a man who wrote hundreds of articulate pages about himself?

Of course, the question could also be posed about Marcel Proust, whose *A la recherche du temps perdu* also straddles the boundary between fiction and autobiography, and yet it is answered by the bounteous accounts of the French novelist created by George D. Painter, Jean-Yves Tadié, and William C. Carter. Like translation, biography is repudiated neither by competing renditions nor by autobiography. Many versions of Henry Roth remain to be told. Mine is the story of a Galician Jewish transplant who in 1964, at age fifty-eight, suddenly became famous for being unknown. Thirty years after its publication, *Call It Sleep* was rediscovered as the classic of immigration fiction, a brilliant attempt to adapt Joycean techniques and Freudian insights to American experience, the finest of the proletarian novels of the 1930s, and the harbinger of American Jewish literature after World War II. If, as Hemingway quipped, all modern American literature begins with *Huckleberry Finn*, American Jewish literature could, with slight exaggeration, be said to stem from *Call It Sleep*. Today, the novel is admired for its pioneering embodiment of multiculturalism and multilingualism. Its author was abruptly thrust out of obscurity as a wildfowl farmer in Maine and into the literary canon, a figure revered by readers and scholars not just in the United States but in Italy, Spain, France, Germany, Israel, the Netherlands, and many other countries as well.

Like Ralph Ellison, Roth suffered a legendary writer's block, ostensibly becoming a textbook demonstration of F. Scott Fitzgerald's remark that American lives lack second acts. In fact, Roth's long life (1906–1995) offers enough acts to please the most prolix of playwrights and to challenge the most assiduous of biographers. In 1994, sixty years after *Call It Sleep*, Roth finally published his second novel, *A Star Shines Over Mt. Morris*. It was the first installment in a projected series of six volumes that, despite crippling arthritis, Roth struggled heroically to complete before he died, on the eve of his ninetieth birthday. The first four of those volumes have been published, under the collective title *Mercy of a Rude Stream*. Through physical and emotional agony, completion of the task brought Roth redemption at last.

"Nobody can write the life of a man, but those who have eaten and drunk and lived in social intercourse with him," declared Samuel Johnson.[7] I never met Roth, but after publishing a few pieces on his work, I was approached by his editor, Robert Weil, and his agent, Roslyn Targ, with the suggestion that I become his biographer. I did not jump at the chance but away from it. For a year and a half, I pondered the many reasons that I, trained originally in the New Criticism to trust the tale and not the teller, ought not to proffer chatter about the author of *Call It Sleep*. Busy with other projects, I was wary of sacrificing a few years of my own life to Roth's extended, tormented one, and I was anxious about the added responsibility of being the first biographer, the one who sets the terms of a continuing conversation.

I had initially read *Call It Sleep*—avidly, compulsively—in 1964, in the new Avon round-cornered paperback with the photo of a tenement that bleeds off the cover. The story seemed written in my blood, which also flows from Eastern Europe. It was the start of winter break, and, sitting in the back of a bus returning me from college to my own family, I lost myself in David Schearl, the young protagonist. Though I was then ten years older and two generations younger, David's brutal domestic drama could have been my own. My grandparents—whom I related to more easily than their children—came, like the Schearls, from Galicia, and they too became Americans on the Lower East Side. But you do not have to be Jewish to absorb the novel's transcendent power. I have taught *Call It Sleep* to a wide variety of students, in California, Israel, Soviet Georgia, Bulgaria, and Texas, and I marvel at how many readers recognize their own experience in Roth's account of dislocation and dread. If biography demands elective affinity with the subject, then I was qualified to write about Roth, but so, too, were many others. Why had the biography remained unwritten?

I became convinced that someone had to do it, and soon, while it was still possible to speak with people who knew Roth. Like Emily Dickinson, the sacred eremite of American poetry, or Edgar Allan Poe, the boozy pedophile and connoisseur of the macabre, Henry Roth had been mummified into legend. His popular (unwritten) biography was a portrait of the artist as a young man shattered by indifference to his early masterpiece. This self-taught Roth abjured his rough magic to rusticate in Maine for thirty years, until a miraculous rediscovery suddenly brought him fame, fortune, and a passion to resume writing, which he did in a final fierce creative sprint. He became the proverbial Rip Van Winkle of modern authors.

This myth of Roth as American literature's spurned prodigy, whose debut was dazzling and departure luminous but whose center was a black hole, distorts and simplifies the truths of a complex life. Roth in fact received enthusiastic reviews for his first book, signed with the celebrated editor Maxwell Perkins to produce a second book, and kept on writing, even publishing stories in *The New Yorker*, during the "silent" years. He was a far more complicated—and interesting—figure than his legend would admit. Mooring Roth (whose first years in America were actually passed in Brooklyn) on the Lower East Side, where he spent just four of his eighty-nine years, is no more accurate than anchoring Thoreau (whose sojourn lasted only two years) in Walden Pond. Moreover, Roth's occupations would have to include not only novelist and waterfowl farmer but also newspaper peddler, messenger, bus conductor, soda pop vendor, plumber's assistant, ditchdigger, English teacher, precision tool grinder, firefighter, maple syrup vendor, blueberry picker, woodcutter, psychiatric hospital attendant, and tutor in math and Latin. He moved from a secularist belief in internationalist communism to Zionism and a renewed embrace of his Jewish identity. And Roth's life is haunted by painful memories of incest with his sister and a cousin—a guilty secret that is crucial to understanding his literary paralysis and his final quest for regeneration.

Yet an effective biography must also pay attention to the shifting landscape of American literary culture throughout the twentieth century. Born in Tysmenitz, Galicia (a historically contested region of Austria-Hungary), he was brought to New York before his second birthday in the tidal wave of immigration that crashed into America's shores before World War I and utterly transformed its society. *Call It Sleep* must be understood not only as a prototype of immigration fiction but also as a creature of the social aspirations and disappointments of the 1930s. Its wildly fluctuating reception offers a case study in the fickle mechanism of literary reputations, in the eclipse of cultural leftism, and in the invention of ethnicity. The rehabilitation of Roth—due primarily to the efforts of Harold U. Ribalow, Leslie Fiedler, Irving Howe, Alfred Kazin, Roslyn Targ, and Peter Mayer—cannot be understood apart from the validation of American Jewish literature and the need to anoint an exemplary ancestor to Saul Bellow, Bernard Malamud, and Philip Roth.

While critics rejoiced in the discovery of what they considered the "missing link" to contemporary American Jewish literature, Roth himself despaired of finding any clear or logical pattern to his own existence. In the posthumously published *From Bondage*, Roth's alter ego, Ira Stigman, puzzles over the "grave and disabling discontinuity"[8] that followed the completion of his ambitious first book.

Brought as an infant out of Eastern Europe and wrenched, as he saw it, as a boy from the Lower East Side, Roth perceived his own life as utterly disconnected, constructed like Frankenstein's monster from disparate shards of experience. How does one reconcile the misanthrope slaughtering waterfowl in rural Maine with the gregarious young Village radical who mingled with many of the era's most influential intellectuals and artists? And how to reconcile these with the arthritic old man in Albuquerque who yearned for death while conjuring up his life? The challenge Roth faced in writing his autobiographical opus—in which the octogenarian author Ira Stigman frequently interrupts and competes with the story of Ira in his teens and twenties, bifurcating narrator and protagonist—was to find a figure in the tattered carpet that covers the dust of almost nine decades. Of course, the prospect of finding subtle continuity amid the fits and starts of any human life is the Grail of all biography. It is particularly elusive when the subject is Roth. Yet I found Roth's dying struggle to make connections inspiring enough to enlist me in the effort. I approach Henry Roth not as a puzzle to be solved but as a mystery to be pondered.

A clue to continuity can be found in a letter Roth sent shortly before *Call It Sleep* was first reissued in hardcover by Pageant Books in 1960. Discussing his inability to write another book, he told Harold U. Ribalow, a literary impresario who was instrumental in finding a new publisher for Roth's neglected novel, "There is one theme I like above all others, and that is redemption, but I haven't the fable."[9] In 1994, sixty years after *Call It Sleep*, Roth finally found his fable, in his second novel, *A Star Shines Over Mt. Morris*, which aroused widespread interest and brought immense personal satisfaction. It was the first installment in Roth's final, courageous, redemptive effort to complete the cycle conceived under the collective title *Mercy of a Rude Stream*.

A quest for redemption is the fable that denies the discontinuities of a life afflicted by chronic depression. It is the tie that binds one fragment to the next. Roth's fiction affirms that he suffered from self-loathing; but so does his silence. For sixty years, shame kept him from

extending his fable beyond the ordeal of a hypersensitive little immigrant boy. Yet redemption is also the engine that drives much of his
later fiction, and the quest for continuity is the only thread he found
to link a patchy life. So disappointed in himself that he welcomed
death, Roth used his later writing to exorcise his revulsion. From Galicia to New York to Maine to Albuquerque, the arc of Roth's eighty-
nine years was classic in both its abomination and its cathartic
redemption. His final, excruciating effort at expression gave life to his
self-loathing, even as it put to rest an old man's mortal pain.

I ACCEDED TO the proposal by Robert Weil and Roslyn Targ, and
Roth's editor became my editor, his agent my agent. Roth's executor,
Larry Fox, has also encouraged this project, ensuring access to the
eighty-two cartons of Roth Papers housed in the archives of the American Jewish Historical Society in New York. Additional papers,
including the manuscript of *Call It Sleep* scrawled on college blue
books from New York University supplied to Roth by Eda Lou Walton, are located in the Berg Collection and the Manuscripts and
Archives Division of the New York Public Library. I am grateful to the
staffs at both institutions for their courteous, efficient assistance.
Throughout the years in which the New Criticism discouraged
research into authors' lives, agents of the Federal Bureau of Investigation maintained the tradition, if not the standards, of biographical
scholarship. Responding to requests under the Freedom of Information Act, the FBI, which kept Roth under sporadic surveillance for
two decades, provided me with documents recording his political
activities.

I am particularly grateful to Felicia Jean Steele, who worked closely
with Roth in the final years, for guidance on the man and his manuscripts. Her careful reading of an earlier draft kept this book from
more errors than it no doubt has. While ambivalent in many ways
about his father, Hugh Roth, the younger son, has been extremely
helpful and forthright in responding to my questions and supportive
in supplying necessary documents. David Bennahum, Roth's physician

and friend, and his wife, Judy, served as gracious guides to Albuquerque, New Mexico, as Roth knew it during his last twenty-seven years. My friend and colleague Bonnie Lyons published the first book-length study of Roth, *Henry Roth: The Man and His Work* (New York: Cooper Square, 1976), and generously allowed me access to her taped conversations with him. I am also indebted to the following people for sharing their parts of the story: Rudolfo A. Anaya, Ben Belitt, Ruth Bookey, Ted Bookey, Daniel Cil Brecher, Stanley Burnshaw, Avery Cheser, Bill Daleski, Grace B. Davis, Morris Dickstein, Vicky Elsberg, Brian Errett, Julian Farb, Elizabeth Frank, Alan Gibbs, Sam Girgus, Peter Gregory, Noah Harris, Rosalie Heller, Suzanne Henig, Shirley Kaufman, Peter Lataster, Petra Lataster-Czisch, Lesley M. Leduc, Philip Levine, Penny Markley, Peter Mayer, Leonard Michaels, John Miller, Helen Mitchener, Pauline Nadler, Meir Ribalow, Virginia Ricard, Carole Roth, Chris Schultis, Leslie Schultis, Dorothy Silfen, Carla Silver, James Thomson, Allen Tobias, Gerald Vizenor, Joy Walker, James Weaver, Scott Wilkinson, John A. Williams, Lori Williams, Hana Wirth-Nesher, and Digby Wolfe.

The University of Texas at San Antonio provided me with invaluable release time from teaching in the form of a Faculty Development Leave and a Faculty Research Grant. Welcome support also came from the National Endowment for the Humanities in an "Extending the Reach" grant, and from the S. T. Harris Foundation. I owe debts of gratitude to Larry Fox for his continuing advice and assistance; to Tom Mayer, a resourceful editorial assistant at W. W. Norton; to Micah Fitzerman-Blue, an assiduous editorial intern at Norton; and to my copy editor, Ann Adelman. But most of all, I cannot thank Roslyn Targ and Robert Weil enough for their contributions to Henry Roth's life, and for their support, from beginning to end, of this literary life.

Despite the cooperation I have received from Roth's executor, editor, agent, and many members of his family, this is not an "authorized" biography. There is no need to wax Roth, a man who reveled in revulsion. Nor is there need to denigrate a courageous author who, anxious for redemption and burdened throughout his life by irredeemable guilt, was harsher toward himself than any observer could be. This biography is not likely to please Al Bierce, who, inhaling the clear air of the mountains above Taos, disdained turbid literary fervor. Unlike D. H. Lawrence, Henry Roth did not beat horses and women, but he did beat the long odds against literary renown.

—Steven G. Kellman
San Antonio, Texas
October 2004

Part I

Chapter 1

"ANOTHER WORLD"

כל ההתחלות קשות

(All the beginnings are difficult).

—INSCRIPTION BY HENRY ROTH IN A NOTEBOOK USED
TO TEACH HIMSELF HEBREW, 1978[1]

SIXTEEN-YEAR-OLD Chaim Roth made his way alone, by foot and by train, from Tysmenitz to the North Sea coast. The journey from this Galician town, where 36 percent of the seven thousand residents were Jewish, took six days. A fugitive from his tyrannical father, Shaul Roth, Chaim was now on his own, headed for America, which he envisioned as the land of freedom. A restless, querulous, scrawny little fellow whose height did not exceed five feet one, Chaim dreamed of playing fiddle for a klezmer ensemble: the jazz of Eastern Europe might endow a diminutive, restless Jewish lad with stature and power. However, Shaul Roth, who managed a distillery for a wealthy baron, had more practical intentions for his youngest son—apprenticeship to an artisan in wrought iron. In that iron, however, young Chaim foresaw the shackles that would confine him for the rest of his life if he did not take immediate action. Two of his brothers, Gabe and

Sam, had already gone off to the United States, starting anew in the burgeoning midwestern city of St. Louis; a third brother, Jacob, had settled in Chicago. If they had marshalled the resolve to break free of Galicia, Chaim knew that he could, too.

Located along a tributary of the Dnieper River at the edge of the Carpathians ninety miles south of Lvov (then Lemberg), in a contested parcel of Europe that switched flags so frequently they had no time to become tattered, Tysmenitz had long been a part of Poland. In 1772, it was appropriated by Austria; later, after the last remaining Roths, Chaim's sisters, Chaya Scheiner and Feiga Ritzer, were exterminated by the Nazis, it would be absorbed by the Soviet Union. Today, it lies within the borders of independent Ukraine.

Galicia had long been a place where cultures and melodies collided. But even as the larger population slowly opened up to the trickle of modernization, many in the Jewish community tried to insulate themselves from the pollutants of the goyishe world. Changes were occurring, invisibly, yet Jewish Galicia at the end of the nineteenth century to an outsider might not have seemed noticeably different from Jewish Galicia at the end of the seventeenth. Nevertheless, a dramatic transformation occurred in the mid-nineteenth century, when socialism, Zionism, and secularism began to draw the Jews of Eastern Europe onto the world stage. The birth of Jacob Freud in Tysmenitz in 1815 heralded one of many changes in the way Jews thought. Roth family lore would later claim his son Sigmund as distant kin.

By the time of Chaim Roth's birth, in 1882, Tysmenitz was known as a center of Haskalah, the Enlightenment movement that was attempting to inject the values of rationalism and modernism into Ashkenazic culture. Its proponents were known as *Maskilim*, or "enlightened ones," and while insisting on respect for traditional Jewish worship and study, they embraced the spirit of reform blowing in from the West. The Haskalah movement made it easier for Shaul Roth to relate to the Gentile baron whose beer he brewed. For Chaim, a taste of modernity only whetted his appetite for more.

Conditions within the Austro-Hungarian Empire were not nearly as oppressive as in the Russian Pale of Settlement, where tsarist authorities instigated deadly pogroms, yet a Jew from Tysmenitz still faced hostile Gentiles and severe restrictions in employment and education. And Jewish fathers like Shaul Roth could demand unconditional obedience from their restive sons. But in part because of the lurid Wild West novels of Karl May, the most widely read author ever to write in German, at the turn of the twentieth century the United States seized possession of the European imagination. Stories about Andrew Carnegie, a poor Scottish immigrant who managed to amass one of the world's largest fortunes, circulated widely. "To the Eastern Jew, the West signifies freedom, justice, civilization, and the possibility to work and develop his talents," wrote another literary Roth from Galicia, the novelist Joseph Roth, who died an alcoholic in Paris in 1939. Observing the shtetls of Eastern Europe after World I, Roth noted: "Here Jews live in dirty streets and collapsing houses. Their Christian neighbor threatens them. The local squire beats them. The official has them locked up. The army officer fires his gun at them with impunity."[2] The land of Buffalo Bill and Thomas Alva Edison beckoned as a vast New World of open borders and immense opportunity. Horatio Alger's popular novels insisted that pluck and luck were the sole limits to accomplishment. Chaim's older brother Gabe had become a *makher*, a veritable big shot, in St. Louis. Sam was also living there after defying their father's wrath and running off with another man's wife. Chaim longed to set out for America. After mustering enough courage to pilfer the money from the despotic, parsimonious Shaul, he too slipped out of Tysmenitz, heading west.

Beyond the exhilaration of being at last on his own, it was a lonely experience for a runaway teenager to make his way overland to the Dutch port of Rotterdam and then, ignorant of the local language, to negotiate passage on the Holland America Line's *Maasdam* across the Atlantic Ocean. But Chaim Roth was hardly alone. Between 1881, the year in which the assassination of Tsar Alexander II triggered anti-Semitic repression and violence, and 1924, when the isolationist Johnson-Reed Act set stringent new quotas against "non-whites"— those coming from parts of Europe that had rejected the Protestant Reformation (most Asians had always been excluded)—more than 28 million immigrants attempted to start their lives afresh by crossing the Atlantic. Most came from eastern and southern sections of the continent—Russia, Poland, Italy, Greece, Romania, Hungary.

Chaim's voyage took more than a week, and a country boy's initial thrill at sailing on the open sea was soon dispelled by nausea, squalor, and boredom. On September 6, 1897, the *Maasdam* entered New York Harbor. On its way to Ellis Island, the ship glided past the Statue of Liberty, a gift from France only eleven years earlier. It is tempting to imagine that Chaim stood on deck to see the Statue of Liberty—his adolescent body trembling with the promise of a new life that seemed to be embodied in this colossal emerald monument. But it is more likely that Chaim saw only the dank and cramped interior of the steerage hull. Not until he disembarked at Ellis Island (which in 1892 had replaced the cramped Castle Garden processing center at the tip of lower Manhattan) could Chaim glance up to see the statue that now loomed over the line in which he stood for hours awaiting admittance to New York. The solitary greenhorn from Tysmenitz knew no one in the city and did not speak its language; yet his arrival added one more body to the total of 2.5 million Jews—more than a third of European Jewry—who emigrated to the United States within four decades. Even Sholem Aleichem, the beloved voice of Yiddishkeit, left Europe for New York in 1914, two years before his death.

By the time Ellis Island ceased operations in 1924, 12 million foreigners would have entered the United States through it after detention, inspection, and registration. During its busiest period, from 1898 to 1915, the center processed as many as five thousand new arrivals in a single day. *An American Tail* (1986), Don Bluth's animated feature about a family of Russian Jewish mice who arrive in New York in 1885, has a scene in which disdainful bureaucrats cavalierly change the names of immigrant mice to something easier for them to pronounce. Tanya Mousekewitz emerges from the process as Tillie. In fact, translators were available at Ellis Island; many of the clerks were themselves foreign-born, and they in any case filled out entry papers by transcribing information directly from the ship's registry. Name changes were more likely to have occurred at the port of embarkation or else at an immigrant's request. Whatever the circumstances, when he emerged from Ellis Island, Chaim Roth, whose first name was the Hebrew word for "life," began new life in America anglicized to Herman. His one-syllable surname, derived from a Middle High German word for "red" and doubtless a red-haired ancestor, remained. Herman's brown-haired son would perpetuate the family name.

He had traveled far through space but also through time. New York City, which absorbed the sovereign municipality of Brooklyn as one of its five boroughs in 1898, seemed to embrace the coming century more passionately than any other place on earth. A greenhorn from gas-lit Galicia who arrived in New York in 1897 might encounter motion pictures, automobiles, electric stoves, and even comic strips and zippers, all for the first time. He might have paused before the pushcart from which Italian immigrant Italo Mariony was selling ice cream in the conical waffles he had invented just the year before. Within a few years, vacuum cleaners, washing machines, radio receivers, refrigerators, paper clips, and cellophane would be showing up in New York, decades before they reached Tysmenitz. During the profound social transformations of the late nineteenth century, New York had overtaken Boston as the engine of American culture and—as F. Scott Fitzgerald maintained in 1921 in a letter to Edmund Wilson—was supplanting London as the global "capital of culture."[3] When he stepped off the ferry from Ellis Island, a lad from Tysmenitz effectively stepped into *yene welt*, some other world that operated according to the laws of a frenetic physics as yet unknown in Eastern Europe. Young Herman's reaction was less euphoria than vertigo. Overwhelmed by the tumult of New York from the moment he arrived, and unable to find suitable employment, he contacted Gabe and Sam in Missouri. Gabe sent him money to join them in their adopted city, "The Gateway to the West." Young Roth was soon traveling again, unaccompanied on his long train journey except perhaps by flittering images of Winnetou, May's fierce Apache warrior. St. Louis was at that time rebounding from the worst disaster in its history, a cyclone that, in the space of fifteen minutes on May 27, 1896, destroyed or damaged more than 8,800 buildings and left 38 victims dead. But the catastrophe was only a temporary setback to the half million people who inhabited the fourth largest city in the United States.

St. Louis in those years was run by its second consecutive Republican mayor, Henry Ziegenhein. His predecessor, Cyrus P. Walbridge, was a reformer who had tried to clean up the spoils system of the Democrats by establishing procedures for hiring city employees on the basis of merit; yet there were still abundant opportunities to use political connection for personal advantage. Defying religious discrimination, Gabe Roth was becoming a power player in the local Republican Party, and he was later able to provide his brother Sam, as well as Sam's son, with positions in municipal government. Eager to expand his influence and register another Republican voter, Gabe persuaded Herman to apply, fraudulently, for American citizenship. Pretending to be twenty-one (he was not yet eighteen), Herman Roth swore allegiance to the United States of America on September 25, 1900. His son would derive his own citizenship from Herman's naturalization.

As a (somewhat) legal citizen, Herman was eligible for a wider range of employment. Gabe managed to place his brother with one job after another. Bullheaded, impetuous, reluctant to submit to another's authority, Herman would not be satisfied, and he would never be able to maintain steady employment. It especially rankled him to have to rely on Gabe. Nothing seemed to please the fitful younger brother, who seethed under the strict supervision that Gabe insisted on maintaining. But the young man had not escaped bondage to Shaul Roth in Galicia in order to be enslaved by Gabe Roth in Missouri. Their falling out would mean more than a decade of silence between the two brothers.

In 1902, Herman set off for New York to control his own fate. It was not the work that troubled him, Herman believed, but the fact that he had to answer to Gabe—the fact that he could not take charge of his own fortunes. Success in New York would secure his future in America. Far from both Tysmenitz and St. Louis, he could set his own terms for how he lived his life.

In short time, he failed, establishing a pattern of bungling that would characterize the rest of his life. The circumstances are not clear, but Herman, his English still shaky, struggled for a foothold in Manhattan entirely on his own. He was suspicious and peevish, loath to take direction but all too quick to take offense. Resentment battened on disappointment, and disappointments for immigrants in New York were as plentiful as needles in a sweatshop. Sweet may be the uses of adversity, but adversity further soured Herman Roth, who, choking on the pride he swallowed, returned to Galicia.

In 1903, a defiant Herman metamorphosed back into the compliant Chaim and reported for duty at Shaul Roth's distillery in Tysmenitz. But once back in the old country, Chaim found himself facing a crisis. During his travels, the young Galician Jew had neglected to register for Austrian military service. Chaim had assumed that in New York and St. Louis he was beyond the reach of Viennese authorities and that his American citizenship would protect him from conscription into a European army. Once back in Tysmenitz, however, he was arrested and thrown into jail. Though released after a few nights of sharing a cell with three other men, he realized that only marriage and paternity could exempt him from military service. Instead of another stint in prison, he consented to a life sentence in the brig of matrimony.

IN NEARBY VELJISH, twenty-two-year-old Leah Farb had incurred the wrath of her father, Benzion, a stern, observant Jew who ran a general store. She had fallen in love with a goy. Though their insular world was on the verge of collapse, the Jews of Eastern Europe had maintained their distinct identity and survived physically by keeping to themselves. The lands of their prolonged exile were controlled by Christians taught to believe that Jews were aberrant, deicidal people who must eventually either convert or disappear. It was much safer for a Jew to trust only in the tribe. Exogamy meant sleeping with the enemy, a betrayal of the traditions that enabled Jews to remain Jews, that they had cherished and preserved throughout two millennia of wandering and persecution.

Leah Farb's predicament echoes a 1905 installment in Sholem Aleichem's famous cycle of Yiddish stories about Tevye the Dairyman. Chava, Tevye's favorite daughter, secretly marries a devout Christian. Tevye is inconsolable, and the effect on the entire family is devastating. Refusing ever to have anything to do with his beloved Chava again, her father sits *shiva*—the ritual seven days of mourning—for her as if she had died. Leah Farb's forbidden romance was a similar *shande,* or disgrace, one that threatened the futures of all her nine unwed siblings. The only way to minimize the damage to the pious Farb family was to marry off the tainted *maidele*, already approaching an age when girls ceased to be marketable, to a Jewish boy as soon as possible. Chaim/Herman Roth, himself a problem to his parents, was conveniently available, and he was soon induced to sign a *ketubah*, a wedding contract.

The *shadkhan* (matchmaker) was as essential as the rabbi and the *shokhet* (ritual butcher) to traditional Jewish communities. The enduring union between Sholem Aleichem's Tevye and Golde was an arranged one, though the freely chosen love matches preferred by most of their daughters reflect dramatic changes in shtetl life at the end of the nineteenth century. Despite its origins in strategem, not passion, Tevye and Golde's alliance matured into a marriage built on trust, affection, even love. But the marriage arranged between Chaim Roth and Leah Farb in real life was a continuing calamity, an abusive relationship poisoned at the outset by the personal regret and rancor that accompanied each party to the altar and the bedroom. A long and early separation when the groom went to America and the bride remained in Europe living with in-laws she disliked further handicapped the couple's prospects. The wedding was contrived in such haste that, though a rabbi presided over the ceremony on January 10, 1905, the couple neglected to file any documents with the civil authorities, so that their union was technically illicit. According to strict interpretation of secular law, their offspring would be *mamzers*— bastards.

Whatever its legal status, when Chaim Roth and Leah Farb met under the ritual canopy, their match was made in Galicia, a long fall from heaven. Love never had a chance to transform strangers into soul mates. Though it lasted fifty-five years, the marriage remained a mixture of oil and fire. The spouses were separated by only two years in age but eons in temperament. Leah was a romantic, predisposed to disappointment, and she found much to be disappointed about in her blundering husband. The birth of their first child, Herschel, on February 8, 1906, did not reconcile husband and wife. (The name Herschel was Americanized to Henry in New York; in order to enroll the child in public school before the prescribed age, Leah would later claim her wedding date as his birthday.)

Leah felt trapped into the role of helpmeet to an ogre, and her emigration to America, where she never mastered the language and retreated into the citadel of domesticity, would only exacerbate Leah's melancholy. Popular immigrant success stories have eclipsed the trauma of relocation experienced by thousands of Europeans who never quite adjusted. "And this is the Golden Land," says Genya Schearl, in Yiddish, her first words in America, at the outset of *Call It Sleep*.[4] *Goldene Medinah*—Golden Land. The phrase was steeped in irony for newcomers who found their dreams of a better life colliding with the harsh realities of crowded tenements and mingy wages in oppressive sweatshops. To the pious, America was the *treife medinah*, the unkosher land that lured good Jews away from their faith and their culture. According to a cynical joke that immigrants told against themselves, immigrants came to America expecting the streets to be paved with gold. They discovered that the streets were, in fact, unpaved: The immigrants were hired to pave them.

After several months as a married man, Herman, who had lost his entire stake in a horse-trading venture, determined yet again to make a new life in the New World. Early in 1906, he set off alone for New York. It was common for families emigrating to America to dispatch the husband first to scout the landscape, set up housekeeping, and earn enough to send back fares for ocean passage for the wife and children. Generous to none and frugal to a fault, Herman saved and dispatched just enough for Leah and little Herschel to sail to New York in August 1907, as he had, in steerage. Traveling on a cut-rate ticket, Leah had to come up with additional cash to supply her hungry child with milk.

Launched less than a year before, the *Kaiserin Auguste Victoria* was the largest seagoing vessel in the world; it could hold almost three thousand passengers. They occupied first-, second-, and third-class berths, but hundreds were also crammed into the bowels of the boat. Part of the Hamburg America Line, the ship sailed from Hamburg to New York with stops in Dover and Cherbourg.

During an era in which the rich booked berths on majestic new ocean liners as much for the glamour and luxury as for the transportation (the *Titanic* would set forth and sink just five years after Henry Roth crossed the Atlantic), steerage was the shabby bargain basement, a dreary place to warehouse tattered human freight out of sight of smoking jackets and evening gowns. Originally designed to carry cargo but modified to accommodate the rabble, steerage was located between the upper deck and the hold. For about thirty-four dollars,[5] passengers could expect basic transport without any frills, not even bedding or food. One undifferentiated, cramped compartment served as bedroom, dining room, and living room for all the steerage passengers, the huddled masses who, after one to two weeks at sea without ventilation and only icy ocean water with which to bathe themselves, would certainly be yearning to breathe. By the time Leah and her toddler, Herschel, arrived in New York, on August 31, they were thoroughly sick of the sea. Weary of travel, they were terrified of the New World.

In Abraham Cahan's novella *Yekl* (1896), as in Roth's own *Call It Sleep*, the reunion on Ellis Island between an Americanized husband and the greenhorn wife and child he barely recognizes is tense, and one can suppose that Herman was not ecstatic over suddenly being encumbered again by a wife he hardly knew and a one-and-a-half-year-old child. Leah and Henry set foot on American soil in 1907— the same year that David and Genya Schearl show up at Ellis Island at the beginning of *Call It Sleep*, and the peak year for immigration through New York. Of the 1,285,350 immigrants from Eastern Europe who arrived in the United States that year, 149,180 (11.6 percent) were Jewish.[6] Roth and his mother formed part of the massive influx that boosted the Jewish population of New York sixteen-fold in thirty years, from 80,000 in 1880 to 1,250,000 in 1910. By 1918, when 10 percent of all Jews in the world lived in New York, the *Jewish Communal Register* was listing 3,997 Jewish *organizations* in the metropolitan area—more than the total number of Jews in Tysmenitz.[7] New York was on its way to displacing Lemberg, Odessa, Vilna, and Warsaw as the capital of the Diaspora. By the end of a century that saw the revival of a Jewish state in the Middle East, even Tel-Aviv, founded two years after Roth's arrival in America, would not surpass New York in the size of its Jewish population.

Observing these dramatic transformations, the fastidious Henry James, who had abandoned Protestant Old New York for Europe, cringed. After a twenty-year absence, he returned to the city in 1905 and, in *The American Scene*, found it "swarming" with "a Jewry that had burst all bounds." Particularly sensitive to distortions of his cherished language, the Master recounts his visit to the Lower East Side, whose cafés he describes as "torture-rooms of the living idiom." Yet James does not entirely condemn this immigrant culture; he merely concedes that its virtues elude him. "Who can ever tell, moreover, in any conditions and in presence of any apparent anomaly, what the genius of Israel may, or may not, really be 'up to'?"[8] Up to 1,037,000 Jews arrived in the United States during the first decade of the twentieth century, but it would take several decades before their genius flourished in English.

The master narrative of the American immigrant experience is a story of triumph over adversity: a Yiddish-speaking youngster named Israel Baline who fled the Russian pogroms to reinvent himself in New York as the composer Irving Berlin—prolific, rich, beloved author of "God Bless America." However, there are other stories rarely told and hard to quantify, about immigrants who found more in America to curse than bless. "*A klug tzu Columbus!* (A pox on Columbus!)" declared more than one disgruntled newcomer. If, for the pious, America was the iniquitous country that seduced Jews away from the life of Torah, for others, its promise of opportunity was mocked by sweatshops and tenements. Many immigrants—as much as a third of other ethnic groups—were so disheartened by what they found in the United States that they gave up the struggle and headed back home. To be sure, many had never planned on making America their permanent home, but saw it as a place to acquire a fortune and from which to return triumphant to their country of origin. Yet "home" had always been temporary and perilous for Jews of the Diaspora. Those who showed up again in anti-Semitic Eastern Europe risked their lives in ways that returning Italians and Greeks did not. Cheerful or miserable, about 95 percent of Jewish immigrants remained in the United States.[9] Those who failed to adjust withdrew into an internal Atlantis, a psychological island submerged somewhere between Europe and America. Leah Roth was one of these, and she would spend most of her life emotionally tied to an absent world, incapable of participating fully in the new world around her.

Most Jewish women became specialists in domesticity, feeding their families, laundering their clothes, cleaning their apartments. In 1907, only 1 percent of wives who came from Eastern Europe worked outside the home.[10] The stereotypical Jewish mother, notorious for dispensing large portions of gefilte fish and guilt, ruled through the stomach. However, for Leah Roth, the kitchen became her cloister as much as her throne. Pining over shattered dreams, and wary of the outside, English-speaking world, Leah invested her energies in doting over her firstborn child, her only son. When he eventually left the household to live with a Gentile, and Leah was forced to deal with Herman on her own, she lost her mind, flitting in and out of mental wards during her final, failing years. Her grandchildren saw a woman whose long stretches of lucidity were interrupted by arias of uncontrollable, unintelligible screaming that seemed to sum up a stunted life. The psychopathology of Leah Roth resembles that of another Jewish author's possessive immigrant mother. Naomi Ginsberg, whom her son, Allen, memorialized in his famous Beat elegy *Kaddish,* came to New York from Russia in 1905, little more than a year before Roth and his mother arrived. The love with which each mother smothered her son protected neither woman against delusion and despair.

Until the children were old enough to hold a paying job, Herman was the Roth family's sole breadwinner, and because of his spotty employment record and his constitutional stinginess (a trait his son would share), the bread was often very thinly sliced. Herman's refusal to provide his wife with what she considered sufficient cash for household expenses was a continuing source of friction. Their son would remember how his mother used to hoard and hide money from Herman and how the two clashed bitterly over family finances. On occasion, Henry even heard Leah disparage her spouse's sexual endowments. Moody, abrasive, and sometimes violent, Herman was quick to take offense and inclined to find malice even in innocent actions. He stockpiled grievances as if they were pieces of silver. Leah, whose behavior toward her adoring son was lovable and loving, brought out the worst in Herman, and the worst stayed out even after her death in New York in 1960. While their son was the mother's favorite, his sister, Rose, born in 1908, was the father's. Both became hostages to domestic combat. Henry recalled Herman as "a timid, frightened, frustrated little guy, and that's the best I could say about him."[11] His prose would say much worse.

From the beginning of their stay in America, Herman subjected his family to hardship and grief. Most Jewish immigrants settled first on Manhattan's Lower East Side before moving on to one of the outer boroughs, the less congested streets of Brooklyn or the Bronx. Completion of the Manhattan Bridge in 1905, to complement the nearby Brooklyn Bridge, which had opened in 1883, facilitated movement across the East River from Manhattan to Brooklyn. But the Roths reversed the pattern; they began in Brownsville, then a modest neighborhood in Brooklyn inhabited mostly by working-class Jewish families. To Leah Roth or any other traveler from Eastern Europe, Brownsville, in the outer reaches of an outer borough, must have seemed like an American Siberia—or at least Bierobidjan, the quasi-autonomous enclave to which Joseph Stalin would try to relocate his own country's Jews.

The esteemed literary critic Alfred Kazin, who would champion Henry Roth's fiction when it was neglected by almost everyone else, grew up in Brownsville, too, and he immortalized his adolescence there in *A Walker in the City* (1951). In his journals, Kazin, who was born in 1915, nine years after Roth, likens living in Brownsville early in the twentieth century to homesteading in the wilderness: "How far removed we were even from the rest of Brooklyn, where 'New York' was another world. We had been dumped by real-estate speculators into the farthest recesses of far-out Brooklyn, near unknown unapproachable Queens on one side, and on the other what was still the wasteland of Canarsie, Jamaica Bay, the great Atlantic itself."[12]

Brownsville served as the cradle of several other noted Jews, including Aaron Copland, John Garfield, Joseph Hirschhorn, Danny Kaye, the physicist I. I. Rabi, and the art historian Meyer Schapiro. Like many another urban district, Brownsville would undergo an ethnic evolution; by the end of the century, challah would be replaced by poori, its European Jews by immigrants from India. But to both Roth and Kazin, the area seemed a self-contained Jewish outpost, distinct from New York and even Brooklyn. "All I knew," recalled Kazin, "was that my immediate world was Jewish, that everyone and everything was Jewish, Jewish all day long."[13] In Roth's *Call It Sleep*, a little boy asks: "Didja ever live in Brooklyn?" Five-year-old David Schearl, who is actually living in what he calls "Bronzville," replies: "No."[14] Less than a decade after relinquishing its independence to become one of five boroughs comprising New York City, Brooklyn still seemed a faraway frontier for recent Jewish arrivals. Though its population was the largest of the boroughs, residents of Brooklyn would continue to defer to Manhattan as "the City."

It was in Brownsville that Rose, the second and final Roth child, was born on March 21, 1908. The American child, two years younger than her brother, would be her daddy's daughter. Unable to adjust to her new surroundings, Leah never learned fluent English. A borderline agoraphobe, she rarely ventured out into the clamorous, alien streets. Henry, born in the Old World that broke and kept her heart, would always be her favorite, a living totem of the life—and love—young Leah left behind.

At the time of Rose's birth, Herman was working as a press feeder in a neighorhood printing shop. Like most of his other jobs, this one would not last very long. Quick to quarrel with his bosses and fellow workers, Herman just as quickly found himself out on the street searching for new employment. To Henry, he became the very model of a fierce but feckless father. After the printing shop in Brownsville, Herman was hired by the Borden Company in Manhattan to deliver milk in a horse-drawn truck. In 1910, in order to be closer to Herman's work, the family moved into a fourth-floor walk-up in a redbrick building at 749 East Ninth Street, on the corner of Avenue D. They had become residents of New York's Lower East Side.

Now a fabled realm and an increasingly gentrified historical landmark, the section of Manhattan east of the Bowery between 14th and Canal Streets was then a cluttered, bustling dominion of tenements, synagogues, pushcarts, trolley cars, and sweatshops. Deprecatingly dubbed "Jewtown," it was a highly pressurized decompression chamber for entry into America, where a Yiddish-speaking newcomer could live for months without encountering many goyim. In the year the Roths moved in, 1910, the neighborhood recorded what would be its largest Jewish population ever: 542,000.[15] Remembering his experience as a boy on the Lower East Side, Henry would emphasize—and exaggerate—the homogeneity of the neighborhood. His belief that East Ninth Street constituted an urban shtetl populated almost entirely by Jews is mirrored in Joan Micklin Silver's film adaptation of Abraham Cahan's *Yekl.* "Where in America is the Gentiles?" Gitl asks her husband, Jake, in *Hester Street.* For all its wretched poverty, the neighborhood that Roth remembered was a lively community of Eastern European immigrants who could now live without fear of anti-Semitism, because they rarely saw a Gentile, more rarely still an anti-Jewish bigot.

The Lower East Side was then the site of the highest population density—about 600,000 in less than two square miles[16]—of any spot on earth. In this, the Progressive Era, muckrakers, armed with pen and camera, made frequent visits to document the overcrowded hovels, the absence of clean air and water, the high infant mortality rate, and the incidence of typhoid, scarlet fever, diptheria, and tuberculosis. Already, Jacob Riis, himself an immigrant from Denmark, had published an illustrated exposé of conditions on the Lower East Side,

How the Other Half Lives (1890). And for the half of American society that lived in comfort, its revelations were appalling.

The immigrant district of lower Manhattan was a fertile breeding ground for disease, crime—and nostalgia. Recollecting their emotions in the relative tranquility of California, Florida, and suburban New York, later generations could sentimentalize their family's toehold in America, forgetting the squalor of their first neighborhood. The Lower East Side became the Jerusalem of the American Diaspora, what one scholar, Hasia R. Diner, has called "the central metaphor of American Jewish memory."[17] Roth would remember it fondly, claiming in *Shifting Landscape*, long after he and most other Jewish residents had abandoned the area, that "the only time he ever felt a sense of belonging to both a place and a people was during the short period when he lived in a Jewish mini-state, and he didn't know it."[18] Far from their tormentors in Eastern Europe, it was a safe cradle in which to nurture Jewish memory.

Jews were not the first immigrants to settle on the Lower East Side. The Irish, fleeing famine, came there in the 1840s, and by 1870 the neighborhood contained enough Germans, refugees of their civil wars, that it was sometimes known as *Kleindeutschland*. The catastrophic loss of more than a thousand lives, mostly local German residents, when the pleasure boat *General Slocum* sank in the East River in 1904 left many vacant rooms to be filled, hastily and inexpensively. By the time the Roths arrived, the Tenth Ward in particular—one of three political units of the Lower East Side—was known as "New Israel." A half century later, when Roth returned to visit in the 1960s, Spanish was the language of the street, spoken by the largely Puerto Rican residents. But during his childhood, Yiddish was the lingua franca, and it was spoken in the dissonant accents of Russia, Hungary, Poland, Lithuania, Romania, and other addresses in Eastern Europe.

Even though pogroms, harsh restrictions, military conscription, and poverty had provided compelling reasons to leave, Jewish immigrants continued to identify with the lands they left behind. *Lantsleit*—newcomers from the same shtetls—often settled on the same block, attended the same schul, and regarded Jews from other origins as aliens. To some, intermarriage between a Galicianer and a Litvak was tantamount to miscegenation. But, however inflected, Yiddish was enough of a communal glue that immigrants from throughout Eastern Europe mingled in more than a dozen live theaters clustered along the Bowery and, later, Second Avenue, eager to hear melodramatic stereotypes as well as Ophelia and King Lear express themselves in Yiddish. Yiddish newspapers, including the Socialist *Forward*, the Communist *Freiheit*, the religious *Morgen Journal*, and the Zionist *Tag*, sold hundreds of thousands of copies a day; at its peak, in 1927, Yiddish press circulation reached 598,347.

When not feared and disdained, the Lower East Side became the object of curiosity, sympathy, and charity; but few Americans found much potential for artistic excellence among these uncouth aliens. One who did, the editor and novelist William Dean Howells, befriended and encouraged Abraham Cahan, the editor of the Yiddish *Forward*. In 1898, while warning his readers that Cahan's collection *The Imported Bridegroom and Other Stories of the New York Ghetto* was "foreign to our race and civilization," Howells added: "No American fiction of the year merits recognition more than this Russian's stories of Yiddish life, which are so entirely of our time and place. . . ." Cahan's English-language novel of immigrant assimilation, *The Rise of David Levinsky* (1917)—which Howells hailed as "an artistic triumph"[19]—brought a melancholic twist to the Horatio Alger formula. Material success leaves its protagonist haunted by regrets over having sacrificed his Jewish identity. Howells observed that: "Very possibly there may be at this moment a Russian or Polish Jew born or bred on our East Side, who shall burst from his parental Yiddish, and from the local hydrants, as from the wells of English undefiled, slake our drouth of imaginative literature."[20] Howells would never meet that Jew, but his name was Henry Roth.

In addition to Cahan, others, including Michael Gold, Samuel Ornitz, and Anzia Yezierska, spun the straw of their immigrant experiences into golden texts. In her popular autobiography *The Promised Land* (1912), Mary Antin celebrated her successful transformation from child of a Russian shtetl to Boston literata. But it is Roth, the transplanted fruit of Yiddishkeit, who, by immortalizing the Jewish Lower East Side in supple English prose, most dramatically fulfilled Howells' generous prophecy. According to Irving Howe, as formidable a literary arbiter for the conclusion of the twentieth century as Howells was for its dawn, Roth grew up to create "one of the few genuinely distinguished novels written by a 20th-century American."[21]

By the time that Howells published his prediction, however, in 1915, the Roths had already left the Lower East Side, when Henry was only eight. The abandonment of East Ninth Street when he had just completed the third grade was, he would later insist persistently, the most traumatic event of his entire life. New York neighborhoods often feel, especially to a child, like autonomous villages, and relocation one hundred blocks north, at the other end of Manhattan, was more wrenching to Roth than his journey, as an infant, from Galicia to the United States. Against his will, the boy was uprooted from a vibrant, cohesive Jewish milieu and forced to fend for himself far uptown, on a street where he was treated as an unwanted stranger. It was the root cause, he claimed, of many of his grown-up woes and of his long, notorious silence. Between his childhood on East Ninth Street and the rest of his life, Roth would assert, stood a "desolating discontinuity."[22]

Though his residence on the Lower East Side ended after a mere four years, emotionally Roth never left its tenements. Roth spent far more time in Maine and New Mexico, but memories of East Ninth Street were the literary capital on which he drew most powerfully. "Ha-adam ayno elah karka erets ktanah," wrote the Hebrew poet Shaul Tchernikhovsky; "A man is nothing but a little plot of land." Despite aliyah and his passionate commitment to Zion, that land remained the steppes of Eastern Europe for Tchernikhovsky. "Everything I have written I knew of or I had heard of before I was eight years old,"[23] declared Gabriel García Márquez. Henry Roth, who was snatched from Ninth Street at the age of eight, might have said the same. He lived out the truth that however far one wanders, one never leaves home. For Roth, the homeland was always his first neighborhood in Manhattan.

The second neighborhood was determined by the arrival of his mother's relatives just before the outbreak of a European war. On July 2, 1914, the *Kaiserin Auguste Victoria*, the same grand ocean liner that had transported Roth and his mother to New York seven years before, deposited another load of passengers on Ellis Island. The Farb family, Leah's clan, was among them. In order to ensure that they would be provided with kosher food, unavailable in steerage, patriarch Benzion had spent almost all the proceeds from the sale of his Veljish general store on second-class tickets for the family. Of his seven surviving children, only Genya stayed behind in Galicia, nursing a new baby. (She would die a few decades later, an inmate in a Nazi camp.) In addition to Leah, two of the other Farb children—Bertha and Morris ("Moe")—had already moved to New York. Now three others—eighteen-year-old Sara, sixteen-year-old Max, and fourteen-year-old Harry—were abandoning Veljish, accompanied by their father, fifty-two-year-old Benzion, whom everyone called "Zaida," and their fifty-year-old mother, Minka, known as "Baba."

Reunion with her family must have aroused mixed emotions in Leah. Though Zaida had coerced her into a marriage that was increasingly troubled, the Farbs were also a reminder of happier times in the Galician countryside. Once in New York, Zaida naturally wanted to live in a community with adequate support—synagogues, kosher markets, *mikvot*, religious schools—for a pious Jewish family. Already experts on America, Moe and Saul, two enterprising Farbs who later became partners in a restaurant, had scouted out suitably Jewish sites for the rest of the family. They found a convenient apartment across the street from where their sister Bertha and her husband, Joseph Kessler, were already living, at West 115th Street, between Park and Madison Avenues, in Harlem, a solidly Jewish section of town.

By 1926, when Carl Van Vechten, a white patron of black culture, published his flamboyant novel about life in northern Manhattan, he

titled it *Nigger Heaven*. But in 1914, a decade before the flowering of
the Harlem Renaissance, the neighborhood was still home to several
different ethnic groups. It was not exactly Jewish heaven (nothing
earthly ever is), but parts of Harlem contained so many Jews that the
Forward, in 1910, called the district "a Jewish city, inhabited by tens of
thousands of Jews." It abounded with synagogues, more than a dozen
of which would, following the exodus of their members, be converted
into churches. But during World War I, Harlem was home to an estimated 175,000 Jews.[24] To move from East Ninth Street to the neighborhood north of Central Park might not have made much difference in
1914, since, as the *Forward* reported, Harlem was "as lousy and congested as our East Side, with the same absence of light and air."[25] But
during the first three decades of the twentieth century, more than a million blacks abandoned the rural South for the urban North. Between
1920 and 1930, while Harlem was receiving 87,417 new black residents and losing 118,792 white ones, it became the most famous
African American neighborhood in the world. It had not yet earned that
fame when the Roths moved north within Manhattan, though by the
time they left, in the early thirties, it had become a deteriorating black
ghetto, home to more than 165,000 African American residents. Unlike
the Jews, who moved out of the Lower East Side as they began to pros-
per, blacks were trapped by discriminatory landlords into staying in
Harlem as it became ever more congested and impoverished.

Between the dissolution of Jewish Harlem and the formation of
Black Harlem, the United States fought a brutal war in Europe. The
Great War closed the door on everything that had come before, just as
Roth's move to Harlem, following the arrival of the Farbs, cut off the
years at East Ninth Street from the remainder of his life. *Call It Sleep*,
which begins on Ellis Island in 1907, ends as its eight-year-old protagonist drowses off, in early August 1913. Roth's second novel, *A Star
Shines Over Mt. Morris Park*, published after an anxious pause of sixty
years, awakens early in fateful August 1914, barely a year after *Call It
Sleep* concludes. Anyone who would understand the life of Henry Roth
must scrutinize the interval between those two books, just as anyone

who would understand the shape that the modern era took must magnify the moment before a shot was fired in Sarajevo in June 1914.

The assassination of Archduke Francis Ferdinand occurred only four days before Benzion Farb set foot on Ellis Island. Among early, obscure casualties of the war that ensued was Herman Roth's father, Shaul, who died that fall in Tysmenitz, from injuries inflicted by invading Russian soldiers. A dour sepia portrait of the old man in Orthodox earlocks continued to glare at his wayward son in New York.

Benzion Farb's decision to move his family to New York in 1914 is hardly evidence that the patriarch foresaw the onset of a catastrophic world war that would cost more than 10 million lives and count among its casualties the settled shtetl world of Eastern Europe. The Farbs were in fact slower than many other Ashkenazim to accept the truth that there was no future for a Jew within the Austro-Hungarian and Russian empires. But by 1914, Zaida was convinced that New York, home to more than one thousand Orthodox synagogues, might be the kind of Jewish community he desired for his children and grandchildren. Had he waited just a few more months, the conflict might have kept them from crossing the Atlantic. Had he waited just a few more years, restrictive quotas in the United States might have forced the Farbs, if they were lucky, to settle in Mexico or Argentina. And had he simply stayed in Veljish, most of the family still alive in the 1940s would have shared the gruesome fate of his daughter Genya.

When the Farbs arrived at Ellis Island, barely 1 million of New York City's 6 million residents were white, native-born, and Protestant. Close to half of the population of the United States consisted of immigrants or the children of immigrants. The lands they had abandoned were in turmoil, and it required an adroit foreign policy in Washington to avoid being pulled into Old World conflicts. Jews, in particular, were troubled by the imminent hostilities. What effect would overt war have on the communities they had left behind? Already victimized within the European countries they called home, Jews would surely suffer enormously in the crossfire between the great powers. "When two monarchs are at war, and one scourges the other's Jews," observes the mother in one of Roth's novels, "the second one says, 'Since you scourge my Jews, I'll scourge your Jews.'"[26]

Though their opinions ranged from pacifism through jingoism, Jews in the United States were uneasy about taking sides in an international conflict that could not be good for Jews and might place in doubt their own national loyalties. President Woodrow Wilson, who included Louis Brandeis and Bernard Berenson among his close advisers, promised to keep the United States out of the European war, easing Jewish anxiety for the moment, a moment at which the Old World, as well as Roth's eight-year-old world, was being torn asunder.

When they left the Lower East Side in 1914, the Roths at first settled one block away from the Farbs—three small, airless rooms at 114th Street and Park Avenue, in the Jewish part of Harlem. Herman had gone into the milk delivery business for himself, and the new lodgings had the added advantage of being closer to his supply depot in the freight yards on West 125th Street. However, a few weeks later, in order to economize, and because Leah missed having a window facing out onto the street, Herman moved the family again, to cheaper, drabber quarters. They would now occupy a railroad flat of four contiguous rooms located one flight up, just above Biolov's drugstore, in a five-story tenement at 108 East 119th Street.

The apartment was shaped like a dumbbell, and Henry's bare, tiny bedroom served as the narrow link between the kitchen in the back and his parents' larger bedroom. The parlor stood just beyond, closest to the street. For a rent of twelve dollars a month, about the cost of steerage, one could not expect hot running water, steam heat, or a private bathroom. To get to the communal toilet, the Roths had to walk through the dingy corridor adjoining all the apartments on the floor. It was not until five years later, when the rent was raised by three dollars a month, that the gas fixtures were replaced with electricity.

The Roths' new parlor, however, did offer a window onto 119th Street from which Leah could gaze and dream. Outside a second window lay a fire escape from which on sweltering summer nights her son could watch the parade of New York–New Haven Pullman cars on the nearby railroad overpass as he drifted off to sleep. Henry's own bedroom was a cheerless chamber dubbed by Leah the *kaiver*—the tomb. The boy hung his clothes on nails that jutted from the wall. The only exposure to the outside world was a grimy pane of glass over an airshaft, rats scurrying through the trash below. (Roth always resented his father as a stubborn skinflint who, in order to save a few dollars, forced the family to live in primitive, austere conditions. Yet he would later make his own wife and children brave the winters of Maine without central heating or plumbing. He regularly embarrassed his own younger son by gleaning discarded produce from the grocery; and in old age he became notorious for buying day-old bread for a quarter.)

The boy suffered from the bleakness of the home at 119th Street but even more from being forced to live in a part of Harlem that held few Jews. Most of the residents were Irish or Italian, and a Jewish interloper did not feel welcome. At first, in order to save the money necessary to purchase his own milk truck and horse, Herman discontinued Henry's religious instruction. Not only was young Roth severed from the vital Jewish culture he had not yet had a chance to absorb fully; he was now the target of anti-Semitic remarks and actions by neighborhood boys.

However, by 1920, 119th Street had acquired a kosher butcher, a Jewish tailor, and Jewish produce, dairy, and hardware stores. Thus, during the final years that Roth, in his twenties, still stayed with his parents and sister, he was again living on a Jewish block. By the last decades of the twentieth century, his old building on 119th Street had been razed and the block was pocked with desolate, weed-strewn lots. Like most other New York neighborhoods, it would later mutate once again, this time into a Puerto Rican one.

Though memory was the foundation of his imagination and he recalled details throughout his life avidly, vividly, and obsessively, Roth claimed to remember nothing from his infancy in Galicia. But details about his earliest experiences in East Harlem, where Jewishness made him feel a pariah, were etched indelibly in his memory. By the time 119th Street turned kosher, the damage had been done. Roth's formative years were over, and it was too late to restrain the shock waves radiating from his primal dislocation. Living among the Irish and Italians remained a sharp reminder that East Ninth Street— like childhood—could never be restored.

Chapter 2

HENRY IN HARLEM

Ah, heart of me, the weary, weary feet
In Harlem wandering from street to street.
—CLAUDE MCKAY[1]

BEFORE HE MOVED from the Lower East Side to Harlem, Henry Roth had just begun his career at *cheder*, the schoolroom where Jewish boys were provided rote religious instruction. A supplement to public secular education, these were often dismal, despotic operations, in which an indigent immigrant scholar eked out a living by browbeating a horde of unruly urchins into studying Torah. *Call It Sleep* would immortalize just such a misplaced *melamed* in the figure of Reb Yidel Pankower, a foul-smelling martinet who tries to batter his indifferent charges into religious erudition. Yet for all the teacher's unappealing traits, Roth also offers some sympathy for the pathos of displacement, for a learned man from Vilna who feels condemned to live out the rest of his life among Yankee savages who disdain what he holds most dear. "What was going to become of this new breed?" asks Reb Pankower. "These new Americans? This sidewalk-and-gutter generation? He knew them all and they were all alike—brazen, selfish, unbridled. Where was piety and observance? Where was learning, veneration of parents, deference to the old?"[2] Later, in *From Bondage*, the third volume of *Mercy of a Rude Stream*, Roth would portray another pious Old World Jew, Ira Stigman's grandfather, who laments the erosion of Jewish tradition in the Americanization of his own grandchildren. Likening himself, oddly, to a Christian saint, Augustine, Ira's Zaida describes himself within his own family "besieged by the barbarians, the Goths, the Vandals, the Teutonim."[3]

At the beginning of their initiation into religious instruction, pupils were required to memorize scriptural passages in Hebrew without understanding them. Though it was not much more than gibberish to him, Roth was so adept at negotiating the Hebrew texts that the *melamed* praised him to Leah, assuring the doting mother that her son would some day be a great rabbi. But relocation to Harlem abruptly ended Roth's *cheder* experience, before he had reached the stage of deciphering the mysterious Semitic phrases that he was reading and repeating. In later years, it was the untimeliness of his enforced departure from the Lower East Side that would trouble him as much as anything else. Just as he was beginning to establish fragile ties to Jewish tradition, through a *cheder* located a few doors from his home, those ties were broken.

However, during the Harlem years, Roth, adopting the values of his new environment, felt revulsion toward the world of *cheders* and schuls that he had left behind. Expelled from his childhood "Jewish mini-state," he embraced its negation. In East Harlem, he eventually did resume *cheder* studies but only reluctantly, under pressure from his parents, and he never became truly literate in Hebrew. At thirteen, on February 8, 1919, Henry underwent a bar mitzvah. Inwardly he rejected the ritual even as, dressed in a new blue serge suit, he performed his public role, reciting from the Torah scroll in synagogue and greeting the guests who crowded into his parents' inhospitable apartment for celebration. "But the Bar Mitzvah," Roth would later write of his fictional alter ego, Ira Stigman, "brought the realization he was only a Jew because he *had* to be a Jew; he hated being a Jew."[4]

Erased in the move to Harlem was Roth's once instinctive sense of membership within the Jewish community. As he wrote in "No Longer at Home," an essay published in *The New York Times* in 1971: "Continuity was destroyed when his family moved from snug, orthodox Ninth Street, from the homogeneous East Side to rowdy, heterogeneous Harlem; normal continuity was destroyed."[5] Though Roth's experience on the Lower East Side seemed to him hauntingly brief, for most Jews the neighborhood was just a way station between Eastern Europe and other American addresses. According to one estimate, the average length of residence by Jewish families on the Lower East Side was fifteen years, before they moved on to Harlem, Washington Heights, the Upper West Side, the outer boroughs, and the suburbs.[6] Few stuck around for the kind of continuity whose loss Roth lamented.

As if reveling in the trauma inflicted by his move to Harlem at age eight, Roth proclaimed himself an atheist at fourteen. He always believed that, but for the abandonment of the Lower East Side, he might have been a Talmudic scholar. "Now it's very likely," he mused in 1986, "that, had I stayed there, I could have become a rabbi. But I didn't."[7] However, if he could not be ordained, Roth was determined to be an *epikoros*, an infidel, to scoff at the faith he could not fully embrace. Even after a late conversion to Zionism in 1967, he would never have much patience for Jewish theology or ceremony. Like Ira Stigman, who boasts, "Here's a Jew who doesn't give a damn about Judaism,"[8] Roth attended class at CCNY on Yom Kippur, the holiest day in the Jewish calendar. Still later, in 1939, Roth would be razzed by his fellow workers—Irish, Italian, and black—as the only Jew to show up on Rosh Hashanah to dig ditches for the WPA. His disavowal of Judaism had practical advantages; on the mean street where young Roth lived, it did not do for a timid child to be an observant Jew. "I wanted to adapt to this Gentile Irish neighborhood," he recalled long after leaving Harlem, in 1972.[9]

Roth would not raise his sons, whose mother was in any case a Gentile of impeccable New England lineage, to be Jews. Yet he remained wistful about an identity that was aborted by the exodus from East Ninth Street. "Do you realize," he later told his wife, "if my folks had stayed on the East Side all these years, I could have been present when a whole people melted away. Language and all. Boy, what a saga."[10] Yet Roth did become the chronicler of a dying culture. Through the figures of David Schearl/Ira Stigman, his elegiac novels trace an American Jewish life shaped by profound loss.

Like Reb Pankower, Roth the aborted rebbe perceived himself to be in exile among savages. In hostile Harlem, he internalized the malicious stereotypes about Jewish avarice with which the callow Christians taunted him. "Make money, *oy*," sneered "Irishers" at the lonely, indigent boy, very like the boy whom Roth describes in *A Star Shines Over Mt. Morris Park*, the first volume of *Mercy of a Rude Stream*. Some of Roth's antagonists even learned enough Yiddish to gibe, "*Makh geldt*,"[11] as if making money were the sole goal of the young Jew's greedy breed. Roth absorbed and sustained the insults. "Their scorn helped make Judaism repugnant," he would recall in 1983.[12] "I came to believe that we were all the things the goyim called us."

Even more vulnerable was Roth's Uncle Harry, a Veljish bumpkin who was barely six years older than his Americanized nephew. Baba, Harry's mother, looked to Roth to provide her son with guidance in the ways of American education. So even though it was out of their district, and even though it ran only through the sixth grade, Roth's grandmother enrolled Harry in the younger child's grammar school, P.S. 103. The newcomer immediately became the continuing butt of anti-Semitic taunts, pranks, and assaults. To the roster of regrets that Roth was compiling he had to add the fact that he failed to come to the defense of his tormented uncle. In fact, he secretly shared his Gentile schoolmates' disdain for a Jewish misfit.

Harry was not even particularly useful to Roth in deflecting animosity. When Roth appealed to his mother for sympathy and protection, Leah explained that they must resign themselves to his *meshuggener* father's decision to live in Irish Harlem, and that the boy had best just learn to fend for himself. A lively, outgoing child became introverted and withdrawn. Henry's school grades suffered (by the seventh grade, his report card was still recording Ds in deportment, effort, and proficiency), and so did his self-esteem. The boy put on weight, exacerbating his relations with the neighborhood ruffians, who chanted:

Fat, fat, the water-rat,
Fifty bullets in your hat.[13]

When not dubbed "Fat, the water-rat" or just "Fatty," the chubby, awkward Henry, who much preferred to be known as Hank, was labeled "Cockeyes" on account of his glasses. Inept at marbles and team sports, he was the last to be chosen for pickup baseball games. He wept easily and sometimes wet his bed as late as age twelve. When attacked by hostile children, he retreated, mewling, to the arms of his mother.

Leah, the only literate woman in their building, read aloud to her son and a neighbor from Yiddish books. Of course, English was the exclusive medium of instruction at the two grammar schools Henry attended: P.S. 103 (at 116th Street and Madison Avenue) through the sixth grade, and then P.S. 24 (at 128th Street and Madison Avenue) until high school. His English soon eclipsed his Yiddish. He lost command of his native tongue, while Leah never became comfortable in the language of her new homeland. Part of what Roth would call his "terrible truncation"[14] was a linguistic loss. The boy felt forced to discard his native Yiddish in favor of the language spoken in the streets and schools of Harlem but not in his home. One of the most striking features of the "virtual Jewish mini-state" that Roth remembered was that "All transactions, work, and play, were conducted in Yiddish."[15] It was through his mastery of English that Roth acquired power; but his most powerful writing would be haunted by traces of his *mama loshen*, the mother tongue he left behind on the Lower East Side.

Primed by his bookish mother, the pudgy, pensive youngster indulged in endless jags of reading, absorbing stories published in English he found in the public library. He regularly visited four different branch collections, but was particularly fond of the one on

124th Street, across from Mt. Morris Park, a ten-acre plot above the northeast edge of Central Park, on the frontier between the Upper East Side of elegant Fifth Avenue mansions and scrappier East Harlem. The promontory that gave Mt. Morris Park its name was more of a hill than a mountain, but satisfactory for a boy who loved sledding through the snow. If he climbed the granite steps that led to the summit, about fifty feet above the city streets, he could walk around a great wooden belltower that had once been used to sound fire alarms.

"The tower was a small pavilion, rather like a toy bandstand, and from it you'd gaze down the Avenue to where it vanished in the gauze of distance," recalled John Sanford, the novelist and screenwriter, who was born Julian Schapiro, just across from Mt. Morris Park, at 2 West 120th Street, in 1904. Sanford's memoir *The View from Mt. Morris: A Harlem Boyhood* evokes Kuck's Saloon and Schorr's Candy Store on Seventh Avenue and 119th Street, Reid's Drug Store on Seventh and 118th, Nick Stano's Shoe Repair on Seventh and 117th, and even the anti-Semitic proprietor of Bachrach's Ice Cream Parlor on Seventh between 119th and 120th, with wistful precision. His account of growing up Jewish in Harlem is much more affectionate than Roth's, though both men, who do not seem to have known each other, evoke Mt. Morris as a young boy's Sinai, a mystical habitation for transcendental vision. In the first volume of Roth's culminating work—whose title, *A Star Shines Over Mt. Morris Park*, is a tribute to his childhood haunt—the promontory offers intimations of a young man's special destiny. And an impressionable Sanford records that the view from the summit offers a glimpse of both heaven and hell: "Off to the west, the Hudson lay hidden by Morningside Ridge, but westward across the island, you could see sunlight weaving the waters of Bronx Kill and Hell Gate."[16]

Across the street from the park, Henry lost himself in the books on the shelves of the Mt. Morris branch library. Indifferent to other genres, he devoured every fairy tale and legend he could find—Norse myths, *contes* from the Brothers Grimm, and tales of Camelot were favorites. They brought the troubled boy solace and escape. In "Somebody Always Grabs the Purple," the second story he published in *The New Yorker*, in 1940, Roth provides some sense of his own penchant for fantasy, as well as his frustrations. When the hero, Sammy Farber, a stocky youngster of eleven or twelve whose surname echoes Leah's maiden name, enters a library in Harlem, he immediately seeks out *The Purple Fairy Book*. Though the librarian attempts to interest him in adventure books, he is intent on reading only fairy tales. Sammy fails to cajole another boy, who beat him to it, into letting him have *The Purple Fairy Book*. The story concludes as he leaves the library, his longing still unsatisfied. Young Roth himself delighted in the Victorian children's series by Andrew Lang, which included *The Green Fairy Book*, *The Violet Fairy Book*, *The Pink Fairy Book*, *The Lilac Fairy Book*, and *The Orange Fairy Book*. (There never was a *Purple Fairy Book* for anyone to grab.)

Henry nevertheless discovered other kinds of fiction, but only when he mistakenly picked up a copy of *The Adventures of Huckleberry Finn*, assuming from the title that it was a fantasy. From Twain, he moved on to Jack London, Victor Hugo, and other adult authors. He wept copiously over *Les Misérables*, not because of the lachrymose story but because the novel was drawing to an end. He cherished the experience of vanishing into a book and sought to prolong it as much as he could. Absorbed in the exotic dramas of *The Count of Monte Cristo*, *The Three Musketeers*, or *The Prisoner of Zenda*, he was able to forget his own predicament in East Harlem. He likely found kinship with the picaresque, autodidactic protagonist of London's *Martin Eden*, and *David Copperfield* must have stimulated comparisons with his own background. But Roth could revel in R. D. Blackmore's *Lorna Doone* and H. Rider Haggard's *She* precisely because they conjured up worlds remote from his own miserable circumstances. Reading removed him from Harlem, and ever further from the streets of the Lower East Side. Roth's account of young Ira Stigman's love of books reflects his own escapism at that age: "All he asked of a book was not to remind him too much that he was a Jew; the more he was taken with a book, the more he prayed that Jews would be overlooked."[17] Like a spurned lover, he now embraced the antithesis of Yiddishkeit.

Apart from his father's abusive behavior, young Henry most resented Herman's role in his expulsion from East Ninth Street. Now, in 1917, Herman was plotting further displacement. He traveled alone back to St. Louis to scout out business prospects. He was certain that, under the patronage of his brother Gabe, the cafeteria that he hoped to open in City Hall would thrive. Herman wrote to Leah in New York, in Yiddish, insisting that she and the children join him in St. Louis. She refused. Leah had grown accustomed to her window ledge overlooking an active New York side street, and she could as easily imagine retreating to rustic Veljish as to a distant western town named St. Louis. In addition, now that her family was settled in New York, Leah did not want to be separated from them again. Experience had taught her to be cynical about her "no-goodnik" husband's inflated expectations. She also seemed to enjoy the schadenfreude of exasperating Herman.

Fuming, Herman returned to 119th Street convinced that Leah and the children had sabotaged his success in America. If only she had followed him to St. Louis, thought Herman, whose mind often assumed the shape of the subjunctive, their lives would have taken a dramatic turn for the better. For the rest of his life, Herman resented Leah's lack of faith in him, and relations between husband and wife deteriorated further. Leah felt trapped in a foreign land with a brutalizing husband who took out his frustrations on their firstborn child. Herman preferred Rose, his Brownsville-born daughter, to the son who came from Europe and often bore the brunt of his father's hostility toward an Old World wife. Herman's belligerence usually took the form of cruel remarks, but his recourse to corporal punishment was so frequent and severe that it might have earned promotion to sergeant. "He was completely mad," Roth later recalled. "He used to beat me."[18]

Sometimes, as when he pounced upon Henry after an Irish neighbor accused the boy, unjustly, of hitting her son, Herman became so violent that Leah had to intercede. Weapons of choice were mop handles and stove pokers, but Herman used whatever was at hand, including his own hands. One day when he lost his temper at a restaurant where he was working (until that incident), Herman hurled a pitcher at a mirror.

The more the son reminded him of his own frailties and failures, the more Herman struck out at him. "He would go completely berserk," Roth recalled in 1994. "Jesus, he would beat the hell out of me."[19]

It is a monstrous thing for a young boy to be assaulted by a grown man, especially if the man is his father. Even if the beating seems unfair, the boy knows better. He must have done *something* to deserve the licking. The agonizing shame outlasts the scars. Roth eventually grew to a height of five feet eight, but even when he towered more than half a foot over his father, and even when the old man ceased to be anything but a loony nag and then a memory, Herman continued to torment him.

So did Harlem, long after he had moved on, to Maine and then New Mexico. Though Roth remembered the neighborhood he lived in between the Brownsville and the Harlem years as a safe, cohesive Jewish hamlet, it is largely Harlem—rowdy, coarse, perilous—that he depicts, disguised as the Lower East Side, in *Call It Sleep*. By 1968, he was telling Byron Franzen, a graduate student at McGill University, that his first novel offered a more accurate view of Harlem, almost six miles north of where the events are said to take place, than of the Lower East Side. *Call It Sleep*, he wrote, was

> but a barbarous East Harlem impinged upon an inoffensive ghetto, when in fact the East Side was really quite cosy, quite snug and homogeneous, while a barbarous, goyish, Irish-infested, Irish-plagued and benighted Harlem, where I spent most of my youth, impinged upon the East Side, where I spent only a few years of earlist [*sic*] childhood, and thereby distorted an essentially benign environment, violated it gratuitously, disfigured it into a new grim vision recognizable to neither Jew nor gentile, with the result that neither, in the vernacular, bought it.[20]

In a journal entry, he noted:

> You superimposed an alien, a hostile Harlem slum on a benign East Side ghetto. You concocted some kind of farrago out of the two that

was true to neither one, did justice to neither one; in which you posed as victim, and you were no victim, but a kid like the others, maybe with more imagination, but a ghetto gamin like the others.[21]

Through the eyes of David Schearl in *Call It Sleep*, the Lower East Side is a terrifying riot of unfamiliar sights and sounds. Beyond the protective gaze of his adoring mother, Genya, lurk hungry rats, malicious brats, and electrified trolley rails. Older Gentiles, such as the lascivious Catholic Pole Leo Dugovka, menace the Jewish child. Even within the haven of the family apartment, David is tormented by his overbearing, raving father, Albert. David Schearl's is not a happy childhood, except that retrospection transforms all childhoods into shattered idylls. Through his first novel, an older Roth remembered his four years on East Ninth Street as an opportunity squandered and a paradise lost, a brief exception to the long ordeal of his life. "I would not hesitate to sacrifice *Call It Sleep* for a happy childhood, adolescence and young manhood," the rueful author told an interviewer in 1969.[22] But in writing the novel, he in fact reconstructed part of his childhood to *eliminate* its happiness, forcing the East Side years to conform to the troubled Harlem period.

Yet Harlem for Roth was not unmitigated horror. In "Petey and Yotsee and Mario," a story published in *The New Yorker* in 1956, when the world thought him silent, Roth recalls an urban childhood summer spent swimming in the Harlem River off 130th Street. The nostalgia is undercut by details of how the narrator, a novice swimmer nicknamed "Fat" by the street-smart boys who live on his block, almost drowns. But not only do Petey, Yotsee, and Mario save him from drowning; they also help him save face by pretending that rather than floundering in the river he was trying to dive to the bottom. The narrator's grateful mother, determined to reward her son's Gentile saviours, bakes them a spice cake. Mortified by his family's obvious Jewishness, the narrator is afraid that his mother's *haimish* offering will be rejected. But the boys devour the gift, and the story concludes on a note of ecumenical amity: "What kind of people would they be if they didn't like Jewish cake?" asks the mother.[23] Their Christian neighbors do like Jewish cake, and the story becomes either a memory or a fantasy of Harlem as a place where the way to disarm the anti-Semites was simply to let them eat cake.

Sensitive throughout his Harlem years to distinctions between Jew and Gentile, Roth himself was introduced to rare, expensive goyish delicacies when, at thirteen, he took an after-school job at Park & Tilford, a fine foods emporium located on 126th Street. When the letter arrived announcing that his son was hired, Herman, disdainful of the boy's bookishness and rankled by his desire to extend formal schooling beyond the sixth grade, was unusually affable. The young schlemiel he taunted as a *melamed* would at least be doing something constructive for the family. Although most of Henry's classmates at P.S. 103 went directly to a full-time job after graduation, Leah encouraged the boy to continue his studies, yet another source of strife between husband and wife. For Herman, a workingman thwarted in his own attempts at advancement, Henry's academic precocity provoked embarrassment tinged with envy. For Leah, limited in both her own schooling and her familiarity with American schools, it remained a mystery.

Working as a stockboy and delivering sumptuous steamer baskets to clients able to afford them, the young Roth discovered anchovies, caviar, kumquats, and capers. Already his résumé included stints at hawking Yiddish newspapers, delivering groceries, making buttons, and serving as factotum at Biolov's drugstore. Now Henry duly handed over his salary—five dollars a week—to Leah, who gave him back 50 cents for spending money. The assignment at Park & Tilford was an education in how the privileged lived, as well as in how the working-class adults he toiled beside thought, spoke, and behaved— often crudely. But it ended when Park & Tilford was forced to close its Harlem outpost, a victim of changing demographics as affluent whites began moving out of the neighborhood, and of Prohibition, which outlawed the store's lucrative trade in liquor.

Meanwhile, Herman was extending his own spotty pattern of employment. After failing in his attempt at an independent milk delivery business, he followed the lead of Leah's brothers Moe and Saul,

taking a job as busboy in the restaurant that employed them as wait-
ers. But, impatient for promotion, Herman quarreled with the manager and left the job before he had a chance to work his way up to
waiter.

THE DECLARATION OF WAR by the United States, on April 6,
1917, following attacks by German U-boats on American shipping
and a secret proposal—the Zimmermann Telegram—sent by the German government to assist Mexico in recovering territory north of the
Rio Grande, posed a particular challenge to Jewish immigrants and
their offspring. More than at any previous time, it tested their commitment to an American identity. Socialist and universalist, much of
the Yiddish press before 1917 portrayed war as an instrument of capitalist exploitation and insisted that the solidarity of workers of the
world trumped national allegiances. However, after the United States,
proclaiming its intention to "make the world safe for democracy,"
went to war against the intolerant monarchies of Eastern Europe, and
especially after war put an end to Russia's despised tsarist regime,
Jews were eager to support the cause. Of the 2 million U.S. soldiers
sent to Europe during 1917 and 1918, up to 250,000 were Jews. Of
those, 40,000 volunteered for military duty, offering tangible proof of
patriotism to a nation many had but recently adopted. Jews served the
American war effort in numbers disproportionate to their percentage
of the total population, and their sacrifice was disproportionate as
well; 3,500 American Jews were killed in action or died of wounds
during the relatively brief time that the United States took part in
World War I. Though only 3 percent of the U.S. population, Jews constituted 5 percent of the death toll.[24]

Herman Roth, who had barely escaped conscription into the Austrian army, was not especially eager to don a Yankee uniform. He
took a dim view of nationalist fervor, and he realized that in any war
Jews would be fighting and dying for both sides of the conflict. Save
for his own initiative, he might now be wearing an Austrian uniform.
He knew that American troops would be attacking hapless shtetl

youths coerced into defending a government whose anti-Semitic policies were indefensible.

Choosing from a list of occupations—including dockworker,
welder, farmer, fisherman, and transport worker—classified as essential to national security, Herman sought deferment as a trolley car
conductor. His assignment, to the Fourth and Madison Avenues line,
which passed along 119th Street, could hardly have been more convenient. Yet Herman, who made a career of temporary employment in
permanent positions, soon walked away from this job, too. He developed chronic cramps and diarrhea and became convinced they were
induced by the bumps and shakes he experienced throughout the day
as his trolley lurched along its route. Not even combat, he thought,
could cause so much torment. Though now vulnerable to the draft,
Herman never did hear from the War Labor Resources Board, and he
spent the rest of the war in non-essential private employment, working as a waiter.

Morris Farb, who was headwaiter at a popular dairy restaurant on
the Lower East Side, was drafted and sent to Europe. Leah's favorite
brother, "Moe" was a husky, handsome fellow, whose blue eyes and
fair hair confounded current stereotypes of the Jew. Leah felt especially close to Moe and had suffered from their separation after she
and her infant son went off to join her husband in America. When
Moe followed her to New York, a few years before the other Farbs,
he initially boarded with the Roths in their flat on East Ninth Street,
providing emotional support for his sister. He developed a special
fondness for his nephew, often treating Henry and himself to Hershey
bars at the candy store that was located below their apartment and
owned by an elderly Jewish couple.

Moe was a sweet-tempered, guileless man; when he was ordered off
to war in France, the elder Farbs were inconsolable, dreading what
would happen to their son amid the general slaughter. However,
standing erect in a spiffy uniform of the United States Army, Moe also
filled the Farbs with pride. Though an immigrant and a Jew, he was,
as they saw it, a genuine American. Henry was thrilled to receive bat-
tlefield souvenirs—artillery shell casings, iron crosses—and Parisian

opera glasses from his gallant Uncle Moe in France. Some of the family's apprehensions might have been allayed had they realized that Moe's work experience in New York helped sew three chevrons on his sleeve: appointed mess sergeant, he spent the harrowing war doing more feeding than fighting. When he returned unscathed from Europe in 1919, Staff Sergeant Morris Farb was welcomed back to Harlem by his entire exultant clan. Moe returned to the civilian restaurant business, but his thirteen-year-old nephew dreamed of wearing a uniform just like his beloved uncle's. Another uncle, "Uncle" Louie, who was actually Herman's nephew, wore a mail carrier's uniform; an ardent socialist, he tried to puncture the boy's romantic illusions about war.

At about the time his son was learning to inventory fancy foods and delivering them to wealthy customers, Herman Roth was working as a waiter at the Wall Street Stock Exchange Club, whose exclusive membership included Bernard Baruch and J. P. Morgan. He supplemented his income by serving diners on an ad hoc basis at banquets held elsewhere in the city. But in 1920, Herman—a demon to his son but to all the world a *schlimazel*, as deficient in commercial acumen as in congeniality—decided to try once again to go into business for himself. He opened a small delicatessen on 116th Street, and once again he failed.

On Armistice Day, November 11, 1918, Henry Roth was not yet thirteen when he joined the crowds lining Fifth Avenue to celebrate victory, and he idolized his Uncle Moe for valiant service in the battle against the European tyrants. The boy was troubled when, returning to a hero's welcome in Harlem in 1919, Moe broke down weeping. And he wondered about the fate of Tysmenitz, the birthplace he could not remember.

Most Jews in the United States rallied to the Allied cause. A flamboyant exception, Emma Goldman, spent twenty months in prison before being deported that same year for conspiring against the draft. Though they grieved over the destruction of Jewish communities in Europe (in Galicia alone, 600,000 Jews were driven out of their homes when Russian forces occupied the area for ten months),[25] World War I affirmed for first- and second-generation Jews an American identity most had not felt before. By 1920, when they constituted more than a fifth of the city's residents (1,164,000 out of a total population of 5,620,000), Jews could feel much more secure in New York City than anywhere else in the world. Nevertheless, a Jewish New Yorker born in Galicia could also find reasons to be anxious during and after the war, when nativist xenophobia became pandemic.

The Ku Klux Klan, hostile to blacks, Jews, Catholics, and other outsiders, enjoyed a resurgence (though not in New York), swelling to a membership of more than 4 million during the 1920s. Vladimir Lenin proclaimed his plans to spread communism beyond the new Soviet Union, and a postwar Red Scare in the United States targeted Jews and immigrants, especially immigrant Jews, such as Goldman and her anarchist companion, Alexander Berkman. In late 1919 and early 1920, Attorney General A. Mitchell Palmer ordered nationwide raids that resulted in more than ten thousand arrests of people, disproportionately Jewish or immigrant or both, whom he and his assistant, J. Edgar Hoover, accused of sedition. Though charges against most were eventually dismissed, several hundred suspects were deported. The U.S. House of Representatives refused to allow Victor L. Berger, a Jewish Socialist from Milwaukee, to take the seat to which he was elected, and he was sentenced to twenty years in prison for sedition before the Supreme Court intervened, in 1921, to overturn the verdict. Wary of their alien ideas, the New York State Assembly expelled five of its elected members, and an increasingly isolationist Congress refused to allow the United States to join Woodrow Wilson's League of Nations. In 1922, Henry Ford's *Dearborn Independent* launched its shrill campaign against alleged Jewish control of American life. Ford disseminated copies of the anti-Semitic canard *Protocols of the Elders of Zion* to his autoworkers.

"America must be kept American," proclaimed Calvin Coolidge on December 26, 1923, signing the Johnson-Reed Act, which stanched the massive influx of foreigners such as the Roths and the Farbs. According to the new law, immigration quotas, based on nationality, would be set at 2 percent of the population of a particular nationality living in the United States in 1890, just before newcomers from Eastern and Southern Europe began arriving in the hundreds of thousands at Castle Garden and then Ellis Island. If the 1924 immigration law had been enacted earlier, Nicola Sacco and Bartolomeo Vanzetti, two Italian anarchists who became leftist causes célèbres when condemned to death in 1921, would probably not have made it to Massachusetts, where they were convicted of killing a paymaster and a guard while robbing a factory. And Henry Roth might, like Joseph Roth, have grown up in Galicia.

The case of Sacco and Vanzetti aroused public passions throughout most of Roth's high school and college years. They were the focus of editorials, speeches, demonstrations, and chatter: "In the room the women come and go, talkin' of Bartolomeo," Roth would write about a cocktail party in 1927.[26] The case became the focus of Edna St. Vincent Millay's poem "Justice Denied in Massachusetts" (1927), of Upton Sinclair's novel *Boston* (1928), and of two Maxwell Anderson plays, *Gods of the Lightning* (1928) and *Winterset* (1935). Though the literary community reacted in outrage to the death by electrocution in 1927 of both immigrants, opinions in general were sharply and bitterly divided over whether Sacco and Vanzetti were indeed guilty of murder, or whether, as radicals and foreigners, they became innocent victims of a nation that had turned reactionary and xenophobic.

Roth would use Sacco and Vanzetti as the subject of an assignment in a public speaking class in college. In *From Bondage*, he describes how his alter ego Ira Stigman researched the case in the public library and "came away more convinced than ever that the two men were innocent of killing the paymaster of the shoe company in South Braintree, Massachusetts, as charged." In 1961, ballistics tests conducted on the pistol found on Sacco led forensic historians to conclude that Sacco, if not Vanzetti, was probably guilty after all. But during the 1920s the case was Roth's initiation into political passion, "the first time he spoke with conviction, spoke the truth about discrimination and oppression."[27] It would not be the last.

So the anti-Semitic bullies who terrorized East 119th Street were not the sole reason an immigrant Jewish boy with leftist leanings might have felt threatened at the beginning of the third decade of the twentieth century. However, during the summer of 1920, when he was fourteen, Roth found brief relief from his distress. He was hired to assist the projectionist at the Fox Theater, a vaudeville house downtown at 14th Street that alternated live acts with silent movies. Roth's job was to fetch the films from the distributor and to rewind reels after they were shown. During action on the stage, he was supposed to train a spotlight on the performers. But it was not the job itself that later caused Roth to look back on that faraway summer as idyllic. It was the narrative authority that the work bestowed on him.

In *Nature's First Green*, an autobiographical anecdote that constituted his second published book (a limited collector's edition published in 1979 by the noted editor William Targ), Roth describes how his summer vaudeville job made him "the reigning comedian of 119th Street in East Harlem."[28] Every evening when he returned from work, neighbors—Irish, Italian, and Jewish—would crowd around him to be regaled with accounts of the day's events at the theater. No longer "Fatty" or "Cockeyes," Roth became an urban Scheherazade, enthralling his audience with tales of dancers, crooners, and comics, as well as versions of their songs and steps and jokes. Decades before flickering images of Milton Berle, Sid Caesar, and Ed Sullivan illuminated rooms on 119th Street, Roth was the impresario of his own live—albeit borrowed—variety show. The gawky Jewish boy had metamorphosed into a star of the warm Harlem nights.

Roth's magnificent new role as retail *badchen*, the secondhand vaudevillian of an inglorious neighborhood, offered temporary redemption, as well as intimations of the majestic powers of the storyteller. The embryonic novelist was beginning to learn his craft. But, like so many of Roth's other fumbled escapades, "nature's first green" quickly turned to gray. A true son of Herman Roth, he was fired from his theater job for bungling the spotlight.

In the autumn of 1920, Henry Roth began his freshman year at Peter Stuyvesant High School, the famed New York public school that still specializes in science, math, and technology. It was named for the last Dutch governor of New Amsterdam—a dour, intolerant man who tried, unsuccessfully, to keep Jews from settling in his colony. In 1654, a group of twenty-three Sephardim, descendants of Jews expelled from Spain by the Inquisition in 1492, fled from Recife, Brazil, when Portugal seized control of the Dutch colony. Upon their arrival at Stuyvesant's settlement, the governor petitioned the Dutch West India Company for authority to ensure "that the deceitful race,—such hateful enemies and blasphemers of the name of Christ,—be not allowed further to infect and trouble this new colony."[29] Stuyvesant was rebuffed in his efforts, and some of the most eminent graduates of the high school named in his memory have been Jews, among them the actor John Garfield, the sculptor George Segal, the labor leader Albert Shanker, and the civil libertarian Aryeh Neier.

Founded in 1904 as a manual trade school for boys, Stuyvesant High, which did not enroll its first girl until 1969, would, by the end of a century in which it produced three Nobel laureates (all of them Jews), surpass most other schools in the United States in academic distinctions such as Merit Scholars and Westinghouse Science Talent Search winners. A magnet school for gifted young New Yorkers, many of them immigrants and the sons of immigrants, it welcomed enrollment of qualified male students who lived anywhere in the city. Demand for a spot in its freshman class would become so intense that Stuyvesant, whose annual acceptance rate is now only 5 percent (800 out of 16,000), eventually instituted a competitive exam for admission. However, when Roth was applying, the requirement for matriculation was merely a minimum scholastic average of 75.

Before it had moved even farther south, to Battery Park in 1992, attendance at Stuyvesant meant a daily journey to 345 East 15th Street, just beyond the upper reaches of the Lower East Side. For Roth, that required a trip all the way down from Harlem on the Lexington Avenue subway line. Split sessions necessitated by overcrowding also meant that freshmen did not begin their school day before noon. Henry was not especially interested in engineering, then thought to be the school's particular strength, but he had no clear notion of what he did want. He was willing to suffer the inconveniences of a long commute and awkward hours for one compelling reason: camaraderie.

Two years before, when Henry was still in seventh grade, an Irish Catholic boy named Francis V. J. (Frank) Hussey transferred from a parochial school, St. Thomas's, to P.S. 24, in the old Harlem neighborhood. He was handsome, athletic, and self-assured, and nebbishy Henry was immediately attracted. Henry and Frank soon became best friends. At last, Roth found someone worthy of his admiration who seemed to accept him as he was and was not bothered by his Jewishness. Though the huge wave of Irish immigration—about 1,600,000 from 1847 to 1854—precipitated by the Great Famine of 1845–49 had preceded the arrival of Eastern European Jews, Roth, who was aware of the history of oppression common to the Irish and the Jews, was always drawn to Irish Americans. He and Frank spent much of their time together, sharing homework assignments, hitchhiking into the suburbs to visit Hussey's relatives in New Rochelle, or just loafing.

Though Roth was gauche in every sport except football, where his bulk was not a disadvantage and he proved an adequate punter, Hussey was a star competitor, especially in track. The high points of Hussey's athletic career would come in 1923, two years after the boys stopped seeing each other, when he tied the world record of 9.6 seconds in the 100-yard dash, and in 1924, when he formed part of the American foursome that took an Olympic Gold home from Paris for the men's 100-meter relay race. Roth took great pride in his blond-haired, blue-eyed classmate's accomplishments. Hussey's exploits as a sprinter made him a popular figure at school, and Roth basked in his friend's reflected glory.

Hussey's father was an undertaker in Harlem whose quiet demeanor offered a stark contrast to the moody, strident Herman Roth. Henry, who would choose a converted mortuary for his own final house in Albuquerque, spent many hours at his friend's home, the Hussey Funeral Parlor, a prominent establishment on 129th Street. Accepted by the Hussey family, he enjoyed their *treyf*—non-kosher fare such as sliced pork and corned beef on buttered bread. Sitting with Frank beside his phonograph, Henry developed a taste for recordings by the legendary Irish tenor John McCormack and a life-long love of opera.

When Frank opted to attend Stuyvesant High School, Henry, too insecure to strike out on his own, determined that he would follow his friend downtown to East 15th Street. The decision would prove a disaster, and brought an end to the friendship. Henry Roth's brief tenure at Stuyvesant turned out to be a devastating disgrace. Fulfilling the resentful Herman's judgment that his bright son was doomed to failure, Roth never adjusted to the competitive atmosphere and began experiencing academic trouble from the outset. At the conclusion of the first semester, he received a failing grade for every subject except English. The boy never overcame the feeling of being an outsider at Stuyvesant, an institution he was attending only because of his friend Frank Hussey. Compounding the stress of entering an elite high school in a distant neighborhood was the fact that Roth found himself the repeated victim of petty theft—books, pens, even his briefcase. The loss of these items, gifts from parents and other relatives that he could hardly afford to replace, exacerbated the persistent sense of helplessness.

In frustration, Roth himself began to snitch pens from classmates. Since he kept his booty hidden at home, the thefts served no purpose except private revenge on a hostile world. Although they assuaged his feelings of ineptitude, the crimes also created a terrible burden of guilt. Roth knew very well that stealing was wrong, and the fact that he continued, compulsively, to pilfer at school reinforced a growing sense of his own depravity. He both dreaded and courted exposure, which would surely summon the punishment he realized he deserved.

Even a professional writer would have had no use for the quantity of pens that Roth appropriated. It is difficult to believe that he stole primarily because he coveted the possessions of wealthy classmates rather than because taking them satisfied an unacknowledged urge for degradation. In March 1921, Roth snatched a particularly alluring and expensive silver-filigreed fountain pen from an affluent boy whose father had given it to him as a present for grade school graduation. Instead of hiding or hocking this most splendid of plunder, he flaunted it. When Hussey admired the pen, Roth insisted on giving it to him. The legitimate owner saw it in Hussey's pocket and Roth's crime spree came to an ignominious halt.

Confronted by the indignant owner, Hussey asked Roth for an explanation. He suggested that, in order to avoid problems, he would be willing simply to surrender the pen to the other boy. But Roth insisted that the pen had truly been his to give away. He left no alternative but to play out an agonizing process of humiliation. Had he allowed Hussey to return the pen, Roth's life could have moved in an entirely different direction; or he might merely have found some other means of debasing himself, of proving to the world that he was indeed unworthy of Hussey's friendship and Stuyvesant's trust. Hauled before the assistant principal, he finally confessed, sobbing, to the entire string of thefts. He was ordered to bring his father into the office the following morning.

This surely vindicated all Herman's rancor toward his son. Worse than a *lemekh*, a feckless fool, this momma's boy was a *gonif*, a common thief. Better that Henry, with pretensions of becoming more learned than his parents, should have gone to work full time than waste his days in high school and dishonor his father. Herman now had to take time from his job to deal with this distressing business at Stuyvesant. It was of course true that Herman had stolen from his own father in order to come to America and that he himself had been sacked from several jobs in disgrace. But being caught with another student's pen was particularly shameful for a bookish boy with ambitions for education, and it demonstrated to both father and son that Herman's negative assessment was accurate. In Roth's autobiographical novel *A Diving Rock on the Hudson*, Ira Stigman reacts much as the author must have done. "The Devil laughed today," wrote Roth, unable to share the joke, in his notebook on March 23, 1921—in indelible pencil.[30]

Walking all the way back home from Stuyvesant to Harlem, Roth wandered along the banks of the Hudson. According to the account published seventy-five years later, the young pariah lingered beside a diving rock that jutted out of the Hudson around 100th Street and

was used by underprivileged local boys as a platform to leap into the
river. The waters of oblivion were tempting. The deep currents might
cleanse, if not redeem him. Yet Roth chose instead to live in torment:

> He turned around on the block of stone, turned his back to the river.
> So now suffer. Everything. The outcries at home. The expulsion
> from school. The shame. That was only the outside, the outside
> wreckage. What he was, what he already was inside, he would have
> to bear. He didn't know what he meant, only that the agony would
> be worse, and he had chosen to bear it, bear the havoc of himself,
> the only thing true. . . .[31]

The only thing true about this account, according to Roth's own
later testimony at eighty-eight, was that he ended up back at 119th
Street, confessing to Leah and Herman. The aging author denied that
at fourteen he seriously contemplated suicide by diving off a rock into
the Hudson River. "I didn't do that," he declared, insisting that his
novel fictionalized autobiographical facts. "I just walked and walked
and went home." Then, and later, he believed that his survival would
serve some purpose as yet unknown.[32] Nevertheless, the reader has a
right to wonder: Why *did* Roth portray his wretched alter ego on the
verge of ending his own life? Did not the scene reveal a truth about a
personality who throughout his long life suffered from bouts of abject
depression? Perhaps the dishonored thief had sunk so low in self-
esteem that he felt incapable even of making the dramatic gesture of
flinging himself into the "rude stream" that flows beside Manhattan.
The boy made his way back to the family apartment, still alive but
overwhelmed by self-loathing.

In the morning, both father and son were told that it would be best
for all concerned if Henry's record at Stuyvesant were expunged. He
would never again set foot in that high school, but he could enroll elsewhere free of external stigma. It would be harder to obliterate Roth's
own feelings of unworthiness. Wracked by guilt not only over stealing
but also over lying about it, thus abusing the trust of his best friend, Roth

could not face Hussey again. Though he followed Hussey's career from afar, noting how he set a citywide record in the 100-yard dash, led the Stuyvesant team to a championship in 1923, and triumphed at the Olympics, Roth found it impossible to resume their casual intimacy, compounding his guilt with this further failure of friendship. It would take him two months to overcome his shame enough to speak to Frank, at a track meet where the sprinter starred. Then, although Hussey seemed to bear no grudge, Roth just drifted out of his life. When Roth walked out of Stuyvesant into the frigid March air, the assistant principal's parting words, rendered in fiction, would echo through the years. "I suggest that in the future you try to control your impulses."[33]

If Henry Roth's life had been a novel (as it became when he finally composed the autobiographical *Mercy of a Rude Stream*), its author might have noted the appropriateness of the targets chosen for his youthful kleptomania. Would stealing umbrellas constitute evidence of ambitions in meteorology? But for a future writer, even one who as yet had no inkling of that future, appropriating another person's pen is a symbolic form of plagiarism, the desperate act of someone who has not yet found his own style. At fifteen, Henry Roth was still a defective dictionary; he lacked definition.

The boy worked for a while, unhappily, in a law office and then in the warehouse of a toy company. But in September 1921, he returned to the classroom, this time at DeWitt Clinton High School, where no one knew about his sordid history. Unlike Stuyvesant, DeWitt Clinton, the oldest high school in New York City, was not a specialized institution, but it was then all-male. Until 1928, when it moved to the Bronx, the school stood just north of the tough Hell's Kitchen neighborhood, on the site, at 59th Street and Tenth Avenue, now occupied by John Jay College. Though the 1903 building was massive and ornate, it could not accommodate all of the school's six thousand students, and freshmen were assigned to an annex more than a mile away, on 88th Street east of Park Avenue. Among thousands of others enrolled at DeWitt Clinton during Roth's high school years were Mortimer Adler, Countee Cullen, Ernest Nagel, Lionel Trilling, and

Nathan Weinstein (who, unlike Roth, felt compelled by the anti-Semitism of the time to adopt a nom de plume, Nathanael West).

On the strength of a feat of superb marksmanship during his first interscholastic meet (which he never came close to duplicating), Roth became a mainstay and eventually the manager of the DeWitt Clinton rifle team. Yet until his senior year, when he began to do well enough in the sciences to contemplate a career in them, he remained an indifferent student—uninspired and undistinguished in almost every academic subject. Roth was living refutation of the school song that described the ideal DeWitt Clinton student:

> He worked with a will
> And exceeding skill
> To honor the name he bore. . . .[34]

Schoolwork bored him, although geometry, in which he exulted and excelled, was always an exception. The abstract purity of mathematics, an alternative universe whose rules one could learn and master, appealed to an adolescent whose life seemed untidy and beyond control. It would also gratify the older Roth, who continued throughout his life to study math on his own and to amuse himself by tackling formal problems in calculus. Plane geometry, the sole subject at Clinton that truly stirred him, was, as Ira Stigman reflected, "the only entire, pure world that offered him unquestioning sanctuary, benign, set before him a problem or a proposition, shared with him his rapture that the solution should be so inevitable, so wondrously spare and immaculate—and so ingenious, even dazzling sometimes."[35] Roth's attraction to mathematics resembled the aesthetic detachment for which he was later to disparage James Joyce. It is reflected in the meticulous prose of Call It Sleep. Abandoning the tangle of human languages for the precision of equations was, for Roth, like getting away from his scrapes in New York. "Math," observes Morris Dickstein, a leading scholar of modern American fiction, "was a version of Maine—an escape into abstraction from whatever problems he had."[36]

During the summer of 1922, sixteen-year-old Roth worked as a bus conductor, collecting fares on a double-decker. Though it was tempting and easy to pocket fares for himself, he was scrupulous about turning over to management all the cash he collected. However, his fellow workers were skimming for themselves, and the larger daily tally from the young newcomer made them look like crooks. They threatened violence unless he too cheated on the bus company. To get the job in the first place, Roth had had to pay a hundred-dollar deposit, which he borrowed from his father. With memories of the mortifying expulsion from Stuyvesant still vivid, Roth dreaded Herman's fury if he had to forfeit the deposit because he was caught stealing again. But he also feared reprisal from the other conductors. So he quit the job and was able to return to Herman his hundred dollars. When the bus company went bankrupt a few months later, none of the other conductors was able to recover his deposit.

Roth found his next job hawking soda pop at New York Giants baseball games. He was hired by the H. M. Stevens Company, which controlled refreshment concessions at the Polo Grounds in northern Manhattan. It was high-pressure work that rewarded most those most nimble and aggressive. Roth was not a natural, but he kept at it, in the Polo Grounds as well as in Yankee Stadium—newly opened in the Bronx in 1923 with profits from the tremendous popularity of slugger Babe Ruth, whom the Yankees had acquired from the Red Sox in 1920. He returned to the job during the fall and winter, for football games and for boxing matches at Madison Square Garden.

The end of summer ushered in another difficult academic year. Roth signed up for an elocution course in his senior year at DeWitt Clinton, but misplaced eloquence almost got him suspended from school on the very first day of class, in September 1923. Because a teacher was late in returning from a summer trip to Europe, two elocution classes were combined in one room. Students had to double up on desks, and Roth found himself seated beside a suave young stranger. The two exchanged wisecracks and began to hit it off, becoming so absorbed in their own banter they failed to notice that class had begun. The furious teacher evicted Roth from the room, and only a tearful plea from the young delinquent, fearful of reliving his ordeal at Stuyvesant, averted harsher punishment.

About a month later, Roth was able to talk more freely with his new acquaintance. "He was a very, very handsome middle class boy—polished, worldly, well-groomed"[37] was how Roth remembered Lester Winter, a dramatic foil to the maladroit immigrant Jew. Winter was a bright companion Roth could look up to, not simply because he stood three inches taller but because he seemed able to take for granted his position in the American middle class. Fully aware of his own failings, Roth was amazed and pleased that someone he would depict as "so handsome, gifted, poised, charming, no sense of smirch about him"[38] would want to be his friend. Still smarting from the break with Frank Hussey, Roth imagined that here at last was another companion he could trust, who would not be ashamed to be seen with an unrefined Jew. And Roth was astonished to discover that Lester Winter himself was a Jew.

A fourth-generation American whose great-grandparents on both sides had immigrated from Hungary, Winter was a kind of assimilated Jew Roth had never encountered before. Though he knew German and Hungarian, Winter did not speak Yiddish, and, though he taught Sunday School—an institution quite unlike *cheder*—at Temple Beth-El, a fashionable midtown showcase of Reformed Judaism, he knew no Hebrew. Winter lived with his family in a building in the Bronx that his father, a successful dry goods merchant, owned. Feeling uncouth and unworthy, Roth was persuaded to be their guest for a Friday night dinner. Everything about the experience—the tasteful furnishings, the civil conversation, even the creamed spinach—impressed Roth as a contrast to life on 119th Street.

If Roth valued Winter as an entrée into a foreign world of American Jewish affluence, Winter valued Roth precisely because he believed him free of the avarice and hypocrisy he hated in his usual social circles. And it was gratifying when Roth treated Winter as his mentor, an expert guide to modern secular culture. Winter was an amateur actor, who appeared in their high school production of *The Pirates of Penzance*, as well as an aspiring poet. Roth had never met a poet before and, though quite familiar with Tennyson, Longfellow, and Keats, relied on Winter to introduce him to the work of such contemporaries as Robert Frost, Vachel Lindsay, and Edna St. Vincent Millay. Winter scorned fellow members of the Jewish bourgeoisie for their materialism and opportunism. Yet for all his artistic interests and aspirations, he was also quite practical. In order to ensure financial support for a cultivated life, Winter planned to be a dentist. Roth, who was then hoping to be a zoologist, was encouraged by Winter to believe that reconciling Mammon and the Muses need not be a problem.

One other problem plagued, and silenced, Roth for most of his life. "A canker in the soul," as he would diagnose it in a novel,[39] it was a loathsome secret he did not dare to share for almost seventy years. A biblical abomination, it was both cause and symptom of Roth's inability to mature and of his persistent self-loathing. He had begun furtively indulging in incest with his sister, Rose. When Roth was a senior at DeWitt Clinton, Rose was attending the newly opened Julia Richmond High School, on East 67th Street. As early as age twelve, when Rose was only ten, Roth had been groping with his sister; but by the fall of 1922, when he was sixteen and she fourteen, their relationship evolved into full sexual intimacy. Roth would later claim that his fictional accounts of Ira Stigman's activities with his sister, Minnie, were exaggerated to intensify the revulsion he felt over his own behavior with Rose. The actual incidents were neither as frequent nor as sordid as he would depict them in his final novels. However, he affirmed that they did occur and were the basis for his literary renditions, a potent factor in his lifelong self-loathing. "It was," he explained in *A Diving Rock on the Hudson*, "like a sneaky mini-family, a tabooed one, and discovered by him, by cunning exploitation of accident, to seal off a little enclave within, utterly unspeakable, vicious, yes, near brutally wicked, oh, wicked was too insipid, all the evil consummate, rolled up, concentrate, essence, wild, and made him feel so depraved that anything went, anything he could think of. . . ."[40]

Occasionally, on Sunday mornings, when Herman was off waiting on breakfast banquets and Leah doing her weekly shopping, brother and sister would repair to their parents' bed together. Henry knew very well that they were indulging in a forbidden activity, but the thrill, as the teen saw it, was intensified by the terror of discovery. More than once their mother returned to the apartment just as an encounter was ending. More than once a broken condom or a delayed menstruation terrified the young Roths into resolving to put an end to their illicit couplings. But danger only heightened the excitement, and the sexual liaison continued throughout Roth's senior year in high school and into his college years.

Surreptitious sex with Rose was not the only source of Roth's lingering guilt. When he was eighteen, during his first winter in college, he attended a family *bris*, a ceremony in Flushing, Queens, to celebrate the circumcision of his Uncle Saul and Aunt Ida's infant son. During the festivities, he led his fourteen-year-old first cousin, Sylvia Kessler, downstairs into a freshly cemented basement and seduced her. Plump, with wavy blond tresses and blue eyes, Sylvia was the daughter of Leah's sister, Bertha. The oldest of the Farb grandchildren, Roth was a favorite of Aunt Bertha and her husband, Joseph Kessler, who always encouraged him to visit them in their apartment on West 112th Street, rewarding him for his trouble with a dollar. He now found more compelling reason to journey the eight blocks across town to spend an evening with his Farb relatives. And it was tempting for the visitor, "throbbing with rut,"[41] to slip away to an empty room for a few lascivious minutes with Sylvia. As the Stuyvesant official who had warned the boy to control his impulses sensed, Henry could not resist temptation. Fear of detection, especially by Zaida, the pious old patriarch who was now living with Bertha and Joseph, intensified the thrill of being more than kissing cousins.

Roth would claim that his account in *A Diving Rock on the Hudson* of the sixteen-year-old Ira Stigman's visit to a black prostitute is not autobiographical.[42] Until he took up with Eda Lou Walton when he was twenty-two, Roth's sexual activity was largely endogamous—and ignominious; it stayed within the house and outside the proprieties. And repulsion over his carnality inhibited Roth's social and sexual contacts. He was late in learning to dance and to relate in other ways to grown-up women outside the clan. "Henry Roth never had a normal sexual relationship," his younger son, Hugh, would later conclude, denying normalcy to his own parents' marriage.[43]

In addition to incestuous relations with his sister and his cousin, Roth was troubled by forbidden feelings toward his mother. When Herman Roth went off to scout business possibilities in St. Louis in 1917, Leah, lonely, asked her eleven-year-old son to share her bed. According to the account Roth conjured up for *A Star Shines Over Mt. Morris Park,* the boy awakened with an erection pressed against her body: "He was playing bad against Mom's naked legs, lying on his side and pushing, rubbing, squeezing his stiff peg between Mom's thighs."[44] Roth notes that he kept to his own bed in the future, but "playing bad" would be the source of the crippling guilt that plagued him until his death.

As a child, Roth associated sexuality with filth and stealth, the naughty rites of children comparing nether parts. Once, when he was about ten, a stranger picked him up in Mt. Morris Park and took him for a trolley ride to distant Fort Tryon Park, in northern Manhattan. There, while trying to force the boy to expose himself, the man was interrupted by some passersby. Roth returned home untouched, but, convinced of his own shame in this episode, he never told his parents. Nor did he tell them about the advances of Mr. Danroe, the man who taught him high school Spanish.

The taboo against homosexuality was almost as strong as the one against incest, and the mere possibility of physical gratification with another man disturbed Roth. In 1938, an initial impression that the composer Muriel Parker was a lesbian would cause him to ignore her. In 1939, while living in Los Angeles, he would reject a man's invitation to share a weekend in San Francisco because of the—erroneous—suspicion that the friend intended a sexual encounter. Often hypersensitive in his conversations about sexual orientation, convinced, as late as 1981, that homosexuality was "a degeneration,"[45] Roth stated during his final years that he had never had sex with a man.[46]

The fractious marriage of Herman and Leah Roth hardly provided their son with a healthy model. The first volume of *Mercy of a Rude*

Stream, published after all the other principals were dead, even hints that Leah's passions were aroused not by her insufferable husband but by her favorite brother, Moe. When another of Roth's uncles, Herman's nephew Louis, attempts to seduce Leah, he pleads: "I'm not your brother. . . . Give me what I yearn for: Your love. Satisfy me!" But she rejects Louis, insisting that she is *ausgebrendt*, all burned out. And she explains that her sexual ardor was dissipated in incestuous longing: "I beheld my brother Morris in his nakedness once, and I became consumed. I confess it. It's shameful. . . ."[47]

The shameful bane of incest is a family disorder, and it brought particular disorder to the family Roth. Moreover, at the end of *Requiem for Harlem*, the fourth volume of *Mercy of a Rude Stream*, Ira Stigman learns that his father too has been sexually assaulting his cousin Stella. If the book is read as personal history—translating Chaim Stigman into Herman Roth and Stella into Roth's first cousin Sylvia—then the startling revelation merely magnifies the family curse. Roth in fact affirmed the equation to Felicia Steele, who assisted in the preparation of his final books.[48]

Incest is a dramatic manifestation of immigrant insecurity, the newcomers' inability to invest their emotions in anything beyond the reassuring confines of the clan. Forbidden sibling love among Italian immigrants is a theme in Gian-Carlo Menotti's opera *The Saint of Bleecker Street* (1954), in the tense relationship between Annina and her brother Michele. Similarly, tragedy in Arthur Miller's *A View from the Bridge* (1955) is precipitated by longshoreman Eddie Carbone's desire for his young niece, Catherine, and his jealousy of her attentions toward Rodolpho, a more recent arrival in Brooklyn from Sicily. Though Alexander Portnoy is a second-generation native of the United States, the erotic fantasies that Philip Roth's notorious onanist entertains toward his sister, Hannah, among others, epitomize his anxieties over being an ambitious Jew in a Christian society. Anaïs Nin, who was born in France but moved to New York at the age of twelve, maintained sexual relations with her father over the course of many years. And what she called "The House of Incest," in the title of a 1936 novel, is the private sanctuary that a fearful immigrant might construct within an alien and unnerving land.

If growing up is a matter of growing out into the world, continuing attachment of the libido to a parent or a sibling clearly signifies a failure to mature. Up to a certain age, Roth's relations with his sister might not even have been as peculiar as he thought. According to one student of the subject, Vernon R. Wiehe, "as many as 53 out of 100 children abuse a brother or sister, higher than the percentage of adults who abuse their children or their spouse."[49] Certainly Roth knew enough of the Bible to cite its prohibition against sibling incest. In Leviticus 18:11 and 20:17, his behavior with Rose is castigated as a flagrant sin. And as Roth certainly also knew, violating the social taboo against incest is repugnant to modern sensibilities. As much as his embarrassment over crude immigrant parents, the secret horror of Henry Roth's domestic life discouraged him from inviting strangers, particularly anyone as debonair as Lester Winter—with what he imagined as his "seraphic luster"[50]—to the fouled nest on 119th Street.

Roth's incestuous liaisons troubled him deeply—all the more because of his own contemptible failure to refrain. Repeated, immediately regretted, his trysts with each girl had the character more of obsession than elation; and despite hasty withdrawal and the protection of doubled condoms, the torment was compounded by fear of conceiving an inbred bastard. The excruciating memory of illicit sexuality was a secret made unbearable precisely because it could not be bared.

Eventually, Rose, who studied at Hunter College (then all-female) and went to work for Macy's department store, married David Broder, whose résumé included firefighter and salesman of chop suey noodles. After several miscarriages, the couple adopted a girl and a boy. (The boy was born to Louis's brother and his wife. When the brother died young, his distraught widow hanged herself, leaving their son an orphan.)

Rose seems to have been able to repress her incestuous memories until, when both were in their eighties, her famous brother recalled the details in print. For Henry, the incest was a physical growth that festered throughout his life: "Jesus Christ," exclaims Ira Stigman, "what a sinister cyst of guilt that was within the self, denigrating the *yontif*, denigrating everything within reach, exuding ambiguity, anomaly, beyond redemption now."[51] Redemption might come through maturation. But Roth's inability to form heterosexual attachments outside the family was evidence of arrested development, what he would diagnose in Ira Stigman as "his continued, his prolonged *infantilism*. . . . He had been fixed in infantilism as deep as a bronze boundary marker was fixed in the ground, deep as a utility pole."[52] More than twenty years before publishing details of his vile secret, Roth, at sixty-six, would admit, obliquely, to an interviewer: "I think I just failed at maturity, at adulthood."[53]

Chapter 3

CITY BOY

Most people are shaped to the form of
their culture because of the enormous
malleability of their original endowment.
They are plastic to the moulding force of
the society into which they are born.

—RUTH BENEDICT[1]

THE COLLEGE OF the City of New York (CCNY), which Roth
entered as a freshman in September 1924, occupied an imposing
Gothic complex on 138th Street and Convent Avenue. CCNY was
founded, in 1847, expressly to provide higher education to working-
class and immigrant students. Until 1976, when a municipal fiscal crisis forced it to begin charging tuition, the school maintained a policy
of offering college degrees free of cost. Women were excluded from
enrollment until 1952. But for a struggling young Jewish man born in
Galicia and living in Harlem in 1924, the College of the City of New
York (its name was changed officially to City College in 1929) was
very accessible—both geographically and financially. Though it would
be Roth's destination, it was not his only option.

With vague plans for a career in biology, perhaps as a teacher, Roth
had applied, during his senior year at DeWitt Clinton, for admission

to a special program in the sciences at Cornell University. The private Ivy League institution lay 230 miles north of Manhattan, in the arcadian college town of Ithaca, New York. In June, Roth took a competitive scholarship exam and placed twenty-third among twenty-five qualifying scores. He was offered complete tuition at Cornell for four years, as well as the opportunity for part-time employment to cover incidental expenses.

After some deliberation, Roth declined the offer, rationalizing that even with the generous scholarship he would still have difficulty paying for room and board. Herman, frugal to a fault and stingy to his only son, whose academic opportunities he mistrusted and resented, refused to help cover expenses. But money was not the only reason Roth did not attend Cornell. He could have found a part-time job to supplement his scholarship. Though he had managed to muster enough impetus to apply for the scholarship, Roth's refusal to accept it stemmed again from his tormented sense of self. Did he, an immigrant Jew who had bungled his chances at Stuyvesant High School, really belong at an Ivy League campus? In a diary entry for July 1, 1971, Roth would explain that he renounced the opportunity to study in Ithaca because he "lacked the enterprise to go."[2] His decision not to leave home—where he continued the incestuous relationship with Rose even after commencing a second with Sylvia—was another symptom of Roth's "prolonged *infantilism*."

In *A Diving Rock on the Hudson*, Ira Stigman berates himself for the "craven reply" he sent to the admissions office at Cornell: "For craven it was, formulated by a mind that knew itself craven, craven and puerile, devoid of self-reliance and initiative."[3] In *Requiem for Harlem*, Ira, distraught again over relations with his father, regrets his choice of college and recognizes that attendance at the Ivy League school might have been a kind of liberation. "If only I'd got away from here and gone to Cornell when I had a chance!" he exclaims.[4] However, Ira also senses that some inchoate intimation of destiny was guiding his decision to stay at 119th Street and attend CCNY: "Within the murky slough of his self-indulgence, he seemed to discern that if he had any hope of escaping from his abject slavery to his contemptible personality into some kind of freedom or self-respect . . . ,"[5] he needed to work things through in Harlem. Had he accepted a place in Cornell's freshman class, it seems unlikely that Roth would have had the kinds of experiences that transformed him into a novelist.

During the period between the two world wars, CCNY was commonly known as "the poor man's Harvard" because of its populist mission to educate avid scholars of modest means. A majority of the twenty thousand young men in its student body were, like Roth, Jews, excluded from Harvard, Yale, and other prestigious American institutions not only by financial barriers but also by restrictive ethnic quotas. By one calculation, 80–90 percent of the student body at CCNY was Jewish during this period.[6] In order to erase traces of the ghetto from its many Yiddish-inflected undergraduates, the college required four years of Public Speaking as a condition for graduation. Post-alveolar pronunciation of "s"—almost as if it were "sh"—was a shibboleth that stigmatized and handicapped Ashkenazic Jews. Roth's own sibling, Rose, would be denied employment in the New York City public schools because of her aberrant sibilants. By requiring Public Speaking courses as a condition for graduation, City College attempted to acculturate its students to the wider community and to deal on some level with the ambient anti-Semitism that denied Jews access to many professions.

William Barrett, a Catholic who attended City College during the 1930s, estimated that about 95 percent of his classmates were Jews. He remembered CCNY as "a combination of noise, crowding, and dirt that nostalgia cannot possibly glamorize," yet he also recalled that: "at that particular time the students, though in their own grubby and ill-mannered way, were probably the most dedicated body of undergraduates in the country."[7] Many of these students came from Yiddish-speaking homes where CCNY or another secular university was revered as a second Ellis Island, a portal into the Promised Land.

Barrett was one of a very loose cohort of critics and scholars, most of them Jews and graduates of CCNY, who became known as the New York Intellectuals. Leading figures in political science, sociology, and literary criticism during the second half of the century, they included Daniel Bell, Nathan Glazer, Irving Howe, Alfred Kazin, Irving Kristol, Melvin Lasky, Seymour Martin Lipset, William Phillips, and Earl Raab. The young intellectuals clustered in the different alcoves of the campus cafeteria not by fraternity membership but according to political allegiance. Alcove number 1 was reserved for the anti-Stalinist left, number 2 for Stalinists. In the capitalist America of breadlines and Hoovervilles, what serious thinker would not line up on the left? Students honed their intellectual and rhetorical skills on fierce polemics about the nuances of socialist theory and praxis. In a different generation and on a different continent, they would have been Talmudists.

Roth entered college about half a dozen years before the ideological ferment that produced the vintage New York Intellectuals. However, by 1924, the year of Roth's matriculation, the pugnacious thinker Sidney Hook had already graduated (in 1923) and the legendary philosopher Morris Raphael Cohen had begun leaving his mark on generations of bright young City students. Roth, alas, would not be one of them. He lacked the self-assurance and intensity of those ardent Jewish scholars. After earning a C- average during his first semester, he wondered whether he might not have fared better at Cornell, whose Gentile student body would not have provided the fierce academic competition that unnerved Roth about City.

From the outset, Roth started falling behind, jeopardizing his ability to graduate in four years since, lacking seniority, he was unable to enroll in the courses required for a biology major. CCNY, where he never felt rapport with his professors, was a disappointment, and Roth the student was a disappointment to his professors and himself. "My college career was simply a calamity," he recalled. "I retch in retrospect."[8] His first transcript showed Cs in Art, French, Philosophy, and Military Science. But in Math, as in Hygiene, he could manage only a D. His mind already muddled by domestic lechery, Roth found it hard to concentrate on trigonometric functions or irregular French verbs.

During the second semester, his grades improved, albeit slightly. He received an A in Chemistry, a B in Hygiene, and a C each in Military

Science, Public Speaking, and French. Though he received a D in English, as in Art, it was a Pyrrhic defeat, a short-term disaster that would eventually amount to a long-term triumph. Therein lies a story—in fact, the story of a story, "Impressions of a Plumber."

The English course was a required freshman class in composition that newcomer Roth had been closed out of for his first semester. The instructor was named Arthur Dickson, and his term paper assignment was an expository essay about how to construct something complex. Roth decided to draw on his experiences during the previous summer as a plumber's helper on a construction site in the Bronx. The piece that he turned in—just at the deadline, obligingly typed by his sister, Rose—is a dramatic account of one day in Roth's own life, performing hard labor as apprentice to a rugged professional named Hymie. Their job was "roughing," which, the essay explains, means installing the pipes that lead from the bathroom and kitchen to the sewer. While "Impressions of a Plumber" is not exactly Zola conjuring up the experience of working a shift in the coal mines, it is vivid, effective writing. Dickson gave the paper a D, however, because it dodged his assignment; it was impressionistic narrative, not at all the objective exposition he had explicitly demanded. With his earliest writing, as with his last, Roth could not help filtering every subject through his own personal experience. He was unable to envision any perspective other than his own, shaping all prose into a form of autobiography.

Still, he was duly shocked when, on the final day of the semester, Dickson singled his work out in class and read it out loud. It was a transforming event for the anxious undergraduate to hear his own words pronounced by the instructor, as if the author were Keats or Tennyson. Dickson announced that he was recommending "Impressions of a Plumber" for publication in the campus literary magazine, and the essay appeared in the May 1925 issue of *Lavender*. It was the first work by Roth to appear in print; and except for an undistinguished exercise in literary criticism that showed up in an obscure journal in 1930, it would be the only piece Roth published until his first novel went on sale nine years later.

Despite the miserable grade his assignment earned, the experience was gratifying. Like laying pipe, lining words up into sentences, sentences into paragraphs, satisfied Roth's fundamental urge to organize his environment. Publication by *Lavender* acknowledged a job well done. It made the author wonder whether he was being called to some career other than biologist. At approximately the same time that Roth was receiving a dubious D for freshman English, William Faulkner was washing out of the University of Mississippi, John Steinbeck out of Stanford, and Langston Hughes out of Columbia. All four were drifting toward a place in the pantheon of academic duds who attained literary glory. Before writing programs became almost as common as football teams at American universities, departments of English made themselves hospitable toward talented authors, but only if they were dead.

While Roth struggled to keep up with his classes at public CCNY, his more affluent friend Lester Winter was attending the private New York University. With a spacious, majestic site perched atop the Harlem River in the northern Bronx, NYU, as it was already known, also maintained satellite operations at a campus downtown in Greenwich Village. Washington Square Park and its surroundings formed a unique college environment, one so enticing that NYU would eventually abandon its attempt at academic seclusion and sell its uptown facilities. By 1924, seven years after Marcel Duchamp, John Sloan, and other rebel artists sneaked to the top of the Washington Square Arch and proclaimed Greenwich Village "a free and independent republic,"[9] the vibrant neighborhood of cafés, bookstores, theaters, galleries, and brownstones was already celebrated and reviled as a center for political, social, and cultural radicalism. "The Village," as the downtown neighborhood was affectionately known, was a magnet for reformers, revolutionaries, and artists who chafed at the conventions of a Puritan, mercenary America. It beckoned, especially, as the capital of sexual liberation, where the free spirits—or at least bodies—of Mabel Dodge, Max Eastman, Floyd Dell, Djuna Barnes, Edna St. Vincent Millay, and others flaunted multiple liaisons in and out of marriage. If you were young and gifted and randy but could not get to Paris during the decade following the signing of the Treaty of Versailles, Greenwich Village beckoned as the only place to be.

Like Concord, Massachusetts, 150 years earlier, the Village proved a crucial battleground in the wars that shaped the United States. This was where the motley irregulars of Modernism met—and vanquished—the tidy regiments of Victorianism. "Make it new," proclaimed Ezra Pound, though he made his demand for novelty by echoing ancient Confucius and as an expatriate to the Old World. No part of the New World was more receptive to the spirit of renewal than the city called New York, where 40 percent of the population in 1920 was foreign-born. By the time Roth abandoned New York in 1945, the metropolis he grew up in would be the site of modernity's most recognizable urban icons, including the Brooklyn Bridge, the Statue of Liberty, Wall Street, Times Square, Rockefeller Center, and the Empire State Building. With its new publishing houses, galleries, and concert halls, it had displaced Boston as the center of the American culture industry and was the local address for the new era that Henry Luce, whose global media empire would radiate outward from midtown Manhattan, dubbed "the American century."

Unscathed by the combat that had devastated European capitals during the Great War, New York in the twenties was a prosperous, boisterous laboratory for developments in the arts and culture, where, encouraged by the Nineteenth Amendment, ratified in 1920, newly enfranchised women dared to bob their hair. Emboldened to defy the Eighteenth Amendment, ratified in 1919, New Yorkers became scofflaws, flocking to speakeasies to flaunt their rebellion against the proprieties of Prohibition. Of course, free thought, free verse, and free love were not universally cherished, even in New York during what F. Scott Fitzgerald called "the Jazz Age." Anthony Comstock's New York Society for the Suppression of Vice vigorously, flamboyantly, but, in the end, unsuccessfully opposed the spread of modernism. When Margaret Sanger tried to open her first birth control clinic in 1916 in a storefront on Amboy Street in Brownsville, she was carted off to jail and sentenced to thirty days at hard labor. And earlier, the 1913 Armory Show, the provocative exhibition of more than thirteen hundred works by insurgent artists including Marcel Duchamp, Henri Matisse, Constantin Brancusi, and Francis Picabia, was assailed by *The New York Times* as "*pathological!*" and by the *New York Herald* as "unadulterated cheek."[10] Writing in *The Outlook* on March 29, 1913, former President Theodore Roosevelt, a native New Yorker, complained that "In this recent exhibition the lunatic fringe was fully in evidence, especially in the rooms devoted to the Cubists and the Futurists, or near-Impressionists."[11]

Greenwich Village, "home of half the talent and half the eccentricity in the country,"[12] was the hub of American modernism. For the immigrant Roth, a child of the ghetto desperate to find his bearings, the creative tumult would ultimately prove too much to bear. The Village was where Lester Winter, along with other privileged students enrolled at NYU Downtown, attended classes. The student body at the Washington Square campus was then 93 percent Jewish,[13] a higher percentage even than at tuition-free CCNY; but these were more advantaged Jews, predominantly middle class and an additional generation removed from immigration. NYU did not require Public Speaking courses. And whereas Roth was frustrated about being closed out of classes required for graduation, Winter encountered no difficulty in signing up for whatever courses he wanted at NYU. Although he was preparing for dental school, Winter found himself more and more drawn to literature, and particularly excited by one extraordinary instructor named Eda Lou Walton.

A petite, olive-skinned woman, with large, doleful eyes, Walton was a vibrant, generous teacher and literary impresario. At a time when the academic study of literature ignored contemporaries, Walton, herself a poet and an anthologist, advocated the work of living authors, introducing her awed students to Hart Crane not just on the page but in person. Decades before it became fashionable, she taught a course at NYU on women authors. She co-edited a hefty collection, *This Generation* (1939), which was one of the few anthologies of its time to include the voices of ethnic minorities. Walton was a champion of modernism, a scourge of banality, and a passionate defender of genuine originality. "The clear poet in her hated the spaghetti of contemporary prose," recalled Claire Burch, one of her students.[14] Walton encouraged Winter in his own creative writing, and she appointed him secretary of the NYU Arts Club, an organization that met monthly to encounter and discuss recent poetry.

Roth was amazed to hear about Winter's stimulating experiences at NYU, so different from his own dreary ordeal at CCNY. Roth's instructors remained aloof, forbidding scholars, but Winter spoke of his as if they were intimates. Walton, in particular, defied the formalities that governed academic life, consorting with her students beyond class time and the classroom. In fact, as Winter soon confided to his old high school pal, Walton had become his secret lover. In the 1920s, when addressing a professor by first name was a shocking breach of etiquette, universities had no need to codify rules about sexual contact between faculty and students. It was simply unheard of—even if it did occur. Though her behavior was scandalous, Eda Lou Walton remained above suspicion as long as her colleagues did not imagine that an instructor at NYU would indulge in sexual relations with a student. An untenured woman in a department run by men, Walton, though, had reason to be wary. The ignominy for a female authority figure caught sleeping with a younger man, especially a Jew, would have been much greater than for a male professor who bedded a female student.

Astounded by his own good fortune, Winter shared details with Roth of his extracurricular lovemaking. He insisted that it was love. Winter adored his teacher and was eager to marry her and abandon the veneer of middle-class respectability. He would scuttle his plans for dentistry and devote the rest of his life to art and Eda Lou Walton. Winter's parents were flabbergasted that their beloved son, who could surely have his pick of wealthy Jewish women, was about to jettison his auspicious future for a bohemian *shicksa* almost half again his age. In order not to burden his family or pose a threat to Walton's tenuous, tenureless position at NYU, Winter decided that he would finish up his studies at tuition-free CCNY.

Roth was stunned by these revelations, though not quite in the way that Winter, who had no inkling of his friend's squalid sexual secrets, might have anticipated. Far from being put off by Winter's unconventional behavior, Roth envied the comparative normalcy of this romance between student poet and poetry instructor. If only he could break the shameful chains tying him to his family, he too could dream of an exalting, exogamous passion.

Winter was eager to show his friend from CCNY the Village avant-garde he had infiltrated, as well as to show off his romantic conquest. But when he invited Roth to attend a session of the NYU Arts Club, Roth, beset by his old sense of unworthiness, declined. In such sophisticated company, any step of his, he feared, would be a faux pas. He was not part of the NYU community, but merely a freshman at unglamorous CCNY. He was not even an English major and had so far taken only one course in English—required composition. Besides, what would he wear? Winter answered the last question by giving Roth a smart English tweed jacket from his own wardrobe. Still, Roth put off from month to month making an appearance at the Arts Club.

FINALLY, ON A CHILLY NIGHT in March 1925, Roth made his way down to MacDougal Street and tried to slip inconspicuously into the teahouse where the Arts Club was meeting. Though Greenwich Village was adjacent to the Lower East Side, Roth was entering a different universe from the one in which he had grown up. What would these suave literati, who commanded flawless English, make of a bumbling upstart whose syllables betrayed the vulgar guttural Jewish jargon he still spoke at home? The featured speaker for this occasion was Léonie Adams, who, though only twenty-five, was already editing the magazine *Measure* and writing poetry powerful enough to draw the well-known anthropologist Margaret Mead down from Morningside Heights to hear her read that evening.

Roth, for whom poetry was a matter of printed texts by long-dead authors such as Wordsworth and Coleridge, felt like Cinderella suddenly lifted out of an ash-strewn hovel and propelled into the palace. He was awkward making small talk with clever NYU students, and the pontifications, during the public discussion, about niceties of contemporary verse left him lost. Nor did he feel secure even about his command of Ashkenazic Jewish culture. When Roth recreated that evening many years later in *A Diving Rock on the Hudson,* Ira Stigman is introduced to the granddaughter of Sholem Aleichem, the most famous and beloved of Yiddish authors. "I don't know who he is,"[15] says Ira, either out of woeful ignorance or a lame attempt to mock a group of assimilated American Jewish literati he resents for condescending to him. In either case, he feels like a *grobyan*—a dolt.

But Winter insisted on introducing Roth immediately to Walton, a gracious host who put the outsider at his ease. The woman's restless energy seemed to burst out of her frail frame. Walton was not put off by Roth's obviously rudimentary grasp of modern literature, and, gazing intently at him with her large brown eyes, encouraged him to pursue the subject further. Walton often held classes in the apartment on St. Mark's Place that she shared with another instructor, Iola Reid, and she invited Roth to attend a session in April. She also urged him to come along whenever Winter visited her. When Roth finally stepped back out into MacDougal Street, the Harlem home that awaited his return seemed more grim than ever.

During the months that followed, Roth, tagging along beside Winter, was a frequent visitor to St. Mark's Place. He served as chaperon to legitimize the couple's outings together. On one Sunday in late May 1925, he and Winter joined Walton and Iola Reid for a boat trip up the Hudson to picnic on Bear Mountain. The situation encouraged a double romantic pairing; but Roth, disabled by his squalid secret, could not accede to the symmetry. He and Reid talked, while Winter and Walton kissed. On this and other occasions, whenever the worldly, comely lovers embraced, Roth remained merely an awkward observer. "God, I just felt like a toad!" he recalled.[16] Thinking of his own tawdry couplings with his sister, Roth might have wished himself into one of his public library storybooks in which the amphibian is transformed by a timely kiss.

Walton had only recently arrived in New York, and to Roth she represented an America of wide, open spaces that a Jewish child of the eastern slums could only imagine. Her background could not have seemed more unlike his. Walton was born in Deming, New Mexico, in 1894, twelve years before Roth's birth in Tysmenitz and eighteen years before New Mexico came into the Union. Her father, William Bell Walton, a lawyer born in Pennsylvania, was an important figure in territorial politics. He served in each house of the New Mexico legislature and as the new state's representative to the U.S. Congress, from 1917 to 1919. He and his wife raised their three children (Eda Lou was the eldest) in Silver City, where he owned and edited a newspaper called *The Independent* and presided over the Board of Regents of the New Mexico Normal School. An active Democrat, William Bell Walton ran for the U.S. Senate in 1918 but was defeated in the general revulsion against Woodrow Wilson's failures. He turned to alcohol and took up with another woman. His abstemious wife took their children with her to California. While his eldest daughter lived in the Village, William Bell Walton was still serving Silver City as district attorney, from 1926 until 1932. He died in 1939.

Though Eda Lou Walton initially trained for a career as a concert pianist and even worked for a while as a musical accompanist for silent movies, her hands were simply too small for the grand task of filling a recital hall. She enrolled at the University of California at Berkeley and graduated summa cum laude and Phi Beta Kappa. Walton pursued her graduate work at Berkeley in both anthropology and English, pioneering the study of American Indian culture. At a time when "creative writing" had not yet become commonplace at American universities, she was also one of twenty-three students in Witter Bynner's legendary course in poetry writing. Bynner, a native New Yorker who had recently come to California, held his classes as often as possible either outdoors, in a grove just below Berkeley's Greek Theater, or else at his residence in the Carlton Hotel, a redbrick edifice on Telegraph Avenue at the corner of Durant where Rupert Brooke had stayed five years earlier.

Intent on living his life poetically according to the fin-de-siècle poetics of Stéphane Mallarmé and Oscar Wilde, Bynner created a distinctive quasi-Oriental ambience within his rented lodgings. In a poem written in tribute to her teacher, Walton attempted to evoke the atmosphere of Carlton's Room 221, presided over by Bynner:

Your Chinese den is green and white
And red, lit with a golden light,
And everyone I know has been
Made welcome by your genial grin
To pass an hour's pleasant flight.[17]

Bynner's custom of fortifying the geniality by serving his students cocktails and wine led to a stern reprimand from Charles Mills Gayley, chairman of the English Department, and the decision not to rehire him after a single semester in 1919. After lingering some months in Berkeley, where he continued as an unofficial impresario of poetry, Bynner moved to Santa Fe, where, until his death in 1968, he remained a prominent figure in the arts community, and a model to many for refusing to conceal his homosexuality, until his death in 1968.

Bynner nourished Walton's literary talent and considered her the one young poet under his tutelage most likely to succeed. In 1919, a year before receiving her doctorate, Walton won the University of California's prestigious Emily Chamberlain Cook Prize for her own poetry. Her dissertation, "Navajo Traditional Poetry, Its Content and Form," the product of long and loving familiarity with southwestern tribal customs and language, broke new ground in academic scholarship. Her translations of Navajo and Blackfoot songs in *Dawn Boy* (1926) would, like Ezra Pound's translations from the Chinese, enlarge the possibilities of modern American poetry. "Miss Walton," wrote Bynner in a patronizing Introduction he provided, "a poet not only bred in Indian terrain but well versed in her art and well attuned in her spirit, has brought into more congenial English than any other interpreter has found, the simplicities, the serenities, the grave and happy mysticism of Indian song."

After Berkeley, Walton taught at Fresno State College, before accepting a position at NYU in 1924, just as Winter and Roth were commencing their college careers. Soon after arriving in New York, she was befriended not only by poets such as Léonie Adams, Louise Bogan, and Genevieve Taggard but also by leading anthropologists, including Ruth Benedict and Margaret Mead. Like Walton herself, most of these women were migrants to Manhattan. They were also examples of the "New Women" who, in the aftermath of the Nineteenth Amendment, were asserting themselves in ways—from bobbed hair to free verse to sexual experimentation—that an earlier, unenfranchised generation would not have dared. Walton attended occasional meetings of Heterodoxy, a women's discussion group that had been founded in 1912 and met twice weekly in the Village. Many, but not all, of the group's fluid membership, which included Margaret Sanger, Elizabeth Gurley Flynn, Fannie Hurst, Zona Gale, Frances Perkins Gilman, Mabel Dodge, and Susan Glaspell, were radical feminists and/or lovers of other women.

Benedict and Mead, who maintained a long-term romantic and sexual relationship even while each was married (Mead three times), had met at Columbia University. Like Alfred Kroeber, Walton's mentor at the University of California, both had studied under Franz Boas, a German-born Jew who was the first professor of anthropology at Columbia University. In addition to pursuing their pioneering fieldwork in ethnography, both women wrote poetry. Mead's sojourn in the South Pacific would result in her best-selling *Coming of Age in Samoa: A Psychological Study of Primitive Youth for Western Civilization* (1928). A provocative account of how a healthy non-Western culture encourages its adolescents to be sexually active, the book made Mead one of the most famous intellectuals of her time. It was the most widely read work of anthropology written by an American in the twentieth century, though it was later in part discredited when another scholar revealed how much of her story Mead had confabulated. Benedict's *Patterns of Culture* (1934) would become a fundamental text in the discipline of anthropology. Of particular interest to Walton, as a native of the Southwest and a scholar of American Indian poetry, was the fieldwork that Benedict conducted in New Mexico during the summers of 1924 and 1925, which resulted in *Tales of the Cochiti Indians* (1931) and the two-volume *Zuñi Mythology* (1935). Walton often joined Benedict, Mead, and their friends for poetry evenings at which they drank bootleg liquor, recited verse, and played rhyming games.

At the end of her first May in New York, Walton set sail for Europe, where she spent most of the summer traveling through France and Italy. In the vivid letters that she sent back almost weekly, not only to Winter but to Roth as well, Walton described the sights she saw and the foods she ate—or did not eat. Suffering from chronic colitis, which sometimes disabled her for an entire day, she was forced throughout her life to be fastidious about diet. That summer Winter worked as a recreational director at a resort hotel in the Catskill Mountains, north of New York City. When Walton returned from abroad, she and Winter spent two weeks together in a lovely stone cottage loaned by an NYU colleague, in Woodstock, at the foot of the Catskills. They invited Roth to join them, and, despite some unease, he did. He would have to control not only how he spoke but also how he ate—*fressen* (gorging) and *chompken* (chomping) might be tolerable on 119th Street, but they surely had no place in polite company.

The geometry of the triangle was anything but plain, yet Walton, Winter, and Roth became increasingly a threesome. Roth warily kept his own sexual secrets to himself, but Winter felt no qualms about confiding intimate information to his friend. In *From Bondage*—the third volume of *Mercy of a Rude Stream*, which would be published posthumously in 1996—Larry Gordon, a fictional version of Lester Winter, reveals to Ira Stigman that premature ejaculation was marring his relationship with his lover, the NYU professor.[18] And Walton openly discussed with Roth her earlier romantic episodes and the barriers to advancement that she and other women faced in academe. Except for the ineluctable fact that she was a *shicksa*, she might, Roth learned, have married Shmuel Hamburg, a Socialist and Zionist who had left his kibbutz in Palestine to study agronomy in California. And though she had received her doctorate and was already distinguishing herself as scholar, translator, and poet, Walton found NYU reluctant to grant women tenure-track positions.

Roth was now known to others as Harry; Walton called him "child," both in droll recognition of the twelve years that separated their ages and in genuine, maternal tenderness. Roth played the part of loyal attendant to Winter and virtuous knight-in-arms to Walton.

He realized that the only reason that Winter and Walton tolerated, even encouraged, his presence was their belief in his innocence, though he in fact felt sullied by irredeemable depravity. Yet again, Roth's "prolonged *infantilism*" made him accept the role of dispassionate witness to others' passion and led others to adopt him as an amiable eunuch. "It was that," observes a Roth character in a virtually identical situation, "that made him a safe confederate at his friend's wooings, such as they were."[19] Compounding the infantilism was his own awareness that this eunuch was a covert debauchee within his home in Harlem.

During their Woodstock idyll, Walton introduced Winter and Roth to a notorious book that she had smuggled back from Europe. In 1925, James Joyce's *Ulysses* was literary contraband in America. Episodes had been judged obscene in 1918, when Margaret Anderson and Jane Heap attempted to publish them in *The Little Review*, produced out of their Washington Square Bookstore in the Village, and no American book publisher now dared touch the novel. When Sylvia Beach, the proprietor of Shakespeare & Company in Paris, brought it out in 1922, *Ulysses* quickly became a smart export item. Not until 1932, when Judge John M. Woolsey of the federal district court in New York ruled that Joyce's novel possessed artistic merit and was not obscene, would a domestic edition, published by Random House, be sold legally in the United States.

Winter tried briefly to read the novel but concluded that the flashy prose demanded too much effort for too little reward, and he had other matters on his mind at Woodstock. Besides, his interests were shifting toward theater and sculpture, and he was beginning to lose his enthusiasm for modern literature. Roth, by contrast, picked up the book with the powder blue cover and found its account of one day— June 16, 1904—in the lives of Leopold Bloom, Molly Bloom, and Stephen Dedalus impossible to put down. If anything, it gave him something to do while the two lovers were preoccupied. Years later, he would turn against Joyce's doctrine of aesthetic autonomy, reviling him as "the Pied Piper of Dublin with his verbal virtuosity leading his spellbound followers to the ultimate cavern,"[20] and berating Joyce for the bogus, stereotypical Jewishness of Leopold Bloom. But in 1925, *Ulysses* was a profound revelation to Roth. In turn, Roth's affinity for Joyce impressed on Walton that he was a young man of exceptional, undeveloped talent well worth nurturing.

As with most other readers, many of the literary allusions eluded him. But Roth, who grew up in an Irish neighborhood, was dazzled by Joyce's ability to endow his vulgar Dublin characters with vibrant verbal life. *Ulysses* taught Roth that the plots and characters of fairy tales need not be the only formula for literature and that, scrutinized carefully enough, ordinary urban existence could bear the gravity of myth. "What I gained," Roth would recall, "was this awed realization that you didn't have to go anywhere at all except around the corner to flesh out a literary work—given some kind of vision, of course. In stream of consciousness I recognized that my own continual dialogue with myself could be made into literature. It was a tremendous impetus toward writing."[21]

Joyce's background was no more privileged than Roth's own. One of sixteen children in a family whose deteriorating fortunes led them through a dozen different Dublin addresses, the Irish author grew up in misery, determined to escape the nets of kinship and nationality. It was through mastery of English prose—"it was language, language, that could magically transmogrify the baseness of his days and ways into precious literature,"[22] wrote Roth—that Joyce was able to transcend his shabby origins through a consummate, enduring book. Could Roth not do the same? Raised in Yiddish, he would have to do it in the purified language of another tribe. Yet even the squalor and horror of his own Harlem life might, through the power of English, be redeemed.

During the fall of 1925, Roth made another crucial literary discovery. In order to make room for Iola Reid's boyfriend to move in with her, Walton moved out of their shared apartment on St. Mark's Place and into a noisy basement flat on Eighth Street, several blocks away. Winter, who was now, like Roth, a student at CCNY, often brought his buddy along to visit her there. During these evenings, Winter would toil on a statue of Walton while Roth pored over the extensive collection of contemporary poetry on Walton's shelves. One poet in particular, T. S. Eliot, challenged and fascinated Roth, who committed much of *The Love Song of J. Alfred Prufrock* and *The Waste Land* to memory.

Eliot's jagged, jazzy rhythms and his discordant urban imagery were revelations to a young reader whose poetic education had ceased with Keats and Tennyson. Here was a contemporary whose "Unreal City"— in *The Waste Land*, published just three years before—might have been Roth's New York as much as dismal London. "The river's tent is broken" might as easily describe the Hudson as the Thames. Of course, Roth was not the only reader to fall under the spell of a magisterial poet and critic who, from 1922 until his death in 1965, dominated British and American literature. Born in St. Louis with an impeccable patrician pedigree, the erudite Eliot belonged to a far different species from his indigent immigrant Jewish admirer. Yet Roth accepted the opening lines of *Prufrock*—"Let us go then, you and I"—as a personal invitation. He could respond to the self-loathing of a narrator who does not dare to eat a peach and to the sexual malaise that Eliot's Tiresias, "Old man with wrinkled female breasts," has "foresuffered." Weary himself of things Jewish, Roth acknowledged and unconsciously accepted the casual anti-Semitism that led Eliot to print "jew" with a disdainful lower-case "j" and to write with contempt in *Gerontion:* "And the jew squats on the window sill, the owner / Spawned in some estaminet of Antwerp." Roth responded directly to the poet's desolate vision of the modern world, whose fragments the artist must shore against his ruins. Through the fractured planes of Eliot's poems, he discerned "a mood made up of futility and timidity, frustration and emptiness, loneliness, misunderstanding, self-distrust,"[23] and it was a mood that corresponded directly to Roth's own state of mind.

It also appealed to Eda Lou Walton, a transposed westerner who, like Eliot, was discovering poetry in dingy urban settings. In 1929, she would publish *The City Day: An Anthology of Recent American Poetry*, a collection that acknowledged Henry Roth and another acolyte named Isadore Silver "for assistance in proofreading and other clerical help."[24] The book organized poems—by Léonie Adams,

Louise Bogan, Hart Crane, David Greenhood, Margaret Mead, Lynn Riggs, Genevieve Taggard, Mark Van Doren, and Marya Zaturensky, among others—to capture the full diurnal cycle of life in the metropolis. "Students need poetry that responds to their increasingly urban experience," Walton explained, in words that also justified Eliot's revolution in sensibility. But Winter was bothered by a poet who so thoroughly repudiated the ideals of classical beauty, and he argued with Roth about Eliot. However, Roth was in awe of the poet's ability to transform the same ennui and alienation felt by his young Jewish reader into redemptive art. "I would say," said Roth in 1979, "that Eliot was the major influence on my life."[25]

Throughout the 1925–26 academic year, Roth's life continued in an ugly muddle. Monday evening sallies to his cousin Sylvia sometimes kept him from joining Winter at Walton's apartment in the Village. But a Sunday-to-Friday job as cashier/clerk at a Loft's candy shop in the Bronx disrupted the old routine with Rose, who was in any case adjusting to adolescence and growing restive in the role of sibling concubine. She boasted to her brother about the "normal" boyfriend she had acquired. Roth was paid sixteen dollars a week for the job at Loft's, and when he was unjustly docked ten dollars for money stolen by an agile thief, he made up the difference by pocketing ten dollars in candy sales without leaving any record of the transaction. However, when a fellow worker urged him to cooperate in a clever scheme to skim the store's profits, Roth, mindful of his disgraceful departure from Stuyvesant High School, refused. In the summer of 1926, when he finally quit the job, he left Loft's with a clear conscience.

WHILE ROTH REAPED huge benefits from his growing friendship with Walton, his newfound literary awareness had virtually no effect on his formal education. The dispenser of sweets at Loft's had soured on CCNY, where he was at best a mediocre performer and soon abandoned plans for a career in biology. Roth's most important literary training came through Eda Lou Walton, her books, and her writer friends. Though he had received an A in Military Science during the fall, he received a D for the same subject in the spring (sympathetic to the international disarmament movement, City students were agitating against keeping the subject compulsory). Roth did get an A in English and a B in Economics, but in almost everything else—French, History, Hygiene, Chemistry—the grade was C. For Public Speaking, he earned a C in the fall and a B in the spring. He dropped a class in Math, and earned a C in the French course that, in order to make up for missing credits, he took during the summer of 1926.

Walton spent that summer visiting her father in Silver City, and Winter, who now anticipated a career in the theater, worked as an entertainer at a Catskills hotel. Walton returned to New York with a special present for Roth: an antique Navajo turquoise ring. In the fall, she invited Roth, alone, to her apartment. It had become increasingly clear that Walton was disappointed in Lester Winter—not just sexually. The way he had flitted from literature to sculpture to theater convinced her he was a dilettante, not the gifted and dedicated young poet who had captured her heart when he entered her NYU class a year and a half earlier. And Roth's reverence for his princely friend, now that he too was enrolled at CCNY, had gradually evolved into first envy and then rivalry. It would have been unimaginable just a few months before, but Walton, a universal magnet with particular power over men, seemed now to take more interest in Roth than in Winter. So, when summoned for a private tête-à-tête, Roth may have floated down to Eighth Street on romantic expectations.

It turned out that Walton needed him, again, to be her confidant. She asked to speak to him alone because she trusted him to be a harmless witness to her own passion. It was the kind of trust that must have exasperated Roth, who played the part of virtuous squire while seething with secret depravity. Walton confided that she had fallen out of love with Winter and into love with someone else. She must have been aware of the effect she was having on her ardent listener. However, her sweetheart, she revealed, was a man named Luther Cressman. A sociologist who taught at Roth's own college, Cressman was the husband of Margaret Mead, whom he had first met in Doylestown, Pennsylvania, where his brother was her high school math teacher. Mead had persuaded Cressman, a Presbyterian, to switch churches and to become an Episcopal priest. When, after a five-year engagement, they wed in September 1923, Mead and Cressman agreed to an open marriage, in which Mead would keep her maiden name and each party would grant the other a divorce on demand. "It would be an insult to both me and my husband to expect marital fidelity on the part of either of us," declared Mead, who avoided insulting Cressman in that way.[26] Throughout the four years of a relatively passionless marriage, Mead had flings with other men and women.

Mead had left Cressman behind while she traveled to the South Pacific to do the research for *Coming of Age in Samoa*. On the ship coming back, she fell seriously in love with Reo Fortune, a psychologist from New Zealand. While his wife was in Samoa, Cressman spent time in Europe, where, despite his marriage vows to Mead and his romantic attachment to Walton, he fell in love with an Englishwoman named Dorothy Cecilia Loch. When Roth entered the story, Cressman was unable to choose between Loch and Walton, even while still emotionally in thrall to Mead.

Walton continued to confide in Roth throughout the academic year. She was grateful for a discreet listener, and she told him of her sexual intimacy with Cressman and her anxiety about losing him to Loch. She also expressed misgivings about her old friend, Margaret Mead. After returning from Samoa, Mead had moved into an apartment on West 24th Street with four other women—two of whom, Léonie Adams and Louise Rosenblatt, were poets. Yet Mead and Cressman were in no haste to terminate their four-year marriage. When they did eventually divorce, Mead married Reo Fortune and, eager to assuage her guilt, tried to pair Cressman with Walton. But at the moment, Walton was convinced that Mead was using her continuing hold over her husband to alienate Cressman from her.

Roth was flattered and flustered by the trust that Walton placed in him. It was so different from the relationships he had with his sister, cousin, and mother. Walton's own distress prevented her from noticing—too much—that her young confidant was neither detached nor dispassionate. The smitten, dependent Roth was convenient compensation for being spurned by Cressman. An interloper among the intellectuals, Roth was amazed at how articulately these sophisticated thinkers could rationalize the predicaments that passion led them into. In Greenwich Village, the bastion of sexual liberation, despotic libido had wreaked as much havoc as it had in unenlightened Harlem. Samoans seemed far more civilized than American intellectuals in how they handled the urgencies of sex.

When, during the spring of 1927, Cressman decided to sail to England in order to weigh his options with his other lover, he discussed everything with Walton. She had an accurate premonition that Cressman's decision to go to Loch meant she would lose him to her rival. However, she insisted on seeing him off, which involved a long, dispiriting trip to and from the port in Hoboken, New Jersey, where Cressman's ship, the SS *Leviathan*, was docked. For emotional support, she asked Roth to come along. After parting from Cressman at the pier, Walton was distraught, wondering whether she would ever see Cressman again. Roth tried his best to dispel the gloom during the cab trip back to Manhattan. But Walton was still despondent when they arrived at her apartment, and Roth decided to try to comfort her by staying for the night. Stretched beside her in her bed, Roth slept chastely—a very perfect, gentle knight.

Roth was receiving an advanced education in matters of the heart, but he still had another year to go before graduating from CCNY. He spent the summer of 1927 at the repair barn of the Interboro Rapid Transit Company (IRT), a huge edifice that held eighty subway trains and employed hundreds of rugged laborers, few of them with any college credits. Respected and resented by the others, the City College scholar worked as a grease monkey for $28.50 a week, squirting oil into the engines of the trains. Throughout his employment at the IRT barn, Roth was wary of a devastating jolt from the third rail—something like the apocalyptic electrocution he would later conjure up for David Schearl while the eight-year-old plays on the streetcar tracks of the Lower East Side. After nine hours each day toiling for the IRT, Roth rushed off to 138th Street for four hours of evening classes. At summer school, he earned predictable Cs in Geology, Government, and Public Speaking.

In September, Cressman returned to New York engaged to his lover in England. But that did not stop him from taking up with Walton again. And Walton turned once more to Roth for emotional support, confiding her continuing passion for Cressman, deftly manipulating the younger man's emotions. When she became pregnant, unexpectedly, she summoned Roth to share the secret, and he showed up at her apartment hours after she returned, ashen, from an abortion. Walton bemoaned her fate, assuring Roth that she had had it with Cressman, Winter, and men in general. As she expected, this specific man was a sympathetic listener.

By this time, Walton had moved to a more tranquil and spacious location in the West Village. Her new apartment, on the first floor of a brick, Greek Revival building at 61 Morton Street, was just a couple of blocks from $75\frac{1}{2}$ Bedford Street, a three-story building that was known as the narrowest house in New York City; it was even more famous for being the residence, in 1924–25, of America's most flamboyant woman poet, Edna St. Vincent Millay. Like Walton, Millay was a free spirit and an alluring figure who collected and discarded lovers. She had even inspired a marriage proposal, rebuffed, from Walton's old poetry professor, Witter Bynner, in spite of his sexual orientation.

Nearby, at 139 MacDougal Street, was the Provincetown Playhouse, where new works by Eugene O'Neill, Sean O'Casey, and Gertrude Stein were regularly performed. One of Roth's many temporary jobs was as scene shifter for the Provincetown Players. Also in the neighborhood, at 86 Bedford Street, was Chumley's, a leftist literary speakeasy. Beyond its purposefully plain, unmarked door congregated a veritable pantheon of writers. Today, long after the repeal of Prohibition in 1933, patrons need no longer speak easy in order to procure alcohol, but Chumley's is still conspicuously inconspicuous. Inside, it advertises that its clientele has included Djuna Barnes, Willa Cather, E. E. Cummings, John Dos Passos, Theodore Dreiser, James Farrell,

Ring Lardner, John Steinbeck, Upton Sinclair, Edmund Wilson—and Henry Roth.

But 61 Morton Street itself soon became a gathering place for eminent artists and thinkers. During the 1940's, long after Walton and Roth had vacated the premises, avant-garde filmmaker Maya Deren would make her home at the same address. During the decade that Walton lived at 61 Morton, the house frequently became a salon whose doors were open to an uncouth undergraduate from CCNY as much as to illustrious intellectuals. A young Jew whose only publishing credit came in a student magazine, with a piece on—of all things—plumbing, could meet as peers such literati as Louise Bogan, Kenneth Burke, Hart Crane, James T. Farrell, Horace Gregory, Lynn Riggs, William Troy, Mark Van Doren, and Thomas Wolfe. "Actually, I wasn't on their level," Roth recalled. "I mean, I scarcely had any business *being* there. What I am trying to say is that I saw talents there that were really exceptional."[27]

For Walton, an exceptional scholar of the Navajo, Roth was in effect a noble savage, who offered a refreshing contrast to the Village intellectuals she introduced him to. Alfred Kroeber, Walton's dissertation adviser at Berkeley, had given shelter to Ishi, the last surviving Yahi Indian. He had also turned him into a museum exhibit, and Ishi, who died of tuberculosis in 1916, did not survive his collision with modernity by more than five years. Roth, in effect, was Walton's Ishi—an interloping primitive she hoped to initiate, more gently and benignly, into the ways of civilization. A much more promising protégé than the middle-class Lester Winter, he had more raw talent and a more malleable personality. Though her disappointments in Winter and Cressman had led her, briefly, to forswear any further entanglement with men, Walton was ready to take on Henry Roth. A popular play by George Bernard Shaw produced in 1914 dramatized a modern Galatea's revolt against her master sculptor. In 1927, Walton, an American academic who shared the civilizing mission of Professor Henry Higgins, took on her role as Pygmalion.

Several weeks after Walton's abortion, Roth, in grotesque symmetry, found himself panicking over his cousin Sylvia's missed menstruation. Frantic at the likelihood that she was carrying their child, he appealed to Walton for help. Sparing no seamy detail, he confessed everything about his chronic incest with both Rose and Sylvia. Walton reacted with compassion. Censure would have clashed with the official Village creed of tolerance and would have been inconsistent with Walton's assurances to Roth that, as their friend Mead had been discovering, sexual experimentation was common among young people in many cultures. It was also an opportunity for Walton to increase Roth's emotional dependence on her. She affirmed her own disdain for Puritan conventions, and she offered the services of her doctor for Sylvia. Though Sylvia turned out not to be pregnant after all, Roth's cathartic confession brought the two closer together and demolished an invisible wall that had hitherto kept them apart. Henceforth, they would live within the same walls, on Morton Street.

Winter pleaded with Roth not to let their shifting relationships with Walton destroy their friendship. From the time they shared a desk in an elocution class at DeWitt Clinton, Winter and Roth had accumulated a treasury of common memories, and Winter was loath for them to go their separate ways. But upon moving in with Walton in December 1927, Roth broke with Winter, abruptly and brutally. He did feel pangs of anguish about leaving 119th Street, especially since Leah, who suffered from recurrent catarrh, complained of a roaring in her head—perhaps an early sign of her later mental illness. And Herman was still tormenting his mother. Much of Roth's continuing resentment toward his own father would be reflected in his description of Ira Stigman's father as "a mean, stingy, screwy little louse."[28] But Rose, who had been rejected for a teaching position on account of her pronunciation, had taken on a steady office job. If Roth did not escape the bondage of his family now, he believed he never would.

Thirteen years after leaving Ninth Street, Roth left Harlem for what was in effect the Lower West Side. He was still a senior at CCNY and would have to commute back up to Harlem to attend classes. In fact, because of poor grades and insufficient credits, Roth would not receive his B.S. for another ten months. But from now on, he would keep a proper distance from both cousin and sister.

The move from Harlem to Morton Street put an end to one phase of Roth's prolonged infantilism. As Thomas Wolfe—whom Roth would later meet through Walton—famously put it: "You can't go home again." Roth would return regularly to East 119th Street, but only as a visitor. After almost twenty-three years, he had finally taken steps to put behind his childhood, through the dubious means of sub-stituting mothers, Eda Lou for Leah.

In one sense, Roth was only now beginning to take charge of his destiny. But in another, he was beginning the process of recursion that would dominate the rest of his long life. Again and again Roth would return in his mind to 119th Street. The Harlem years provided him with the emotional capital on which he drew for almost all his fiction, even when the setting appears to be the Lower East Side. A departure from Harlem is the final scene of the final pages of *Mercy of a Rude Stream*. The theme for everything from now on, throughout a seventy-year fixation on the immigrant boy in a dysfunctional household, could be borrowed from what became the title of his last book: *Requiem for Harlem*.

Chapter 4

KEPT MAN

My mother's voice and my father's fists are
the two bookends of my childhood, and they
form the basis of my art.

—PAT CONROY[1]

HENRY ROTH DEPARTED Harlem in the same year, 1928, that
Claude McKay published his best-selling *Home to Harlem*.
Even though he wrote the novel—about a black soldier's return from
Europe after World War I—in Paris, McKay formed part of a lustrous
constellation of artists and thinkers at first known as the New Negro
Movement and then the Harlem Renaissance. If Roth had any contact
with McKay, Langston Hughes, James Weldon Johnson, Arna Bon-
temps, Countee Cullen, or any of the other black writers who con-
verged on Harlem during the 1920s, it would more likely have been
downtown on Ninth Street, at one of Mabel Dodge's eclectic evenings,
than uptown on 136th Street, at the salon called the Dark Tower that
A'Lelia Walker, flamboyant heir to her mother's cosmetics fortune,
hosted. Zora Neale Hurston was a regular guest at Walker's salon as
well as, like Margaret Mead, a student of anthropology at Barnard

under Franz Boas and Ruth Benedict. Hurston published her first novel, *Jonah's Vine Gourd*, in 1934, the same year Roth published his first book, and her work too languished in neglect for decades before being rediscovered posthumously and canonized. Despite her acquaintance with Mead and Benedict, however, there is no evidence that Hurston and Roth ever met through Walton.

The Roths remained in Harlem even as Jews and other whites were abandoning the neighborhood for other parts of New York and the suburbs. Blacks, many of them part of the Great Migration that brought close to 2 million African Americans from the rural South to the urban North between 1914 and 1930, were moving in. By 1930, the black population of Harlem had swelled to 164,566. They soon discovered that housing discrimination elsewhere in the borough prevented them from moving out of Harlem as others had. And by 1930, a combination of economic adversity, landlords (black and white) willing to exploit captive tenants, and declining morale turned the area into an infamously wretched ghetto and put an end to the Renaissance.

However, while Roth was an undergraduate at CCNY on 138th Street, Harlem was hot. Yet there is no evidence that, throughout the decade now dubbed the Jazz Age, Roth visited Small's Paradise, Connie's Inn, the Cotton Club, the Savoy Ballroom, the Apollo Theater, or any of the other spots in Harlem where Duke Ellington, Louis Armstrong, Fats Waller, and other African Americans were inventing a new musical idiom. Italian opera maintained its hold on his affections. The fictional prostitute whose Harlem apartment Ira Stigman visits in *A Diving Rock on the Hudson* is black, as are the three young thugs who harass Stigman and his cousin Stella in the balcony of a movie theater in *Requiem for Harlem*. So is the driver, unnamed except as "the Negro," whose battered Chevrolet truck ties up midtown traffic in the short story "Broker." Otherwise, the black population in Roth's fictional New York is extremely sparse. Roth's resuscitation, in his eighties, as the chronicler of his own earlier life in upper Manhattan could be termed a kind of private, minor Harlem Renaissance, but the Harlem that he conjured up is very different from the capital of

African American culture. Uptown was just coming into vogue when Roth moved downtown to live with Walton, and he was too absorbed in his own personal renaissance to pay much heed to the cultural efflorescence of the neighborhood he fled.

Eda Lou Walton was prolific as an author, critic, and editor, but even while composing poetry, compiling anthologies, writing reviews, and teaching, she expended abundant energy on a range of friendships. At Morton Street, Walton provided Roth with a room of his own, a study facing the backyard garden, and she kept him amply supplied with food, clothing, and affection. Yet she also welcomed a steady stream of visitors, some overnight. Walton, a divorcée who had been married briefly, in 1920, to a man from Michigan named Otto L. Tinklepaugh, made no attempt to hide her attachments to other—mostly young—men. To one, a promising poet, David "Clink" Greenhood, she temporarily provided another room in the house. To another, the labor lawyer David Mandel, she eventually provided her hand in marriage.

During the thirties, the erotic versatility of Henry Miller could be considered charmingly wicked. But a woman was held to different standards, even in New York's bohemia and even by an anthropologist famed for defending sexual experimentation among Samoan adolescents. Margaret Mead, whose younger brother and first husband each ended up in Walton's bed, had little sympathy for her friend's sexual activity. When Roth met up with Mead about forty years later, she said of Walton: "Her promiscuity was desperate. Far beyond anything necessary to establish her right to an equal sex life with men."[2] For *This Generation*, an anthology of modern American literature that she co-edited, with George K. Anderson, in 1939, Walton contributed a headnote on the poetry of Edna St. Vincent Millay. A brief, wistful sentence there could serve as an epitaph not only for the meteoric Millay but also for other contemporary women writers, including Dorothy Parker, Elinor Wylie, Dawn Powell, and Eda Lou Walton herself, who loved not wisely but too well: "Love was always her chief subject matter, and one cannot forever be falling in or out of love."[3]

Grateful to Walton for salvaging him from the lower depths, Roth was in no position to make demands on her. Sexual freedom seemed to be a prerogative of independent literary women in downtown Manhattan, and Roth was keenly aware that his own odious experiences had hardly equipped him as an arbiter of healthy sexuality. He accepted that Walton's relationship to him was often more maternal than connubial. "She was both a mistress and a mother," he later recalled. "It was good, and it was bad. It was maybe good for the writer, but it was bad for the person. He fell in the habit of not being an independent, mature individual who was willing to face the world on his own and make his own living."[4] The older woman persisted in calling him "child" and "lad." ("Laddie" was the way that Lester Winter signed love letters to his teacher/lover.) Writing to Walton from California five years after moving in with her, Roth analyzed the dynamics of their connection: "Know then that another reason why I love you is that I can pour things out in a jumble and you'll listen to me as patiently as you would (or would you?) to a child."[5]

Walton had in effect adopted Roth away from his troubled biological family. Despite the fact that Walton was Gentile, Leah recognized that living with the other woman might benefit her son. At the very least, it put him beyond the reach of Herman's violent tantrums. "When I became her lover, it was as if she adopted me," Roth told an interviewer in 1987. "She was a great admirer of talent, and she thought I had exceptional talent, even though, in those years, I hardly opened my mouth, I was so very shy! So, it was she who said, 'I will support you.' She gave me everything."[6]

The poet and translator Ben Belitt was also a beneficiary of Walton's largesse. It was not sexual, but Belitt, who was homosexual, likened his experience with the accomplished older woman to Roth's: "We were both orphans adopted by Eda Lou Walton." In Belitt's case, he was not just being metaphorical. He had actually grown up in the huge, Dickensian Hebrew Orphan Asylum on 137th and Amsterdam Avenue, directly across the street from CCNY. After outgrowing the orphanage, Belitt went off to attend the University of Virginia. It was in Charlottesville, in 1932, that he first heard from Walton, in an enthusiastic letter praising his poetry and announcing that she intended to publish it in *College Verse*, which she edited. At her invitation, Belitt visited Walton and Roth whenever he was in New York, and in July 1936, after graduating from Virginia, he became their neighbor, moving into an apartment down the block at 48 Morton Street. "We were three," he recalled. "We were a family."[7]

Belitt acknowledged that he felt closer to Walton than to Roth. She was the mother of them all, and Roth, five years Belitt's senior and "ambiguously installed as foster-son and prentice-prodigy," was like an older sibling rival whom the younger man often found aloof and difficult to approach. "He had no identity. He needed to create one through *Call It Sleep*."[8]

Walton helped secure Belitt an appointment as assistant literary editor of *The Nation* and later, in 1935, as an instructor at Bennington College. Like Roth, he was an object of Walton's persistent beneficence. "I now think of Eda Lou Walton," he wrote afterward, "as a Protectress engaged in a search for *protégés* in the Gallic sense of that word— vulnerable and besieged talents in their nonage or orphaned states."[9]

Roth was still an undergraduate when he moved in with Walton. Commuting from Morton Street up to the CCNY campus in Harlem, he continued his desultory progress toward a degree. Low grades and a deficiency of credits, which he would later blame on his distress over the incest, caused him to graduate half a year later than his classmates. But in September 1928, Roth finally received his B.S. from City College. Though Leah was eager to see her only son accept his college diploma, Roth refused to attend the graduation ceremony, as he had after completing DeWitt Clinton High School. In one of the most painful scenes in *A Diving Rock on the Hudson*, Roth describes the anguish Ira Stigman causes his doting mother when he insists on showing up for his job at Madison Square Garden instead of allowing her the satisfaction of watching him graduate from high school. Many years after her death, Ira, regretting his cruel stubbornness, wishes he could make it up to his mother. But it is too late: "The grave is a barrier to all amends, all redress."[10]

Once awarded his bachelor's degree, Roth began, during the fall of

1929, to do graduate work in English at City College, but he lasted only one semester, receiving three Bs and a C. Roth's live-in professor from NYU was a more effective teacher than anyone he encountered in his classrooms uptown.

Eda Lou Walton was an exceptionally generous woman, and her service to callow acolytes was not always erotic (though, in a fictional reconstruction, Margaret Mead quips that sex with Edith Welles, Walton's alter ego, was an extension of hospitality).[11] She delighted in discovering and nurturing unconventional talent. Many besides Roth discovered that 61 Morton Street functioned as Walton's private academy, a center for continuing education where visitors could wrestle with the latest ideas and engage with the latest texts, often by encountering their authors. Belitt recalled 61 Morton Street as "a special pantheon of begetters." Under Walton's auspices, he encountered a wide variety of guests, including "card-carrying communists, avowed or clandestine, fellow-travellers, russophiles and voyeurs of the 'liberal' persuasion, zealots committed to the utopias of Trotsky or Marx or Franklin Delano Roosevelt, 'non-political' *examens de conscience* in the manner of Thomas Mann or the hermeneutical calculus of Caudwell and Kenneth Burke."[12]

The Morton Street salon was more stimulating than any class that Roth had found at CCNY. With Walton's tutelage, Roth embarked on a regimen of reading that was more ambitious and intense than anything he had experienced since his boyhood discoveries at the public library opposite Mt. Morris Park. Though it had taken him four and a half years to complete three years of college Spanish, he was now studying Italian, Latin, German, and Greek.

It is remarkable how many of the men whom Walton befriended, either as mentor or lover or both, were Jewish. In addition to Roth, Winter, Belitt, and Isadore Silver, they included Shmuel Hamburg, whom she knew in California, as well as another lover, Hamburg's friend, Zev Hassid, also a Zionist agronomist. In a letter to Roth in 1930, Walton herself noted her predilection for young Jewish men. She wondered why she was always attracted to men much younger than she was, especially if they happened to be Jewish. Why, she asks Roth, does she keep finding herself drawn irresistibly to people from his background?[13] Though the biblical reference was a little askew, Belitt too called attention to Walton's penchant for adopting stray Jews: "Eda Lou Walton, no bigger than a wren or an ember in a hearthbed, with a phoenix's tolerance for combustion, had long ago come to a hard decision which drew her to Ishmaelites like myself and Henry in search of their patrimony."[14] Walton's own patrimony was the Protestant American establishment, and by translating songs from Navajo and Blackfoot and courting the sons of Abraham, Isaac, and Jacob, she was rebelling against the world of William Bell Walton. "I am more / Than ever he bargained for," she wrote of her father.[15] But by embracing Indian poetry and Jewish men, she was also extending the jurisdiction of her father's territorial tribunals.

David Mandel was a Jew, which was why he chose the law as his profession. An English major at Princeton, Mandel was advised that because of his religion he could never hope to be a professor. This was two decades before Lionel Trilling's breakthrough at Columbia University in 1945, when he became the first Jew awarded tenure in the English Department of a major American university. Decades after Jews, at least in limited numbers, were accepted as anthropologists, physicists, and legal scholars, the stewards of English were still wary of allowing upstarts, whose ancestors spoke some exotic guttural tongue, into their profession. So Mandel attended law school instead and went into practice in Perth Amboy, New Jersey.

After he became involved with Walton, whom he met in 1932, Mandel would often commute from New Jersey to Morton Street to spend weekends with her. Perhaps because of his own frustrated ambitions or the new acquaintances he made through Walton, Mandel was magnanimous toward literary people and would play a crucial role in Roth's debut as a novelist. With Mandel in town, Walton's house was a *ménage à trois*—or *quatre* or *cinq*—yet one that managed somehow to maintain domestic peace. Asked once whether he, Walton, and Mandel ever slept together, Roth laughed. "Eda Lou was not that libertine," he told his last editor, Robert Weil. "She was a one-man-at-a-time woman." Henry quickly learned that he simply had to stay in his own room when the dapper Mandel came to visit.[16]

To support her ambition to write a long narrative poem, Walton was invited to spend the summer of 1930 at the MacDowell Colony. Located on 450 hilly, bosky acres in Peterborough, in southwestern New Hampshire, the MacDowell Colony was designed by its founder, Marian MacDowell, widow of the American composer Edward Mac-Dowell, to provide "working conditions most favorable to the production of enduring works of imagination. . . ."[17] Since its opening in 1907, many eminent figures in the arts, including Willa Cather, Aaron Copland, Ben Shahn, Thornton Wilder, and Elinor Wylie, had been attracted by the community of solitude that the MacDowell—with its isolated studios and convivial dinners—provided. Residents during the summer of 1930 included Amy Beach, Morris Raphael Cohen, Padraic Colum, Douglas Moore, Edward Arlington Robinson, Constance Rourke, and Helen Santmyer. Tagging along with Walton, Roth got to meet many of them. He had already run into Cohen at CCNY, where the charismatic philosophy professor had a devoted following. *From Bondage* recounts a public debate in 1927 on compulsory military training at the university in which Cohen, "a Jewish thunderhead,"[18] appears so arrogant and intolerant that he arouses sympathy for his adversary, a major in the campus ROTC program. Santmyer, a young poet from Ohio, would anticipate Roth's own crepuscular creativity when, in her eighties in 1984, she published a best-selling novel, . . . *And Ladies of the Club.*

Iven Hurlinger, a friend of Roth from CCNY, agreed to drive Walton and Roth up to Peterborough. Roth returned to New York with Hurlinger, but he rejoined Walton a few weeks later. As a mere companion to one of the artists, he was not allowed to stay overnight on the grounds of the colony. Instead, Walton deposited him, at her expense, just down the road, at the Peterborough Inn. While she worked on her poetry (the narrative poem metamorphosed into a sonnet sequence) at MacDowell, Roth too began to write.

His only venture into publishing, since "Impressions of a Plumber" back in 1925, had been an essay on Lynn Riggs, a thirty-year-old playwright he had come to know personally through Walton. It would also be his only attempt at formal literary criticism. Roth wrote it at the playwright's behest, to help publicize his work. "Lynn Riggs and the Individual," which appeared in a collection called *Folk-say: A Regional Miscellany* (published in 1930 by the University of Oklahoma Press), traces the thematic development throughout Riggs's modest oeuvre. The most notable of his works remains *Green Grow the Lilacs*, which Richard Rodgers and Oscar Hammerstein II later adapted as the musical *Oklahoma!*

Roth, who had never yet ventured west of New Jersey, stressed Riggs's success in capturing the richness of life in Oklahoma, but he also insisted on the play's universality. Though anguish would pervade his own fiction, Roth noted and seemed to endorse "one of Riggs's strongest beliefs, that joy is the true nature of man, a sign of his true development, and tragedy the defeat of his true nature." Though he himself would soon be tailoring fiction to conform to Marxist principles, he praised Riggs's characters precisely because they were not mere vehicles for ideology—"none strains toward absolutes; none is driven by ideas." Roth's conclusion was that Riggs "is already by imagination and sensitivity of equipment the best poet writing for the American stage, and by depth of meaning and definiteness one of the most important dramatists."[19] Was Riggs really a better "poet" than Eugene O'Neill or Thornton Wilder?

ROTH WAS PROBABLY more valuable for his friendship than his literary analysis. But despite scant evidence, Walton remained convinced of Roth's untapped talent and urged him to develop it. She supplied him with "blue books," the blank eight-page pads with blue covers used for exams at NYU and other universities. And he decided to spend his time in Peterborough writing his autobiography—a work that would set out his own story, from birth in Tysmenitz to rebirth on Morton Street. Immigrant memoirs had enjoyed a vogue, and Roth might have hoped for the success that Mary Antin had found two decades earlier with *The Promised Land* (1912), an account of her own journey from a childhood in a Russian shtetl to American literary celebrity patronized by William Dean Howells. As Roth later

explained to Irit Manskleid-Mankowsky, "the very original conception of the book was to include my entire trajectory—from ghetto
child to Greenwich Village. . . ."[20] Scrawling in pencil in Walton's blue
books (some of the covers, in truth, were pink), he began a first-
person rendition of his life. Those official exam booklets could easily
give an anxious writer the sense that his prose if not his existence was
waiting to be graded. However, after seventy-five pages, the narrative
began to assume another life.

In a moment of catalytic inspiration, Roth grabbed a fresh blue book
and sketched the outline for quite a different kind of story. It would still
draw directly from his own experiences as a young Jewish immigrant,
but it would transmute them into fiction. Abandoning the first person,
the work would concentrate on a tiny Galician newcomer named David
Schearl. Afflicted by his own unspeakable sibling angst, Roth made the
boy an only child, airbrushing Rose out of the picture. Memories of his
mother, Leah, would be projected onto two separate characters: David's
mother, Genya, and his Aunt Bertha—"All I had to do was remember
Mom in her contemplative moments and she was Genya; in her irritation, anxieties, and angers she was Bertha." In order to augment paternal menace, Roth transformed the short and scrawny Herman Roth
into the hulking bully Albert Schearl: "I had to increase his magnitude
and dimension. I had to fictionalize a character not based on the petty,
little man my real father was."[21] But relinquishing the full trajectory of
Roth's twenty-six years, the author kept the book's protagonist prepu-
bescent. The story ends in the summer of 1913, when the boy is eight.
David Schearl never leaves the Lower East Side.

The shift from autobiography to fiction was liberating. Henceforth,
recollection would not squelch imagination. The author had set himself
a formidable task, one that certainly could not be fulfilled during a few
weeks at the Peterborough Inn. But Roth, a creature of frail will and
hazy identity, now had a purpose. He believed in a destiny that would
redeem the loss of the Lower East Side and expunge the shame of expulsion from Stuyvesant and of incest with his sister and his cousin. Day
after day, Roth toiled away at his job as strenuously as if he were still
in the IRT repair barn. "Really you know," he wrote Walton, on pages

torn from a blue book, while one of them was out of town, "the artist is just a maniac who somehow evades the bug-house."[22]

Walton's apartment in the Village became a kind of beneficent bug-house, in which Roth maniacally wrote himself into some degree of sanity. Although he erased Rose from the story and concluded it before David gets old enough to share his author's sexual transgressions, Roth would ultimately recognize that incest was the engine that drove his composition. Writing was a way to assuage guilt—he would note in his fictionalized journals—"it was all those unclean loves Augustine talked about that propelled the only novel he ever wrote, day after day, page after page, for over three years."[23] Though he lacked self-control in other areas, he always approached writing as a rigorous discipline. The neophyte novelist never attended a writing workshop, and he refused to show his manuscript to anyone, even Walton, until it was finished. But Roth on Morton Street proved an extraordinary example of a writer who methodically, day by day, week by week, year by year, learned to write by writing.

During this period, Ben Belitt found Roth withdrawn and self-absorbed, reluctant to say anything about his literary project. In his own collection, *The Five-Fold Mesh*, Belitt in 1938 dedicated a poem to Henry Roth whose title, "The Enemy Joy," hints at the glumness of his brooding neighbor. Roth's spirit was never exactly blithe; but Stanley Burnshaw, a poet and editor who met him during the thirties, remembered Roth as particularly morose. "In all the times I spent with Henry," he observed, "I can't recall his ever having laughed."[24] Of course, these were not universally happy days. Following the stock market crash of September 3, 1929, few were immune to endemic hardship and despondency.

By 1933, the depth of the economic crisis, about 16 million Americans—one third of the labor force—were unemployed. Yet, while so many other Americans were losing their jobs, their homes, and their hopes, Roth remained free to fill Walton's blue books. Thanks to what, in a late fictional manuscript, he would acknowledge as Walton's "endless bounty matched by an equal possessiveness,"[25] Roth did not have to contend with breadlines, soup kitchens, and

Hoovervilles. Though he returned to Harlem for family visits a few times a month, Walton's generosity insulated Roth from the onslaught of the Great Depression and distracted him from his own depression. But his dependence on her maternal munificence was another form of infantilism. Fixated on fictionalizing childhood, the would-be writer felt suspended in his growth. "And I was being supported by Eda Lou, so I didn't have to mature," Roth later concluded. "It was a real continuation of infancy to be supported by a woman so long."[26]

PERHAPS INEVITABLY, as Roth's sheltered years at Morton Street multiplied, his gratitude toward his benefactor became tinged with resentment. Roth's self-loathing gradually developed into anger at the forceful woman who made him feel like a parasite. Desperate to affirm his autonomy, he might well have nourished a desire to desert—or even hurt—Eda Lou. A similar dynamic was being played out with a prominent novelist whom Roth had met through Walton and who for a time even shared a faculty office at NYU with her, Thomas Wolfe. Roth himself would later share an editor with Wolfe—Maxwell Perkins. Soon after his arrival in New York from North Carolina, the young, ambitious Wolfe was taken up as an artist and a lover by Aline Bernstein, a stage designer eighteen years his senior. Without her inspiration, advocacy, and money, Wolfe would never have enjoyed the spectacular literary career that he did. But once he attained some success, he abruptly and cruelly dropped Bernstein, venting his hostility in anti-Semitic abuse. Though Roth and Walton inverted the ethnic components of the relationship, theirs too would end in acrimony, and a less than gentle abandonment by the writer of his older muse and lover.

Outfitting him with a Dunham pipe and English tweeds, Walton took on the task of reinventing her young urban foundling as an urbane intellectual. She accompanied him to performances of *Carmen*, *Petrushka*, and *Tristan und Isolde*. She encouraged him in his autodidactic forays into Homer, Virgil, Dante, and Goethe. Together they attended readings by Robert Frost, T. S. Eliot, and W. B. Yeats, and saw Arturo Toscanini conduct at Carnegie Hall. A letter that

Louise Bogan sent to the critic Morton D. Zabel during this period gives some sense of Roth as Walton's Galatea, as well as her efforts to endow him not so much with aristocratic tastes as artistic ones. Describing New York's Poetry Ball, Bogan reports:

> Eda Lou Walton gave her ticket to the P.B. to Henry Roth and bought him a full dress suit to go to it in (actually: she may have rented the suit, but it was tails, I believe, and an opera hat, and everything). She wanted him to see what the upper classes are really like. That's the honest truth, although hardly anyone in their senses would believe it. Well, Henry went, and came back, having observed that the upper classes didn't know anything about Dante (Henry can read him in the original, I have been told), and that they get drunk, and that the upper class women looked cruel and heartless and frightened him. So I suppose Eda Lou's money really wasn't wasted, after all, Dear God.[27]

Ben Belitt remembered this as the time when Roth finally attained maturity. "Writing *Call It Sleep* was his act of liberation from Eda Lou Walton,"[28] he observed. But the only way Roth could have written his liberating novel was to become dependent on her.

In 1932, Roth found an opportunity to return to New England, where he had started his novel, this time free of Walton. A poem of hers had appeared in *Poetry Folio*, whose editor, Stanley Burnshaw, asked Walton for non-literary advice. His wife's sister, a senior in high school, was pregnant, and it was thought best to spirit her out of New York City and up to Smithfield, Maine, where Burnshaw owned a cabin and an acre. But Burnshaw himself could not get out of town until later, and neither his wife nor his sister-in-law could handle a car. Did Walton know anyone who might drive them up to Maine in Burnshaw's Model A?

Walton introduced Burnshaw to Henry Roth in May, and her protégé made an immediate impression.[29] Despite the warm weather, Roth wore pigskin gloves during his visit to Burnshaw's apartment. Whenever the host left the room, he found Roth muttering snatches of Dante and Gerard Manley Hopkins to himself upon his return. Roth agreed to drive Burnshaw's wife and sister-in-law to Maine in return for lodging in their cabin, as a resident chauffeur. In the fresh country air far from Morton Street and its puzzling muse, he hoped to make headway on his novel.

The journey up to Maine proved almost fatal. Though she herself stayed behind, Walton sent along a household pet, a black and white cat named Popeye. Roth and the animal were not especially fond of each other, and when the driver stopped by the side of the road in New Hampshire to let everyone stretch, Popeye darted off. Tracking the cat through the bushes, Roth eventually grabbed it, swung it in the air, and bit into its belly. Popeye bounded off with a screech, never to return; Roth was left with a large, bleeding gash on his hand. He stanched the flow with a rag and drove on to a hospital in Waterville, where he was kept for four days. Twice put under ether, he was treated against tetanus, rabies, and blood poisoning, before eventually making it safely to the Burnshaw cabin. But, after teaching another guest how to handle the Model A, Roth moved out on his own. Seven decades later, Burnshaw was still pleased to take credit for getting Roth to Maine to write *Call It Sleep*, and he marveled at how a cat very nearly got the nascent writer's tongue.

On his own in Maine, Roth rented a room in a farmhouse in Norridgewock, a few miles from the Burnshaws' cabin in Smithfield, for seven dollars a week. He got his laundry washed for an additional 50 cents. Walton, as usual, paid Roth's expenses. But another older woman, a widow in her seventies named Mrs. Fletcher, took charge of his life, in effect adopting him into her extended family, which included Enid, a teenager, and a younger boy, Malcolm. She urged Roth, who helped with family chores, to stay on beyond the summer and think of living permanently in Norridgewock; she even offered to waive Roth's rent, though he declined. But Roth did stay there through the winter, finishing up the bulk of his book in pencil in the blue books supplied by Walton. "It was a wonderful place for me to do the writing,"[30] he observed, remembering idyllic days in rural

Maine spent conjuring up the Lower East Side. He was no longer an uncouth tenement golem contending with witty intellectuals, no longer the Jewish court jester to Walton's Village salon.

IN THE PRISTINE New England environment of Norridgewock, Roth felt free to recreate his Galician immigrant childhood: baptized with a new identity, he now felt he had at last left the old one behind. "Incidentally, do you know, I'm not taken for a jew here?" he wrote back to Walton. "I stalled them off the one time we got on religion and I'm taken right into the midst of the family without reserve. As a result, I'm invited to Sunday school and completely accepted by the neighborhood. It's swell. It gives me a chance I may never have again. From now on I'm a Baptist with a capital Bap."[31] Far from the dense metropolis in which he had spent virtually his entire existence, Roth reinvented himself by rewriting his life, purged of Jewishness.

Whenever he filled up a few batches of blue books, Roth mailed them off to New York to Rose, who sent them back promptly, typed. The little sister whom Roth had expunged from his story by making David Schearl an only child was the one who created a fair copy of it. In 1977, Roth would tell an interviewer that "there is another person here involved here, my sister, and yet for me she scarcely existed. . . . She was never important."[32] More important than Roth was yet prepared to admit, the sister was in fact a crucial figure in the family narrative.

The letters between Roth in Norridgewock and Walton in the Village are frank and affectionate. Walton shared gossip about friends in New York, while Roth bemoaned the frigid New England weather and, though he reported ogling local high school girls, his enforced celibacy. In March 1933, when the temperature reached 8° Fahrenheit, he noted that the ramshackle privy fifty yards from the Fletcher house made him yearn for constipation. Indoor heating was augmented by a fellow boarder, a man named Kellogg with whom Roth shared a bed, and whom he described as "a furnace." "He's a big, natural, good-humored simpleton—and what outstanding genitals. So I sleep with Kellogg and don't even have a chance to masturbate."[33]

"Finishing is an obsession with me,"[34] Roth wrote from Maine, sixty years before the final sprint that would conclude his writing and his life. By spring, Roth was back on Morton Street, and his novel, with the working title of *Cellars Under the Street*, was nearing completion. Before Walton left in late May to visit her ailing father in New Mexico, he showed her a first draft. Bursting into tears, his benefactor declared: "You are so much greater an artist than I am."[35] It was not quite Emerson greeting Whitman "at the beginning of a great career," but it was a remarkably magnanimous instance of an older poet conceding that her disciple had exceeded her. Walton enlisted David Mandel to help get the book published, and he took the manuscript to several prominent editors, without success. Both Maxwell Perkins at Scribners and Marshall Best at Viking turned it down. Anticipating rejection, as well, from Harcourt Brace, Roth wrote Walton in New Mexico: "Well, I did the best I knew. I put into it everything I had and could conceive limited by critical discipline. It stinks and I am ready to depart. That was lousy."[36] But that was not the end of the story.

Roth continued to revise the text and to waver between self-confidence and self-doubt. He was disgusted with the novel when he wrote Walton in New Mexico: "There's so much about it that seems to me bad and that can't be remedied that I want to forget it."[37] But on September 14, Roth could write in his journal: "The novel is finished."[38]

He also continued to keep Walton informed of his summer in New York. In a letter dated June 3, he described serving as witness at Louise Bogan's wedding to the critic William Troy, reporting that the couple put off purchasing a ring until the final day. After Roth's frugal suggestion that they make do with a trinket from a nearby five-and-ten, he served as their chief negotiator with a gem merchant: "So we went and I jewed a jeweler down and we bought an 18 karet [*sic*] gold ring (cost me 14 dollars mister, I should live so, but for you I'll sell it for five etc.) So we bought it for $3.50."[39] On the verge of completing a masterpiece of American Jewish fiction, Roth tried to camouflage his anxiety over ethnicity by mocking a hoary Jewish stereotype. Sixty years later, embracing Zionism and his identity as a pioneering Jewish author, Roth would presumably cringe at the flagrant anti-Semitism of the verb "jewed down."

Early in June, Roth, who expressed concern about his weight, now over 155 pounds, also recorded erotic longings. "Sexually, I've been abstaining which may be not be a good thing since it makes me hungry for the real thing."[40] But two days later, he wrote again to say that he had had sex with a salesclerk in a department store, a friend of Rose, and that the condom broke, apparently without serious consequences. Roth also reported visiting his parents and his sister. By June 23, they had moved to 144th Street in Jamaica, Queens, and Roth provides his first requiem for Harlem in these curt terms: "We lived 14 years in that hole in 119 Street and now we'll never rest again."[41]

Meanwhile, though Harcourt Brace had turned him down, David Mandel refused to rest until Roth's book found a publisher. With $2,000 of his own, he bought an interest in a Fifth Avenue publishing firm founded by Robert O. Ballou in 1932. Ballou, a Chicagoan who had written for several publications and worked for several publishers, had been technical manager at Cape & Smith in 1929 when that company published William Faulkner's *The Sound and the Fury*. Ballou's new independent house had already brought out John Steinbeck's third novel, *To a God Unknown*, and *The Golden Mountain*, a collection of Hasidic tales retold by Meyer Levin. After Mandel provided an additional subsidy of $1,000, Ballou agreed to take on Henry Roth. He scheduled Roth's novel for release in December 1934. Steinbeck, whose *Tortilla Flat* Ballou turned down, described the publisher as "a fine man and a sensitive man but I do not think he is fitted to fight the battle of New York. He is a gentleman. He can't bring himself to do the things required for success."[42]

While the gentle capitalist was preparing Roth's novel for print, the novelist himself was joining the Communist Party. During the Great Depression, when the global crisis seemed to call for radical solutions, that was not in itself a remarkable act. In 1935, Earl Browder, leader of the Communist Party of the United States of America (CPUSA), claimed 31,000 dues-paying members.[43] Less than twenty years after the Bolshevik Revolution, many idealistic Americans still regarded the Soviet Union as a magnificent experiment in social and economic democracy. Jews, in particular, welcomed an end to the tsarist regime that promulgated discriminatory restrictions and quotas and fomented pogroms. They believed, naively, that its Marxist successor, many of whose leaders came from Jewish families, meant to put a stop to the virulent anti-Semitism that had for centuries blighted Eastern Europe. In the United States, where jobs were often insecure, dangerous, and underpaid, and where lynching was still commonplace, the Communist Party promised an end to economic and social injustice.

Dedicated to the principle that artists should side with workers in the current class war, the John Reed Club—named for the flamboyant American literary radical who was buried beside the Kremlin wall—was founded by Joseph Freeman and Michael Gold in 1929 to advance the cause of the CPUSA among the intelligentsia. The original John Reed Club, the one that Roth joined, was based in the Village, in drab quarters at 430 Sixth Avenue. It was a site for poetry readings, exchange of manuscripts, and debates over the social role of literature, as well as for the sore eyes of idealists distressed by what they saw in contemporary society. For many high-minded and able-bodied second-generation New Yorkers, the John Reed Club was a place to pick up lessons in political theory—and members of the opposite sex. Aside from the doctrine and the camaraderie, a few young men were attracted to meetings by the presence of the redbrick Victorian structure across the street, the Women's House of Detention, whose inmates sometimes bared themselves to passersby through the window bars.

By 1934, thirty John Reed Club chapters had spread throughout the United States. Their manifesto called upon "all honest intellectuals, all honest writers and artists, to abandon decisively the treacherous illusion that art can exist for art's sake, or that the artist can remain remote from the historic conflicts in which all men must take sides."[44] At this point, Roth became convinced that he wrote his first novel under that "treacherous illusion," and he resolved to change his ways. Henceforth, he would use fiction not to make a fetish of rarefied art but to advance the interests of the working class. Enlistment in the cause might dissipate the shame that burdened him, as if political revolution meant personal redemption. "Here I was—warm, taken care of, well-clothed, well-fed, doing what I wanted to do—and outside all that turmoil, all that suffering," he recalled.[45] Using his pen to address that turmoil and that suffering might relieve him of the discomfort he felt over his unmerited fortune. As Roth later explained: "I think that one of the reasons I joined the Communist Party was to feel that I was doing something to redeem myself. . . ."[46]

Though she herself would eventually join as well, Eda Lou Walton initially tried hard to dissuade Roth from becoming a Party member. Once, he woke up in the middle of the night to find her weeping over his determination to cast his lot with the Communists. Walton was certain it would destroy him as an artist, and her concerns were, in the short term, prophetic. His attempts to enlist literature in the service of ideology would result in frustrating failure. Roth's conversion to communism did not improve his fiction; indeed, it contributed to his literary drought, even as it generated dozens of pages of prose by FBI agents assigned to his surveillance during the next two decades. Belitt remembered Roth during this period as preoccupied with the class struggle. "He was saturated, obsessed with politics. He was a real Communist zealot."[47]

But so were many of his most creative contemporaries. From 1936 to 1938, Joseph Stalin staged elaborate show trials in Moscow of more than a dozen leading Kremlin *nomenklatura* on specious charges of treason. Most were convicted and executed. In the West, the legal proceedings were widely viewed as a cynical ploy by Stalin to eliminate rivals and consolidate personal power. However, 150 American artists and intellectuals endorsed a public statement of support for the Moscow Trials. Roth signed onto the list, along with Nelson Algren, Harold Clurman, Malcolm Cowley, John Garfield, Dashiell Hammett, Lillian Hellman, Langston Hughes, Dorothy Parker, Irwin Shaw, Raphael Soyer, and Richard Wright, among others.

After Leon Trotsky, the principal theorist of the Bolshevik Revolution, was purged from the Soviet leadership and fled into exile in North America, John Dewey headed up an independent commission of inquiry into whether Stalin had committed an injustice against his chief rival as Lenin's heir. An "Open Letter to American Liberals" condemned the Dewey Commission in print. Its signators, according to Earl Browder, comprised "the most distinguished list of names ever gathered on a single document in America in support of the Soviet Union."[48] Henry Roth was one of the least prominent of those names. In a short essay of his own, "Where My Sympathy Lies," published in *The New Masses* on March 2, 1937, Roth reaffirmed his confidence in the guilt of the Moscow show trial defendants, his commitment to the struggle for human liberation from exploitation, and his conviction that "the Trotskyite mentality" was an obstacle to that liberation. "Whoever hungers for justice," he wrote, "must ally himself, if only in sympathy, with all those forces that struggle to liberate humanity from slavery and want."[49] In 1937, Roth identified those forces with Stalin. By supporting the purge of Trotsky (né Lev Davidovich Bronstein), he, like many other American Stalinists, also followed a familiar pattern of repudiating his own Jewishness.

Many of the artists and intellectuals who signed these petitions and joined the John Reed Clubs acted out of a combination of lofty ideals and cynical self-interest. Marxism promised a more equitable distribution of the world's resources and more meaningful lives for the mass of workers. It was also a modish way to affirm one's political virtue and to facilitate romantic encounters. The clubs were known as a good place to pick up a date. The left fell in love with the idea, if not the reality, of the proletariat. For refined Americans during the depression, the most savory spice was salt of the earth. Aaron Copland was not alone—merely late, in 1942—in composing a fanfare for the common man. The surest means to confirm one's credentials as an intellectual was to be nostalgic for the working class.

Roth's situation during his years with Walton compounded this paradox. His membership in the Communist Party aligned him with many of the bookish people that he, a cultural parvenu, felt so awkward with. It also allowed him to assert some independence from

Walton. Yet Roth was a genuine product of the working class, not just a Bleecker Street salon proletarian. And when he donned a blue collar to work as a plumber's assistant or as a grease monkey for the IRT, it was not in order to affirm affiliation with the intelligentsia. Though Walton clothed him in tweeds, the fit was never right. Throughout his ten-year sojourn in Greenwich Village, Roth never overcame the sense that he was an uncouth intruder from the slums who was obliged to prove himself. At times, the ordeal of civility was impossible to disguise. Frustrated while struggling with his novel, Roth sent Walton a *cri de coeur* on June 23, 1933. "I'm sick of looking at it [the manuscript] and sick of all literary people, including myself. I'm not going to see andother [*sic*] intlectual [*sic*] outside of yourself more than once a week if I can help it. They're nothing but a gnawing barrenness. They juggle aridities."[50] It was impossible for Roth to honor this vow while living with Walton in the Village. Only his removal to Maine and New Mexico would extricate him from the painful embrace of intellectuals.

"I ONCE SAW Israel Amter plain," wrote Allen Ginsberg in his poem *America*. "Everybody must have been a spy." Few of the literary leftists of the 1930s and 1940s were spies; but many would have endorsed Ginsberg's suggestion—echoing Robert Browning's awestruck question: "Ah, did you once see Shelley plain?"—that a glimpse of Amter was like the sighting of a saint. Roth signed a nominating petition to put Israel Amter on the ballot as a Communist in the race for governor of New York State in 1942; the following year he signed a nominating petition for Carl Brodsky, a Communist candidate for the City Council of New York, and served on the defense committee for Morris Schappes, a Communist who was dismissed from his position in the English Department at City College and sentenced to prison for almost two years.

While most American Jews were not Communists, many American Communists were Jews; according to one estimate, "close to 50 percent of the aggregate of those who appeared regularly in Party-affiliated publications and joined Party-led organizations such as the John Reed Clubs and League of American Writers" were Jewish,[51] just a shave and a haircut removed from Orthodox piety. The Party, with its prophetic rhetoric and its organizational discipline, provided them with a secular substitute for religious life. In part to camouflage the Ashkenazic coloration of the CPUSA, it even provided them with new names that sounded more indigenous. The nom de guerre assigned to Roth was "Berry." For the precocious atheist who nevertheless remained nostalgic over *cheder* days in his Jewish mini-state on the Lower East Side, joining the Communist Party was like belonging to a schul. Berry/Roth accepted its dogmas longer than most others. But eventually, like the heretics Louis Fischer, André Gide, Arthur Koestler, Ignazio Silone, Stephen Spender, and Richard Wright, who in 1950 published a collective recantation entitled *The God That Failed*, he too would recognize that he had been worshipping false idols of a fickle tribe. Disillusioned with the Party, Berry would finally sour more than thirty years after joining.

Roth's infatuation with communism led to an intense relationship with a particular Communist—a proud, pugnacious worker named Bill Clay. Though a hook took the place of his right hand, mangled in an industrial accident at a Nabisco plant in Los Angeles. Clay was admired as the leading salesman for the *Daily Worker*, the paper of the CPUSA. Born in the heartland, in Cincinnati, in 1888, Clay, who came of German stock, was echt American in ways that a Jewish immigrant could never be. He was illiterate, which distanced him not only from the intellectuals Roth mistrusted but also from the people who defined themselves by a book, the Bible. Pleased to pass as a Christian in Maine, Roth was thrilled to sit at the feet of Clay. At first, he revered the older man as a labor hero. Claims that Comrade Clay had been a middleweight boxer and even an armed robber merely enhanced the revolutionary romance. Though Roth tried to teach him to read, it was Clay who served as mentor and scourge. Clay's own son would lose a foot fighting the fascists in the Spanish Civil War, but for Roth, Clay—like Herman—became a figure of paternal torment. Playing on Roth's self-loathing, Clay continued to berate him for bourgeois tendencies. Roth came to believe that those tendencies had inspired his first novel, and he determined to abandon the treacherous illusion of art for art's sake and create fiction grounded in historical circumstances that would advance the cause of the working class. He began to conceive of a novel based on the life of Bill Clay.

On May 13, 1934, while attempting to persuade dockworkers to shift their allegiance from the accommodationist American Federation of Labor to the more radical Congress of Industrial Organizations, Roth was attacked and badly beaten by AFL supporters. For future self-defense, he began taking boxing lessons and would later claim that he became so proficient with his fists that he might have had a career in the ring. But in early June 1934, Roth fled to Norridgewock for a few weeks with the Fletchers. Then, on the Fourth of July, he set out from New York with Iven Hurlinger to drive across the United States. During the 1930s, while an army of transients was riding the rails, writers, photographers, painters, filmmakers, and musicians who were not expatriated in Paris were out discovering America. Thomas Hart Benton, Walker Evans, Woody Guthrie, Dorothea Lange, Carl Sandburg, John Steinbeck, Preston Sturges, and many others all fanned out across the country in search of common truths among the common people.

Roth's first book was confined to a few square blocks within the immigrant enclave of lower Manhattan. But he would expand his canvas to include Harlem, the Village, Maine, and New Mexico. In the immediate aftermath of his journey, Roth would even try to set a novel inspired by Bill Clay in contemporary Cincinnati and the frontier Dakotas. Traveling in a car at Walton's expense, Roth was hardly part of the horde of hobos who scattered across the landscape during the Depression, but the trip did introduce him to a new world west of the Hudson River.

Yet he still headed for places associated with Walton. The first extended stop was Berkeley, California, where she had been a student, and the return route included a visit with Walton's father in Silver City, New Mexico. In Berkeley, Roth and Hurlinger rented a room on Woolsey Street, south of the university campus, for three dollars a week. While there, he paid a visit to Shmuel Hamburg, Walton's former lover, in Los Banos, a rural community southeast of the Bay Area.

Born in Russia, Hamburg had come to California from what was then the British Mandate of Palestine in order to study agricultural methods that would be useful in the colony of Jewish pioneers he planned to return to in the Middle East. However, Hamburg stayed on in California and made a fortune out of farming. When Roth encountered him, he commanded 5,300 acres of cotton and wheat.

Hamburg still pined for Walton, but Roth's letters back to her offered a caustic portrait of "a manical [sic] looking duck" with a three-day growth of beard, who smoked incessantly, picked his nose, and spoke atrocious English.[52] In another letter, Roth described Hamburg as a bundle of contradictions: "Quite a seething personality— great sentimentality and great canniness, sympathy for the oppressed and a first-rate exploiter of Mexican peons." And Roth, the honorary Christian in Maine, specifically applied hoary Jewish stereotypes to analyze Hamburg's position as agricultural capitalist: "One eye looks at the land with all the hunger of the landless Jew, the other with all the avarice of the pawnbroker."[53]

By August, Roth and Hurlinger had moved on to Long Beach in Southern California, where Hurlinger's mother lived and where Roth savored swimming in the Pacific. Page proofs of his novel had been sent on to California, and on August 10 he began correcting them. Hurlinger, a physics major, helped. Roth needed to come up with a new title more effective than *Cellars Under the Street*. He sent his publisher several alternatives suggested by Hurlinger—*Play, Little David*; *The Old Melting Pot*; *Escape Little David*; *East Side Inferno*; *God Shed His Light on Thee*; and *Ankle Deep in Lightning*—reporting that he was particularly taken with *Ankle Deep in Lightning*, which he called "both provocative and visual" and "a Wow!" However, *Ankle Deep in Lightning* apparently did not work for Walton, Mandel, and Ballou. Asked to do better, Roth responded with exasperation: "About that damned title again, just call it anything you like from *A Pain in the Neck* to *Sleep*. I'm too thoroughly confused and demoralized about it to know what I like anymore."[54] They chose to call it *Sleep*, and that is how, echoing the incantation in the novel's final paragraph, the book became known as *Call It Sleep*.

The jacket was being designed by Stuyvesant Van Veen, a New York friend of Roth. It would feature a drawing of three slum children standing by a fire hydrant, two of them peering down a sewer grating, one off to the side by himself. Roth insisted on including a dedication page that stated "To Eda Lou Walton," though he acknowledged in private that such a gesture could hardly repay his enormous debt to her.

On August 24, Roth and Hurlinger began the drive back to New York. Roth was so inspired by Arizona, where they paused to visit the Grand Canyon, that he wrote a rhapsodic poem that has not survived. In New Mexico, they stopped in Silver City to pay their respects to William Bell Walton, who could spare only half an hour to speak with his daughter's companion. They spent two days along the boundary between Texas and Mexico, crossing at Eagle Pass. Roth, the child of New York slums, wrote Walton of the Mexican border town of Piedras Negras: "I have never seen such poverty." They attended a bullfight, and Roth was revolted: "It's pitiful, disgusting and it stinks, and so does Mr. Hemingway for pearling it over with glamor." (*Death in the Afternoon*, Hemingway's tribute to bullfighting as tragic ritual, had been published in 1932.)

After hundreds of miles and thousands of hours together, relations between Roth and Hurlinger grew strained as the two travelers drove up through San Antonio, east to New Orleans, and north into Alabama. Roth, himself no paragon of self-confidence and stability, wrote of Hurlinger: "I had never realized the length and depth of his neuroticism and his inferiority complex."[55] However, three days later, on September 6, their situation changed dramatically. Hurlinger's ulcer began hemorrhaging in Birmingham, Alabama, and Roth rushed his friend to the hospital. He stayed by Hurlinger's side for several days until the patient was well enough to risk travel. Then he put Hurlinger, chafing at the doctor's insistence he use a wheelchair, at the boarding, on a train for New York. On September 11, Roth set out alone by car from Birmingham on the final leg of his trip back to Morton Street. Awaiting him was another sort of hemorrhage, a life's blood transfused into a book called *Call It Sleep*.

Chapter 5

CALL IT SLEEP

The profession of book-writing makes
horse racing seem like a solid, stable business.
—JOHN STEINBECK[1]

THE 559-PAGE NOVEL that Robert O. Ballou published in a
turquoise cloth cover in December 1934, three months after the
author's return from California, was strikingly different from the fac-
tual memoir Roth had begun to scrawl in blue books at the Peterborough Inn in 1930. Though *Call It Sleep* is obviously based on Roth's
own childhood experiences, he had just as obviously reshaped these
into intricate literary art. Most of the names have been changed,
though the mother's sister, like Roth's real aunt, is still called Bertha.
Roth's young alter ego is given the name of the psalmist, David, suggesting he is indeed the protonovelist. Like the biblical David, he is
also a tiny champion of wits and heart against his galoot of a father,
Albert, who is inflated beyond the puny physical dimensions of Herman Roth.

The novel begins with a short Prologue set in May 1907 describing the arrival of two-year-old David Schearl and his mother Genya at the immigration center on Ellis Island. David's father had already settled in America, and, suspicious about the date of birth of a son he had not seen before, he offers a harsh reception to the new arrivals. The Prologue alerts the reader to the fact that this is to be a story about outsiders, a dysfunctional immigrant family in which the young son seeks refuge in his mother's arms from the hostility of his cruel father. Arrival at Ellis Island is not something that Roth, who was himself an infant when Leah brought him to America, could remember. In fact, he wrote the Prologue to *Call It Sleep* after completing everything else. In the earliest versions, the novel opened in a Brownsville tenement very like the one the Roths inhabited for three years before moving across the East River to Manhattan.[2] Ellis Island, however, anchors the intimate experiences of the Schearls in the broader immigrant experience. It also serves as the site of a second delivery for the infant David, whose innocence and frailty are set against the tumult of the gangplank and the brusqueness of his unfamiliar father.

Every image in the novel augments the terror and squalor that Roth's protagonist must endure. In the opening paragraph of the first chapter, a bead of water falls ominously from the kitchen faucet in the Schearls' Brownsville flat, evoking not wonder but apprehension in the barely verbal boy. If the author of *The Metamorphosis*, who had died ten years before, were not still unknown in America, the scene might be called Kafkaesque. Where did the water come from that lurked in the curve of the brass? Where did it go to, gurgling in the drain? What strange world must be hidden behind the walls of a house?

The text itself is arranged as a cluster of images that inspire dread or bafflement in David: "The Cellar," "The Picture," "The Coal," and "The Rail" are the totems for each of the four sections of *Call It Sleep*. And throughout the book, details that might otherwise seem petty are magnified by refraction through the mind of an anxious child. Roth employs stream of consciousness to intensify the sense of an unformed mind trying to assimilate the varied sensations that assault it. The family apartment on the crowded Lower East Side is a haven for David—as long as his father is not home and his doting mother can lavish her affections on him. When the boy ventures out into the clamorous streets, he feels threatened, by rodents as well as humans. He is frightened and confused by sexual advances from a little girl called Annie and, later, by the attempts of an older Christian boy, Leo, to use him to gain access to David's female cousins in order to "play dirty" with them.

A coming-of-age story about a hypersensitive Jewish boy who is forced to cope alone with the mysteries of sex, religion, and love, the novel focuses on David's troubling experiences during the years 1911–13 as a stranger in a strange land. Not the least of his troubles is the enmity of his father, Albert, a surly, abusive man who is embittered by disappointment. Albert is forever falling out with fellow workers and forced to seek new employment, first as a printer, then as a milkman, and he is particularly harsh toward David, about whose paternity he has doubts.

When he is old enough to attend public school, David is also sent to a drab *cheder* where Jewish boys are made to undergo rote instruction in a Hebrew Bible they cannot understand, and he is confused and inspired by Isaiah's account of the angel with a burning coal. Eavesdropping on fragments of a conversation, mixing Polish and Yiddish, between his mother and her sister Bertha, he misconstrues an explanation for why Genya, disgraced after being jilted by a Gentile, married Albert. Out of Genya's account of her forbidden romance in Eastern Europe, young David, a nascent novelist, concocts a sensational story of his own origins. And when the Polish boy Leo persuades David to introduce him to his cousin Esther, David is overwhelmed by shock and guilt over the sexual liberties that his older friend takes. He is also fascinated by Leo's rosary and crucifix and by the symbolism of Christian salvation.

By the final section of the novel, meticulously constructed by crosscutting among different characters who ultimately converge and collide, Albert's simmering rancor toward David has dramatically increased. Esther's father, complaining about David's collusion with Leo, arrives at the apartment at the same time as David's *cheder* teacher, Reb Yidel Pankower, who has come to investigate the boy's fantastic claim that he is an orphan. When he then sees David holding an alien rosary, Albert erupts in violent rage. Fleeing his brutal father, David is shocked into unconsciousness after touching the live rail of a streetcar. Faced, like the reader, with sensory overload, little David collapses. He might as well call it sleep, embrace temporary oblivion as restoration after a long, disorienting day.

Roth may have been disingenuous when he claimed ignorance of Sigmund Freud before writing *Call It Sleep*, a book about a clanging family triangle that echoes with resentments and recriminations. It was easy to soak up the new psychoanalytic thought in which Greenwich Village was awash. Freudianism rivaled Marxism as the official local language of the Village, and "Freuding parties," in which guests found entertainment by probing one another's psyches, were a fad. As early as 1914, Mabel Dodge—the benefactor of D. H. Lawrence and indirectly of Henry Roth—was hosting evenings devoted to "The New Psychology" at her stylish salon at the corner of Fifth Avenue and Ninth Street. By the time Roth came on the scene, fifteen years later, Freudian jargon flowed freely from the lips of every Village dilettante. "You could not go out to buy a bun without hearing of someone's complex," recalled the playwright Susan Glaspell.[3]

Roth pioneered literary techniques and themes often associated with Freud—stream of consciousness, a lethal family triangle in which father and son vie for the affections of the mother, emphasis on childhood development, preoccupation with sexuality, and belief in the restorative powers of sleep. Yet the novelist was always wary when questioned about the founder of psychoanalysis. "I don't know much about Freud and I never did," Roth told an interviewer in 1965. "If I'd known about things like Oedipus complexes I probably never would have written the book at all."[4] While working on the book, Roth might have learned about Oedipus complexes as well as incest from Eugene O'Neill's *Strange Interlude* (1928) and *Mourning Becomes Electra* (1931). Strongly influenced by Freudian theory, O'Neill's theatrical career was launched with the Provincetown Players, who began in Provincetown and moved to the Village. In Roth's time, the Provincetown Playhouse was on MacDougal Street, a few blocks from 61 Morton. However, Roth could also have drawn on his own raw experience to teach O'Neill and Freud a thing or two about Oedipus and incest.

Whether Roth appropriated or merely anticipated Freudian theory, it is impossible to ignore the powerful Oedipal bond between mother and son, as well as the almost patricidal strife between Albert and David. Modern literature offers few more potent moments of domestic dread than the violent confrontation when the enraged, deranged father, fearful that his young son will eventually be the death of him, assaults the child with a clotheshanger, ranting: "Those hands of his will beat me yet! I know! My blood warns me of this son! This son! Look at this child! Look what he's done! He'll shed human blood like water!"[5] Albert himself feels guilty of patricide for not having done anything to save his own father from a rampaging bull. To find a father-son relationship in American literature as charged with terror as the one between David and Albert, one would have to turn to Mark Twain's Huck Finn and his Pap or Eugene O'Neill's Ephraim and Eben Cabot. Roth anticipated the way in which Theodore Roethke, in "My Father's Waltz," evokes the fierce love-hate that links a little boy and his brutish father:

> You beat time on my head
> With a palm caked hard by dirt,
> Then waltzed me off to bed
> Still clinging to your shirt.[6]

The authority of James Joyce is evident in *Call It Sleep*, not only because Roth's account of David Schearl is in effect another portrait of the artist as a young man but also in the lavish use of stream of consciousness and the scrupulous, Symbolist deployment of recurrent imagery. A pattern of radiant figures and biblical allusions supports the story of a child who manages to transcend the shocks and horrors of everyday life into mystical illumination. From the Joyce who wrote *Ulysses*, Roth derived the inspiration to forge sophisticated fiction out of the tawdry material of his own domestic experience, the lesson "that I could talk about urban squalor and develop it into a work of art."[7] Joyce's example gave Roth the confidence to extract straws from his banal existence and turn them into literary gold. However, many years later, when he preferred to minimize and even denigrate Joyce's contribution to his art, Roth hailed another Irish author as his master, insisting that "the foremost of my mentors in the transmutation of a 'base' language (a pun), into a 'noble' one, was none other than John Synge, who first performed the alchemy in his plays; they drew much of their source from the primitive speech of the Aran islanders, a peasant and fishing folk. His *Riders to the Sea* and his *Playboy of the Western World* are supreme examples of that kind of recreation."[8]

Call It Sleep records the traumas experienced when the Old World meets the New, as it did for millions of new Americans during the four decades surrounding the turn of the twentieth century. Many of Roth's immigrants are inspired by the American dream of enlarged opportunity, while others are repulsed by an urban nightmare. *Schearl* means "scissors" in Yiddish, and behind Roth's story of the Schearls is not just his own pain at being cut off from Eastern Europe but, even more, from the Lower East Side he had long since been forced to abandon.

Though the Schearls are Polish Jews, the eclectic slum in which they live serves as home to immigrants and natives from many other backgrounds. It is not exactly the homogeneous "Jewish mini-state" that Roth, later sentimentalizing his lost Lower East Side, would remember. Not the least of his accomplishments is his success at rendering the diversity of David's environs. *Call It Sleep* is attentive to the physical details of life among the tenements of the Lower East Side, a tumult of conflicting impressions that makes it easy for little David Schearl to become lost when he wanders just a few blocks away from home and cannot make himself understood to the kindly Irish cop who tries to help. But the novel is most memorable as a discordant record of culture clash, one that makes its English into a subtle instrument for rendering the collision of languages.

Yiddish is the first language of the Schearls, as it was of the Roths.

But English, German, Hebrew, Italian, and Polish are also spoken, in varying registers, by characters in the story. In a novel designed for English-speaking readers, it would be misleading and demeaning to put fractured English into the mouths or minds of fluent Yiddish speakers assumed to be using their native tongue. That would be the equivalent of the Hollywood westerns that reduce American Indians to stammering puerile pidgin even among themselves. Instead, Roth fashions English prose supple enough to represent the varying speech and thought of those who speak and think in other languages and dialects. In his Afterword to the 1964 paperback edition, the British critic Walter Allen, noting the disparate, cacophonous voices that clamor throughout the work, observed that *Call It Sleep* "must be the *noisiest* novel ever written."[9] And in an essay, "Between Mother Tongue and Native Language in *Call It Sleep*," that was appropriated as an Afterword to a 1991 edition, Hana Wirth-Nesher discusses the novel as a polyglot echo chamber. Studying the variety of languages, dialects, and accents throughout the text, she notes that Roth "makes use of multilingualism and translation in his masterful novel as a way of identifying how the book partakes of more than one literary and cultural tradition. . . ." For Wirth-Nesher, Roth's multilingual text is his "specific response to the dilemma of the self-consciously Jewish author writing in a language steeped in non-Jewish culture."[10]

Roth, who allowed his own first language, Yiddish, to atrophy, remained sensitive to the unique ways in which particular languages refract experience. He was keenly aware of the arbitrariness of verbal expression. In its first manuscript version, the alternative title he was to give his final work, *Mercy of a Rude Stream*, was *Advanced English for Foreigners*. In a sense, Roth's texts are always meant to be read as if in translation, as if the words are never entirely transparent or spontaneous.

Humor pervades a novel in which outsiders are continually blundering their way through circumstances they do not quite understand. The most notable comic figure in *Call It Sleep* is Bertha, Genya's younger sister, who stays with the Schearls for a while after arriving alone in New York. Whereas Genya and Albert are, for different reasons, withdrawn, sharp-tongued Bertha is exuberant and loquacious, and even during her clumsy attempts to find a husband she is a vibrant presence amid the dismal tenements. Impatient with fake sentimentality over the forsaken charms of the Old World, she offers a pungent, irreverent assessment of her native village: "Veljish was still as a fart in company. Who could endure it?"[11] The episode in which Bertha, along with her nephew David, ventures uptown to visit the labyrinthine Metropolitan Museum of Art is a comic gem; exhausted and lost in the endless galleries and corridors, Bertha follows a couple who seem more at ease in this American temple to high culture, only to discover they are just as bewildered as she is. And they are hunting not for an exit but a restroom.

Call It Sleep is significant sociologically, for reflecting a momentous phenomenon—the transformation of the United States into a multicultural nation—that was ignored by most of Roth's respectable literary contemporaries. It marks the emergence of Americans who do not derive from Western or Northern Europe, who are not even Protestant. It is the flagship text for a nation of immigrants—one that speaks also to the descendants of Irish, Poles, Italians, Mexicans, Haitians, and Vietnamese. But to the extent that we are all immigrants, strangers in a strange life, each forced to confront alone the perils of a shifting landscape, Roth's Ur-text mines more precious ore. In its vivid rendition of a child's-eye view, its dramatic exposure of family tensions, and its creation of a rich linguistic texture, his first novel is an artistic triumph. Out of his own disjointed, disgraceful life, Roth drew a story for the entire nomadic human race.

The final, climactic paragraph, a rhythmic prose poem that resonates against the novel's title and recapitulates its images and themes, is not diminished by comparison with the famous conclusion to *The Great Gatsby*. F. Scott Fitzgerald's invocation of the green light and the orgiastic future is as fraught with apocalyptic intimations as is Roth's association of Isaiah with a jolt of electricity from a streetcar in *Call It Sleep*. "I have had my vision" are the parting words of Lily Briscoe in Virginia Woolf's *To the Lighthouse*. Savoring the final lines of Roth's sonorous paragraph, the reader of *Call It Sleep* shares the same sense of redemptive consummation:

It was only toward sleep one knew himself still lying on the cobbles, felt the cobbles under him, and over him and scudding ever toward him like a black foam, the perpetual blur of shod and running feet, the broken shoes, new shoes, stubby, pointed, caked, polished, buniony, pavement-beveled, lumpish, under skirts, under trousers, shoes, over one and through one, and feel them all and feel, not pain, not terror, but strangest triumph, strangest acquiescence. One might as well call it sleep. He shut his eyes.[12]

When Roth died, in 1995, the Jewish population of the United States had been augmented by an influx of half a million Soviet émigrés during the years preceding and following the dissolution of the Union of Soviet Socialist Republics in 1991. But by the last decade of the twentieth century, most American Jews were two or three generations removed from the immigrant experiences he recounted. Yet a vast new wave of newcomers to the United States—primarily from Latin America and Asia and, at 20 million, exceeding the deluge of European humanity that washed up at Ellis Island around the turn of the twentieth century—made *Call It Sleep* seem as timely as ever.

IN 1934, Roth's initial readers, though hardly numerous, were impressed. According to the simplified legend, *Call It Sleep*, like *Moby-Dick*, met with widespread scorn or indifference when first published. The neophyte novelist is thought to have been so disheartened when his magnum opus failed to find readers that he rejected writing entirely and went off to Maine to slaughter ducks. Like Herman Melville, who was rediscovered seventy years after his masterpiece flopped in the marketplace, Roth reemerged as a literary force only after thirty years.

However, the initial critical reception for *Call It Sleep* was in fact as favorable as any author—especially a new one—could hope for. Of the seventeen reviews that appeared in six newspapers and eight magazines, most were highly favorable.[13] Fred T. Marsh of the *New York*

Herald Tribune praised the novel as "a work of superior craftsman-
ship, more than that a work of significance, authority and depth. I
believe it to be the most compelling and moving, the most accurate
and profound study of an American slum childhood that has yet
appeared in this day when, be it said to the credit of our contemporary critics, economic color-lines are no longer drawn in our literature."[14] In *The Nation*, Horace Gregory, a poet who knew Roth and
Walton socially, hailed *Call It Sleep* as a "first novel of extraordinary
character" and "an experience which few readers of contemporary
fiction can afford to ignore."[15] Few new authors would take offense
at being likened to James T. Farrell or James Joyce. In *The New York
Times*, John Chamberlain proclaimed that Roth "has done for the
East Side what James T. Farrell is doing for the Chicago Irish," while
Edwin Seaver in the *New York Sun* called Roth "a brilliant disciple of
James Joyce." Alfred Hayes even contended, in the Communist *Daily
Worker*, that Roth had surpassed the Irish master, that *Call It Sleep*
was "as brilliant as Joyce's *Portrait of the Artist*, but with a wider
scope, a richer emotion, a deeper realism."[16]

During those decorous times when books were still being censored,
at least two critics expressed squeamishness over the novel's squalor.
Yet both acknowledged the author's talents. Joseph Gollomb, writing
in the *Saturday Review of Literature*, called *Call It Sleep* "by far the
foulest picture of the east side that has yet appeared, in conception
and in language"; yet he also conceded that "There is much that is
true in Mr. Roth's novel; he has a sensitive ear for speech; his characters speak from character and in the idioms of their land; he
remembers amazingly and reports photographically."[17] And H. W.
Boynton in *The New York Times*, while noting that "The book lays
all possible stress on the nastiness of the human animal," assured the
reader: "It is the fashion, and we must make the best of the spectacle
of a fine book deliberately and as it were doggedly smeared with verbal filthiness."[18]

A fresh recruit to the Communist Party, Roth must have rejoiced to
read in Hayes's *Daily Worker* piece that "There has appeared in
America no novel to rival the veracity of this childhood."[19] Yet he was

distressed when another Marxist publication, *The New Masses*, dismissed his novel as too subjective and impressionistic to be of much political use. "It is a pity that so many young writers drawn from the proletariat can make no better use of their working-class experience than as material for introspective and febrile novels," complained the anonymous reviewer, who also faulted the work for being at least 200 pages too long, and for focusing on "the sex phobia of this six year old Proust."[20] However, this condemnation of *Call It Sleep* for bourgeois aestheticism provoked a controversy within *The New Masses* that echoed arguments roiling the literary left throughout the thirties and forties.

To what extent should art be regarded instrumentally, as a tool or a weapon of the revolution? Can artistic individualism be tolerated or even encouraged by those committed to class struggle? The question of what, if anything, is the writer's political responsibility became the subject of fierce polemics and internecine feuds within *The New Masses*, *Partisan Review*, and other Socialist publications of the period. Upton Sinclair had just made a credible run for governor of California on the slogan of EPIC (End Poverty in California), and Dartmouth College had resisted intense pressure to destroy the murals it commissioned from José Clemente Orozco depicting capitalist exploitation of the masses. In 1935, Clifford Odets would open a play, *Waiting for Lefty*, designed to rouse its audience to leave the theater shouting: "Strike!"

One week after its original review of *Call It Sleep*, *The New Masses* published a letter to the editor from the poet David Greenhood defending his friend's novel in explicitly political terms. While Greenhood noted the book's formal merits, he did not reject the standards against which it had been judged by *The New Masses*; he merely applied those standards differently. Greenhood's principal point was that any critic who faults Roth's text for lack of revolutionary consciousness has simply misread it: "*Call It Sleep* is about the working-class bottom, written by one of its own naturals who became articulate long before he wrote the novel, and who while he wrote it was engaged, as he has never ceased to be, in the one struggle that counts."[21] The following week, *The New Masses* published two more letters—by Kenneth Burke and Alvah C. Brothers, respectively—about Roth and his reviewer.

On March 5, *The New Masses* published yet another review of the novel, and this time the critic, Edwin Seaver, took the occasion to deplore the effect of ideological absolutism on literary culture. Seaver assailed the doctrinaire demands of other leftist critics that resulted in "the assassination of books which fail to do what the author never intended to do and could not have done with the material at hand." Yet he defended Roth, even within the narrow scope of Marxist formulas, for having created in young David Schearl a budding hero of the working class. "When we close the book," insisted Seaver, "we honestly feel that such a childhood can mature into a revolutionary manhood."[22]

More accustomed to sticks than carrots, Roth got stuck on the first *New Masses* review. None of the praise heaped on his novel affected him as much as the assault on his radical credentials. "I thought I was a good Communist," he recalled. "I thought I was doing the right thing for the Party and the Revolution."[23] Roth internalized the standards of socialist realism and vowed that next time out he would write an exemplary Marxist novel. While conceding that Roth's first work would not "fall readily into the classification of 'proletarian' novel," Gregory in his *Nation* review nevertheless maintained that it "reveals, I think, more of the actual conditions of living on New York's East Side than any other book I have ever read."[24] Although Michael Harrington, a leading socialist intellectual, would later judge *Call It Sleep* "the finest proletarian novel of the Thirties,"[25] Roth continued to disparage his own literary effort as bourgeois—too fixated on the merely personal. Many have been more generous than its own author was, and by 1966, the literary scholar Kenneth Ledbetter was pronouncing Roth's novel "the most authentic and compelling expression the American proletariat has received."[26]

Yet the tendency to read *Call It Sleep* as "aesthetic" rather than "political" persisted, as did Roth's own dissatisfaction. Seventy-five years after its publication, Arthur Miller, surveying the social protest fiction of the thirties, noted: "Very little of the writing of that exciting new dispensation has survived, having died with the issues with which it was so tightly bound up. The few surviving works of high art, like Henry Roth's *Call It Sleep*, while powerfully depicting the poverty and squalor of the city life of working-class people, were essentially aimed elsewhere, at the subjective experiences of the author, in fact, and his personal sensations of life in a certain time and place."[27] As late as 1968, Roth himself still shared some of the first, anonymous *New Masses* reviewer's disdain for work that stood aloof from the struggle for social justice. In a letter to a Canadian graduate student, he accused his own book of being out of sync with its era, an irresponsible throwback to mere aestheticism:

The '30s were a period of polarization, left and right, a period infused with imminence: the coming struggle for power. My novel was a kind of carry-over, was conditioned by a previous a-political, a-economic (if not anti), semi-mystical decade espousing art for its own fair sake, and it appeared belatedly at the acme of partnership. In short it was, or was akin to, an atavism.[28]

Yet, if it was an atavism, *Call It Sleep* was also ahead of its time; either way, December 1934, when unemployment exceeded 20 percent and one of every four American households was on relief, was not the most propitious moment for its debut. Those who had disposable cash to spend were buying Hervey Allen's historical romance, *Anthony Adverse*, and James Hilton's nostalgic salute to a saintly teacher, *Goodbye, Mr. Chips*. It was possible to go to the movies seven times for the price of one novel. *Bride of Frankenstein*, *Mutiny on the Bounty*, *Top Hat*, and *Gold Diggers of 1935* held more immediate appeal to more Americans than an unknown immigrant's first novel about life among the lowly. Ballou initially printed 1,500 copies of *Call It Sleep*, and when they sold well, he ordered another 1,000 copies. However, by the time the second batch was ready, demand was already declining. Most of the second run ended up either being pulped or simply disappearing. Unable to balance books overall, the firm of

Robert O. Ballou ceased to publish them. After lingering for several months, the company finally went out of business on July 22, 1936, and Ballou himself went to work for other publishers. *Call It Sleep* became a phantom, no longer even a title on any house's backlist.

By the end of the century, a single copy of the Ballou edition of *Call It Sleep*, which originally sold for $2.50, would fetch $5,000, but no one seemed to want it at any price in 1935. When an author casts his bread upon the waters and it seems to sink without a trace, the experience can be devastating, even to someone whose self-esteem is not as fragile as Roth's. Lester Winter, now a dentist and married, and no longer a rival in literature or love, congratulated Roth warmly. But the publication of his first novel was not a magical event. Unlike David Schearl's experience touching a milk dipper to a streetcar rail, it brought neither revelation nor transformation. Roth still yearned for redemption.

In 1934, the category of "American Jewish literature" did not yet exist—in bookstore aisles or in the minds of readers and writers. Anti-Semitic propaganda, including the calumny of the spurious tsarist *Protocols of the Elders of Zion*, was being widely consumed. Henry Ford's *Dearborn Independent* in the early 1920s and later Father Charles Coughlin's radio broadcasts made Jews feel wary guests in American society. They were also rare figures in professional sports. But when a young first baseman named Hank Greenberg led the Detroit Tigers to the American League pennant that season, he faced the kind of bigotry that Jackie Robinson, breaking the color barrier in major league baseball, would contend with a decade later. Batting .339 with 139 runs batted in and 26 home runs, Greenberg became a tribal hero to Jewish fans and a lightning rod for anti-Jewish sentiment. On September 19, despite a tense pennant race with the visiting New York Yankees, he refused to play in that day's game. It was Yom Kippur and, though no more pious than Roth, Greenberg chose to affirm his heritage by spending the sacred day in a synagogue. Without their star slugger, the Tigers lost to the rival Yankees, 5–2.

Much later, Roth would recall the casual anti-Semitism common in a baseball park in the early 1920s in *A Diving Rock on the Hudson*.

Ira Stigman and his friend Izzy arrive early at the Polo Grounds and cheer the Giants during batting practice. John McGraw, the Giants' truculent manager, berates the two boys. "Who the hell's askin' you fer yer two cents?" he demands. "If you Jews don't shut up, I'll have you thrown outta the park."[29]

In 1934, advertising a Jewish identity was a risky way to market either athletes or books. Fred T. Marsh did not review *Call It Sleep* as a Jewish book—not because its author regarded Yom Kippur as just another work day but because no one would yet think of placing such a label on an American novel. The critic concluded his discussion in the *New York Herald Tribune* by prophesying: "To discerning readers, I believe, for its profound intensity, its rare virtuosity, its sensitive realism, its sheer weight, its power, circumference and depth, this first novel of this Mr. Roth will be remembered for some time to come. I should like to see *Call It Sleep* win the Pulitzer prize—which it never will."[30] Though the novel was largely forgotten for thirty years, Marsh was ultimately proved accurate in both predictions. The Pulitzer Prize in Fiction for 1935 went to twenty-four-year-old Josephine Winslow Johnson's *Now in November*, a novel that soon became unknown, unread, and unavailable, until republished by the Feminist Press in 1991. Although Walter B. Rideout's comprehensive study, *The Radical Novel in the United States* (1956), would later single Roth's novel out as "the most distinguished single proletarian novel,"[31] *The New Masses* passed over *Call It Sleep* when it bestowed an award for proletarian novel of the year on Clara Weatherwax's *Marching! Marching!*

When *Call It Sleep* was published, American literary culture lacked the elaborate infrastructure of prizes, grants, and reading tours that today encourages and sustains authors both psychologically and financially. In a later era, Roth's book might have been a contender for one of several honors targeted at first novels, Jewish books, or fiction set in New York State. It might have been a contender for the National Book Critics Circle prize. Instead, missing the Pulitzer, it fell into oblivion, and its young author slid into one of the sloughs of despond strewn throughout the landscape of his life.

It seemed too late to take up a career in biology. Roth was a writer, and the natural follow-up to *Call It Sleep* would have been to write a novel about David Schearl—and Henry Roth—beginning at the age of eight. However, for a fiction writer who drew so directly from his own life, that would have meant confronting harsh truths about his high school disgrace and sexual abomination, which Roth would not be prepared to do for another fifty years. Though he did attempt a novel about an adolescent character, he abandoned it after forty or fifty pages and eventually burned the entire manuscript.[32] Instead, he invested his literary energies in a novel about a midwestern proletarian hero modeled on his mentor, Bill Clay, the Communist organizer and salesman for the *Daily Worker*. Roth eagerly embraced the world view advanced by the Marxist critic Granville Hicks that "American life is a battleground, and that arrayed on one side are the exploiters and on the other the exploited."[33] He saw Clay's struggles as an opportunity to portray that stark conflict and to deploy his pen as a weapon on behalf of the oppressed against the oppressors. "It seemed to me," Roth later told an interviewer, "that all I had to do was to explore his life's experiences and exploit the picturesque language that he used and I had a novel."[34]

It was not that simple. Thinly disguising Clay under the fictional name Dan Loem, Roth wrote almost 100 pages. He began the story on the mean streets of Cincinnati, with the young ruffian Loem's attempt to rob the paymaster of a slaughterhouse. Marxism has not yet redeemed him from the loutish life of a hooligan. Roth later went on to write an allegorical prologue—eventually published (1960) as "The Dun Dakotas"—in which Loem's father, a cavalry scout, plays poker with an Indian chief for the right to pass peacefully through his tribal lands.

Roth showed his work-in-progress to Walton and Mandel, and Mandel sold it to Maxwell Perkins at Scribners. Perkins paid Mandel $1,000, the amount Mandel had lost on *Call It Sleep*, as an advance. According to Roth, Mandel spent the sum on an automobile. The most celebrated American book editor of the twentieth century, Perkins counted Erskine Caldwell, F. Scott Fitzgerald, Ernest Hemingway, Ring Lardner, Marjorie Kinnan Rawlings, and Thomas Wolfe among his authors. Though he had rejected *Call It Sleep*, he now had second thoughts. In a letter on July 29, 1935, to his friend Elizabeth Lemmon, Perkins expressed admiration for Roth, mixed with anxiety that "such a writer would make no end of trouble for me on account of his contempt for conventional restraint—much worse than any one we have published. Still, I wrote encouragingly and sent for [his next] book. We are publishers after all."[35] As unrestrained as Roth was, this new project certainly held promise. With the unflagging support of Mandel and Walton, Roth had convinced America's foremost editor that he deserved a place beside leading modern authors. But the novelist never completed the work, and the advance was never returned.

Chapter 6

AUTO-DA-FÉ

I burnt every novel I possessed. Dickens. Cervantes. Dostoevsky. Flaubert. All the great and all the small. I even burnt something I wrote myself when I was too young to know better. I burnt them out there. It took me all day. The sky took their smoke, the earth their ashes. It was a fumigation. I have been happier and healthier ever since. . . . Why should I struggle through hundreds of pages of fabrication to reach half a dozen very little truths?

—JOHN FOWLES[1]

THE NEW BOOK was beyond redemption—and so, its faltering author thought, was he. On a mild May morning in 1935, Henry Roth, disheartened and restless, grimaced at his incomplete manuscript. He was writing to vindicate himself from the mistake of his first novel. He had poured his life into his art, and each, he concluded, was a failure. *Call It Sleep* was too subjective, too involute, too aesthetic—in short, too bourgeois. And it had, to all appearances, vanished into oblivion, more than 1,000 unsold copies doomed to rot in the warehouse of his hapless publisher. This new novel needed to be different. It needed to stir his readers into action, not distanced (and unrealized) appreciation. Yet the second novel, celebrating the exploits of a blustering midwestern working-class hero, felt more fraudulent with every sentence. Instead of spending yet another fruitless day hunched over his desk, Roth set out toward the piers lining the Hudson River. On his way out the door, he grabbed a pile of leaflets from the John Reed Club, the national organization dedicated to spreading the cause of revolution to the working masses. This would be no idle morning stroll beside the harbor. If Roth could not convince dockworkers on New York's piers of his beliefs in person, he had no license to try to do so in writing. He bounded out the door of Eda Lou Walton's home and headed west.

It was four blocks to the Hudson River, and, as he crossed Hudson Street, Greenwich Street, Washington Street, and West Street on his way to the edge of the island borough, Roth passed just north of the route that a restless Ishmael treads in the first chapter of *Moby-Dick* when, setting out to "Circumambulate the city of a dreary Sabbath afternoon," he finds that "Right and left, the streets take you water-ward."[2] Melville's mariner is drawn to the open sea as a way of driving off the spleen, a substitute for pistol and ball. Though Roth held enough spleen to rival Ishmael, his purpose in striding toward the wharves along the Hudson was not to embark on an ocean voyage, much less hunt a whale. He had crossed the Atlantic once, in steerage, and that would suffice for a lifetime. Yet just as he was confined within the bowels of a steamship three decades earlier, Roth now believed himself to be something of a captive again.

It pained Roth, coddled and controlled by Walton, to witness her overactive romantic life and her bourgeois aestheticism. Even though she shielded him from poverty—even though he never had to eat in a soup kitchen or sleep in the street—Roth longed for independence from this academic Circe who was beguiling and enthralling other men as well. As he sat in his Village study relishing the luxury of stringing words into resonant sentences, Roth wondered about the kind of man he had become: was it manly to allow Walton to pamper and support him? He saw his financial and emotional dependency on a female intellectual as a symptom of "degeneracy," and he brooded over how to establish some autonomy.

Joining the Communist Party of the United States (CPUSA), in 1934, seemed to Roth one way to prove his credentials as a member of the working class, not just the parasite of a privileged woman. Through agitation, he sought redemption. Walton had warned him that he was destroying himself as an artist, but her opposition made membership in the Party even more appealing. A few months later, Walton herself would join the CPUSA. Roth was not the only modern intellectual beset by *nostalgie de la boue*, but his nostalgia was not just sentimental; unlike many other Village artists, he was actually born into the working class, and he still felt mired in the mud. An immigrant Jew who had grown up in New York's poorest, most congested neighborhoods, Roth could claim expertise in economic insecurity that was not just theoretical. And though he was a graduate of CCNY at a time when only a happy few pursued a higher education, Roth's résumé already bulged with blue-collar assignments. "I am the eternal plebeian,"[3] he would proclaim in 1987, accepting a prestigious honor, the Nonino International Prize, that was not usually awarded to hoi polloi. Yet, whether digging ditches in Queens or cutting pulpwood in Maine, Roth never quite felt proletarian enough. Every time he brought out his blue collar, it seemed to fade to beige. He always felt tainted by bourgeois values that he was compelled to repudiate—by serving the Party, by subsisting through manual labor in rural New England, or by struggling to compose fiction that extolled the working class.

The Communist Party of the 1930s tendered hope of eliminating exploitation and injustice; impatient with the mere reform of Franklin D. Roosevelt's New Deal, thirty thousand Americans, three fifths of them foreign-born, had joined. Jews, bearing genetic memory of restrictions and pogroms in Eastern Europe and smarting from overt anti-Semitism in the New World, were attracted to the Party in numbers disproportionate to their percentage of the general population. Among the writers and artists Roth knew, membership in the Party was a way to affirm solidarity with manual laborers while enhancing one's standing in the largely leftist intelligentsia. It was also a convenient way for nubile young idealists to make the acquaintance of others willing to share their passions.

But if ideologues and laborers had anything in common during the 1930s, it was the dread of unemployment. In 1935, several years into the Great Depression, 20.7 percent of job seekers in the United States were out of work, and one out of four households relied on government relief. Hoovervilles, the makeshift shantytowns named for the recent president who was widely blamed for economic calamity, still occupied swaths of land along the Hudson and East Rivers. The largest Hooverville in New York, assembled in Central Park near the old Croton Reservoir, consisted of two hundred shacks. The riverfront, Roth's destination on that May morning, was one of the few places where a bit of money could be made. Desperate men could not afford to spurn the paychecks offered on the wharves. Thousands of them assembled three times a day—at eight, noon, and later at four—to be available for the shape-up, the process by which no more than a third or half of those seeking work were selected for an assignment on the docks.

Even during the depths of the Depression, New York Harbor remained the busiest port in the world. On any given day, dozens of ships flying flags from nations in Europe, Latin America, Asia, and Africa lay anchored off the margin of Manhattan. Every day, thousands of men assembled beside these huge vessels eager for the task of loading or unloading the produce, textiles, machinery, coal, and other commodities that fueled global commerce. Hauling crated freight in and out of holds was arduous, even dangerous, physical labor, and no one but executives and stockholders of the shipping companies could expect to get rich from the effort. But it was work that paid.

Men eager for assignments stood in line in front of the hiring boss, who signaled his decisions by tossing brass checks to those he chose for work. Winners and losers returned to compete again the following day. Officially, there was a union, the International Longshoremen's Association (ILA), but its bosses were corrupt. Organized crime would still be trumping organized labor twenty years later, in 1954, when Elia Kazan's *On the Waterfront* exposed mob control of New York Harbor. Roth was in any case convinced that what the oppressed

workers of this world needed more than representation was revolution. Just the year before, authorities had put a violent end to a three-
month strike by longshoremen in San Francisco. In response to the
police action that left two dead and dozens wounded, unions in
Northern California called a general strike, but it did little to improve
the lot of the workers who loaded and unloaded ships. When Roth
walked to the wharves along the Hudson, he hoped to herald the
advent of a classless society. Gifted with a facility for languages, he
had taught himself Italian, and he was proud of the fact that he could
not only recite Dante and sing Verdi but also talk with the dockworkers—most of them Italian, either immigrants or their sons, called
"narrowbacks"—in their own tongue.

Roth marched off to the waterfront in order, as he later explained,
"to feel that I was doing something to redeem myself."[4] Few ship-
workers, however, were especially receptive to the revolutionary message he bore. And the bosses of the docks did not welcome intrusion
by any outside agitator, much less a Jewish Bolshevik. On that May
day, several stevedores, urged on by the business agent for the ILA
local, pounced upon Roth and administered a brutal beating. It is not
hard to imagine the bookish, bespectacled intruder suddenly sur-
rounded by a group of burly, sullen, hostile men. At a signal from one,
fists and cudgels rained down on Roth, who was poorly prepared to
offer much resistance. *Call It Sleep* had made almost no impact on the
world at large, but these union goons were making their emphatic
mark on the body of its vulnerable author.

By the time he staggered back to Morton Street, Roth had lost his
leaflets, his glasses, and his self-confidence as an activist and a writer.
Bruised and swollen from a battering he was sure he deserved, he
climbed the stairs to his study, to the unfinished manuscript on his
desk. A short while later, entering the house with Walton, David Mandel, the lawyer who had negotiated Roth's contract, was stunned to
find the new manuscript being consumed by flames. Though Mandel
lived in New Jersey, he regularly came into the Village to spend a night
with Walton. When the two of them entered Roth's study, they found

Roth, his nose bloodied and broken, reveling in triumphant misery beside the fire.

"When we went to his room," Mandel recalled three decades later, "we found him bleeding, singing the *International* [*sic*], and with his entire manuscript, which was virtually finished, burning in the fireplace." Both Walton and Mandel believed in Roth's talent. Walton had been his benefactor and muse during the six years it took him to complete *Call It Sleep*, and Mandel had provided the capital necessary to get it into print. They were devastated by this destruction of his new work-in-progress. But Roth, having liberated himself from a pointless task, had grown delirious. Convinced that nothing he could write would ever make a difference, he was determined to give up entirely on the literary life. "Henry told me that no one could describe the American scene with imagination and that he was through with trying to do so, and that he did not think that any writers of the first rank could appear in what he termed an abominable society," Mandel recalled.[5] Almost fifty years later, Roth himself would explain to a friend: "I did not want to go on. I began to fool with introductions, with prologues, etc. But to go further I knew I would have to go to the Middle West to pick up material about this guy. Something now developed that I couldn't overcome or perhaps I didn't want to. I just wanted to conclude."[6]

In the torching of literary ambition was born the legend of Henry Roth the master novelist who called it silence for sixty years. According to the familiar story, the anchorite of the Pine Tree State, the Jewish American Rimbaud, abjuring the novelist's rough magic, now endured the longest writer's block of any major figure in American literary history, before recovering his ambition and his powers. But Roth's gesture in burning his own manuscript—at a time when Nazis were incinerating books—was but a single, dramatic episode in a long life that was far more complicated than the legend.

Roth would later draw some other conclusions about abandoning the novel he had promised Perkins. It had to do with his troubled feelings about the main character: "He was the most picturesque character, proletarian character one could imagine. He was illiterate. He had been a brawler and he looked it. He had these tremendous chest muscles, tremendous shoulder thickness. . . ." Roth would later speculate that an unacknowledged sexual attraction toward Clay might have been a factor in his literary paralysis:

> I began to realize there were very strong homosexual hints, shall I call them that, I mean the kind of configurations and the imagery, etc., and I was appalled. To me homosexuality is a degeneration. Or may I say it was. I still don't accept it, and I think that that has [as] much to do with my quitting and not writing anymore as anything.[7]

The Scribner copy disappeared. The sole record of Roth's aborted second novel survives in a fragment that was published in 1936 in a small, ephemeral magazine called *Signatures: Works in Progress*. The author was paid thirty-five dollars for his story. Beginning with its unkosher title, "If We Had Bacon" strays very far from Roth's Jewish childhood on the Lower East Side. His take on a midwestern, Gentile adolescence is, as he himself later admitted, "precious" and "stilted."[8] It is writing from a recipe—one that Roth found more ideologically commanding than artistically compelling. The formulas of socialist realism elicited Roth's respect but did not inspire his creativity. An autobiographical impulse was always the impetus for his most authentic work, and he simply failed to find in Bill Clay—a blustering, goyish yahoo—enough to nourish his art. Even the dialogue, ordinarily one of Roth's strengths, rings false. "I got t' git us some real bacon now," says Dan Loem, in a speech that announces the theme—and demonstrates the stylistic weaknesses—of the entire story. "Er us won't have no breakfas'. An' I'll git real bacon ef I have t' drag it home squealin'."[9]

Roth himself did not have to worry about the next day's breakfast. And, preoccupied with a stable of prominent authors, Perkins put no pressure on Roth to complete the novel Scribners had contracted for. It became apparent to Roth that nothing good would come of his Bill

Clay project, but what would become of him? Chafing under his helpless dependency on Walton, Roth was ill suited to be a Village *flâneur*, just another local dilettante best known for the book he was *not* writing. Still in love with her, he was puzzled and hurt by Walton's continuing liaisons with others. Her generosity filled him with both gratitude and shame. "It was a real continuation of infancy to be supported by a woman so long," Roth, long insecure about his manhood, recalled.[10] Yet, though Mandel had become a continuing presence at Morton Street, the letters that Roth and Walton exchanged when one or the other was away from New York were very affectionate. Each on occasion reported other sexual partners, and Roth even recounted instances of masturbation, yet their correspondence reflects mutual devotion and passion. In a 1935 letter, Walton proclaimed that her love for Roth was boundless. The following year, she wrote that her love for him had lost none of its force.[11]

As late as 1938, Walton was still declaring that she valued Roth even more than her own life, most of the time, at least. Yet Walton also presented herself as liberated from bourgeois notions of sexual possessiveness. She often advised Roth to seek out other women just as she pursued other men. She even recognized that he might finally be better off leaving her for someone else, though a letter in early 1938 suggests ambivalence over that prospect. She wrote that if the proper woman came along, she would gladly surrender the field, though begrudgingly. Walton admitted that she could not pretend to be happy about losing him.[12]

For a while, it seemed to Roth that a proper woman had come along. The name she goes by in his papers is Barbara O'Connell, and Roth fell in love with her sophistication, her wit, her poise in precisely those social encounters at which he felt most gauche. When she refused to take his attempts at courtship seriously, peremptorily dismissing a proposal of marriage, his alienation from the Manhattan intelligentsia was intensified. Still in awe of the salon world Walton had introduced him to, Roth also disdained its arid intellectuals and longed to break away, to some place where he would not have to disguise his plebeian nature—some place like the Fletcher farmhouse in Maine, where he had done most of his best writing. He longed to do something decisive and redemptive.

Chapter 7

YADDO AND
ITS CONSEQUENCES

My despair about the American novel began in the winter
of 1991, when I fled to Yaddo, the artists' colony in
upstate New York, to write the last two chapters of my
second book.

—JONATHAN FRANZEN[1]

HAVING ALREADY PUBLISHED one critically acclaimed novel, Henry Roth, now thirty-two, was invited to spend the summer of 1938 at Yaddo, the artists' colony in Saratoga Springs, two hundred miles north of New York City. Saratoga Springs established itself as a fashionable resort during the nineteenth century, drawing the Vanderbilts and other northeastern gentry to its curative waters, its stylish race track, and its provincial elegance. The Adirondack spa respected social status even more than wealth and in 1869 denied a hotel room to banker Joseph Seligman, who, though very, very rich, happened also to be Jewish. Nearly seventy years later, in May 1938, when Roth drove his Model A Ford up from Manhattan, Saratoga Springs had become a bit tattered but still not much more hospitable to Jews and other outsiders. Roth, however, was welcomed into a refuge for anxious artists.

Opened in 1926 as the legacy of Spencer and Katrina Trask, Yaddo occupied 400 acres just north of Saratoga's famous racetrack. Yaddo was a couple of decades younger than the MacDowell Colony, but by 1938 it could already claim Aaron Copland, John Cheever, Clyfford Still, Stanley Kunitz, Roy Harris, Lionel Trilling, James T. Farrell, and Hannah Arendt among its alumni. According to the Trasks' bequest, the estate was to serve as "a permanent Home to which shall come from time to time . . . authors, painters, sculptors, musicians and other artists both men and women . . . their sole qualification being that they have done, are doing, or give promise of doing good and earnest work."[2]

Walton had scouted out the territory, as had several of her friends, including Witter Bynner and Lynn Riggs. She had already seen to it that Ben Belitt spend time at Yaddo, and she would be instrumental in installing Roth there as well. Nine years earlier, during the summer of 1929, Walton herself had been a guest at Yaddo, working on *Jane Matthew and Other Poems* (1931).

In February 1938, Walton wrote to Elizabeth Ames, the colony's executive director, urging her to take Roth in for the summer. Walton's letter made spurious claims about her protégé's productivity. She assured Ames that Henry Roth was almost finished with his new book, and that it would be appearing in the fall if everything went according to plan.[3] Her contention that publication of his second novel was imminent was extravagantly inaccurate. But if MacDowell changed Roth's life, so too would Yaddo.

It was easy for a guest to feel spoiled by the plush carpeting, ample meals, and abundant leisure. The poet Kenneth Fearing, who was also a resident during the summer of 1938, spent more time drinking than writing, and he remarked repeatedly that the accommodations were much too sumptuous for serious work. But Roth refused to blame the setting for his own lack of productivity. "Yaddo can scarcely be faulted for the barren summer I spent there trying to write," he would note almost forty years later.[4] It can, however, be credited for his marriage and his final break with Eda Lou Walton.

The first residents Roth saw when he arrived at "the Castle," the fifty-two-room mansion modeled after the royal palace in Bucharest that served as the main building at Yaddo, were two women, and something about their demeanor convinced him they were lovers. He would soon encounter other women who seemed more appropriate to his romantic fantasies. In an unpublished autobiographical manuscript, the narrator becomes sexually involved with a young, brown-eyed sculptor from Iowa during her final week at Yaddo but early during his stay (guests held overlapping appointments). The relationship concludes with her departure from the colony. The transient lover remains unnamed, but the actual Yaddo guest who best fits the description was Edna Guck. Two years older than Roth, Guck had already left her mark in New York with a stone bear commissioned by the Federal Art Project and placed in the reading room of the Children's Division of the Brooklyn Public Library.

For the most part, however, when not working in their separate cabin studios scattered in the woods, Yaddo's resident artists came together for softball, charades, and alcohol. Recurrent topics of discussion were the dwindling prospects for the Loyalists in the Spanish Civil War and the idiosyncrasies of the formidable Elizabeth Ames. In 1938, the partially deaf Mrs. Ames, a World War I widow who was hired when the colony began operations, was already twelve years into a reign that would last until 1969, when she finally retired at age eighty-four. Notoriously fastidious, she often sent guests personal notes admonishing them over an infraction of house rules. Roth suspected that she was surreptitiously monitoring his mail. Summoned once by Mrs. Ames to answer for some transgression, he lost his temper and insulted her. But his old social insecurity quickly reasserted itself, and he ended the session in tears, kissing Mrs. Ames's hand. Her romantic involvement with one of the other guests, Leonard Ehrlich, author of *God's Angry Man* (1932), about the abolitionist John Brown, provided further fuel for gossip among the Yaddo artists during the summer of 1938. (In 1977, at the time of Ames's death, Roth would offer a more generous assessment of the old autocrat of Yaddo: "In short, she had many fine qualities, necessarily subordinated to the requirements of personality, which I didn't appreciate then, but do now.")[5]

Other notable residents while Roth was there included B. H. Haggin, Ralph Kirkpatrick, Muriel Rukeyser, Wallace Stegner, Willard Thorp, and Morton D. Zabel. Daniel Fuchs, who brought along his wife and their young son, was assigned family accommodations in a separate cottage. Fuchs was the twenty-nine-year-old author of a fictional trilogy set among first- and second-generation New York Jews in the Williamsburg neighborhood of Brooklyn. Like *Call It Sleep*, Fuchs's novels enjoyed a *succès d'estime* that did not translate into success in the marketplace. His first novel, *Summer in Williamsburg*, published in the same year as Roth's first novel, sold only 400 copies, and so did his second, *Homage to Blenholt*, published in 1936. The third installment in the trilogy, *Low Company*, published just a year before, had fared better, but its sales were still a modest 1,200 copies.[6] Unlike Roth, Fuchs served as breadwinner for himself and his wife and child, and writing novels was not a winning proposition. So he had decided to abandon literature for Hollywood. "You can't live on favorable reviews, especially if you've got a family to support, a child to feed and clothe," he explained in Roth's final autobiographical fiction.[7]

One Sunday afternoon, in a room just off the chapel in the Castle, Roth attended a piano recital by another guest. On the program were pieces by Emmanuel Chabrier and by the performer herself—a willowy woman with fair, bobbed hair named Muriel Parker. A musician of considerable promise, Parker had turned thirty in April. After graduating summa cum laude from the University of Chicago, she had earned degrees in piano and composition at the American Conservatory of Music. She then spent a year in Paris studying with Nadia Boulanger and Soulima Stravinsky. After returning from Europe, where, she would later recall, "You didn't eat enough, didn't bathe enough, and fell in love with all the wrong people,"[8] Parker joined the music faculty of the Western College for Women, an independent school in Oxford, Ohio, founded in 1855 (later absorbed by Miami University, in 1974).

Parker had visited Yaddo for a day in 1937, and she hesitated over an invitation to return the following summer only because she was awaiting the results of an application for a Guggenheim grant. But Yaddo proved sweet consolation for an unrequited try at a Guggenheim. Parker had been teaching at Western for four years and was planning to spend the following six months on leave in New York City studying under the composer Roger Sessions. While Roth sat listening to her perform, he realized that the six-foot Parker was one of the two women he had encountered when he first arrived at Yaddo. Though he had dismissed them from his mind as lesbians, this talented musician merited attention.

For Jewish families in New York, seltzer—carbonated water dispensed by siphon from a thick, tinted glass bottle—was an affordable elixir. Roth remembered it fondly as a fixture of his childhood, beloved of hoi polloi. A deliveryman regularly made his rounds by truck throughout the neighborhood, hauling a wooden case that held a dozen bottles up and down the flights of stairs to customers' apartments. Roth was delighted to discover that bubbly water very much like seltzer gushed out of public fountains in Saratoga Springs. Paper cups were available for a penny each.

Roth began driving into town each day before breakfast in order to partake of the fizz. Eager for company, he invited other Yaddo residents to join him. "I'd sooner drink mud water," snapped Kenneth Fearing.[9] However, one guest accepted Roth's offer: Muriel Parker. For the rest of their stay, it became a merry routine. In their daily run for the hoses in downtown Saratoga Springs, Roth and Parker were flouting two of Mrs. Ames's cardinal rules: No socializing between guests before 4:00 p.m.; and no trips into town before 4:00 p.m. Roth was attracted to a quiet streak of rebellion in his new drinking companion, who mocked her own elite lineage, which led back to the *Mayflower*, by hanging out with a mutinous, impecunious, immigrant Communist Jew.

Though born in Somerville, Massachusetts, Muriel Parker grew up in Oak Park, Illinois, the leafy Chicago suburb that was Ernest Hemingway's birthplace. She was the third of four children born to Frederick and Grace Parker. A graduate of Brown University, where he was an all-American tackle, Frederick Parker was the namesake of an ancestor memorialized in bronze on Boston Common, a captain killed in battle during the American Revolution. After college, the later Frederick Parker was ordained as a Baptist minister and spent a couple of years preaching the Gospel to lumberjacks in logging camps in Oregon. He moved the family to Chicago in order to accept a position as administrative head of the central YMCA. A few years later, he was appointed executive secretary of Kiwanis International, the far-flung association of community leaders dedicated to fellowship and civic virtue. Yet, for all his worthy attributes, he was merely the son of a New York City fireman. And Muriel's mother, whose family was listed in the Social Register and staked its claim to a place in the American aristocracy by descent from the earliest English settlers, was marrying beneath her when she became Grace Parker. Her own father, Stanley Reid, a very wealthy wholesale meat dealer, expelled her from the family when she joined this ragged missionary preacher. She set a precedent for her own gifted, headstrong daughter.

Commuting for water, Parker was playing with fire. Glancing at the woman riding beside him in his Model A, Roth found her, he wrote, as radiant as the morning sunshine. He was impressed by her intelligence and fascinated by her privileged air of restrained confidence. Yet her sly manner of subverting her own gentility drew him to this uncommon Gentile. In the hothouse ambience of Yaddo's "Castle," it was hard to hide the fact that Roth and Parker were keeping company; one of the artists, Antony Martelli, insisted on painting a double portrait. But their courtship, if that is what it was, was founded more on tenderness than passion. "It was hardly a romantic love affair," Roth would recall in 1972. "I feel that Muriel just retrieved me in time. I don't think I would have lived very long; I just didn't feel like it."[10]

Disillusioned with the proprieties and values of her parents' world, Parker made common cause with a man who did the driving but had lost his way. "She came from people who were such white potatoes," her son Hugh would later explain. "Henry was terribly interesting."[11]

Neither Roth nor Parker had ever been to a horse race, and their relationship crystallized during one that they decided to attend together. It was the summer that Seabiscuit, the scruffy equine underdog who became the hero of Depression-weary Americans, was receiving more news coverage than FDR, Hitler, or Clark Gable. The Saratoga track lay at the edge of the Yaddo estate, and one afternoon Roth and Parker walked through the woods to reach a spot where they could watch the competition free of charge. The distant starting gate was barely visible, but as the horses and their jockeys rounded the track, they passed in front of the onlookers. And just as the pack was moving to their right on its way to the finish line, something unexpected happened. A horse and his rider toppled over. The animal had broken its leg. Aghast and afraid of ricocheting bullets, Muriel retreated into the forest. Roth stayed to watch the track crew take charge of the situation. One pulled out a pistol, aimed, and put the horse out of its misery. Roth continued watching until the carcass was hauled away in a truck, and then, having had enough of horse racing for the day, walked back through the woods with Parker.

Two decades later, in 1959, Roth (changing Muriel's name to Martha) would reconstruct this experience as "At Times in Flight: A Parable," a piece published in *Commentary*, the monthly sponsored by the American Jewish Committee. It is hard to fault the author for choosing this tidy little tale of love and death as his favorite among his own short stories. The piece marks a turning point in his own career, serving as a parabolic explanation for Roth's abiding mystery: Why did the richly talented author of *Call It Sleep* renounce the writing life? In a 1986 interview, Roth glosses the stumbled horse as Pegasus, a winged symbol of the arts, and its death as the loss of inspiration. "At Times in Flight" recalls the moment when Roth abandoned exalted dreams of literary glory in order to commit himself to Muriel and to normalcy as he understood it. It commemorates the day that its author dropped out of the race for artistic renown:

> . . . it also implies that in the death of the art there is a beginning of the acceptance of the necessity to live in a normal fashion, subject to all the demands and all the exigencies and vicissitudes that life

will bring. When I say normal, I mean that now he's willing to accept marriage, he's willing now to accept the getting of a livelihood and all that *that* would imply, and so forth.[12]

By the time Roth and Parker had concluded their sojourns at Yaddo, it was obvious to all that they were a couple. As Roth drove back to New York City with his new companion seated beside him, he was ready to turn the page on the life he had been leading as Walton's coddled novice writer.

But first he had to break the news to Walton, and he dreaded the ordeal. For all her affected nonchalance about romantic relationships, Walton had been living with Roth for more than a decade, and her emotional investment in the younger man was much greater than she was willing to admit. Roth dropped Muriel off at the apartment she was sharing with her younger sister, Betty, and Betty's husband, a professional photographer named John Miller. Then he returned to the Village, to the third-floor apartment at 107 Waverly Place to which, in order to be closer to NYU, Walton had recently moved. She was out, and Roth made himself uneasily at home.

When Walton showed up, Roth tried to explain what his stay at Yaddo had made clear to him: He could no longer continue his debilitating dependency on her, especially now that he had finally found another woman who would help him stand on his own two feet. This was, Roth insisted, his opportunity for regeneration, and he refused to squander it. By affirming his commitment to a future with Muriel Parker, Walton's protégé was declaring independence from his Pygmalion.

Walton was proud of her role in transforming Roth from a shy ghetto boy into a full-blooded, independent author. In a letter to Ben Belitt in 1935, she recounted how she took Roth at age nineteen away from his parents—"very poor, almost illiterate peasants, Jewish, of course." She described how, though bewildered by it all, Leah and Herman Roth were instinctively grateful for the opportunities she provided their son. Walton also recognized that the striking success of her experiment at creating an artist meant that, inevitably, "he has outgrown me, too."[13]

Yet, though Walton might have admitted in principle that Roth had grown beyond her, she was not yet prepared to accept the reality. Betrayed by the ghetto child she had rescued and reinvented, she responded now with fury. She would have expected and accepted— even encouraged—a summer fling, but this melodramatic gesture would come to no good. Martelli's double portrait of Roth and Muriel, which Roth had had the effrontery to bring to the apartment, added to her irritation. From Roth's terse descriptions, Walton thought of Parker as a prim midwesterner, and she railed against her rival, insisting that the liaison would mean the extinction of all Roth's literary ambitions. When he reconstructed the scene in his final manuscripts, Roth reported her warning: "You're going to do something you'll regret the rest of your life."[14]

Though Muriel Parker would later allude to how her heart had been broken in Paris and to what was at least a sentimental attachment to a married colleague at Western College, she must have seemed almost virginal to the libertine Village rebel Walton. However, the two had more in common than the older woman, convinced that Parker represented the forces of bland convention, was prepared to acknowledge. Walton had been obliged to abandon her aspirations as a concert pianist and Parker would soon cease composing and performing, yet both received intensive training as professional musicians. Both were the wayward daughters of community leaders, proud agents of the Protestant elite—an elite mistrustful of any indigent immigrant with designs on one of its own. For the insecure young writer, both women were nurturing figures. And both were philo-Semites.

Walton pleaded with Roth not to allow this relationship to destroy his artistic ambitions. If independence was all he wanted, she would arrange, through David Mandel, to set him up in his own apartment, with the sole condition that he stay away from Muriel Parker. For all her solicitude, Walton, no stranger to double standards, was still involved with Mandel.

Guilty over obligations toward his benefactor, yet yearning to break free and join his life to another woman, Roth temporized. He stayed on at Waverly Place, in part because he had nowhere else to go. He even continued to sleep with Walton—whose anguish now exacerbated her colitis—all the while loathing his weakness and his disloyalty to Muriel.

Meanwhile, Herman, Leah, and Rose Roth had recently moved into the ground floor of a two-story house in Brooklyn, where, in another of his abortive entrepreneurial schemes, Herman ran the luncheonette concession within a bakery on nearby Pitkin Avenue. When the balcony railing outside their old apartment collapsed beneath her, Leah was badly injured. An insurance setttlement not only covered her hospital expenses but provided a small additional windfall. Herman attempted to wrest control of the money, but Leah resisted. When Roth intervened on his mother's behalf, father and son fought fiercely again. Herman roared that his son was a wastrel destined to end his own life, but for the moment, as the two men came to blows, homicide seemed more likely than suicide. So Roth now dared not show up at the Brooklyn house while Herman was around, though he made a secret visit while his father was at work. Mother and son discussed Roth's romantic plight, and, though sympathetic to Walton and sensitive to her distress, Leah gave her blessing to the break. She also loaned her son $250, from savings she had hidden from her husband. Leah always kept a secret cache and had tried, unsuccessfully, to use some of it to bribe her son to attend his own high school graduation.

Roth discussed his situation with Muriel as well. He explained that he desperately needed to get away from Eda Lou; merely moving to another part of town would not provide the emotional distance he demanded. And he revealed a plan of escape: He would drive out to California accompanied by Bill Clay, who was intending to relocate there with his wife, Bea, as well as their two young children. One-armed Clay's oldest son, Bill Junior, had recently lost a foot fighting against the Fascists in the Spanish Civil War, and both father and son now sported stumps as emblems of their resistance to oppression. For his part, Roth had not entirely given up on the possibility of writing a novel tracing the life of a working-class hero resembling his rugged, illiterate friend. Traveling with Clay would provide the novelist with intimate knowledge of his model.

In addition, following the advice that Daniel Fuchs had offered in Yaddo, Roth wanted to try his luck in Hollywood. In a legendary telegram sent in 1925, Herman J. Mankiewicz had wired his fellow writer Ben Hecht:

WILL YOU ACCEPT 300 PER WEEK TO WORK FOR PARAMOUNT PIC-
TURES? ALL EXPENSES PAID. THE 300 IS PEANUTS. MILLIONS ARE TO
BE GRABBED OUT HERE AND YOUR ONLY COMPETITION IS IDIOTS.
DON'T LET THIS GET AROUND.[15]

This had of course gotten around among dozens of New York writers—including DeWitt Clinton classmate Nathanael West, who went prospecting on the West Coast. The author of *Call It Sleep* was not the only novelist or playwright who looked to Hollywood as a way to establish financial and emotional independence. Lynn Riggs, whose plays Roth had championed, was already working for a studio, and Roth counted on making contacts in the movie business through him. Parker listened patiently, knowing that his plan meant not only a decisive split with Walton but also separation from her.

On a sunny Monday in October 1938, Roth loaded up his Model A with papers and books, including dictionaries of Latin, Greek, Italian, French, and German. Returning from classes at nearby NYU, Walton made a final attempt to dissuade Roth from his scheme. She again disparaged Parker as a conventional bourgeoise who would destroy him as an artist, and she appealed for loyalty after all that she had done for him for so many years. Walton also pleaded with Roth not to squander his literary talent, which she insisted was for writing novels, not movies.

"You're the most unfitted person for Hollywood I have ever known," she declared, according to a dramatic reconstruction in Roth's final manuscript.

At least in that account, Roth parried every comment, insisting that his dependence on Walton was destroying him as an artist as well as a man: "It's nothing less than regeneration of some sort that I'm after. And neither you nor Mandel can help me. Muriel can."

"Did anyone ever hear of such romantic rot!" Roth's text has her shriek. "Yes, rot!"[16]

Though she had transformed a timorous ghetto boy into an accomplished novelist, Walton had exhausted her role in a life whose theme was regeneration. There was, Roth felt, nothing left to say. He turned to leave, to begin his trip to California, about as far from Walton as the car could take him. Grabbing an exquisite black Navajo ashtray she had brought back from Silver City, Eda Lou hurled it at Roth. It sailed past his right shoulder, struck the wall behind him, and shattered into pieces. "He could only get away, that was all," Roth would write, describing how Ira Stigman finally seizes the initiative to get "the hell out of Harlem."[17] Roth's break with Greenwich Village was as agonizing and absolute as his earlier break with Harlem. In Roth's reconstruction of their parting scene, his abandoned mentor/lover sobs, "You damn fool!" as he sallies forth from Waverly Place and out into the world.[18]

Part II

Chapter 8

FROM VAGABONDAGE

So I went back to the working-class, in which I had been
born and where I belonged. I care no longer to climb. The
imposing edifice of society above my head holds no
delights for me. It is the foundation of the edifice that
interests me.

—JACK LONDON[1]

TRAVELING ACROSS the continent, Roth got to know his companion, Bill Clay, so thoroughly that he soon grew to regret the
arrangement. No man is a hero to his chauffeur, and long before he had
finished driving them both to California, Roth recognized that the
roughhewn comrade he had idealized as a man of iron was really a
boorish, selfish individual. Clay had sent his wife and children ahead
by bus, and the Model A crammed with his household belongings and
Roth's books could barely manage 35 miles per hour on the primitive
dirt roads that, in October 1938, carried the two men west. At about
the same time, John Steinbeck was imagining that some of those same
roads were carrying the Joad family and its belongings; *The Grapes of
Wrath* would appear the following year, 1939.

Roth had been Clay's tutor, trying, with limited success, to teach his
fifty-year-old noble savage the rudiments of reading. But now, during

the countless hours spent together on the open road and in the ragged boardinghouses where they stopped for the night, Roth, rarely known to suffer boors gladly, found himself captive audience to a blowhard and a bully. Clay used their many hours of close proximity to vent his resentments against capitalist exploitation, and he tailored his rants to irk his bookish admirer. Vaunting his own sturdy working-class credentials, he accused Roth—whom he kept referring to by his Party moniker, "Berry"—of bourgeois complacency, but he also blustered about leftist intellectuals who were all theory and no action.

Clay questioned Roth's commitment to the cause of revolution, and, though illiterate himself, disparaged Roth's literary talent. In the fictionalized account of their relationship that Roth wrote late in his life, the other man boasts: "If I could write, I'd be a better writer than youze. Youze can only write about that soft crap is the boojwazie. I'd be writin' about the workin' class, the revolutionary workin' class, an' what they done for Russia, and what they're goin' to do for the world!"[2]

In Roth's manuscript, the proletarian blowhard, renamed Loem, even maligns Muriel Parker. Proclaiming the supremacy of stout proletarian women, hardy enough to bear robust babies to their hardworking men, he suggested that Parker's slim body marked her as alien to the working class. Real men, lectured Loem/Clay, bond with women who have more flesh on their bones. "I'm sayin' the boojwasie chooses the delicate and the flat-chested ones, the ones that can't work. That ain't what the proletariat chooses."[3]

Still loyal to Marxist-Leninist doctrine and anxious about his own position as an economic parasite, "Berry" chose not to dispute most of the content in Clay's interminable, self-righteous tirades. He and Clay were, in the most obvious way, fellow travelers, but the belligerent bombast rankled. The man he had venerated as salt of the earth had lost his savor, and Roth realized that his journey of discovery was going to be an ordeal. His working-class muse was beginning to inspire revulsion.

Roth and Clay faced strained financial circumstances together. Free at last of Walton, Roth could now rely on nothing but his own meager resources. Forced to scrimp throughout the journey, they dined on baloney sandwiches in Washington, D.C., the first day out, and passed their initial, restless night camped by the side of the road. In Cincinnati, Clay's hometown, where they planned to explore the haunts of his youth, they paid twenty-five dollars for a week's lodging in a squalid building infested with roaches and rats. Roth's old Harlem tenement seemed luxurious by contrast. In 1994, Roth would revisit Cincinnati as the honored guest of Hebrew Union College, but he and Clay were now experiencing the underside of the Ohio city. Walking through back alleys past dilapidated brick buildings, Clay recalled the slaughterhouse, the brewery, and the tannery that once dominated the area. Along these harsh streets, before losing his right hand and finding his revolutionary faith, Clay had been a thief and a thug. At the end of a lengthy search for his last living link to the neighborhood, they learned of his aunt's death a year before.

On their final day in Cincinnati, Roth and Clay wandered through Fountain Square, between Fifth and Sixth Streets, in the heart of downtown. In that vibrant civic space, dominated by the 43-foot-high Tyler Davidson Fountain, they came upon a small group of black women gospel singers and paused to listen to "Down by the River." Abruptly, Clay burst into tears, sobbing over memories of his troubled childhood on the banks of the Ohio. It was an uncharacteristic moment of emotional exposure for a man whom harsh experience had taught never to be vulnerable. However, recovering his composure, Clay soon compensated for his apparent frailty by an increasing belligerence, accusing Roth of insufficient compassion for the poor and the oppressed.

Travels with Clay had become a trial; by the time the Model A lumbered into Los Angeles, Roth had arrived at the conviction that the idea of writing a novel based on the other man's life was "a colossally romantic delusion." Further experiences in California would confirm that the prototype for Roth's aborted second novel was in reality "both a thug and a semi-deranged fanatic."[4]

Clay himself later mythologized the journey by bragging that he had traveled west by hopping freight cars. In Los Angeles, he, Bea, and their two children lived, like Steinbeck's Joads, in the cabin of a motor court. They survived on Bea's relief checks, supplemented by shoplifting, which Clay rationalized by thinking of himself as Robin Hood. He cadged off friends, not only Roth but also Walton, who sent Clay checks by mail. Roth himself lodged in a Spartan boarding-house, staying on a stringent budget. He calculated that, at 17 cents per gallon, the trip to California had cost him $24.25 in gas. Now, without Walton, Leah's piggy bank, or a job, he had to be careful with his money. Instead of paying 17 cents per pack, Roth bought bulk tobacco and rolled his own cigarettes. The only relief he could count on was a government check for $6.25 every two weeks.

In Los Angeles, Roth looked to Lynn Riggs as his link to Holly-wood largesse. The two men had become friends in New York, but Roth had been wary since the evening that the Oklahoman, openly homosexual, had drunk a bit too much and playfully kissed him on the lips. Roth did attempt to contact Riggs in California but, learning that he was back home in Tulsa, decided to try his luck in the movie business on his own. He arranged to meet with a couple of executives at a Hollywood agency and gave them a copy of *Call It Sleep*. They promised to read it and asked Roth to return a week later. At their second meeting, the two men told him how much the novel horri-fied them and that its author displayed scant promise for success in motion pictures.

Roth showed up in Hollywood during what came to seem its Golden Age. *Stagecoach, Ninotchka, Mr. Smith Goes to Washington, Gunga Din, Gone With the Wind, The Wizard of Oz,* and *Wuthering Heights* were either in preparation or production while he came offer-ing his services. None features a character at all like David Schearl or a setting that resembles the Lower East Side of pushcarts and *cheders*. Motion pictures had begun to talk—with a Jewish intonation—only eleven years earlier, in 1927, with the release by Warner Bros. of *The Jazz Singer*. Al Jolson plays a pious cantor's son who chooses to sing in a nightclub on Yom Kippur. The deracination of Jolson's Jakie Rabinowitz, who changes his name to Jack Robin, parallels the his-tory of the great studios, founded by men such as Adolph Zukor, Carl Laemmle, Louis B. Mayer, Jack and Harry Warner, Lewis Selznick,

Samuel Goldwyn, William Fox, and other Jews, born in Eastern Europe or to immigrants from Eastern Europe. They left behind pogroms, but when they came to the United States, they found a society that was openly and casually anti-Semitic. Employment ads advised that only Christians need apply, hotels posted signs warning: "No Jews or dogs," and restrictive clauses in real estate deeds barred Jews from desirable neighborhoods.

Excluded from respectable professions such as medicine, law, and banking, these outsiders entered an infant industry that few others saw much future in, and they succeeded beyond their fondest dreams by searing onto celluloid their versions of the American Dream. Jews defined America—for Americans and others. But the price they paid for marketing a product palatable to the most xenophobic audiences in the national heartland was expunging their Jewish identity. Many of the moguls converted to Christianity, married Christians, or at least shared some of David O. Selznick's distaste for all things Jewish. When Ben Hecht tried to solicit his support for a Zionist fund-raiser, Selznick snapped: "I don't want to have anything to do with your cause, for the simple reason that it's a Jewish political cause. And I am not interested in Jewish political problems. I am an American and not a Jew."[5]

Roth was by now an atheist internationalist who scorned religious and ethnic sectarianism. But his novel was an embarrassing reminder of the immigrant Jewish origins of many Hollywood producers. In the 1930s, when about the only Jews allowed on screen in the United States (German studios were busy propagating vicious anti-Semitic stereotypes) were biblical, the author of *Call It Sleep* was not welcome in the dream factories of Southern California. In later years, the novel inspired several screenplays, and successive options were purchased on the book and allowed to expire. Roth never did succeed in Hollywood; but during his final decades it was not the Jewishness of his material as much as its complex verbal textures and its stream-of-consciousness technique that posed a barrier to adaptation.

In 1938, Roth left the studio office humiliated, and anxious for financial support. His principal motivation for fleeing New York had been to escape from what, in his final manuscript, he would recall as Walton's "ruinous solicitude and my ruinous susceptibility to it."[6] But her judgment that he was totally unsuitable for Hollywood was now validated. Unemployed and unfunded, Roth was so desperate to find the rent for his Los Angeles boardinghouse that he actually wrote a letter to Walton, pleading for help.

On November 20, 1938, Walton replied, with a scathing analysis of her erstwhile lover, a letter whose blunt assessment reads like nothing so much as Franz Kafka's infamous, unsent "Letter to His Father." Just as Franz imagined Hermann Kafka calling him unfit for life and intent on living entirely off him, Walton denounced Roth as "a completely self-engrossed individualist." She berated him as a hypocrite who feigned dedication to the cause of the proletariat only to exploit it for his own selfish purposes. Though she enclosed a check, for ten dollars, to help him with his second novel, Walton reminded Roth of the financial sacrifices she had made, in vain, on his behalf. She asked whether he had ever considered the possibility that she might have found some better use of her own for the money she spent financing his travels. And Walton went on to offer a telling observation about the autobiographical basis to Roth's fiction and the way his art lived entirely and exclusively off his life. Almost sixty years before *Mercy of a Rude Stream*, Walton advised him that since he was lucid about himself only when writing about himself, he ought to do exactly that. She doubted, however, "that you can write of much else."[7]

Though she affected nonchalance, Walton was devastated by Roth's departure. She would still seek consolation in David Mandel and other men; but after thirteen years, Roth had become the great enterprise—if not passion—of her life, and Walton suddenly felt abandoned and physically ill. She was drinking more heavily and suffering from attacks of chronic colitis. Walton must have brooded many hours over the letter she sent on November 20, because she sent another one the following day. In it, she noted her ailments and the suspicion—later dispelled—that she might be pregnant. But the bulk of the second letter is a *cri de coeur*, a heart-rending valediction from a woman who is convinced that she loved a man who proved unworthy of her bounty. Though she tried to believe in his superior qualities, she now castigated herself for having wasted her life on "a complete weakling."[8]

Walton regretted that they did not marry, but berated Roth for exploiting her benevolence. And she blamed herself for encouraging this abuse. She noted that she had been supporting herself financially since age seventeen and lamented allowing herself to be reduced to "an abject, pathetic victim," who justified her life by sacrificing it to his.[9]

Roth was as isolated as he had ever been in his life. He continued to visit Clay, but that relationship had deteriorated into a sado-masochistic ritual of reproach and regret. Moreover, he missed Muriel Parker. Even the most disciplined of novelists might have had trouble writing under the circumstances, and Roth was as low on psycholog-ical resources as he was on finances. In December, Roth reported that his cash holdings totaled three cents. In January 1939, he sold the Model A for fifty-five dollars, and in February, five months after arriving in Los Angeles, he began the return journey to New York, alone and without a car. He left his precious books with Clay, who promised to ship them. He never did.

Throughout the 1930s, thousands of poorly heeled men lined the roads and railroads of America, shielded from despair only by the possibility that a change of place might bring a change of luck. During February, Roth joined an army of itinerants. The landlord of his L.A. boardinghouse obliged by providing a ride southeast to El Centro. Roth paid 50 cents to spend the night in a flophouse near the highway. In the morning, he hitched a short ride east to Holtville, still in California. There he found dozens of rivals on the road with their thumbs extended, and it was twelve hours before a trucker took him to Yuma. Next, he hopped a freight car to Tuc-son, and from there, on February 24, made his way, without a ticket, by rail to El Paso. During a frigid, snowy night huddled in the corner of another boxcar, Roth bonded with a drifter from Texas whom, in a later account, he named Johnny. When they arrived in Fort Worth, Johnny persuaded Roth to accompany him to his cousin's in Dallas. The pair stuck out sore thumbs, but they had no luck trying to hitchhike.

Nearby, in the window of a travel agency, Roth noticed a sign advertising "Detroit by Car $9." Johnny's friendship was getting him nowhere; unable to face another freezing, sleepless night in a boxcar, Roth paid two dollars for the first leg of the trip north by automobile. He parted company with Johnny at 4 p.m. but had to wait until 10 p.m. for the car to fill up and take to the road. Roth was seated in the back, squeezed between two bibulous, bloated Texans, one a poultryman and the other an auto parts salesman. Each would down a pint of liquor before the night was over, but the journey had just begun when, according to an account Roth constructed for his final manuscript, the poultryman asked him: "Are you a Jew?"

"Who, me?" replied Roth. "No, not me."

"Well, then, what *are* you?" demanded the poultryman.

"A Greek Orthodox, from the Carpathians."

Roth had to explain that that meant he was a Slovak from Austria, yet he was sure they knew he was Jewish. For the rest of the night, while the wipers swept sleet off the windshield, Roth was captive audience to a carful of Jew-baiters. "They're the goddamndest no-good skunks that ever walked the earth," declared the driver.

"The goddamn Jews own 74% of the country's wealth," noted the poultryman. "The goddamn bastards, they'd sell their own grandmother if there was a dollar in it. You can't trust any of 'em."

"What the hell do they do with their dough?" asked the auto parts salesman. "The Christians don't see any of it, once the Jews get hold of it."[10]

Only the passenger seated to the driver's right declined to join in the repartee, and only the snores of the two boors in back brought it to an end. In none of his journals, letters, or stories had Roth taken note of Kristallnacht, the night of organized anti-Jewish mayhem that had taken place in Germany on the night of November 9/10, 1938. Nor would he at the time make any written comment on the gruesome fate of European Jews, including his own relatives in Tysmenitz, under Nazi rule. His silence was not unusual among American Jews, at least at that period. Mindful of New World anti-Semitism, they were wary about jeopardizing their own position by any appearance of special pleading. "A Jew did not 'make rishis,'" explained Paul Jacobs. "To 'make rishis' was to stir up a fuss of some kind, and it was a cardinal sin, for it supposedly made Jews vulnerable to the potential wrath of the Christian world. This world was conceived of as something like a potentially sleeping giant who, if awakened by a loud noise, might, and probably would, turn on the disturber of his peace and do him harm."[11]

Even the venerable *New York Times*, owned by the Jewish Sulzberger family, downplayed dreadful information it obtained about the Holocaust. In mid-1942, it reported what it called "the greatest mass slaughter in history"—the Nazi plan "to annihilate all the Jews in Europe," of whom 700,000 had already been slaughtered—not on the front page but deep inside the paper and in a mere two inches of print.[12] Apprehensive about singling themselves out, American Jewish institutions and organizations came late to the effort to rescue European Jews. In their history of *The New York Times*, Susan E. Tifft and Alex S. Jones point to contemporary surveys of opinion that might explain why neither the American Jewish Committee nor the American Jewish Congress raised an institutional voice against the persecution of European Jews: "In five polls taken between March 1938 and April 1940, some 60 percent of Americans thought Jews had 'objectionable' qualities. Another survey taken in 1938 found that the same percentage believed the persecution of the Jews in Europe was either entirely or partly their own fault."[13] In a notorious speech called "Who Are the Agitators?" delivered by Charles Lindbergh in Des Moines on September 11, 1941, the American hero warned the nation against the Jews: "Their greatest danger to this country lies in their large ownership and influence in our motion pictures, our press, our radio, and our government."[14] When Lindbergh cautioned that American Jews were intent on drawing the United States into an unnecessary war with Germany, few such Jews dared take any action that might seem to corroborate his claim.

Marxist orthodoxy insisted that religion and ethnicity were reactionary, vestiges of the primitive tribalism that humanity was destined to outgrow. Roth was a universalist, and even decades later he would still insist that Jews could serve the world best by ceasing to be Jews. But a long trip in tight quarters with indigenous American fascists reminded him that the revolution had not yet come. In that car that night, Roth was still Jewish.

At dawn, the driver stopped in the business district of Kansas City, Kansas, for breakfast. The four other travelers headed toward a diner, but Roth, claiming he needed to stretch, went for a walk—out of sight of his tormenters. Unwilling to continue the journey, he hid out in the streets of Kansas City until he was sure that they had left. Then he posted himself on the highway to St. Louis and attempted to thumb a ride east. After several hours without success, Roth finally gave up. He found a Western Union office and sent a telegram to Muriel: "PLEASE WIRE $25 MONEY ORDER BUS FARE HOME."[15]

Chapter 9

MATRIMONY

So the final product is a hash, and
all my books are botches.
—HERMAN MELVILLE[1]

T HE BUS ARRIVED in Manhattan at 4:30 p.m. on March 1, 1939.
A timely response from Muriel had enabled Roth to make his
way back from Kansas City without incident. Five months on the road
and in California had helped him sever ties to both Eda Lou Walton
and Bill Clay. Divested of those hypnotic influences, he and Muriel
realized that their own relationship had now entered a more mature
stage. Though it was affection more than ardor that drew him to her,
Roth felt his fate unalterably linked to Muriel Parker. In a recollection
that he put into writing during his final years, Roth describes Muriel
seated on a piano stool after playing for him part of her new *Chorus
for Exiles* and declaring: "There are only two things I want: To marry
you, and write music."[2] Half her wishes would come true.

For the moment, a monthly check for seventy-five dollars from her
mother and occasional gigs playing piano for a dance troupe gave

Muriel the financial freedom to focus on her music. Renting a basement apartment in midtown, she took classes in orchestration at Columbia University; to expand her repertoire beyond piano, she also studied the bassoon. Roth hoped to earn a living from his writing, but depended on government relief checks for the tiny furnished room in a boardinghouse at 351 East 51st Street that, for four dollars a week, he shared with the bedbugs. Home Relief required that recipients spend no more than $3.50 per week on lodging, and Roth lived in fear of losing financial support because his wretched dwelling was too costly.

For most of the 1930s, an older woman's generosity had sheltered Roth from the devastating effects of the Great Depression. Roth now sought assistance from the New Deal's most ambitious public employment program—the Works Progress Administration, which would be renamed Work Projects Administration (WPA) later that year. He joined the vast army of 8.5 million workers provided jobs—most of them in the construction and maintenance of the country's physical infrastructure—by the WPA before a booming war economy led to its demise in 1943. In contrast to James Agee, Saul Bellow, Ralph Ellison, Edmund Wilson, Richard Wright, and others hired by the WPA's Federal Writers' Project to write guidebooks, almanacs, and other civic texts, Roth was assigned strenuous manual labor. Ever the proletarian, he relished the assignment. For $55.20 a month, he accepted steady employment digging drainage ditches and sewer lines in Queens. But, after putting aside his pick and shovel, he also toiled away at prose that he attempted to market to commercial magazines. Following Maxwell Perkins's advice, he had even acquired an enterprising young literary agent, Elizabeth Nowell, whom Perkins had recommended as well to Thomas Wolfe. Perkins was not upset that Roth had failed either to deliver his contracted manuscript or to return the advance.

One of Roth's efforts, the short story called "Broker," is a comic study in futility, about which the author could claim some expertise. To write the piece, Roth embroidered on an incident he observed on the streets of Manhattan. When an overloaded, battered truck breaks down in the midst of dense New York traffic, its black driver merely multiplies problems by attempting to move his rig out of the way. Angry reactions from impatient white cops and motorists succeed only in flustering him further. "Every time somebody look at that truck, it get broker!" complains the story's unnamed urban Sisyphus.[3]

Almost forty years later, Roth would report that as he was writing "Broker," at about one or two in the morning, he suffered a devastating anxiety attack:

> Sweat broke out on my brow, and I had a desire to just scream. Those are signs of a nervous breakdown. I knew I had to quit everything I was doing and just walk out on the street and walk, and walk, and walk forever. Finally about three o'clock in the morning I calmed down and came home and went to bed. I think it was about this time that I decided, if I ever finish the thing I'm going to be through writing.[4]

Despite the agony that putting words to paper caused him, Roth stubbornly, courageously continued writing after "Broker." A legend would later grow up about his retreat into silence, but it does not account for his persistence despite repeated failure to find favor with editors. The fate of "Broker" itself proved an exception. Soon after submitting it, Roth received a note from Nowell informing him that William Maxwell, fiction editor of *The New Yorker*, wanted to see him. On a Monday morning in July, Roth met Maxwell in his office and agreed to strengthen his description of the truck wreck in "Broker." The story was accepted for publication in *The New Yorker*, and Roth was paid eighty-five dollars, a windfall that jeopardized his eligibility for public relief but enhanced his prospects for marriage and for living by his pen. Roth was temporarily vindicated in his determination to write.

He seemed an unlikely contributor to the glossy literary magazine that, since its founding in 1925 by Harold Ross, had become the embodiment of midtown Manhattan urbanity. Many aspiring writers despaired of appearing in *The New Yorker*, regarding the magazine, with its elegant advertising for furs and liqueurs, as a showcase of Protestant privilege. *The New Yorker* did in fact publish work by Jews, but writers such as George S. Kaufman, Lillian Hellman, and Dorothy Parker were far removed from Roth's proletarian, immigrant origins. Nor did he write the kind of "*New Yorker* fiction"—chronicles of bourgeois angst—published frequently under the byline John O'Hara.

When "Broker" appeared on November 18, 1939, it was only the second of Roth's publications since *Call It Sleep* in 1934. It helped allay doubts that had become acute since his breaks with Walton and Clay, but Roth still was not convinced that he had the requisite stamina to hack it as a working writer. Much later, he told the Canadian critic Don Bell that the publication of "Broker" encouraged him. "But it seemed such hard work, and without the kind of—I've used the word *possession*—possession, inspiration, whatever you want to call it. . . . It didn't seem worth it as far as making a living was concerned. I could do almost anything else, so why sit and sweat over a story to make it fit *The New Yorker* magazine style?" In a radio interview for WFAU in Augusta, Maine, in 1965, he explained:

> I felt that this particular creative force . . . that had been efficient in *Call It Sleep* was no longer operating anywhere near the same extent; that I could do what others did, that is, trying for commercial writing, trying to write short stories that were salable, and make a living that way. And I did. I sold a few of them, but I found that it was awfully hard work, without that particular feeling of inspiration. And there were easier forms of making a living than that, so I gave it up.[5]

Yet Roth did not give it up entirely in 1939 any more than he had in 1934. Though he managed to publish only three other stories in *The New Yorker* ("Somebody Always Grabs the Purple" in 1940; "Petey and Yotsee and Mario" in 1956; and "The Surveyor" in 1966), the *New Yorker* archives contain an ample file for Roth, consisting largely of correspondence with Maxwell (they addressed each other as "Dear Roth" and "Dear Maxwell") and with succeeding fiction editors Robert Hemenway, Robert Henderson, and Frances Kiernan. The final letter in the file, dated December 1, 1975, is a rejection by Kiernan of a story called "Paradise Lost for Good." Much later, in 1993, Charles McGrath, the magazine's fiction editor before he became editor of *The New York Times Book Review*, would turn down early extracts from *Mercy of a Rude Stream*.

In 1943, Maxwell, curious about why he had not heard from Roth in quite some time, wrote to ask whether the author had any new material to show him. Roth responded by claiming that "writing and I seem to have parted company indefinitely. . . . There's a world of material, but where's the magic wand?" he asked.[6] It would take Roth many years to understand that there is no magic wand, that writing is more a matter of sticking to it. Yet even after abandoning his literary friends and ambitions, he kept close company with writing.

Throughout the years of exile, about a dozen different submissions, including a play called *Oedipus, Meet Orestes*, were turned down by *The New Yorker*. Sometimes the rejections were categorical. In 1956, Maxwell reacted to a science fiction story by advising Roth: "I think you would have better luck in writing about ordinary people in ordinary circumstances."[7] In 1967, Robert Henderson sent back "New England Sampler," a copious manuscript drawing on Roth's sojourn in Maine, explaining: "It struck us as a lifeless piece of work. . . . The feeling here is that a writer's problems are only likely to be interesting to other writers."[8] However, the rejection letters from *The New Yorker* were often more supportive, offering suggestions for revisions that would make the pieces more publishable. In such instances, Roth responded almost immediately, resubmitting the work with the recommended alterations. Yet, though compliant and persistent, Roth never produced a version that passed muster.

On January 24, 1955, for example, Maxwell returned a story called "Finish Line." He later rejected a revision of that story, now called "Remembered Bus Line," on September 27, 1956, and another draft, "Vanished Bus Line," on October 11. If, as he later claimed,

Roth had lost the enterprise to succeed as a commercial writer, he surely would have given up on the story after a third rejection. Yet a little more than two months later, he tried yet again with "Vanished Bus Line," telling Maxwell: "Incidentally, it's been much easier to re-write it than to find the necessary brass to submit it to you again, but I trust you'll forgive me."[9] Maxwell no doubt forgave him, but he promptly rejected the story again. Roth even tried once more, but in March 1957 Maxwell again sent back the story, now bearing its orig-inal title, "Finish Line."

Roth did score one other commercial success a few months after "Broker" was accepted by *The New Yorker*. A short story called "Many Mansions" was published in the September 1940 edition of *Coronet*, a magazine based in Chicago. Founded in 1936, *Coronet*, whose compact physical format resembled that of *Reader's Digest*, was—like *Collier's*, *Saturday Evening Post*, and *Liberty*—part of the crowded field of general interest publications that fiction writers of the period could count on as potential markets.

A slight tale about a young outsider's obsession with the lives of the privileged, "Many Mansions" drew upon a personal anecdote that Roth heard from his friend Gus Ornstein, a dentist and an ardent amateur violinist. For eight years, Ornstein had attended night classes in order to qualify as an engineer; but after receiving his degree, he was told that there were no jobs in engineering for Jews. In "Many Mansions," the narrator recalls how, at the age of ten, he yearned to know everything about the sumptuous residences that lined "Million-aires' Row" along Fifth Avenue. One day, he confronts one proprietor, the patrician Senator Charles Stover, and cajoles him into letting the boy look inside his house. However, fearful of being appropriated as just another fancy object to decorate the mansion, the narrator sud-denly rushes out the door, and the story ends.

Written while Roth was joining forces with Muriel Parker, "Many Mansions" expresses an upstart's ambivalence toward the entitle-ments that he covets. Though Muriel had not grown up in a mansion, her genteel family was more at home on Fifth Avenue than East 119th Street. Roth was in awe of the sangfroid with which the Parkers bore themselves, but he also resented them for what he took to be their Philistine disdain and their anti-Semitism. Like the boy who flees Senator Stover's mansion, he would later break abruptly and rudely with Muriel's parents. "They took to me as I to them: like a carbuncle," he would recall.[10]

Months before she even met Roth, Grace Parker's letters to her other daughter, Betty, a social worker, disparaged Muriel's relationship. Grace had also initially contested Betty's engagement to John Miller, but Betty was convinced that her mother was simply irked that she had had no hand in arranging it. Grace soon took pride in John's accomplishments as a freelance photographer; but she never truly warmed to Roth.

Though Roth's own mother regretted his rift with Walton, she quickly embraced his new relationship. One sultry Sunday in May 1939, while Herman was off at work and there was no danger of another clash between father and son, Roth took Muriel to meet Leah Roth at her home on Glenmore Avenue in Brooklyn—in the Brownsville neighborhood where she had begun her life in America. After a long subway journey, Roth and Muriel were received enthusiastically. Leah ushered them over to the kitchen table and plied them with delicacies, including whitefish, lox, smoked sturgeon, and rye bread with carroway seeds. Muriel was fascinated by the exotic food and grateful for Leah's effusive welcome. Relieved that his two women had hit it off, Roth marveled at the study in contrast they represented—the tall, majestic Anglo-Saxon and the short, plump, working-class Galician Jew.

Their confidence bolstered by the first visit, Henry and Muriel returned to Brooklyn one Saturday night in June. This time, Herman was at home, and he strained to be cordial, even unctuous. Again, several of the items that Leah served for dinner—including gefilte fish, chopped eggs in schmaltz, and challah—were unfamiliar to Muriel. Leah and Herman exchanged brief taunts in Yiddish, but both treated the young couple as honored guests.

Throughout the spring and summer, Roth was a frequent visitor at Muriel's midtown boardinghouse, but he was careful to leave early enough not to violate the proprieties for an unmarried woman living alone. His own place of residence was less appealing. Despite Roth's repeated complaints, the room that he returned to at night and where he toiled away at his writing remained infested with insects. He impaled bedbugs on pins and presented them as evidence.

In the vivid recreation of this incident that shows up in Roth's final manuscript, the elderly Swedish housekeeper is indignant over his complaint. "Well, it won't do to be so fussy," she replies. "You always too classy. You always lookin' to make trouble for me."[11]

However, in September 1939, as war finally broke out in Europe, Roth's situation changed dramatically. In order to accommodate the equipment necessary for John's photographic work, Betty and John Miller had rented a spacious penthouse apartment on the seventeenth floor of a building at 220 East 23rd Street. They invited Muriel and Henry to move in with them. Muriel would have a separate room for her piano, Henry a small one for his writing.

Everyone was enthusiastic about the new arrangement, though Roth was embarrassed to be seen entering and leaving the building dressed in the laborer's duds he wore to dig storm drains and sewers for the WPA. He took to wrapping up his dungarees and denim shirt in a bag and changing back and forth at his work site in Queens, far from the scrutiny of the elevator operator in his apartment building. Shortly after Roth and Muriel began living together under the auspices of the Millers, they faced some formidable new challenges. While still hobbling from surgery to repair the cartilage in a hip joint, Muriel learned that, ostensibly in order to encourage self-reliance (but perhaps also to force a break with Roth), her mother was henceforth cutting off her monthly allowance of seventy-five dollars. Frederick and Grace Parker also announced that they were traveling east on business. They would be staying at the Beekman Towers Hotel and naturally intended to see their daughters, as well as to meet Muriel's beau.

It was relatively easy for Roth to disguise his living arrangements by crashing with an Irish friend for the duration of the Parkers' visit. But meeting Muriel's imperious parents at the Millers' penthouse was an ordeal he dreaded. It took place on October 3, 1939, shortly after the Parkers' arrival in New York. Anxious to make a good impression, Roth put on a clean shirt and tie beneath the gray and black English tweed jacket that Walton had bought him years before.

Mr. and Mrs. Parker were not overtly hostile, but neither were they especially affectionate. Roth would remember Muriel's father as "a brawny, staunch, dauntless American, upright and loyal," her mother as "silkily cunning, politely acquisitive, and sweetly sanctimonious." From the first impression to the last, he was convinced that as far as Muriel's parents were concerned, "I was an alien. It was easy to conjecture what they thought of me: Home Relief indigent, dubious scrivener, Jewish neurotic. A Jew and a ne'er-do-well. What could rate lower on their scale of values?"[12]

Grace Reid had been disowned by her own wealthy father for marrying a quixotic Baptist minister, but now, as Grace Reid Parker, she bristled at signs of independence from her own daughters. She posed pointed questions about John Miller's income and the grimy windows in his apartment. And it was clear, at least to Roth, that she was not in the least impressed by Muriel's choice. The party of six—the Parkers, the Millers, Muriel, and Roth—made their way from the penthouse to a nearby German restaurant, Zum Hofbrau, chosen by Frederick Parker, overruling other recommendations. And it was he who dominated the conversation with remarks about his nineteen years as executive secretary of Kiwanis International, which under his stewardship had burgeoned from five hundred to a thousand clubs. Both Parkers offered disparaging comments about the radical New Deal, but Roth was shrewd enough not to let on that he was digging ditches for the WPA, or that—far worse—as a Communist, he too faulted Roosevelt—for social reforms that were not radical enough.

Muriel and Roth were as good as engaged, and before her parents came to town they had mulled over when and how to formalize the bond. Roth advised marrying immediately; it might in the long run cause less upheaval if the Parkers were presented with a fait accompli upon arrival in New York. Muriel was uncomfortable over such flagrant defiance of family protocol. Betty suggested that the wedding take place during the Parkers' stay in town, but Roth preferred to keep all parents, Muriel's as much as his own, out of the picture. The question was still unresolved when Mr. and Mrs. Parker descended on Manhattan.

Never one to obfuscate, Grace got straight to the point. It was clear that she was not very pleased by the prospect of acquiring this feckless, leftist Jewish writer as a son-in-law. Such opposition was hardly surprising in an era when "mixed marriages" between Gentiles and Jews were, in many social circles, shunned as a form of miscegenation. But sizing up the situation very quickly, Grace realized that since it was too late to prevent her daughter's marriage, she might as well take control of it. She urged an immediate wedding, while she and her husband were around to serve as witnesses. Frederick agreed, offering to recruit the Reverend Harry Emerson Fosdick, of Riverside Church, who was America's most esteemed radio preacher, to preside over the ceremony. When Roth balked at the idea of a Presbyterian wedding, Grace suggested finding a Reform rabbi to substitute for the Reverend Fosdick. But a rabbi was no more appealing to the atheist Roth than a Christian minister, and he offered an argument he was sure would guarantee a secular service: any rabbi, even one from the Reform branch of Judaism, would likely demand that Muriel convert to the groom's religion. Finally Muriel and Roth agreed to be united by a clerk at New York City's Marriage Bureau.

So, at 8:45 a.m. on October 7, the wedding party set out in Frederick Parker's Studebaker for the large Municipal Building in lower Manhattan. The group consisted solely of the bride and groom, Frederick and Grace Parker, and John and Betty Miller. No one from Roth's family was invited or attended. After the principals and witnesses signed the legal documents and the father of the bride paid the five-dollar license fee, a New York City magistrate officially declared Henry and Muriel Roth husband and wife. Henry presented his bride with a turquoise and silver ring, a Navajo ornament that had been brought back for him from New Mexico by Eda Lou Walton. Walton herself had not been informed of the ceremony.

After the formalities were concluded, the party retired to the

Gramercy Hotel to share a wedding breakfast of calves' liver, bacon, and muffins. The conversation turned to literature, the new groom's calling. Grace Parker complained about the sordidness of John Steinbeck's provocative new novel, *The Grapes of Wrath*.

"Why can't writers write of beautiful things?"Roth has her asking in a later manuscript.[13]

Knowing that if she ever managed to obtain a copy of *Call It Sleep*, now out of print, his new mother-in-law would probably find it even more unpalatable, Roth curbed his impulse to proclaim that an artist has a higher allegiance to truth than to beauty. But Frederick Parker wondered why contemporary American literature did not provide its readers with more uplifting stories.

In the account of the wedding breakfast that Roth constructed more than fifty years later, his new father-in-law asks: "Doesn't any writer know anything about the millions of service-minded individuals in the country? Aren't writers interested in character-building at all?"[14]

Though he would have been dismayed to recognize his bond with the Marxist doctrine of socialist realism, Mr. Parker was voicing the same kind of idealist aesthetic—the demand that literature provide positive social models—that had stymied his son-in-law's creativity after *Call It Sleep*. It was precisely in order to offer the portrait of a "service-minded individual" that Roth had attempted his disastrous novel about Dan Loem. Whether the call for edifying art came from Frederick Parker or from *The New Masses*, Roth did not know quite how to respond. For the moment, he held his tongue.

Chapter 10

PRECISION GRINDING

Whoever is able to write a book and does not,
it is as if he has lost a child.
—NACHMAN OF BRATSLAV[1]

ACQUISITION OF A marriage certificate brought the newlyweds reassurance rather than euphoria. It was a relief to send the Parkers back off to Chicago without having yet sparked a family brawl, and it was comforting to resume their domestic lives together. But it was still a struggle to create a space for literature and music during times so lean that Roth had to pawn his Omega wristwatch to keep the couple fed. Health was another concern; still recovering from hip surgery, Muriel also broke a tooth. On October 9, 1939, she turned to Gus Ornstein, the Jewish dentist-cum-engineer-manqué whose childhood anecdote had inspired Roth to write "Many Mansions." While Gus was examining Muriel's mouth, another patient sat down in the waiting room: Eda Lou Walton.

Knowing what they had in common, Dr. Ornstein introduced his two patients, and they greeted each other cordially, if anxiously. Wal-

ton expressed sympathy for Muriel's hip problems, and Muriel understood how difficult it must have been for Roth to leave the older
woman. At the time of this encounter, Walton, like Muriel, was also a
newlywed: she had married David Mandel in April. Muriel reported
her adventures at the dentist to her husband. She urged Roth to write
Eda Lou and suggest that the two couples get together for dinner.

This was not Roth's first contact with Walton since he had walked
out of her Waverly Place apartment and the bitter letters that she sent
him in California. In April, he had showed up at her door to collect
the remainder of his belongings, particularly a gray suit that he
wanted to wear for an interview with the Jewish Social Service Association (later known as the Jewish Family Service). Though Roth
dressed in his best, the agency turned down his application for funds
to purchase a typewriter, forcing him to set aside $10 from a $13.85
relief check in order to buy a used model.

Roth's visit to Walton's apartment, one week after her marriage to
Mandel, was brief and businesslike. The conversation was terse,
remarkable most for what was left unsaid. Roth stuffed as much as he
could into a shopping bag, but it would take one more trip to evacu-
ate the last of his belongings, a bulky overcoat, from Waverly Place.
A few days later, he dispatched Rose, his devoted sister, to perform the
awkward task for him.

In May, David Mandel contacted Roth and arranged a meeting.
Over lunch in a Chinese restaurant, Roth's old literary patron and
rival in love asked him about his current situation. Roth told Mandel
about his job with the WPA and his efforts to write short fiction for
commercial markets. Mandel was disappointed, insisting that Roth
should be concentrating on writing another novel. "Why waste your
talent turning out commodities for slick magazines?" Roth later
recalled him asking.[2] Roth argued that crafting short stories was an
honorable discipline, and besides, he needed the money. Mandel proposed to pay him a subsidy of thirty dollars a month in order to free
him to focus on a novel. Wary of falling back into his old dependency,
Roth declined the magnanimous offer.

Sporadic successes amid consistent failure deepened Roth's frustration with freelance writing. However, before 1939 was over, a lucky connection enabled him to quit his WPA job. The relative of a friend hired Roth to teach night classes in English at Theodore Roosevelt High School. His title, "permanent substitute teacher," was not exactly an oxymoron, since faculty absences were not uncommon in a large public high school. Though the work—mostly a matter of keeping restive students placated while their regular teachers were away—was not especially gratifying, Roth could count on fairly steady employment at the school.

In 1940, Roth took advantage of industrial training programs that were being offered at no cost. Sponsored by the city, instruction was provided at public vocational schools in the late afternoons after regular classes were over. On his way to his evening's assignment at Theodore Roosevelt, on Fordham Road in the Belmont section of the Bronx, Roth would stop off at a dingy building in Harlem to attend a machine shop course. He soon demonstrated an aptitude for precision grinding of gauges, dies, and tools, finding a kind of transcendence in meticulous manual labor: "the pieces of metal were pure abstraction."[3] After mastering the ability to grind metals to one ten-thousandth of an inch, he found skilled work in a series of machine shops in the New York area. These included the Clix Zipper Company, the Master Tool & Die Company, the Federal Machine Tool Company, and the Gussack Machine Company.

Roth's discovery of a new vocation proved timely, because after one academic year at Theodore Roosevelt, a new principal who did not know him or feel any obligation replaced Roth with a choice of his own. Nepotism had provided Roth with the teaching position in the first place, and it now seemed responsible for his ousting. But the principal's favoritism had unintended consequences that Roth could chuckle over. Within a year, the protégé installed to replace Roth would likely be drafted by the army and sent off to serve his nation. As a full-time precision metal grinder, however, Roth was spared the call to arms. Throughout World War II, he held the Selective Service classification 3A: Deferred for essential work.

Roth remained to all appearances unaffected by the plight of Jews under Nazism. Fifty years later, he would fault himself for having been indifferent to the genocide of his own people. But for now, he was a universalist and counted on the Soviet Union to advance social justice for all. In fact, Roth supported the mutual non-aggression pact signed by Joseph Stalin and Adolf Hitler on August 23, 1939, a Faustian agreement that extinguished the hopes of any Jew living on the European continent. Marching in a parade in New York City sponsored by the American League Against War and Fascism, Roth handed out leaflets urging the United States to stay out of the developing conflict. When Germany launched a surprise attack against the Soviet Union on June 22, 1941, Roth followed the revised Party line, that the United States must make common cause with Stalin in the war against Germany. He registered to vote as a member of the American Labor Party, the Socialist splinter of New Deal Democrats that, at least in New York, fell under the domination of Communists and that, in 1938, sent Vito Marcantonio, one of the most radical leftists ever to serve in Congress, to the House of Representatives from the 20th District in East Harlem.

Barely two weeks after Pearl Harbor, on December 23, 1941, Muriel gave birth to a baby boy: Jeremy, soon nicknamed "Jeb." Parenthood put an end to Muriel's music and to Roth's fantasies of supporting his family through freelance writing. In 1941, in collaboration with Corinne Chochem—director of a Jewish dance troupe based in the United States—Muriel did publish *Palestine Dances! Folk Dances of Palestine*. This was a collection of music and dance settings with drawings by Raphael Soyer and photographs by her brother-in-law, John Miller.

By now, the couple had moved out of the Miller penthouse to an apartment of their own at 233 East 77th Street; later, from 1942 until 1945, they would live farther south, at 335 East 69th Street. Both Jeremy and his younger brother, Hugh, born on September 8, 1943, were reared by working parents who struggled under straitened circumstances. Forced in coming years to take on enervating teaching jobs that were sometimes the family's sole source of income, Muriel never complained of having sacrificed her artistic aspirations to be the wife of Henry Roth. Growing up, neither of their two sons would know their father as an author, of *Call It Sleep* or anything else.

Though his starting wage was 40 cents an hour, Roth was earning $1.10 an hour within a year of becoming a precision grinder. In support of the war effort, organized labor in the United States honored a no-strike pledge, but that did not prevent Roth and others from finding different ways, including production slowdowns, to pressure management into improving conditions for employees. In several of the shops at which he worked, Roth was active in organizing his fellow workers, a fact that did not escape the attention of the FBI, whose agents filed periodic confidential reports on him until 1955.

During a summer break in 1944 from work at the Gussack Machine Company in Long Island City, Roth, Muriel, and their two young sons traveled to Cape Cod, to spend a week with Muriel's parents in their cottage on Buzzard's Bay. Fifty years later, the experience remained painfully vivid for Roth. While it is unlikely that the dialogue he conjured up to recreate the tense confrontation with his in-laws is accurate verbatim, it surely captures the sad drama that was being played out that summer. Over dinner early in their stay, Frederick Parker began to expound on the sterling virtues of Kiwanis members, prominent men of accomplishment who volunteered their time and energy on behalf of communities throughout the world.

"We're all dedicated to service, and our members are all well-connected, successful businessmen," he observed. "Of course, while membership in Kiwanis is open to people of all faiths, Jewish as well as others, we don't want any kikes in this organization."[4]

Everyone at the table knew that Parker's son-in-law was Jewish. The implication was that there is a distinction between "kikes" and "Jews" and that the executive secretary of Kiwanis International was willing to recognize—and tolerate—Roth within the latter category. However, the remark rankled; it was presumptuous, abusive, and—even for someone whose sense of Jewish identity had become as attenuated as Roth's—painfully anti-Semitic. But Roth remained silent. His rejoinder would emerge a few days later.

The tide was low, and Roth spent the morning by himself, digging for soft-shell clams on the beach in front of the cottage and filling a pail. He proceeded to steam them. Then, alone in the basement of the cottage, Roth gorged himself. When, about an hour later, the midday meal was served, Roth had no appetite. He told the others to eat without him, but his mother-in-law insisted that he be courteous enough to sit with them at the table anyway.

"I don't see why I have to join you for dinner if I'm not hungry," Roth said.

"It's not a matter of appetite," Grace Parker replied. "That isn't the point. You're part of the family, and dinner is the time when we always join together. That's the custom in the Parker family, and if you intend to become part of it, you'll join us."

It was a collision between two immovable forces. Mrs. Parker spoke with the stern voice of a New England matriarch, and the more challenged she felt by a wimpy, scoffing, interloping son-in-law, the more obdurate she became. For his part, Roth—still smarting from her husband's ethnic slur and from his own failure to respond to it— embraced rudeness as a matter of perverse principle, a way of contesting the small minds that menaced him in the cottage at Buzzard's Bay. Each time Mrs. Parker reiterated the house rule that all assemble at the table for meals, Roth, as if inspired by Melville's defiant Bartleby, preferred not to.

Finally, inevitably, Grace Parker issued her expulsion: "Very well. Then you're no longer welcome here."[5]

With that, Roth gathered up his wife and their two young sons and decamped. He immediately recognized the boorishness of his behavior and how he had once again trapped himself in his own childish rhetoric. But it was impossible for Roth and Muriel not to revel a bit in their own righteous rebellion. Muriel did not hesitate in following her husband. Henceforward, she would be excommunicated from the Parker clan, as her mother before her had been banished by her own father, Stanley Reid. She would never again speak with Frederick Parker, who died of a stroke within a year, after having stricken his elder daughter from his will. Her two brothers, Wesby, later president of Dr. Pepper, and Kent, CEO of Underwriters Laboratories, dutifully cut all ties to their sister. Only Betty would maintain contact with the Roths while Jeremy and Hugh were growing up.

By 1945, *Call It Sleep* had been out of print for a decade, and Roth had ceased his efforts to write marketable short fiction. He had stopped corresponding with William Maxwell, and the break to him seemed so conclusive that when Roth finally resumed contact with Maxwell in 1952, he felt compelled to introduce himself as if he were a stranger. In his cover letter of a submission sent on November 12, Roth began: "Some time ago—quite a while ago, I guess—I was fortunate enough to have a couple of things printed in *The New Yorker*. I mention this by way of introduction."[6] The story he enclosed, "Elegy for Pomarsky," would be rejected.

Yet as World War II drew to a close, Roth no longer chose to see himself as a literary supplicant. He was a husband, a father, and a precision metal grinder, though sometimes haunted by other identities and aspirations. From Harlem to Greenwich Village, New York had become a constant reminder of his failures. Determined to get "as far away from the geographic epicenter of my neurotic frustration as I could," Roth thought about seeking work in the thriving aviation industry that had grown up in Southern California. But in May 1945 he took a job in Providence, Rhode Island, at a firm called the Federal Products Company. A month later, he was working as a toolmaker for the Keystone Manufacturing Company in Boston. After brief stays in nearby Dorchester and Monument Beach, the family found lodging in an Irish Catholic neighborhood in Cambridge, on the top floor of a shabby wooden tenement at 24 Hayes Street, on a block whose Irish urchins brought back memories of Roth's own East 119th Street. Though only a single subway stop away from sophisticated Harvard Square, their new residence was "a true working class warren," whose residents tossed garbage out the windows, drank heavily, and were not especially hospitable to the newcomers from New York. Since the flimsy, cockroach-infested building lacked a fire escape, Roth rigged one up out of ropes.[7]

At work, he was active in Local 246 of the CIO-affiliated United Electrical, Radio, and Machine Workers of America. He edited the

union newsletter, *UE Projector*, and on February 28, 1946, ran an
article that excoriated Keystone for its treatment of an employee who
had just returned from military service and found his wages reduced
and his seniority ignored. In a meeting that took place on April 11,
management dismissed the charges as inaccurate and malicious, but
Roth responded with a temper tantrum that puzzled and embarrassed
the other union representatives. He was still allowed to serve as
finance chairman of their strike committee, but negotiations between
management and labor succeeded in averting a strike. On May 17,
Roth attended a class in union leadership at the Samuel Adams School
for Social Studies, which was cited by the attorney general as a Communist organization. He became president of the Industrial 1-A
(Metal) Branch of the Communist Party of the United States for District 1, Boston.

By 1946, Stalin was no longer America's "Uncle Joe," a steadfast
ally in the crusade against fascism, but rather the incarnation of a per-
nicious, voracious global menace. In the United States, as persecution
and prosecution of leftists and former leftists escalated, Roth, who
was still, despite everything, an unrepentant Communist, began to
wonder whether it might be prudent to become less visible. Family
matters now seemed more pressing, and he was particularly concerned about the stutter that his older child, Jeremy, had developed.
Doctors attributed the problem to the pressures of urban life, and
Roth became convinced that his son as well as the rest of the family
would benefit from getting away from neighbors who casually emp-
tied trash out their windows. Though he should have read enough of
Marx to make him wary of "the idiocy of rural life," he entertained
romantic fantasies of abandoning the city and living off the land. He
recalled his idyllic stay in Norridgewock in 1932, where he had not
only written a large block of *Call It Sleep* but also, beyond the reach
of Eda Lou Walton, first felt freedom and fulfillment.

Beguiled by a real estate brochure, Roth took a train to Maine. He
examined a homestead sitting on a ribbon of 110 acres that, though
merely 200 yards across at the entrance, was about a mile in length.
The price was just $1,200, and the nearest town, Montville, was

located about midway between Liberty and Freedom and only thirty miles from Norridgewock. Roth left a down payment of $600 and agreed to monthly mortgage payments of $100. On Memorial Day, 1946, he sent Muriel and the boys ahead to Maine while he finished up his work in Boston. A week before Labor Day, he resigned from Keystone.

With the relocation to Montville, where Jeremy soon lost his stutter, Roth's rejection of the literary life now seemed complete. "I was consciously trying to get out, away from, a terrific failure, a terrific frustration," he would later explain.[8] In leaving behind the urban landscape that had formed the backdrop of his life and the foundation for his art, Roth was casting off his identity as Jewish immigrant, literary gigolo, and one-book novelist, in order to reinvent himself as a Yankee farmer.

Part III

Chapter 11

EXILE IN MAINE

Do not keep aloof from the community.

—HILLEL[1]

The peculiarity of the New England hermit
has not been his desire to get near to God,
but his anxiety to get away from man.

—HAMILTON WRIGHT MABIE[2]

THE LATE SUMMER splendors of the New England foliage and
sheer relief at fleeing their Cambridge firetrap distracted the
Roths from the grim realities they faced in Maine as they settled in
together on Labor Day, 1946. After forty years of dwelling in tenements and apartments, it was exhilarating for Roth to own a house of
his own, in fact to be the monarch of an expanse that was about a
tenth as large as the entire Lower East Side. However, such sover-
eignty demanded sacrifice: the tumbledown Montville house lacked
central heating, indoor plumbing, and electricity. Indeed, the Roths
were lords of one hundred maples, but they had no car or radio or
telephone and were forced to rely on a wood-burning stove for cook-
ing and warmth and on kerosene lamps for illumination. Feeding a
family in rural Maine proved more difficult than Roth had antici-

pated. "We were as strapped as you can imagine," he would recall half a century later.[3]

Montville, a speck of a town in a sparsely populated state, had no more call for a precision tool grinder than it did for an autobiographical novelist. Unemployment compensation checks for $25 helped a bit at first, as did outings to hunt rabbits and deer and to gather wild cranberries. After purchasing a cow for $125 from a devious neighbor, Roth discovered that the animal was sterile and he had been bilked. Since the man had been storing furniture with him, Roth was able to extort ransom—$20 and an antique lamp—from him. A more dependable source of milk was a small herd of five Toggenburgs—brown dairy goats descended from stock in Switzerland—that he later bought for $110.

Another neighbor, Lysle Littlefield, took pity on the clueless newcomers and offered Roth some work clearing brush and gathering wood with him. For a dollar an hour, Roth helped Littlefield operate a two-man chain saw. To lop off the smaller branches from the tree limbs before and after felling the trunk, they each used hatchets. Roth's career as a woodcutter came to an abrupt end when his hatchet slipped and gashed his ankle. Other local work he took up included raking blueberries, picking apples, and selling maple syrup. He spent two weeks fighting forest fires around Rockland for a dollar an hour.

During the 1947–48 academic year, Roth was paid $1,400 to teach in a one-room schoolhouse. But the experience was as disastrous as chopping wood; after months of trying to educate twenty-four unruly students spread through eight different grades, he quit. Eventually, he managed to find precision tool work, but the job, with the Singer Sewing Machine Company in Dover-Foxcroft, was about sixty miles from Montville and, until he gave up on that as well, Roth was forced to live in a dormitory during the week, returning to his family only on weekends.

Late one October afternoon in 1946, in a plot behind the house on which Muriel had attempted a vegetable garden, Roth ignited a pyre of manuscripts. In the thickening atmosphere of political repression he was anxious to obliterate any documents that might prove incriminating; but he was also intent on marking an end to his identity as a writer. With young Jeremy and Hugh as witnesses, Roth set fire to what he thought to be the total remnants of his papers: journals from the early 1930s, impressions of Mrs. Fletcher's farmhouse back in Norridgewock, an account of his unrequited passion for a literary woman he knew in New York before he met Muriel. (In fact, three large notebooks that he somehow overlooked survived.) Roth had long since lost his passion for reading, and a rare visitor would remark on how, with the exception of a few school texts for the boys, his house was almost devoid of books. At the same time, Roth cut ties to almost all his New York friends and made few new friends in Maine.

But the bonfire of Roth's literary vanities did not entirely set his mind or soul at ease. The austerity of life in Montville exacerbated his tendency toward depression. In one of his bleakest moments—recalled years later with the kind of revulsion evoked by memories of stealing pens at Stuyvesant and stealing embraces from Rose—Roth brutally killed a household pet. The Roths had managed to find homes for all but one of the litter produced by their beloved collie, Lassy. One grim day, while Muriel and the boys were off at a neighbor's, Roth grew desperate over their financial plight. How, while struggling to sustain a family of four, could he possibly feed a mongrel that would probably eventually give birth to other hungry dogs? Roth seized the puppy and hanged her from a makeshift noose. But the victim survived. After bungling the execution, Roth took a club and bludgeoned the hapless creature to death. Like the immolation of Roth's manuscripts, the murder of the puppy was an expression of self-loathing, combined this time with physical cruelty. He buried the victim secretly, expunging yet another bit of Henry Roth. After such mortification, redemption seemed remote.

Young Hugh Roth, who was himself the occasional object of his father's fits of rage, recalled another brutal episode from the time when they were raising ducks in Maine:

Gimpy was the name Daddy gave (and we picked up) to a duckling
born with a turned foot. At every other step it collapsed. We carried
it around when driving the birds from one part of a field to another.
It became sort of a pet. One day he took it to the chopping block
and cut off its head.[4]

The empathetic author who rendered the torments of young David
at the brutal hands of Albert Schearl is the same man who dispatched
the duckling and puppy and also beat his own son. Though Roth had
experienced enough in his own childhood to make him alert to unjust
suffering, he was quite capable of inflicting violence—especially during the dismal period in Maine. The knowledge that he was visiting
the sins of his own father on a fresh group of victims tormented Roth,
even as it drove him to scourge himself by hurting others.

Roth's spirits rose over the prospects of a job teaching math and
science at Liberty High School. The superintendent seemed enthusiastic about hiring him, even suggesting that Roth might also coach one
of the varsity teams. However, when he tried to follow up a few weeks
later, the superintendent suddenly turned cold, denying that there was
an opening and refusing to discuss the matter further. Roth was convinced that the FBI had gotten to the school administrator and poisoned his attitude toward an outsider. He suspected that the hostility
he felt from many of his neighbors was also the result of pressure from
intrusive federal agents.

Suspicion is not always a symptom of paranoia. Roth's sense of
being victimized by surreptitious government operations may have
been justified. FBI files indicate that investigators, alert for any evidence of subversive activity, did interrogate Roth's neighbors and
associates about him. In the process, they probably reinforced the hostility that many already felt toward a stranger with unconventional
customs and attitudes. The FBI documents report that some could
find nothing negative to say about Roth except that, in the words of
one unnamed informant, "They are very quiet people who seem to
remain to themselves and have no friends in that area." However,
another asserted that Roth "was always talking down the American

way of life and favoring Communism because he felt that it was the only plan that helped the working class of people." A third unidentified source told FBI agents that, during the Korean War, Roth insisted: "The Communists in North Korea were fighting for a real cause and are putting into force a worthwhile program."[5]

From 1949 to 1953, while holding a job as an attendant at Augusta State Hospital, Roth tried to organize his fellow workers and to pressure management to improve wages and working conditions. Word of his activities reached the governor of Maine, Frederic G. Payne, who directed state police to investigate. On February 8, 1951, during a meeting with an FBI agent named Thornton, Payne reported that Roth "WAS A QUOTE RABBLE ROUSER UNQUOTE, WHO WAS ATTEMPTING TO ORGANIZE THE EMPLOYEES OF THE INSTITUTION FOR A PAY INCREASE."[6] However, an FBI memorandum on Roth dated October 30, 1953, states: "Recent investigation failed to reflect any subversive activity on the part of subject for the past several years." Nevertheless, in the hope that he might furnish them with information about other suspects, a pair of FBI agents attempted to interview Roth himself on December 29 that year. The two men, whom Roth remembered for their distinctive snap-brim hats, approached him outside his house. Initially friendly toward the strangers, he became angry and defiant when they identified themselves. Thereafter, "Subject stated he would answer no questions, could give the agents no help, turned and got something from his car and entered his home saying on the way in that he had nothing to say to the agents."[7]

The suspicion and hostility that Roth, an avowed leftist, a Jew, and a "foreigner," encountered in isolated, frigid Maine during the Cold War was not unique. Much more dramatic was the case of the maverick psychoanalyst Wilhelm Reich. Like Roth, Reich was a Jew born in Galicia. He was a prominent disciple of Sigmund Freud in Vienna until forced to flee in 1938. Rural, insular Rangeley, Maine, where Reich settled in the 1940s, was not the ideal place for a German-speaking refugee with bizarre theories about orgone energy, and wary locals became convinced that he was a spy. The FBI was active not only in investigating but also persecuting the unfortunate Reich,

whose mind became unbalanced. His books and papers were inciner-
ated after being seized by agents of the Food and Drug Administration, which, citing its mandate to protect the public health, has on
several occasions seized and destroyed literature that promotes alternative therapies. Unlike Roth, Reich did not live to write again. He
died in 1957, harassed to death in Lewisburg Federal Prison.

As the Roths' situation became more desperate, Muriel was able to
secure a job teaching in West Washington at an annual salary of
$1,200. She enrolled both Jeremy and Hugh in the same school, but
because it was about thirty miles from their Montville homestead,
commuting became impractical. During the week, Muriel and the
boys took up residence in an old rented house about 200 yards from
the school, rejoining Roth on weekends. By now, they had acquired a
1931 Model A, and Roth could also look for work beyond the immediate vicinity of Montville.

In January 1949, he finally found employment in Augusta, just
across the Kennebec River from the Capitol. Founded in 1840,
Augusta State Hospital was a formidable psychiatric institution whose
patient population would, in its peak year (1956), number 1,828.
Roth was hired as an orderly at a salary of $26.70 a week. Perquisites
of the job included one hot meal each day, as well as something that
the house in Montville did not provide—adequately heated shelter
from the subzero wintry air. On weekdays, he often stayed overnight
at the hospital. Assigned to the third floor of the Burleigh Building,
which housed about forty inmates, Roth was responsible for writing
reports, cleaning the hardwood floors, changing linen, serving meals,
and bathing the patients. The head nurse was impressed enough by his
performance to recommend that Roth be appointed a supervisor, but
when he tried to unionize the hospital employees he was demoted to
the night shift in the infirmary.

Muriel was then offered a teaching job in Vassalboro, near
Augusta, and it no longer made much sense to hold on to the place in
Montville, thirty-five miles from the capital. They sold the house for
$1,800 and the goats for $60 and, in the summer of 1949, bought 3.5
acres at Church Hill Road—RFD #3—about five miles north of

Augusta. The price was $7,500, payable in monthly installments of $25 over a period of fifteen years. The property included an ancient barn and a brook. The small, drafty, whitewashed house that the Roths now moved into contained electricity and a party-line telephone, but few other creature comforts, initially not even running water. Its insulation was inadequate for winters in Maine, where, Roth recalled, "You could see the nailheads getting frost on them."[8] The Roths were to live there for almost twenty years, but out of a combination of principle and parsimony, the accommodations remained Spartan. Occasional guests would marvel at the absence of curtains, upholstered furniture, hot water heater, and reading lamps— as well as of anything to read. In the women's restroom of the Sears, Roebuck in Augusta where they went shopping together, a visitor from New York noticed how unaccustomed Muriel was to the sensation of warm water on her hands.[9]

Muriel ended up teaching in Vassalboro for seventeen years. Eventually, she became principal of the Riverside Grammar School, but she continued teaching all subjects in the seventh and eighth grades. Later she gave private lessons in piano. Muriel was temporarily sidelined in 1950 with a mysterious paralysis resembling Guillain-Barré syndrome, but she fought back and was soon toiling as valiantly as before. (The condition, an undiagnosable form of myelitis, would recur in later years.) The buttress of the family, Muriel had long since given up on her own musical ambitions in order to support her husband and their sons. She even served as barber to her three men. "My family was more important than a Steinway grand or a career, and oatmeal was more important for survival than a symphony," she later rationalized.[10]

Muriel doted on her husband, much as her mother, Grace, had revered her own husband; and at social gatherings even after fifty years of marriage she would hang on every word he uttered. "They hardly noticed anyone else," recalled a daughter-in-law, Joy Walker.[11] "My life might not be easy, but I have an interesting husband," Muriel told Penny Markley, who studied piano with her from fourth grade through high school.[12] Muriel was admired by all who knew her, but she and her husband were so tightly bound to each other that they left little room for anyone else, even their children (and later, grandchildren). Roth recognized Muriel's love as "the meaning and mainstay of his life";[13] a victim of recurrent, deep depression, he credited her with saving that life. "Once I married Muriel," he later told his editor, "that was it." Noting that he never again slept with another woman, Roth scorned the philandering of a fellow novelist, Isaac Bashevis Singer: "The man could not keep his zipper up."[14]

In January 1952, during a two-week vacation from his hospital duties, Roth attempted to write again. Though he began an autobiographical novel, he was clearly not yet ready for the task. Rejecting the forty to fifty pages he had managed to fill as "trash, miserable trash," he tossed the entire manuscript into the wood-burning furnace in the cellar. If he could not ignite a creative fire, Roth at least knew how to light a destructive one. Though this was not the first time that he consigned his work to flames, he would later describe this moment as "the nadir certainly of my literary endeavors."[15]

By 1953, Roth had begun to feel as if he were an involuntary inmate rather than an aide at Augusta State Hospital, and he resigned his position. Using his brook, his barn, and some help from the boys, he began "Roth's Waterfowl"—a family operation that extracted meat and feathers from ducks and geese. Convinced that his artistry was dead, Roth became an artist of death, the self-taught scourge of waterfowl. Out of discarded washing machines, burners, stoves, and metal shelves that he salvaged from an Augusta junkyard, he constructed the only plant in Maine equipped to slaughter and pluck geese and ducks. To do the job right, he jerry-rigged his own devices to heat, scald, and wax his feathered victims. Above a blood trough fashioned out of scrap metal, Roth hung three killing cones about a foot high each: "You put the bird in there so that the body was squeezed inside the cone but the head projected downward—outward. And then you grabbed the throat. You could feel the windpipe, so to speak, of the poor thing."[16]

Roth, who trained himself in all this by reading books, took pride in his resourcefulness and parsimony in the business of dispatching birds. He boasted that the entire operation cost but a few dollars to assemble, and it even inspired him enough to break his long literary silence. It had been fourteen years since "Many Mansions" appeared in *Coronet*; now, in 1954, he was published in *The Magazine for Ducks and Geese*! "Equipment for Pennies," a brief primer on how to scavenge the local junkyard to create a profitable custom-dressing venture, was not exactly material for *The New Yorker*. But Roth wrote the piece with careful attention to detail and a burst of gusto such as he had not felt for many years. "It was my first intimation that maybe I was coming out of this terrible, terrible bog."[17]

From 1953 to 1963, Roth was bogged down in his personal despondency and in the enterprise of reducing birds to flesh and feathers. Filling up his killing cones with flapping, squawking victims at once intensified the depression and diverted him from his own preoccupations. After snuffing out their lives, Roth dipped bodies into molten wax. Once the wax cooled and hardened, it was easy to remove the pin feathers. Roth would stuff about twenty pounds of feathers into a burlap bag and haul it to the post office to send by parcel post to the wholesaler. "Oh, my God," the postal clerk exclaimed when he saw Roth coming. "Here come the sneeze feathers! I'll be sneezing the rest of the day!" Roth apologized, each time asking, "What else can I do?" The clerk invariably replied, "Go into some other line of business."[18]

Roth's line of business during the postwar years in Maine had the character of a private obsession. He recognized that, with a sufficient labor force, he might have turned the whole operation into a very lucrative enterprise. He charged 50 cents to pluck a goose, 30 cents to pluck a duck, and sold goose feathers for $2.50 per pound, duck feathers for $1 per pound. Ducks and geese could have created a very comfortable nest for Roth and his family. He refused, however, to hire any outside help, relying for assistance only on Jeremy and Hugh, and occasionally Muriel. He commandeered the kitchen to incubate his own goslings, away from the rats and raccoons that prowled the barn. After school until suppertime, and then again well into the night, the two boys would help their father pluck and de-wax, and during seasons when the demand increased, Muriel also helped him with the bloody work of eviscerating birds for the holiday table.

Roth never stuck with the business long enough to allow his income to exceed his expenditures. When he was summoned to meet with an agent of the Internal Revenue Service, it was not to be audited but rather to be asked whether he ever expected to turn a profit. Yet customers came from as far away as New Hampshire to have their birds butchered and plucked by the master. The Maine State Prison even sent a guard and trusties with ducks and geese they raised within their walls, an experience that Roth wrote about much later, in "The Prisoners," published (in Italian translation, in *Lingua letteratura*) in 1987. As patrons were often squeamish about eating their own pets, Roth would oblige by trading a duck or goose that he had raised for one of theirs; hand-fed, the other birds were usually plumper than his anyway.

He came to despise the work, especially the killing. Like bludgeoning a puppy, it was as far as he could imagine from the humane task of writing prose that could change the world. After *Call It Sleep* was rediscovered in 1964, *Life* magazine was eager to photograph the newly famous, neglected author at his exotic vocation. Roth balked when they demanded a picture of him making use of the killing cones. "Nothing doing," he insisted. "I will not do it, that's all!" He told them he resented the attempt to portray him as a freak. "I have a profound suspicion of poses."[19] Yet the enormous, belated success of his first novel would enable Roth to prepare a new response to the question he had posed to the postal clerk: "What else can I do?"

Hugh Roth was still a child when conscripted by his father to help slaughter waterfowl. It was wet, woeful work, and Hugh detested it. He was embarrassed by a frugal father who scavenged amid discarded grocery produce to gather food for his geese and ducks. Hugh came to resent the unnecessary austerity of his childhood, spent in a chilly, somber house that never held a television. While his older brother, Jeb, received a new bicycle for one of his birthdays, young Hughie never did. "Henry Roth shouldn't have had children," Hugh's wife, Carole, would later conclude.[20] Though Roth was nothing like the monster he created in Albert Schearl or endured himself in Herman Roth, Hugh concurred: "My father was unqualified to be a parent."[21]

Roth made no secret of the fact that Jeb, whose temporary stutter was the immediate cause of the family's retreat to Maine, was his preferred son. He later admitted that he mistreated Hugh because his younger son looked more "Jewish." "My aunt and uncle did not treat their sons fairly," observed Rose's daughter, Vicky Elsberg. "Jeremy was the favored one. They just put up with Hughie."[22] Roth described his older son as "shy, gawky, tending to lankiness, clumsy, myopic, and a squirrel for thrift," and his younger one as "round, sleek, friendly dumpling, prodigal when he had the wherewithal."[23]

In "Assassins and Soldiers," a short story written in the 1960s that is so closely based on his own family that Roth does not even bother to change the names Jeb and Hugh, he tried to explain the way he felt about his older son. Roth noted that the older boy's "sagacity, his unusual ability to draw correct inferences, his quickness (and with it impatience with his dawdling father), all endeared him to me, but above all, his resemblance to the woman I so loved, his Mom." However, the resemblance was closer to Roth himself—also shy, gawky, clumsy, myopic, and as thrifty as a pack rat. When Jeremy was twenty-three, Roth acknowledged: "He is stubborn as I am, as obdurate, resists correction as I did, or accepts it with as little grace." He recognized "his Olympian manner, and his fleering, his superiority— and other traits and propensities he has derived from no one else but his father."[24]

Jeremy was a brilliant boy who from the earliest grades excelled at school. The selective, expensive Phillips Exeter Academy awarded him a full scholarship for his final two years of college preparation. Hugh recalled with some bitterness that the only time the family traveled anywhere together was in 1959 when they went to New Hampshire to attend his brother's prep school graduation ceremony. Roth was especially proud of Jeremy's mastery of Latin, in which he had coached him. An outstanding performance in Latin sight-reading earned Jeremy one of his two scholarships to Harvard, from which he graduated in only three years with a degree in mathematics. After a stint of twenty months as a volunteer teacher in what was then Tanganyika, he returned to Harvard for a master's degree in geophysics. He became a professional geologist based in Toronto, with frequent consulting assignments in remote parts of the world.

Hugh distinguished himself in other ways. As a boy his life was punctuated by a series of powerful but passing enthusiasms. With Muriel's encouragement, he studied piano, but then he flitted from the keyboard to trumpet to tubaphone to cello. He also threw himself into spells of weightlifting, judo, skiing, archery, and math. Hugh was accepted for study at the prestigious Eastman School of Music in Rochester but decided to attend Boston University instead. He dropped out of BU, and, over the strenuous objections of his leftist father, enlisted in the military, serving in the Army Corps of Engineers in Germany and Thailand. Hugh also defied his father by embracing Orthodox Judaism. Jeremy identified with the Christian side of the family. Since his mother was Gentile, Hugh, according to *halakhah*, the Talmudic legal interpretation that defines identity by matrilineal descent, was not a Jew by birth. In 1976, he underwent a formal conversion, after marrying Carole Nobel, a synagogue librarian who was the daughter of a rabbi. Teaching himself what he had to know, he found work in the computer software business.

Both Roth and Hugh were often indifferent students, but they compensated for their less than stellar performance in formal schooling by being ardent and successful autodidacts. When, to update her teaching credentials, Muriel took a course in Spanish, Roth studied it on his own as well. Yet mathematics was the subject that most aroused his interest. Only geometry, he had felt earlier in his life, had saved him from madness. Roth had performed abysmally in the course in elementary calculus taken back at CCNY, but when, following a self-taught program in trigonometry, he enrolled in a correspondence course in advanced calculus from the University of Maine at Orono, he earned an A for both semesters. Like his retreat to Maine, a symbolic system of functions and equations distracted Roth from his anguish. He found pleasure in the intricacies of mathematical problems, and working them out provided an escape into abstraction.

His math also provided a practical solution to an immediate problem—how to earn some money to supplement and eventually replace the income from the waterfowl business. Charging $1.50 an hour, Roth began tutoring students from Augusta High School who were falling behind in math. The Soviet Union's successful launch of Sputnik in 1957 stunned Americans into concluding that a national effort was urgently required to surpass their Cold War antagonists in science and engineering, and Roth had as much business as he could handle. During the summers, he spent up to eight hours a day providing help in algebra, geometry, trigonometry, and calculus, as well as English and Latin.

Roth worked his own way through *Calculus and Analytical Geometry*, a standard textbook that concludes each chapter with more than ninety problems, often struggling long into the night before arriving at the solutions. The answers were published at the back of the book, but after retracing his steps several times, Roth became convinced that one was in error. He wrote to the author, George B. Thomas, Jr., a professor at MIT. Conceding that Roth was correct, Thomas thanked him and promised to rectify the error in future editions. Roth and Thomas continued to correspond. (The professor never suspected that the stranger in Maine was anything other than a talented amateur. However, in 1964, Thomas suddenly learned that his correspondent, recently retired from waterfowl farming, was the author of the forgotten masterpiece *Call It Sleep*.)

DURING HIS YEARS at Augusta State Hospital, Roth had kept a private notebook, in which he recorded observations about the patients among whom he worked and lived for much of the week. His comments often reflected uncertainty about the tenuous line dividing him from them. In 1957, Roth's hold on sanity was further challenged by news that his mother had been committed to Bellevue Hospital in New York. For Henry, Leah Farb Roth had been a heroic source of strength. Diagnosed with involutional psychosis—a disorder that is characterized by deep depression, hallucinations, and agitation—as well as diabetes, she seemed finally to have succumbed to the pressures that haunt her son's fiction. Much later, Roth gave intimations of his mother's psychosis in his description of the loud noises that Ira Stigman's mother—and no one else—begins to hear in the third volume of *Mercy of a Rude Stream*: "Now a loud roar, now a soft piping, the volume of the sounds she heard she was convinced depended on the weather. 'The weather is about to change,' she would say. 'The engineer has begun to drive the train like one demented.' "[25] Leah Roth was treated with electroshock therapy and then allowed to leave the hospital.

Disturbed and distraught, Roth invited his mother to spend the summer with them in Maine. Muriel fetched her for the bus ride from New York to Augusta, during which Leah burst out in fits of uncontrollable, inexplicable shrieking. She was lucid for long stretches of time during the summer, though she occasionally began abruptly tossing things on the floor or weeping. She fell in love with bacon, a forbidden food that she had never served at home. She seemed to enjoy visiting her son's family, but she soon missed the window perch from which she liked to watch the tumult of New York City. Augusta was to her as stagnant as Veljish, and she returned at the end of the summer.

Leah Farb Roth's immortality in the form of Genya Schearl, the loving Jewish mama in *Call It Sleep*, was far from assured when she died in New York on March 23, 1960. Sensing that the end was near, Roth had visited her a few months earlier. When news came of his seventy-eight-year-old mother's death, he exclaimed: "Oh, my prophetic soul!" He spared himself a trip back down to New York and did not attend her funeral.[26] But Leah, who brought Henry Roth into the world and accompanied him to the New World, remained a vital presence in her son's imagination. It was she who had stood as a buffer between her ferocious husband and their vulnerable child. Imprisoned for fifty-five years within a loveless marriage, she remained, to Roth, a tragic figure. A reluctant immigrant, who never quite adjusted to the language and the customs of America, Leah was one of the neglected casualties in the successful transposition of the Jewish community from Eastern Europe to the United States.

While Herman, impatient with a dreamy son who seemed no more adept at earning a living than he was, had scoffed at Henry's academic ambitions, it was Leah who encouraged his education. She taught her son to read and was his earliest muse. The only literate woman in their tenement on 119th Street, she read aloud in Yiddish to her son and to a Jewish neighbor who had never learned to decipher writing. *Requiem for Harlem* describes how Ira Stigman's mother keeps both her son and Mrs. Shapiro informed of the latest news as well as the daily installment of a novel serialized in the Yiddish paper *Der Tag*. For Roth, writing novels would be an affirmation of his mother's influence.

Where Rose was Herman's child, Henry remained his mother's son, even after his life diverged from hers and he developed secrets he dared not divulge even to her. When taking college courses and courting a Gentile NYU professor, Henry still felt a special affinity, a bond of temperament, with Leah. "She still understood him," Roth writes of Ira Stigman and his mother, "intuitively, imaginatively, understood him in the realm of feeling." Leah and Henry Roth shared a vision of imperfection, a conviction that one's fondest aspirations are always doomed to failure: "Unknowingly, she had indoctrinated him into tragedy, given him a penchant for it, the tragic outlook. He recognized that fact, now that he had grasped the rudiments of how to form abstractions, to generalize. She was the source of his tragic bent, and that was their bond."[27] Roth grappled with thoughts of how different his mother's life might have been—had she not been forced into marriage with a man she did not love and had her son been willing and able to stand up against his father in her defense. He often wondered whether leaving Herman might have brought her some modicum of happiness. Yet he also would not have wished on her the plight of a middle-aged immigrant woman with no husband and no employable skills. Such regrets became the stuff of fiction, works Roth suffused with his mother's own sense of inevitable disappointment.

Despite their bitter animosity, her departure left a void for Herman, too. To overcome a loneliness he was reluctant to acknowledge, Herman began spending six weeks each summer in Augusta, staying by himself in a little cabin constructed of plywood, cardboard, and Sheetrock on his son's property. In fact, he made a point of never entering the main house, but enjoyed touring the surrounding countryside in a rented horse and buggy. Still intent on going into business for himself, Herman even bought a large restaurant in Manhattan. But when this latest commercial scheme also ended in failure after just a few months, he sold out and resumed the trade of waiting tables. In Maine, the ancient enmity between father and son reasserted itself in recurrent clashes over minor issues. Partial to a diet of sour cream, gefilte fish, and chicken soup, Herman griped about the blander fare that Muriel prepared. "He was still," concluded his proud son, "a miserably, moody, infantile tightwad, a backbiting, spiteful wretch."[28]

A short story entitled "Final Dwarf," published in *The Atlantic* in 1969, provides some sense of the resentments that poisoned Herman's visits to Augusta. The story (whose title derives from a Wallace Stevens poem) recounts a day in which a man called Kestrel drives his elderly father, visiting from New York, around the streets of a New England town on errands. Kestrel clearly has much in common with the author, finding almost no common ground with his father, whose diminutive size and personal pettiness are highlighted. "Final Dwarf" calibrates the excruciating psychological torture that father and son each inflict upon the other. Though critical of his miserly, bigoted, exasperating father, Kestrel, who delights in devising ways to annoy the old man, proves to be an equally mean-spirited adversary. Herman's annual visits to Maine enabled father and son to renew their mutual—and invigorating—belligerence. What Roth would later call "the essential and irreconcilable animosity that existed between us"[29] also seemed essential to the identity of each antagonist.

But it is Roth's description of Chaim Stigman's rabid violence toward his son Ira that provides the most disturbing intimation of just how brutal Herman Roth's paternal rule was. "Provocations I must have afforded in plenty, without any doubt," admits Ira, in *A Diving Rock on the Hudson*.

Roth/Farb family photo, circa 1914. Henry Roth is in the back row on the far right. Leah Farb Roth, his mother, is in the middle of the back row, and his father, Herman Roth, is in the back row, third from the right. Roth's sister, Rose Roth (Broder) is in the front row in the middle. *Courtesy of Pauline Nagel and Hugh Roth*

Henry Roth's mother, Leah Farb (far right), and three sisters. Their father, Benzion, had run a general store in Veljish, Galicia, before his emigration to America. *Courtesy of Joy Walker*

Henry Roth (rifle to his chin) as Dewitt Clinton High School senior with riflery team, circa 1924. He had refused to have his photograph taken for the high school yearbook. *Courtesy Dewitt Clinton High School*

Fire tower atop Manhattan's former Mt. Morris Park, which provided the title for the first volume of *Mercy of a Rude Stream,* where the young Henry and friends played in then-Jewish Harlem. "He passes below the hill on Mt. Morris Park in autumn twilight, with the evening star in the west in limpid sky above the wooden bell tower." —from *A Star Shines Over Mt. Morris Park*
Photograph by Mikael Awake

Harlem branch of the New York Public Library on 124th Street, still standing, where young Henry Roth discovered "the myths and legends he loved so well."
Photograph by Mikael Awake

Eda Lou Walton, NYU
English professor and poetry
critic, muse and lover of
Henry Roth, circa 1930. *From
the Ben Belitt Collection, Howard
Gotlieb Archival Research Center
at Boston University*

First edition of *Call It Sleep*, published by
Robert Ballou in 1934. It has since become
one of the rarest and most expensive first editions in twentieth-century American literature.
Courtesy of Larry Fox, photograph by Tom Mayer

Maxwell Perkins, the legendary editor at
Charles Scribner's Sons who was so
impressed with *Call It Sleep* that he
signed up the young writer for a new
novel. Roth later burned the partial manuscript, of which only one chapter survives.
Courtesy of the Library of Congress

Muriel's mother, Grace Reed Parker. Proud of an ancestry that could be traced back to the *Mayflower*, she was not pleased by her daughter's determination to marry Henry Roth. *Courtesy of Joy Walker*

Muriel Parker, born in Somerville, Massachusetts, as a young girl. She studied musical composition in Paris under Nadia Boulanger before meeting Henry Roth. *Courtesy of Joy Walker*

Yaddo, the artists' colony in Saratoga Springs, New York, at which Henry Roth met musician Muriel Parker. Yaddo Class of 1938: Back row (against door grill): Hubert Skidmore, Kenneth Fearing, Fred R. Miller, unknown, Wallace Stegner, unknown, Joseph Vogel, Charles Naginsky, Henry Roth. Front row: Leonard

Ehrlich, Muriel Parker, Marjorie Peabody Waite, Mary Bernard, Rebecca Pitts, Muriel Rukeyser, Edna Gluck, unknown, Margaret Helene, Elizabeth Ames, Mrs. Willard Thorpe, Susia Fuchs, Daniel Fuchs, Willard Thorpe.

Courtesy of Yaddo

Muriel Parker Roth and Henry Roth (at left), Elizabeth Parker Mills and John Mills IV (at right), shortly after Henry and Muriel's marriage. In 1939, Elizabeth Parker Mills, Muriel's sister, and her husband, photographer John Mills, invited Henry and Muriel to move into their penthouse apartment with them. *Courtesy of John Mills V*

Leah Farb, Henry's mother, who died in 1960. Over thirty years after Leah's death, Roth would reflect about his treatment of her: "Pity all mothers of such sons. The whelp treats its dam better than you did yours, my friend. But you're too late. The grave is a barrier to all amends, all redress." *Courtesy of Joy Walker*

Herman Roth in Henry's refurbished chicken coop in Maine, 1966, four years before his death. Though he was his son's lifelong nemesis, Herman spent his final summers on Henry's farm. *Courtesy of Joy Walker*

This 1964 Avon edition of *Call It Sleep* was the subject of Irving Howe's front-page review in the *New York Times Book Review* and would sell well over a million copies. *Photograph by Tom Mayer*

Peter Mayer, the young editor at Avon who re-published *Call It Sleep*. *Courtesy of Peter Mayer*

Maine, 1966, two years after the rediscovery of *Call It Sleep*. The Roth family: Hugh (born in 1943), Henry, Muriel, and Jeremy (born in 1941) partly visible in chair. *Courtesy of Joy Walker*

Henry and Muriel at the D. H. Lawrence Ranch, 1968. They enjoyed their summer in New Mexico so much that, reluctant to return to another winter in Maine, they moved to Albuquerque. *Courtesy of Joy Walker*

Roth had run a waterfowl farm in Maine at which he slaughtered ducks and geese for neighboring farmers and then sold the feathers. Here he is butchering a steer in New Mexico. *Courtesy of Joy Walker*

Henry and Muriel with grandson Owen in Toronto, 1976, where Jeremy and Joy had settled. *Courtesy of Joy Walker*

Henry, Jeremy, and grandson Owen in the second mobile-home location, on New York Avenue, just outside Albuquerque's Old Town. *Courtesy of Joy Walker*

Muriel (second from left) and Henry Roth (center) with son Jeremy (third from left) and all four of their grandchildren. *Courtesy of Joy Walker*

Henry with Albuquerque friends David and Judith Bennahum. *Courtesy of David and Judith Bennahum, photograph by Peter A. Masley*

Muriel, Henry, and Felicia Jean Steele, 1990. While still in high school, Steele became Roth's indispensable assistant. She was crucial in the editorial preparation of *Mercy of a Rude Stream. Courtesy of Joy Walker*

Henry's final house, a converted funeral home located at 300 Hendrix Road NW in Albuquerque, where the final sections of *Mercy of a Rude Stream* were composed. *Courtesy of Joy Walker*

Joy Walker, daughter-in-law, and Henry, 1993. *Courtesy of Joy Walker*

Roslyn Targ, Roth's devoted literary agent, and Roth, February 1994. Targ's husband, William Targ, published *Nature's First Green*, a small excerpt from *Mercy of a Rude Stream*, in 1978. *Courtesy of Roslyn Targ*

Larry Fox, Roth's literary executor, and Roth, 1994. A successful lawyer and a dedicated bibliophile, Fox was an admirer of Roth long before he flew from New York to Albuquerque in 1987. *Courtesy of Larry Fox*

Roth holding a book, 1995, near the end of his life. Roth had always expressed a desire "to die with one's books on." *Courtesy of Joy Walker*

But the little man, pathetic, deeply troubled little man, frustrated by his inadequacy, haunted by fear of ridicule, undoubtedly a rejected child himself, lost all self-control in administering chastisement. He went almost berserk, seized the first scourge within reach, stove poker, butt of horsewhip, wooden clothes hanger. Mom, in fact, always maintained that the peculiar inward crook of the pinky of my left hand resulted from my trying to ward off some flailing blow. If nothing was at hand to flog me with, he yanked me up from the floor where I lay groveling under his blows, yanked me up by both ears, threw me down again, and trampled me. He himself—scared, resentful, unstable, little man![30]

Though Herman would bequeath his only son an insultingly tiny financial inheritance, in addition to a crooked pinky, the old tyrant's truest legacy was a lifetime of depression and insecurity.

Yet Herman did not provoke antipathy in everyone. "I loved my Uncle Hymie," said a cousin, Pauline Nadler, who recalled with gratitude how when she was a child, Roth's father had pulled her out of a burning house.[31] "He was not really an ogre," insisted Joy Walker.[32] Roth's sister, Rose, adored their father, though her own daughter ridiculed her mother's naïveté. "It's hard to believe that you and my mother grew up in the same home," Vicky Elsberg, who suffered some abuse at Herman's hands, wrote Roth in 1994. "Her vision of reality is so skewed. She still believes and defends her 'good father.' "[33]

Among the Roths' few friends in Maine were Ted Bookey, a poet and translator, and his wife, Ruth, a teacher and singer. The Bookeys offered a parallel to Roth and his teacher-musician wife. Eager to overcome her husband's depression, Muriel encouraged the friendship. Ruth drew Muriel back into music, and Ted drew Roth back into the world. The four became fast friends. Though Roth did not discuss his writing, the Bookeys enjoyed his company, his conversation, and his sense of humor. Roth's sons grew up with no knowledge of the gregarious literary life their father had abandoned in New

York. The Bookeys were an exception to Roth's cultural isolation in Maine. Ted recalled hearing Muriel explain to their younger son: "You see, Hugh, these are the kind of people we used to know in New York."[34]

Almost twenty years after leaving New York, the Roths seemed fully rusticated in Maine. By then the boys had grown up and away, but as far as anyone else could tell, Roth appeared to be going nowhere. The gorgeous foliage that greeted Henry and Muriel when they first moved to New England in September 1946 was deceptive. Making peace with Maine year after year meant learning to adapt to the icy isolation of the sparsely populated Pine Tree State. "One must have a mind of winter," wrote Wallace Stevens, "To regard the frost and the bows / Of the pine-trees crusted with snow."[35] Until 1964 at least, Roth kept his mind on winter.

Chapter 12

BACK FROM OBLIVION

I think I'm finished. It's a rather hard thing to say, especially for someone who once felt, or fancied he felt, a true
creative ardor. But one might as well face facts, and try to
face them as objectively as possible. I do write occasionally, a kind of protracted reminiscence, but it's not worth
much, except psychologically, to discharge some of the
potential that would never go anyway. I have rather limited ability; I relied almost entirely on the imagination and
when that faded, so did I.

—HENRY ROTH, LETTER TO HAROLD U. RIBALOW[1]

A T THE END of the 1930s, James T. Farrell, whose own Studs
Lonigan trilogy constituted an important contribution,
attempted to sum up the era's achievements in fiction. In an essay published in the December 1939 issue of H. L. Mencken's *American Mercury* entitled "The End of a Literary Decade," Farrell lamented that
"many of the works were written by flashes in the pan who didn't
really flash." However, he singled out six authors whose works possessed "genuine merit and value."[2] In addition to Nelson Algren,
Edward Dahlberg, Erskine Caldwell, Daniel Fuchs, and John Fante,
Farrell cited Henry Roth. At the time, Roth himself had turned from
digging ditches in Queens to teaching high school in the Bronx, and
his only novel was unavailable in bookstores. His name was the least
familiar on Farrell's list, and his obscurity only deepened during the
years that followed.

Yet he was never entirely ignored. Over the years, a few authors acknowledged Roth's influence on their work. Howard Fast, for one, admitted that his use of a child's voice in *The Children*, first published as a short story in 1937 and later as a novel in 1947, was inspired by his reading of *Call It Sleep*. However, when William Rose Benét published his *Reader's Encyclopedia of American Literature* in 1948, he included an entry for Eda Lou Walton but not a word about Henry Roth, a one-book novelist whose one book was about as hard to find as its author. For all its favorable reviews, *Call It Sleep* had long since fallen out of print and out of public memory. When the revised third edition of the standard *Literary History of the United States* was published in 1963, Roth still was not mentioned. As late as 1965, the *Oxford Companion to American Literature*, in its fourth edition, offered no companionship for Roth's scattered readers. He would finally appear in the 1966 edition of *Who's Who in America*, but until 1964, he was living effectively incognito in Maine, isolated from the arbiters of literary reputations. His novel was not entirely forgotten, but evidence that it was being read becomes extremely sparse.

One brief exception surfaced in 1942, in a collection of essays edited by Oscar I. Janowsky called *The American Jew: A Composite Portrait*. In "The Cultural Scene: Literary Expression," Marie Syrkin, wife of the poet Charles Reznikoff and prominent in her own right as a leading American Zionist, surveyed American Jews who to that point had made their mark as writers—including Mary Antin, Abraham Cahan, Anzia Yezierska, Fannie Hurst, Meyer Levin, Albert Halper, Michael Gold, Jerome Weidman, and Ben Hecht. She also mentioned Roth, as a master and a mystery: "Judging solely from *Call It Sleep*, Henry Roth has the literary equipment of a major novelist, which can be said of no other American Jewish writer. However, since no other book by Roth has appeared, it is impossible to tell whether he has reached the stature his first book indicated."[3] Within the next twenty years, several Jews would emerge to transform American literature before Roth himself, like some sleeping princess, was brought back to life with a critic's kiss.

Few readers besides Syrkin were yet paying much attention to

American Jewish writers as such. Until the horror of the Holocaust made anti-Semitism suddenly seem uncouth, mainstream publishers had no interest in publishing books with Jewish themes. Edna Ferber was probably the most commercially successful Jewish novelist of the 1930s, but her novels were not Jewish.

During the decade following World War II, critics not preoccupied with such literary upstarts as Truman Capote, Ralph Ellison, Norman Mailer, J. D. Salinger, and Gore Vidal focused their attention on the giants of a previous generation—William Faulkner, F. Scott Fitzgerald, Ernest Hemingway, and John Steinbeck. It would have been inconceivable at the time to place Roth in that illustrious group. In 1956, Walter B. Rideout's *The Radical Novel in the United States* identified *Call It Sleep* as "the most distinguished single proletarian novel."[4] To readers who could not find the book in any publisher's catalogue, it must have seemed like the unearthing of a literary fossil.

That same year brought further sightings. Hiram Haydn, editor of *The American Scholar*, an influential quarterly published by the Phi Beta Kappa Society, organized a printed symposium to honor the magazine's founding in 1932. The topic was: What is the most neglected book of the past twenty-five years? Among several candidates nominated by the eminent literary critics whom Haydn solicited, only one title, *Call It Sleep*, was mentioned more than once. Its champions were two of the most formidable figures in American letters: Leslie Fiedler and Alfred Kazin. Both of them were second-generation Jews, for whom Jewishness was a signficant feature of their identities and a legitimate literary category.

Kazin chronicled his own coming of age in Brownsville in his memoir *A Walker in the City* (1951) and, like Roth, graduated from City College, though in the class of 1935. In the *American Scholar* symposium, he praised *Call It Sleep* as the supreme specimen of tenement bildungsroman, calling it "a wonderful novel about a little boy's first years in a Brooklyn jungle" and "the deepest and most authentic, and certainly the most unforgettable, example of this much-tried subject that I know."[5] Fiedler, who would reiterate his admiration for Roth's novel many times in later years—notably in *The Jew in the American*

Novel (1959) and in an essay, "Henry Roth's Neglected Masterpiece," that appeared in *Commentary* in 1960—proclaimed: "For sheer virtuosity, *Call It Sleep* is hard to beat; no one has ever distilled such poetry and wit from the counterpoint between the maimed English and the subtle Yiddish of the immigrant. No one has reproduced so sensitively the terror of family life in the imagination of a child caught between two cultures. To let another year go by without reprinting it would be unforgivable."[6]

Roth himself appeared willing to forgive. Another four years went by without a reprint of *Call It Sleep*, but the author had scant interest in any literary exhumation. Unaware of the attention he was receiving, he had tried to make his fragile peace with oblivion. Yet he had never entirely ceased approaching *The New Yorker*, and William Maxwell at long last put him back in print on July 14, 1956, with "Petey and Yotsee and Mario," Roth's fictionalized memoir of how three neighborhood Gentile boys saved him from drowning in the Harlem River. Under the editorship of Harold Ross and then William Shawn, *The New Yorker* did not indulge then in the practice of publishing photographs of its contributors or biographical information about them, so the author of *Call It Sleep* remained unknown.

In 1958, Charles Angoff made a further assault on Roth's anonymity. Born in Russia, in 1902, Angoff was a novelist, poet, and journalist, the former managing editor of Mencken's *American Mercury*. He was already a leader in the attempt to highlight and canonize American Jewish literature, and while lecturing on the subject at a Jewish community center in Queens, New York, he mentioned *Call It Sleep*, whose author, Angoff told the audience, had somehow disappeared. Rose Broder, who had typed that novel from the handwritten blue books, happened to be in the audience. After the lecture, she came up to tell Angoff that her brother was alive—and where to find him.

Angoff in turn told Harold U. Ribalow. A short, stocky man of prodigious energies and catholic interests, who "looked like Mickey Rooney but acted like Jimmy Cagney," Ribalow was a fund-raiser for several Jewish causes and an active impresario of American Jewish culture. He published *The Jew in American Sports* in 1955, when

Brooklyn Dodger pitching ace Sandy Koufax was just a rookie and the title might have seemed as absurd as the hoary joke about a one-page dissertation on "Humor in German Philosophy." As an enterprising and astute anthologist and editor, Ribalow was responsible for publishing Bernard Malamud, Harry Golden, Cynthia Ozick, and Isaac Bashevis Singer before they became widely known. Like Ozick, he too had studied under Eda Lou Walton at NYU (he was there in the late 1930s, Ozick in the 1950s), and he was excited about the possibility of meeting the author of *Call It Sleep*.[7]

Ribalow wrote to Roth in Maine, but the response was not encouraging. Ribalow, however, was not to be deterred—as his son remarked. "It was impossible not to pay attention to my dad." He was able to coax a story out of Roth—"At Times in Flight: A Parable," the account of the horse race that Henry and Muriel witnessed at Yaddo that is also a parable of creative paralysis. Ribalow saw that it got published in the July 1959 issue of *Commentary*.

During that summer, Ribalow took his family on vacation to Maine and found it not inconvenient for them all to drop by Church Hill Road. Meir Ribalow was about twelve at the time, and he was stunned by the rural poverty in which the Roths were living. The household was bare, and the residents as laconic and dour as if they were native New Englanders. "You wouldn't have known Roth was a writer," he recalled.[8]

Proclaiming his great admiration for *Call It Sleep*, Harold Ribalow urged Roth to try to get it back into print. At the very least, he needed to renew the copyright, which was on the verge of reaching a twenty-eight-year limit and entering the public domain. Bitter and scathing about almost everything, Roth insisted that nobody cared about his novel. The only positive words he had were for Phillips Exeter, from which Jeremy had just graduated. The Ribalows were so impressed by Roth's glowing description of the New Hampshire prep school that young Meir, who had never even heard of the place before, applied and later attended it.

Roth remained sullen and detached. But if Harold Ribalow wanted to do something about his work, Roth would not stand in his way. He gave Ribalow power of attorney and the blessing to do what he wanted with the novel. Although they were at first not aware of it, Scribners still held the rights to *Call It Sleep*, part of the deal in which Roth was offered a contract for the Dan Loem novel. After protracted negotiations and the intercession of Rose Broder, Scribners sold the rights to Ribalow for $500. They regretted that they were not able to sell their missing copy of Roth's unfinished second novel, too. Maxwell Perkins himself had died in 1947, but as Ribalow explained to Roth, another veteran editor at Scribners remembered "the manuscript you destroyed as one of the best they ever read."[9]

Ribalow had had no experience with marketing a novel to major publishers, but he discussed the problem with Henry "Chip" Chafetz and Sidney B. Solomon, proprietors of Pageant Books, founded in 1945. The retail business occupied several locations on Fourth Avenue's "Book Row," until moving later in the 1960s to 109 East Ninth Street, fewer then twenty blocks north of where most of David Schearl's adventures occur. With the encouragement of Shep Rifkin, a part-time employee at Pageant who also published mystery novels with Knopf and other publishers, Chafetz and Solomon had become intrigued by the idea of reviving *Call It Sleep*, since the price of a used copy had soared above $100, and they created a publishing imprint, Cooper Square Editions, expressly for that purpose. In September 1960, after an absence of almost twenty-six years, Roth's novel was back in circulation, in an attractive hardcover edition priced at $5.95. To ease the way back, Ribalow included three essays. Introductions by Maxwell Geismar, Meyer Levin, and Ribalow himself were designed to orient the reader to an extraordinary novel recovered from oblivion.

A minuscule new imprint, Cooper Square Editions was not able to compete with large, established houses in generating publicity, and the reaction was underwhelming. Although the reviews of *Call It Sleep* in *The New York Times* and several other papers had been rhapsodic in 1934, the reprint in 1960 was largely ignored. A column on the publishing industry in *The New York Times Book Review* made brief mention of the book. Reviews in half a dozen other publications did little to challenge its status as a neglected novel, although in an uncharacteristic burst of earnestness, especially about something related to her own Jewish background, Dorothy Parker declared in *Esquire*: "I think that this is the finest book about new Americans I have ever read."[10]

Few others seemed to be reading the book. A radio audience was introduced to atheist Roth's novel on November 30, when NBC broadcast a half-hour adaptation, by Shimon Wincelberg, on the Sunday morning religious program *Eternal Light*. A spread on Roth in the December 5 *Kennebec Journal* did little more than blow his local cover: Maine neighbors now knew that a novelist, if not a Communist, had been living in their midst. But by April 1961, only 2,300 copies of the new edition of *Call It Sleep* had been sold. Roth had earned $387.35 in royalties, which he divided equally with Ribalow. His conviction that no one cared seemed to have been vindicated.

A year or two before Cooper Square brought out *Call It Sleep*, Peter Mayer, a young man of German Jewish background, was earning his way through graduate school by driving a taxi for George's Cab Company. At the time, he lived at East Eighth Street and Avenue D. When Mayer's shift ended, at about 4 a.m., he and a fellow cabbie named Eddie Adler, who also lived on the Lower East Side, would leave their vehicles at the company's garage in Harlem and make their way back home by subway. Sometimes, in order to unwind after eight to twelve hours of driving cabs through New York, Mayer would accompany Adler in the early morning hours as he walked his dog through the neighborhood.

"This is where David Schearl grew up," Adler observed one night, gesturing to the streets around them.[11]

Mayer had never heard of David Schearl, and Adler (who would himself later write a novel called *Notes from a Dark Street*) told him about the legendary *Call It Sleep*. Mayer's curiosity was piqued; the following day he went to the New York Public Library on 42nd Street to hunt down a copy. He returned each day for about a week, and at the rate of about fifty pages a session made his way through Roth's novel.

In 1963, Mayer was hired by Frank Taylor as "education editor" at Avon, a paperback imprint founded in 1941 and acquired by the Hearst Corporation in 1959. At a time when most paperbacks were westerns, mysteries, and other mass-market genres packaged in lurid covers and distributed, like magazines, on racks in drugstores and bus depots rather than bookstores, Avon was now attempting to do what respectable houses did in cloth, except at lower prices. A few other paperback houses had already been publishing more prestigious titles, but, by placing Mayer in charge of "the better socks and shoes," Taylor was hoping to enhance Avon's lowly reputation.

"What can I do that is creative and cheap?" Mayer asked himself. Avon allowed him to spend up to $2,500 to obtain any title, a sum that even then severely limited an acquiring editor's options. "I was the most junior kid in the company," he later recalled.

Mayer remembered the novel that he had read in the New York Public Library, since published by Cooper Square in a hardcover reprint. He also knew about the edition published, to warm reviews and tepid sales (after negotiations by Roslyn Siegel, later Roslyn Targ, who was becoming a major force in the Roth revival), by Michael Joseph in London in 1963. The twenty-five-year-old bookman sought out Chafetz and Solomon at Pageant Books. Over a lunch of bagels and cream cheese, he offered to buy *Call It Sleep* for Avon, on one condition: that the paperback edition be allowed to drop the prefaces by the three Jewish critics, Ribalow, Geismar, and Levin.

"I wanted to position the book differently," he explained later. "This is a great *American* novel."[12]

Refusing to pigeonhole the book as "Jewish," Mayer appropriated an Afterword by Walter Allen, an English Gentile who was an authority on the American novel. It pronounced Roth "a master of the novelist's art, a master of sympathy, humor, detachment and deep poetic insight into the immigrant's lot and into the mind of childhood."[13]

Chafetz and Solomon were perfectly willing to settle for $2,500 for the paperback rights to a book whose author had given up on it and that had earned them very little. Publication was scheduled for October 1964. Mayer wrote to Maine to ask Roth whether he wanted to make any changes in the text, but Roth declined to play an active role in this fourth attempt at launching his novel. He in fact replied that he did not even want to read the book again. At the time, a paperback book was not considered worthy of review, any more than the new line of toothpaste with which it shared the drugstore shelves. However, Mayer set out aggressively to promote *Call It Sleep* as if it were an original hardcover from Doubleday, Random House, or Scribners. He did not disguise the fact that the book was a reprint, but he wanted to signal that it was something special. Mayer prepared bound galleys and sent them out to potential reviewers, and he paid personal visits to book review editors to encourage them to cover *Call It Sleep*. David Mandel knew Francis Brown, editor in chief of *The New York Times Book Review*, and he too made a personal appeal on behalf of Roth's novel.

In late September, Mayer received a call from Eric Wensberg, an editor at *The New York Times Book Review*, asking whether Avon planned a large press run for its book. Prodded over why he was asking, Wensberg eventually revealed that not only had the *Times* decided to review *Call It Sleep*; but they planned to run the review on the cover of the October 25 edition. This was astonishing news, since never before had *The New York Times Book Review*, the most influential reviewing organ in the United States, devoted space to a paperback on any of its pages, let alone the front page. And it would have been glorious news for Mayer—except that Avon had decided without consulting him to postpone the book's debut for another month. Their publishing schedule was crowded with titles shepherded by senior editors with much more clout than Mayer. He now dreaded the disaster of a *Times* review appearing before any copies were available in bookstores.

Mayer begged Taylor, his boss, to print *Call It Sleep* immediately, and he agreed. After a frantic call to Avon's printer, W. H. Hall, a limited run of 15,000 copies was produced in a few days. When 1,000 copies, shipped by air, arrived, Mayer hired twenty cabs and with the help of Avon staff distributed them to bookstores throughout Manhattan. Copies of *Call It Sleep* would be available at least in New York when the tsunami of a front-page *Times* review broke on Sunday, October 25.

A week or two before that date, Mayer obtained an advance copy of the review. It could not have been more favorable had Mayer written it himself. Of all the titles scheduled for publication in the last week of October, none had seemed worthy of the coveted position in *The New York Times Book Review*. When the editors huddled to make a choice, Raymond Walters suggested to Francis Brown that they might as well go with *Call It Sleep*. No stronger candidate emerged, and they invited Irving Howe to write the review. He had heard of the novel and was delighted to accept.[14] Ribalow was asked to contribute a brief biographical sidebar.

A leading New York intellectual who, like Roth, was a graduate of both DeWitt Clinton High School (class of '36) and City College (class of '40), Howe was an ideal choice to provide an informed and sympathetic reading. A founding editor of the Socialist journal *Dissent*, he published widely on politics, European and American modernism, and Jewish—especially Yiddish—culture. (In 1976, he would achieve both popular and critical success with *World of Our Fathers*, a detailed, affectionate account of the American Jewish immigrant experience.) In his decisive review for the *Times*, Howe praised Roth for his evocation of that experience, but contended that the Lower East Side was Roth's Yoknapatawpha County—synecdoche for Everyplace. By 1964, the general public was much more receptive than it had been in 1934 to stories about the Jewish experience. Nevertheless, a Jewish critic writing in a newspaper owned by Jews about a Jewish work of fiction still felt insecure enough to try to avoid the appearance of parochialism. Like Mayer, who eliminated the Jewish critics included in the Cooper Square edition, Howe insisted on the novel's universality: "And to be drawn into Roth's trembling world, the reader need have no special knowledge about Jewish life, just as he need have no special knowledge about the South in order to enjoy Faulkner." His verdict was unequivocal and non-sectarian: "It was a splendid book, one of the few genuinely distinguished novels written by a 20th-century American."[15]

Armed with the galley proofs of Howe's encomium, Peter Mayer braved an autumn snowstorm and flew up to Maine.

"You're a very young man," said Roth, dressed in a red and black mackinaw, when he met Mayer at the airport. "And you're undermining my position." The author said nothing about his novel until several hours later. Over dinner, Mayer eventually got him to take a look at the Howe review. "Do you think we'll make any money on this?" asked Roth, who had been working on his Spanish and wanted to know whether he and Muriel might now afford to visit a Spanish-speaking country. The next morning, when they drove into Augusta, Mayer bought Roth a recorded "How to Speak Spanish" course by Linguaphone, as small down payment on his later success.

Mayer was struck by how few books Roth's house contained and by the fact that Jeremy, with whom he shared a room overnight, knew less about his father's writing than he, a stranger, did. Over a beer, Roth stated that his reading was largely confined to *The Saturday Review of Literature* and *The Bulletin of the Atomic Scientists*. He was not exactly pleased by the prospect of becoming famous. He had chosen silence, exile, and waterfowling, and he sensed that his life in Maine would soon no longer be the same.

Nor was Muriel entirely pleased by the tidings that Mayer brought. "Isn't this all simply marvelous?" he asked her before returning to New York in the morning. "Marvelous for you, Peter, maybe marvelous for Henry, not marvelous for me," she replied. "The book was dedicated to Eda Lou Walton, and I've lived with Henry all these years and he's never written a book. Can you imagine, Peter, how I feel?'

The Avon edition of *Call It Sleep* was physically distinctive. A photograph, by Jay Maisel, of tenement roofs bled to the edges of the cover. It was compact (seven by four inches), with rounded corners—an unusual touch that added a bit to the publishing costs. Though priced at 95 cents (on the last page an Avon edition of John Barth's *The End of the Road* was advertised for only 50 cents), copies flew out of stores as soon as *The New York Times* hit the stands on October 25. The Sunday paper also contained a review, written by John M. Brinnin, of *The Enemy Joy: New and Selected Poems* by Ben Belitt, a fellow Walton protégé. As it happened, the title poem, written in the thirties, was dedicated to Henry Roth. Topping the *Times* best-seller list in an era when serious fiction could still be found there was *Herzog*, by Saul Bellow.

The dramatic effect of Howe's review is without parallel, except perhaps in the ability of Oprah Winfrey thirty-five years later to anoint a best-seller merely by discussing a book on her popular daytime TV show. A first printing of 25,000 copies sold out almost immediately, followed quickly by a second of 50,000, a third of 75,000, and a fourth of 100,000. Within five weeks, Avon was ordering a sixth printing. Though it came out late in the year, *Call It Sleep*, according to *Publishers Weekly*, outsold all but four other paperbacks for the entire year of 1964. It was number six for 1965. It would soon sell more than 1 million copies, in over thirty printings. Thirty years after the first copies of his novel rolled off its first presses, Henry Roth was an overnight success. At the age of twenty-six, Peter Mayer was appointed editor in chief at Avon. (He went on to become head of the Penguin Group, before beginning a second career running Overlook Press—a distinguished independent house publishing original works as well as occasionally reviving neglected books, as he had done with *Call It Sleep*.)

If 1934 was an inopportune time to market a novel about immigrant Jews, 1964, the year in which the Ecumenical Council of the Roman Catholic Church exonerated Jews for the killing of Jesus, was much more receptive. Revulsion over the Nazi death camps had driven American anti-Semitism underground, and, two years after the execution of Adolf Eichmann, a large cohort of third-generation American Jews was coming of age without having to feel defensive about their ethnic identity. In fact, "ethnicity" was fashionable; black was beautiful, and Jewish was cool. The venerable ideal of the melting pot, a metaphor coined by Israel Zangwill, an English Jew, was being challenged by a new model of pluralism. The political, economic, and cultural power of the old Anglo-Saxon ascendancy was descending, and other groups—among them Irish, Italians, blacks, and Jews—were rising to the occasion. The age of the Kennedys, Frank Sinatra, and the Supremes was more hospitable to Henry Roth than the age of Henry Ford had been.

Though the work of Jewish composers and lyricists—among them Richard Rodgers, Lorenz Hart, Oscar Hammerstein II, George and Ira Gershwin, Jerome Kern, and Irving Berlin—had long dominated Broadway, it rarely risked overtly Jewish content. But *Fiddler on the*

Roof, *Funny Girl*, and *What Makes Sammy Run?*—each with overtly Jewish content—opened successfully during the year that *Call It Sleep* returned. Similarly, Hollywood was created and controlled largely by Jews, but until the end of the 1960s they tended to stay behind the cameras or else to camouflage their identity. "Around this studio," declared Harry Cohn, the autocrat of the Columbia back lot, "the only Jews we put into pictures play Indians."[16] Though he worked for another studio, 20th Century Fox, Jeff Chandler (né Ira Grossel) did in fact specialize in roles in *Broken Arrow* (1950), *Battle of Apache Pass* (1952), and *Taza, Son of Cochise* (1954) requiring face paint and feathered headdress. Release of *The Pawnbroker* in 1965 ended what was in effect an unofficial embargo on movies about American Jews.

The Avon edition of *Call It Sleep* was published eight years after Leon Uris's *Exodus* had popularized a heroic image of Israeli Jews and eleven years after Saul Bellow's *Adventures of Augie March* became the first Jewish novel to win the National Book Award. It appeared in print after Bellow, Bernard Malamud, and Philip Roth, for all their differences, had established themselves as leading American Jewish novelists and had validated the category of American Jewish fiction. In 1964, Bellow enjoyed enormous commercial and critical success with *Herzog*, a book about an anxious Jewish intellectual. Other contributions that year to the category of American Jewish literature included Bruce Jay Friedman's *A Mother's Kisses*, Harry Kemelman's *Friday the Rabbi Slept Late*, Meyer Levin's *The Fanatic*, Wallace Markfield's *To an Early Grave*, Arthur Miller's *Incident at Vichy*, Karl Shapiro's *The Bourgeois Poet*, and Isaac Bashevis Singer's *Short Friday and Other Stories*. By the time *Call It Sleep* resurfaced, American Jews were demonstrating a vibrant contemporary culture. Roth provided convenient proof that they also possessed a magnificent tradition. The rediscovery of Herman Melville and Walt Whitman in the 1920s, when the United States, a young imperial power, was challenging ancient players on the global stage, absolved anxious Americans of the charge that they had no usable past. Similarly, *Call It Sleep* came along—again—at just the right moment to prove that American Jewish literature, for all its genuine accomplishments, was not just a flash in the pen. Henry Roth provided the ancestry it needed.

Rose, Roth's invisible accessory, who had typed the novel, promoted it, and helped secure the rights for republication, rejoiced in his success. She wrote him that his new celebrity had made her happier and more thrilled than she had ever been.[17]

But the woman most responsible for the existence of *Call It Sleep* never learned of its belated success. Eda Lou Walton had died, in Oakland, in 1961. Roth last saw her in New York in 1943, and the meeting was cordial. Her marriage to David Mandel collapsed when he fell in love with and eventually married someone else. However, Walton continued to inspire eager acolytes at NYU for almost two more decades. Gerald Vizenor, who would himself become a professor at Walton's alma mater, the University of California, and a prolific novelist, poet, and critic, took a class with her in 1956. He recalled that Walton changed his life, as she had Roth's: "She made me believe that I could write."[18] In Vizenor, who grew up in Minnesota of mixed Anishnabe and European heritage, Walton saw a future American Indian poet like the ones she had collected in *Dawn Boy* thirty years earlier. She encouraged him to continue his studies in New Mexico, where as a pioneering scholar of the Navajo she had begun hers. Though Vizenor did not move to the Southwest, specifically Santa Fe, until much later in his career, he paid tribute to Walton's influence in his memoir, *Interior Landscapes* (1990): "Eda Lou Walton was a most considerate teacher; with pleasure she raised the beams on literature, praised imagination, peeled the seals on precious prose, healed wounds, and she allowed me to shout and brush the wild nation with descriptions in the manner of Thomas Wolfe."[19]

Even after Lester Winter, Henry Roth, Ben Belitt, and her other young men moved on, Walton's instinct to nurture was irrepressible, and she legally adopted a motherless child. He was a fourteen-year-old Irish lad named Tom whom Mandel had been taking care of just before the boy's father, active in a labor union that Mandel represented, died. Mandel sought to place Tom in an orphanage, but Walton insisted on assuming custody of him shortly before moving back to Northern California, where she had spent her student years and where her brother, William, now lived.

Walton existed in straitened circumstances, supported by Social Security and a modest pension from NYU, where the student roster in her last class had included Cynthia Ozick. "Sleepless nights and constant dreams of loss, of *houselessness*, form a distinct symbolic story of how much this has hurt me," she wrote to Ben Belitt from Oakland in one of her final letters. "I don't know what the next move will be. The story remains sordid and neurotic."[20] She was drinking more heavily than ever, and her five-o'clock cocktails were replenished throughout the evening. Famished as a result of a largely liquid diet, she would raid the refrigerator around midnight. One morning in December 1961, Tom found Walton's lifeless body on the floor. She had apparently fallen after choking on a predawn sandwich. It was not quite ten years since another spunky Village poet, Edna St. Vincent Millay, woozy from alcohol and Seconal, had tumbled down a flight of stairs and broken her neck.

"I just regret that I didn't have finally made [*sic*] some kind of amends," Roth said of Walton in 1972.[21] Guilt over abandoning his benefactor had been added to Roth's burden of self-loathing. The dedication "To Eda Lou Walton" was at the front of the Avon edition of *Call It Sleep*, as it had been for the Ballou and Cooper Square editions. But the woman who transformed Roth from a gawky ghetto youth into a major American novelist, who furnished him with blue books, financial security, and emotional sustenance, died lonely and obscure.

Belitt did memorialize Eda Lou Walton, dedicating an oblique elegy to her. "The Cremation: New Mexico," published in his collection *The Enemy Joy*, conjures up the image of "a slight body" like "the flower on a cactus's thistle."[22] However, in 1999, when a dual biography of Walton's friends Ruth Benedict and Margaret Mead was published, it mentioned her only once, briefly, misspelling her name as "Edna Lou" in both text and index.[23] Of all the talented students—including Genevieve Taggard and Hildegarde Flanner—who participated in his poetry workshop at the University of California, Witter Bynner considered Walton the one whose work would most endure: "With her quiet humanness and individual style," he wrote, "she has always seemed to me sure of a place in the poetry of her time,—thus far, if my other students will forgive me, the most likely of them all."[24] For all of Walton's accomplishments, however, her name would vanish from almost all reference books, except as the muse of Henry Roth.

Barring an unlikely revival of interest in her poetry, Walton will survive most vividly in the character of Edith Welles, who compels attention almost as soon as her name (obviously derived from Eda Lou Walton) is first mentioned, about two thirds of the way through *A Diving Rock on the Hudson*, the second volume of *Mercy of a Rude Stream*. Excited by the literary ferment at NYU, Larry Gordon is particularly enthralled by his instructor in a course called "Outlines of English Literature," a poet and critic from New Mexico whom he describes as "extremely girlish in appearance, dainty and petite, with the tiniest hands and feet he had ever seen on a grown woman. . . . She was so sensitive, so fine and discerning, it was really a shame," says Larry, "that such an exceptional person should waste her energies lecturing on English literature to a bunch of premeds and predents, who don't give a damn about literature and about poetry."[25]

Like his prototype, Lester Winter, Larry is a young predental student who falls in love not only with English literature but also with the extraordinary instructor. And, like Roth himself, Ira Stigman is immediately won over by the attention that Welles, a "petite olive-skinned woman, turning away with winning and receptive mien, smiling countenance like a dark-hued source for rays of generosity, sympathy, smiling countenance with prominent, sad eyes," devotes to him, an uncouth City College biology major, when he first encounters her at a meeting of the NYU Arts Club. He is astonished by her frankness toward an undergraduate twelve years her junior, and grateful for her confidence when she begins writing him candid personal letters while traveling that summer through Europe. Like Walton, Welles eventually drops Larry Gordon and, after each comforts the other over erotic ordeals, invites the City College student to take his place. Getting "the hell out of Harlem" is the final action in the final volume of *Mercy of a Rude Stream*, but what determines it is of course Ira's decision to move downtown, into Edith's Morton Street apartment. Ira's mother concedes that, in leaving her, "At least you'll be in better hands."[26]

As Roth acknowledged in the dedication to his first novel, Walton made *Call It Sleep* possible, but she also made *Mercy of a Rude Stream* necessary. Walking out on her after a decade together added to the burden of guilt from which Roth found relief only through writing his final sequence of novels. Moreover, Walton was his first confessor, to whom he confided seamy details of incest with his sister and cousin. In a sense, much of *Mercy*, as an old man's final revelations, is a reenactment of Roth's disclosures to Walton almost seventy years before. In Edith Welles, the affectionate portrait of a generous, talented, and passionate woman, Roth repaid his debt to a benefactor, teacher, and lover.

IMMEDIATELY AFTER READING the review of *Call It Sleep* by Irving Howe, Ted Bookey wrote his friend these playful and prophetic words:

> Like it or not, 'enry, you are going to be a remembered episode in American and world literature. How interesting it will be to see your anonymity grow, this time from an entirely new direction. Imagine the crap, the falsifying, deluging crap, that's going to be written about you by industrious PhD's and tender-loving critics (some already apparant [sic] in the *Times* review), think of the bull market for Roth's disgarded [sic] shoe and socks and the relics that will be sold. On a thousand typewriters the myths are raining. But the book will be read.[27]

For the rest of his life, Roth would indeed be besieged by strangers. He received a steady stream of fan mail, all of which he answered, and of invitations to autograph books, give talks, contribute essays, write blurbs, and submit to interviews. But the book was read, not only in the new paperback but also in translations into about a dozen other languages. Perhaps the clearest confirmation of Roth's elevation to genuine celebrity status was a letter from Brian M. Sietsema, an editor of the *Merriam-Webster Dictionary*, asking the author how to pronounce his last name.[28]

This sudden hazard of new fortune might have seemed like something lifted out of the fairy tales that young Henry had devoured in the public library back in Harlem. He was Cinderella again, condemned to drudgery after a taste of glamour but then magically restored to the opulent palace. Yet what might have been regeneration felt to Roth more like intrusion. Jane Howard was one of many strangers who soon showed up on Roth's doorstep. When she flew up to Maine on November 17, 1964, to interview the neglected novelist for *Life* magazine, she found him dazed and wary about his unexpected, unwelcome fame. "Now that it has happened, I don't know what I'll do," he told her. "It kind of scares me."[29]

Howard's profile, which appeared in the January 8, 1965, issue of *Life*, contributed to the myth of Henry Roth as the Rip Van Winkle of American literature—an important author now being forced to reawaken after thirty years of voluntary poverty and obscurity. When Martha MacGregor, of the *New York Post*, called him, she too found Roth a reluctant celebrity:

> In a telephone interview, Roth answered questions patiently, courteously. But you had a feeling he wished the reporter would hang up and go away. You even had a feeling he wished the book would go away. "It came out of such a different kind of life," he said. "It seems as if I had spent all these years since in a kind of repudiation of that life."[30]

And when a reporter from Maine, Frank Sleeper of the *Portland Sunday Telegram*, asked Roth how he felt about all the attention he was receiving, the response was not cheerful:

> I was at first depressed when all this hullabaloo started with the Avon publication a few weeks ago. When you get used to living like an average guy, you find it's not too bad. I was comfortable and then I was being dislodged all over again. I resented it at first. My pins were being taken out from under me.[31]

Roth's stock reply to questions about *Call It Sleep* was to deny any continuity in his identity between 1934 and 1964. He insisted to Ted

Bookey that "I'm not the one who wrote that book."[32] It was a position he would maintain until his death. Interviewed by David Bronsen
for *Partisan Review* in 1969, Roth declared: "But as far as literature
is concerned, I am in reality no longer alive. The renewed interest in
Call It Sleep is being witnessed by a dead author who still happens to
be ambulatory."[33] As late as 1987, he was still asserting in a letter:
"Incidentally, I have to warn all the admirers of *Call It Sleep*, that
they're directing their praise to someone who has ceased to be."[34]

Among his journals, Roth kept a list of one-book authors, figures
whose reputations rest on a single splendid work. The category has
come to include Humphrey Cobb (*Paths of Glory*), Ralph Ellison
(*Invisible Man*), Thomas Heggen (*Mister Roberts*), Harper Lee (*To
Kill a Mockingbird*), Margaret Mitchell (*Gone With the Wind*), and
Tess Slesinger (*The Unpossessed*). After spectacular success in 1997
with her first novel, *The God of Small Things*, Arundhati Roy, like an
officeholder pledging to abide by self-imposed term limitations,
announced she had no intention of producing a second. In 2003,
Mark Moskowitz released *Stone Reader*, a film in which he documented his quest to discover what became of Dow Mossman, whose
first and only novel, *The Stones of Summer* (1972), had fascinated
him thirty years earlier. Along the way, Moskowitz tracks down Leslie
Fiedler who talks on camera about the case of *Call It Sleep*.

Searching for other parallels in American literature, one might
think of Norman Mailer. Mailer and Roth have little in common
except for their New York Jewish background, yet they shared what
Mailer has called "second-novel panic." Unlike Roth, Mailer became
a celebrity with the publication, fourteen years after *Call It Sleep*, of
his first novel, *The Naked and the Dead*, and throughout a prolific
career continued to seek and bask in public attention. But like Roth,
Mailer also traveled to the Midwest—Indiana, not Ohio—in a futile
attempt to write a second novel about labor activists. "I spent four to
five weeks getting ready to begin, made a great push on the beginning,
worked for two weeks, and quit cold," he recalled. "I didn't have the
book. I didn't know a damned thing about labor unions."[35] Except
for the fact that Mailer immediately abandoned the effort and man-

aged to publish a second novel, *Barbary Shore*, within less than three years, this might have been Roth talking about his Dan Loem book.

Roth, who probably never read Mailer, likened himself to the Romantic poets: "Keats, Byron, Shelley, Wordsworth—they succeeded young too, and then, one way or another, they petered out," he told Jane Howard.[36] Openly voicing doubts he would ever publish anything again, he saved a clipping from the *Boston Globe* that quoted Ezra Pound at 77: "I will never write another line."[37] In his Preface to the paperback of *Call It Sleep*, Walter Allen countered: "Even so, to have written *Call It Sleep* is enough to make any man's reputation."[38] By 1964, Roth's reputation was made on the freakishness of having signed his name to one great book.

When John Keats, in a famous sonnet, expressed "fears that I may cease to be," he was apprehensive about premature oblivion. Roth embraced oblivion and pretended to be completely resigned to the chasm between the eager young novelist on Morton Street and the middle-aged farmer on Church Hill Road. Yet the world outside Augusta was fascinated by the broken link between the two. "How could he give up a God-given talent and fool around with chickens and ducks?" asked his own sister, Rose.[39] The question echoed in the minds of hundreds of thousands of readers.

Biography is built upon the premise of a coherent, continuous self, and Roth's interrupted life defies even a casual observer's urge to connect the dots. What *had* he been doing for the past thirty years? Did he really give up on writing? If so, why? Would he ever write again? "Henry Roth" had become the site for ardent speculation about what constitutes a literary career, American Jewish identity, and a life worth living.

Chapter 13

AFTERMATH

All of us who grew up before the war are immigrants in
time, immigrants from an earlier world, living in an age
essentially different from anything we knew before.
—MARGARET MEAD[1]

Why is it hard for a Jew to forget for one second that he
is a Jew? All that history, the constant tug of the past.
—ALFRED KAZIN[2]

IN 1951, Frederic G. Payne, the governor of Maine, had targeted
Roth as a suspicious subversive and directed state and federal
agents to investigate him. But fourteen years later, on January 24,
1965, Governor John H. Reed saluted the achievement—or at least
the sudden national fame—of a fellow Maine resident by presenting
Roth with a gold-bound copy of *Call It Sleep*. This was but one of
many tributes that the rediscovered author began receiving. On May
19 that year, he was lured back to New York to be honored with a
grant of $2,500 from the National Institute of Arts and Letters, a
windfall for a man who had recently given up waterfowl farming to
tutor math and Latin. The citation, presented by the institute's president, George F. Kennan, whose family arrived in North America in the
seventeenth century, reads: "To Henry Roth, born in 1906 in Austria-
Hungary, in belated recognition of a passionate and, as is now proven,

a durable work of art, *Call It Sleep*."[3] Also receiving a grant at the same ceremony was his old friend Ben Belitt.

In October, the wayward child returned to his alma mater, City College. Despite a spectacularly lackluster academic career, Henry Roth '28 was received as guest of honor at a luncheon and presented with the Alumni Association's Townsend Harris Medal for Outstanding Achievement. The alumnus who had received a D in the freshman English composition class for which he had written "Impressions of a Plumber" was now invited to address the students of English 90, on contemporary American and British writers.

Roth wrote to the National Institute of Arts and Letters to express his ambivalent gratitude for their award, as well as his apprehensions about opening a new chapter in his life:

> The grant does two things: it seals off a way of life I have known and been more or less content with for the past nineteen years, longer, twenty-five, from the last time I seriously tried to write. It seals it off simply because, together with the reappearance of *Call It Sleep*, it annuls the necessity and even the internal consistency of that way of life. At the same time it sets a seal of confidence on my resumption of a new way of life based on a performance anteceding the old. Understandably I welcome that confidence, but equally understandably I don't welcome the change.[4]

One welcome change was the new financial freedom. The Roths, whose journey to New Hampshire for Jeremy's graduation had been one of the few occasions they ventured out of Maine, were particularly pleased by the opportunity to travel abroad. Roth had become tantalized by a book that Hugh brought home for a school assignment—an abridgment of Henry Charles Lea's *History of the Inquisition of the Middle Ages* (first published in 1877–78). Fortified by the Spanish he had taught himself while Muriel was enrolled in a formal language class, Roth conceived the vague idea of writing a historical drama set during the Spanish Inquisition, when, having wrested control of Iberia from the Moors, the Christian authorities were consolidating their power and enforcing Catholic orthodoxy. The Jews of Spain were forced to choose among three fates: conversion, emigration, or execution. The protagonist of the play that Roth imagined would be a young Marrano, a crypto-Jew who escapes religious persecution in Europe by making his way to Aztec Mexico along with the conquistadors of Hernando Cortés. The material might enable Roth, a European immigrant ambivalent about his own Jewishness, to ponder questions of personal identity and destiny in his own life. Henry and Muriel Roth set out to examine possible North American and European settings for the drama.

In the summer of 1965, they traveled to Mexico to take classes in Spanish administered by the University of Arizona in Chapalita, a suburb of Guadalajara; and in October, after Roth's return to City College, they made their way to Spain. They spent a week at the seedy Hotel Inglaterra in Seville, where they discovered that their study of Castillian did not equip them for the local Andalusian dialect, before renting a four-room apartment for 4,000 pesetas (about $67) a month. From their balcony, they could glimpse La Giralda, the Moorish tower constructed in the twelfth century. Fascinated by the historical layers within contemporary Iberia and hoping to find traces of the large and lively Jewish community that inhabited medieval Spain, Roth wandered through the old part of town, the streets so narrow he could spread his arms across, touching buildings on both sides of the street. He marveled at the huge Cathedral, the Ruinas Itálicas (a third-century amphitheater), and the Church of San Gil, with its unexpectedly erotic statue of the Virgin of Macarena. But, perhaps identifying with the plight of his fictional character, a secret heretic within Catholic Spain, he was overwhelmed by a feeling of oppression. "One suffers at length a kind of reaction to it all, to the overpowering religiosity that surrounds one—at any rate I did," Roth wrote his old friend Iven Hurlinger. "I awoke Monday morning with a terrible feeling of despair. It seemed to me there was no escape from the fearful conformity of Catholicism. It pervaded everything."[5]

Though Roth's abandonment of Greenwich Village had left him wary of companionship with other writers, he did spend some time with two other American authors living in Spain. One was Philip Levine, a Jew from Detroit whose working-class background and leftist convictions gave him much in common with Roth. Levine was still in his thirties, early in a career as poet that would bring him many honors, including a Pulitzer and a National Book Award. In 1965, Levine and Roth talked about *Call It Sleep* and politics. But Levine would recall that Roth never showed an interest in the younger man's poetry.[6]

Another American whom Roth encountered in Spain was John A. Williams, the future biographer of Richard Wright and author of such celebrated novels as *The Man Who Cried I Am* (1967), *Sons of Darkness, Sons of Light* (1969), and *Captain Blackman* (1972). In New York, Williams had been a neighbor and friend of Chip Chafetz and Sid Solomon. As Williams and his wife, Lori, were now living in Barcelona, they urged him to seek out Roth. Williams was already emerging as an important voice in African American fiction and a major inspiration to younger black writers, yet Roth showed as little interest in his work as he did in Levine's. However, Williams was fascinated by the man who wrote *Call It Sleep*, and he was determined to make a short film about him.[7] Roth resisted the idea, but he patiently sat before the camera answering Williams's questions about his life. The result, a documentary profile called *Creative Person 2: Henry Roth*, was broadcast on New York's public television station, WNET, in the spring of 1966. Later, after he and Muriel returned to the United States, Roth wrote Williams that "the film gave a satisfactory impression. Speaking for self in the lead role, wish I were smarter, more fluent, more inspired."[8]

The history of the Spanish crypto-Jews inspired Roth, and he spent many hours in the library in Seville investigating the background for what, in a letter sent to Jeremy, he called his "grandiose ideas for a grandiose play."[9] He found a map that helped him locate the forgotten site of the *quemadero*, the altar where officers of the Inquisition used to burn heretics at the stake—now a neglected spot on a busy urban thoroughfare. However, Roth admitted that he lacked the talent, training, and stamina for scholarly investigation. "It would have taken a lot of research," he said about the period piece he planned but never completed. "I'm the worst researcher in the world."[10] Devoid of genuine historical imagination, Roth wrote most powerfully when stimulated by his own personal memories. Clio was not his Muse, nor was *War and Peace* his inspiration. His literary gift was Proustian, a piece of bagel his *petite madeleine*.

Though he eventually abandoned the Marrano project, Roth's stay in Seville did yield one work of autobiographical fiction, whose plot is the effort to write about a sixteenth-century crypto-Jew rather than the adventures of that crypto-Jew themselves. Originally entitled "My Darling Surveyor," then "Los Españoles," and finally "The Surveyor," the short story that he completed in Seville before the couple left in January 1966 draws directly on his own experiences in seeking out the site of Seville's *quemadero*. An American Jewish couple named Stigman (the same surname Roth would use for his alter ego in *Mercy of a Rude Stream*) calculate the precise spot where the *quemadero* must once have stood in Seville. They insist on laying a wreath in memory of *conversos* martyred by the Inquisition for refusing to renounce the faith of their ancestors. The Stigmans' actions arouse the curiosity of the local police, who take them in for questioning. Asked to explain what they were doing taking measurements on the Avenida del Cid, the couple refuse to say anything except that they were laying a wreath.

Roth was more forthcoming in interrogating himself. "Why had I come to Spain?" he asks in a letter to Iven Hurlinger. He replies that the reason he had given himself—to learn more about the background of his Marrano character—was not quite accurate: "I had come to Spain to reunite with Judaism—via a side door! I wouldn't admit it until now, but that was the reason."[11] He now realized that the obscure force luring him back to Spain, a land that had exiled all its Jews, was a subliminal desire to annul that expulsion and be a Jew. While Roth was reentering the Jewish community through what he called the side door, his long-standing aversion to ethnic particularism was retreating to the cellar.

"The Surveyor," which John A. Williams reprinted in *An Introduc-*

tory Fiction Anthology (1969), marks a significant turning point in Roth's sense of Jewish identity. Throughout most of his adult life, he had been a staunch universalist, insisting on the Marxist doctrine that it was necessary to discard tribal designations; Jewishness was atavistic and counterrevolutionary. Even as a child, Roth responded to the trauma of being wrenched from the Jewish milieu of the Lower East Side by turning his back on the culture it represented. If Paradise was lost, he might as well, like Milton's Satan, embrace Hell. Declaring himself an atheist at fourteen, Roth, who later became a kind of poster boy for the American Jewish experience, long resisted acknowledging his Jewish identity. He even named the surviving fragment of his Dan Loem novel after *treyf*: "If We Had Bacon."

Shortly after his bar mitzvah, Ira Stigman arrives at the realization that "he was only a Jew because he *had* to be a Jew; he hated being a Jew; he didn't want to be one, saw no virtue in being one, and realized he was caught, imprisoned in an identity from which there was no chance of his ever freeing himself."[12] As a student at City College, Ira shows up for classes on Yom Kippur, proud to convey the message: "Ah, here's a Jew who doesn't give a damn about Judaism."[13] And, in 1939, five years after Hank Greenberg skipped a crucial baseball game in order to observe the holiest of Jewish holy days, Roth flaunted his indifference to religious custom by showing up at his WPA job on the sacred Day of Atonement. He was a lifelong secularist whose personal theme was nevertheless redemption.

As late as 1963, when asked to contribute to a symposium in the American Zionist magazine *Midstream* on "The Meaning of *Galut* in America Today," Roth proclaimed that Jewishness was an anachronism that he had discarded, and others should, too:

> It follows therefore that the fairly intensive conditioning of my own childhood with regard to Judaism, with its inculcation not only of special criteria, but also of a state of mind, has been abandoned to the extent possible. I would not dare to generalize on what Jews in general ought to do. I can only say, again, that I feel that to the great boons Jews have already conferred upon humanity, Jews in Amer-

ica might add this last and greatest one: of orienting themselves toward ceasing to be Jews.[14]

Yet "The Surveyor," haunted by the vanished world of Jewish Spain, makes it clear that Roth was gradually orienting himself toward ceasing to be a scourge of his own Jewishness. Following World War II, as Jews achieved material success, abandoned the urban neighborhoods of the immigrant generation, and severed affiliation with synagogues and other communal institutions, Roth's *Midstream* article spoke for many who regarded their Jewishness as an impediment to full participation in American society. His subsequent embrace of a Jewish identity, at the end of the sixties, occurred at the same time that pluralism was replacing the melting pot as the popular model of American culture.

Accepted by Robert Hemenway for the August 6, 1966, edition of *The New Yorker*, "The Surveyor," which Muriel edited and typed, would be Roth's first successful work of fiction after the republication of *Call It Sleep* made him famous in 1964. It was also chosen in 1967 by Martha Foley for inclusion in her annual *Best American Short Stories*. By that time, Roth's literary interests would be managed by an energetic agent, Roslyn Siegel (later Targ), who had been working for the Franz J. Horsch Agency since graduating from college. "I found Roslyn warm honey-blond, charming, intelligent,"[15] recalled the publishing veteran William Targ, and—as Jane Eyre might have put it—Reader, he married her. In 1969, she would buy Horsch's business and rename it the Roslyn Targ Literary Agency. In addition to Henry Roth, Roslyn Targ over the years would represent the foreign or domestic rights of Chester Himes, Harold Robbins, John Dos Passos, Erich Maria Remarque, J. D. Salinger, and F. Scott Fitzgerald, among others. She was particularly active in securing foreign sales for American titles. Her husband, William, editor in chief at G. P. Putnam's, considered *Call It Sleep*, along with *The Great Gatsby* and *An American Tragedy*, one of the three great American novels of the twentieth century.[16] Bill Targ was a distinguished figure in publishing whose keen commercial eye enabled him to foresee success with Mario

Puzo's *The Godfather*. Though a bon vivant who dined at three-star restaurants and the White House and traveled widely, he developed a close relationship with Roth and would offer crucial encouragement for his final burst of creativity.

As soon as Harold Ribalow received power of attorney to negotiate with Chafetz and Solomon over reprinting *Call It Sleep* under their Cooper Square imprint, he had in effect assumed control of Roth's literary interests and legal ownership of his novel. Roth, who did not expect much from any new edition, seemed content to let Ribalow function as unofficial agent and promoter if that was what he wanted to do. Though Ribalow urged Roth to reclaim possession of his own book, he declined. The income from the Cooper Square edition was modest, but when Avon paid an advance of $2,500 ($1,250 to Pageant Books and $1,250 to Roth) for the paperback, Ribalow was still taking a 50 percent cut of Roth's share, a commission that was highly unusual in a business in which agents usually receive 10 to 15 percent. He also took 50 percent of the advance on the Italian translation of *Call It Sleep*, published in the same year as the Avon edition. However, by October 19, 1964, Roth had become uncomfortable with the partnership. While insisting that "I preen myself on ignoring fiscal amenities,"[17] Roth asked Ribalow to reconsider their fifty/fifty arrangement. Ribalow wrote back two days later with the suggestion that he be paid 10 percent as Roth's agent and 15 percent as his publicist.[18] Four days later, Roth responded by asking Ribalow to decide for himself whether to take 50 percent or 25 percent of the proceeds from his novel.[19]

Ribalow apparently never got to exercise that option. Shep Rifkin, the Pageant employee and mystery writer, recommended another literary agent: Roslyn Siegel, who had become known as "the queen of foreign rights."[20] Siegel also negotiated the rights with the Milan firm of Garzanti for Mario Materassi's translation of *Call It Sleep* into Italian, the first and most successful of versions in eleven other languages besides English. On January 25, 1965, Roth anointed the queen of foreign rights, Roslyn Siegel (she became Roslyn Targ on July 30), as his legal agent. When Ribalow, relinquishing his role as unofficial representative, suggested that he might at least become Roth's biographer, the novelist resisted. "That involves material I would rather not disclose—yet," he explained.[21] It would take Roth almost another thirty years to disclose that material.

Materassi, an Italian academic born in Bologna but based in Florence, held a Fulbright appointment at Columbia University during the 1961–62 academic year. In a dentist's waiting room, he happened to read a copy of the article in *Commentary* in which Leslie Fiedler had extolled *Call It Sleep* as a neglected masterpiece. His curiosity piqued, Materassi made a point of seeking out the novel, and the result resembled young Peter Mayer's exhilaration when he sat in the New York Public Library reading about David Schearl's experiences on the streets of the Lower East Side where Mayer drove a cab. "The very next day I found a copy of *Call It Sleep* at [a bookstore] on Fourth Avenue," Materassi told an interviewer later. "For the next three days I hardly ate or slept till I finished the book."[22] On December 7, 1961, Materassi wrote a letter to Roth requesting permission to translate the book into Italian. A tall, slender man of twenty-six, the Italian traveled to Maine to meet Roth, and each immediately found the other *molto simpàtico*. "Almost miraculous that we should have spent our lives so far removed from each other and subject to such differences of environment, and yet find thoughts so matching," Roth marveled.[23]

Materassi would serve as Roth's translator, advocate, adviser, editor, and confidant for almost thirty years; and as Roth's relationships with Jeremy and Hugh deteriorated, he became a surrogate son. "*Figlio*" is the Italian term of affection with which Roth would begin letters to Materassi. The responses were addressed: "Dear Father." Eventually, this father-son relationship, too, would degenerate into bitterness.

The sudden fame that followed rediscovery of *Call It Sleep* in 1964 did not dim Roth's political passions. As early as March 1965, when Lyndon Johnson's administration was still beginning its buildup of forces in Vietnam, Roth sent a letter to Maine's Senator Edmund Muskie urging an end to American military actions in Southeast Asia.

Roth's opposition to the war in Vietnam, complicated by the fact that each of his sons was now in uniform—Jeremy in the National Guard and Hugh in the Army Corps of Engineers—became more strident as American involvement became more massive. He contributed his name and his money to an anti-war ad designed by the literary couple Denise Levertov and Mitchell Goodman that ran in *The New York Times*, and in private, in a mischievous letter to Materassi, he declared his identification with the enemies of the United States. "I'm a Vietcong or a North Vietnamese," Roth wrote his Italian friend. "The bigger the toll they take of us, the better I like it."

In conversations and letters, Roth remained a cantankerous contrarian. In the 1960s, while Newark, Detroit, Watts, and other urban areas exploded in racial riots, Roth took heart at the rise of black militancy. "I not only hope it becomes the great stumbling block, even a paralyzing one, of American society, but its ultimate undoing," he wrote Materassi, whose first wife was African American. "I don't believe the American society, taking it by and large, deserves to exist morally; and if it doesn't morally it doesn't deserve in any other way."[24] FBI agents might have found many other pungent remarks to insert in their reports had not the bureau, following the fall of Senator Joseph McCarthy, ceased to take an interest in Henry Roth.

ROTH HIMSELF had not lost interest in the fate of Spanish Jews. After returning from Spain, with side visits to Morocco and Italy, he still nourished plans to write about a covert Spanish Jew who sails with Cortés to the New World, though he now conceived of the project as a novel rather than a play. In 1967, he planned to spend the summer doing further research in Mexico. Roth asked his friend Ted Bookey to house-sit his property in Maine and baby-sit his father, who had been spending summers there. Bookey got on famously with the old man, whom he found "totally, totally charming." He remembered Herman as "a great raconteur," who regaled him with stories drawn from a wide range of experiences. Yet the elder Roth also belittled his son, calling him "a schmo who had married a shiksa and didn't amount to anything."[25]

In May 1967, Roth and Muriel drove their Ford Falcon down from Maine to Mexico. At first they settled in San Miguel de Allende, an antique town of narrow, cobblestone streets that, at an elevation of 6,000 feet, is a treasure of the Sierra Madre. Long a haven for *norteamericanos* attracted to the quaint setting and modest living expenses, it had, by the late 1960s, become a kind of Haight Ashbury South, a capital of the youthful counterculture. Roth met Ken Kesey, the author of *One Flew Over the Cuckoo's Nest*, who, as the leader of a group known as the Merry Pranksters, had assumed the role of hippie Pied Piper. Kesey and his gang were just about to drive their psychedelic bus to other places and other adventures, as documented in Tom Wolfe's *Electric Kool-Aid Acid Test*.

Roth, who drank socially and liberally, smoked pot once but was unimpressed. Though he was astrologically an Aquarian, both Roth and Muriel felt profoundly out of sync with the so-called dawning of the Age of Aquarius, antiquated and alienated among the drugged-out young dropouts who congregated in San Miguel de Allende. The United States was mired in a costly, divisive war abroad and racked by urban strife at home, and Roth's deepest impulse was to confront these problems through direct political action, not by retreating into an alternative realm of altered consciousness.

The millenarians of San Miguel de Allende were oblivious to a developing crisis in the Middle East that Roth found particularly disturbing. Violent border raids into Israel from Syria and Jordan were increasing, while Egyptian president Gamal Abdel Nasser mobilized his military units in the Sinai, closed the Gulf of Aqaba, Israel's only outlet to the Indian Ocean, and demanded the removal of United Nations peacekeeping forces from Suez. Roth was making little progress on his historical novel but, while trying to imagine the eradication of the once vibrant Jewish community in Spain, he found his emotions passionately invested in the fate of the contemporary Jewish state. He was beginning to think of himself as a Jew again.

After a month in San Miguel de Allende, the Roths moved on to Guadalajara, which, though Mexico's second largest city, retained much of the ambience of the Spanish colonial period. On the second floor of a building catty-corner from a remarkable old church, they rented a three-room apartment that they shared with a horde of cockroaches. It was there that the Roths followed avidly, as best they could in Spanish, daily developments in the Middle East. The Soviet Union was supporting the Arab countries and, as a Communist, Roth would have been expected to oppose the Israelis as capitalist imperialists. However, he could not help but feel enormous anxiety. He feared for the fate of a vulnerable remnant of 1 million vastly outnumbered by hostile neighbors whose avowed goal—announced repeatedly in public declarations—was to drive the Jews into the sea. He dreaded the impending annihilation.

On June 5, 1967, Israel swiftly eliminated the threat of Arab airpower. Within three days, it took control of the Sinai Peninsula. By June 10, when combat concluded, Israel had captured Jerusalem and the West Bank of the Jordan River, and gained a strategic hold on the Golan Heights. The Six-Day War was an unexpected, sweeping victory for the underdog Israelis, and Roth was overjoyed. "When Israel defeated the Arabs in a matter of a few days, my exaltation knew no bounds," he told an interviewer ten years later. "I felt at last that Jews had redeemed themselves by self-sacrifice and sheer valor."[26]

As Roth explained in numerous interviews and in authorial asides in his later fiction, the war traumatized and Zionized him; and, rejecting Marxist universalism, he now saw his identity inextricably bound with that of the Jewish people. David Bronsen, the author of a biography of Joseph Roth, published a conversation with Henry Roth in *Partisan Review* in 1969 in which Roth recalled how, following events from Mexico, he was transformed by Israel's trial by combat:

I found myself identifying intensely with the Israelis in their military feats, which repudiated all the anti-Jewish accusations we had been living with in the Diaspora, and I gloried in the establishment of themselves as a state through their own application and resources. An intellectual excitement seized hold of me that forced me to set down what was going through my mind, to record my thoughts about Israel and my new reservations about the Soviet Union. What I wrote seemed to reflect a peculiar adoption. Israel did not adopt me; I adopted my *ex post facto* native land.[27]

Israel's unexpected rout of its Arab adversaries struck Roth with the force of revelation. "Here," he wrote later in *Midstream*, in 1977, "was regeneration, tenable, feasible, rational—not in the direction of grandfather's medieval orthodoxy, but in the direction of a renascent Judaism, a new state." By 1967, the state was not exactly new, and the apocalyptic language is probably more appropriate to the 1948 War of Independence, about which Roth had said nothing, than the more recent conflict. But the regeneration that he found in Israel was a version of the creative renewal that he himself was starting to experience, and that he credited to inspiration from the Jewish state. "And it was Israel," wrote Roth in 1977, "a revitalized Judaism, that revitalized the writer, his partisanship a new exploration into contemporaneity, a new summoning of the word—however inept in the service of a cause."[28] The Israeli Defense Forces had begun to break one of the most notorious writer's blocks in American literary history.

Only four years earlier, Roth, still oddly unaffected by the Holocaust, had written in *Midstream* that Jews ought to be "orienting themselves toward ceasing to be Jews." Fourteen years later, he used the same magazine to proclaim his solidarity with Jews (at least the assertive new Israelis, who defied the victimhood of Diaspora Jews) and to diagnose his embrace of Jewishness as the antidote to his own creative impasse. If Israel could be revived from the edge of extinction, so could he. "What the hell was he waiting for? Here was a people reborn—*his* people—regenerated by their own will. Was he mad not to share in that regeneration?"[29] By 1979, Roth was claiming that he felt more Jewish than American.[30]

Roth's public embrace of Jewishness and Zionism was such a stunning reversal that it elicited a caustic letter from David Mandel in 1971. More than thirty years earlier, Mandel had found Roth broken and bleeding after a futile effort on the New York docks to help unite the workers of the world in a utopia that transcended class, nationality, race, and religion. In response to Roth's newfound Jewish partisanship, Mandel wrote: "Unbelievable. The lapsed Catholic resumes the faith, the internationalist goes nationalistic."[31]

Yet Roth remained skeptical of religion and, sympathetic to the plight of Palestinian Arabs, wary of Israeli government policies. While affirming his Jewish identity, he remained skeptical of Judaism. Responding to an author's questionnaire in 1994, he filled in the space for religion: "None." Roth longed for redemption from his own creative paralysis, and he rejoiced to find it in the Jewish state: "Only Israel had sundered his well-nigh impervious preoccupations with his psyche, burst open the pod of his self-engrossment, and had sent predilections flying—as if his partisanship were an accelerator."[32]

Though early intimations of Roth's transformation can be found in his fascination with Jewish victims of the Inquisition, it was not Spain but Israel that awakened the author of *Call It Sleep* from the dogmatic slumber of his Marxism and from literary hibernation. Roth would later extol "the midwife of his rebirth: *Israel.*"[33] This curious maieutic metaphor begs a few questions. If Israel was the midwife, who was the mother? Who the father? And how exactly did the Jewish state perform this delivery? Did the Land of Milk and Honey also serve as wetnurse? It is moot whether military victory in 1967 actually represented a national rebirth; post-Zionists have argued that it resulted in complacency and arrogance as well as the conditions of colonialism that actually undermined the state. But in proclaiming that "Israel's regeneration inspired mine,"[34] Roth would credit Zion for his literary resurgence.

It did not occur immediately. In the short term, Roth remained stymied by the writer's block that had already lasted more than thirty years. He abandoned the Marrano project, and the Roths made their way home, to Maine—despite a missing license plate on their Ford

Falcon. On September 15, 1967, they were back in New York for Jeremy's wedding to Joy Walker, a tall, vibrant painter he had met through Penny Markley and Barbara Field, two of Muriel's music students. Joy grew up on a farm in Oregon and came east to pursue a career in art. Like Muriel, she was a talented Gentile tying her fate to a Roth (and like her new in-laws, she would much later be invited to Yaddo). Though her fiancé was a scientist, Joy was delighted to discover that Muriel was a musician and Henry a writer. Indeed, she adored and revered them: "To me they were this ideal, wonderful couple—intelligent, witty, and charming," she recalled. She was beguiled by what seemed their delightfully unconventional life in Maine. "I didn't realize their children hated it," she observed. "And I didn't realize that Muriel was in anguish over not composing."[35]

Intent on an unconventional wedding, Joy arranged for an al fresco evening ceremony at the northern edges of Central Park, not far from the Mt. Morris that had been such an important setting for Roth's childhood. Roth himself was appalled. In 1967, New York City was a battleground of class and race. Muggings had become commonplace in the park, and Roth, wary of danger from what was now a largely black and Puerto Rican community surrounding the park, was convinced that a wedding party after dusk was just inviting trouble. But a large contingent of New York City police ensured that the ceremony went ahead without incident, except for a thwarted attempt by a neighborhood youth to snatch the Protestant minister's bicycle.

The bride, the groom, and their guests then made their way to a reception at a friend's apartment. Roth was stunned when Kent Parker, the younger of Muriel's two brothers, came up and introduced himself. Following the Buzzard's Bay episode, Kent, like every other Parker except for Betty, had severed all communication with Muriel. Roth had never met him, and he was indignant that now, twenty years later, the man, perhaps alerted by Betty, would dare show his beaming face as if nothing had happened. Never, even during her bout with myelitis, had her brother shown any concern for Muriel at all. Now he and his wife, Marni, were behaving with impeccable and insufferable politesse.

In the version of the incident that Roth reconstructed in a final manuscript, Kent extended his hand to his brother-in-law and announced, "I'm glad to meet you."

Because of Muriel, "because I owed her the immense debt of regeneration," Roth felt compelled to shake that hand. But according to his later account he also replied: "I'm not sure I'm at all glad to meet you," and then retreated to another part of the room.[36] Roth's reaction did not seem to faze the Parkers, who continued to mingle cheerfully.

Hugh, ever resentful of his favored older brother, showed up at the ceremony wearing blue jeans. Hugh's own wedding in 1975, when he was thirty-two and his observant bride twenty-eight, would take place under a *khupa*, presided over by an Orthodox rabbi. His marriage would produce three children, but end in divorce.

Joy Walker acknowledged that the Roths were so in love with each other that they neglected their children, yet her affection for Henry and Muriel would survive her divorce in 1983 from Jeremy, who settled in Toronto. She and their only child, Owen, lived in Brooklyn.

Hugh's Orthodox wife, Carole, never developed the affection for Muriel and Henry that Joy had, and she did not like Jeremy, whom many other members of the family found distant. While she loved Henry's sister, Rose, Carole Roth was bothered by all the adulation heaped on the author of *Call It Sleep*.[37] Yet she also took pride in being married to the son of Henry Roth, and she was a beaming presence at New York City's Henry Roth Day on February 29, 1996.[38] Nevertheless, she regarded her father-in-law as a flawed parent who should never have had children, complaining that he and Muriel neglected their grandchildren, as if they belonged to an entirely different family.[39]

Family ties and shackles distressed Roth throughout his life, even as family provided him with his richest literary capital. It was to escape the toxic atmosphere of his parents' household in Harlem that

Roth moved in with Walton in Greenwich Village. But he was still in New York City, still within the gravitational field of Herman Roth. Rose's daughter, Vicky Elsberg, was convinced that Roth moved to Maine in the first place "because he wanted to put distance between himself and the family."[40] By leaving Maine, he was now about to widen that distance.

Part IV

Chapter 14

NEW LIFE IN NEW MEXICO

"Brightest New Mexico. In that vivid light each rock
and tree and cloud and moutain existed with a kind of
force and clarity that seemed not natural but supernatu-
ral. Yet it also felt as familiar as home, the country of
dreams, the land I had known from the beginning."
—EDWARD ABBEY[1]

WHEN HE FIRST encountered New Mexico, in 1922, D. H.
Lawrence called it "the greatest experience from the outside
world that I have ever had."[2] When Roth moved to New Mexico
forty-six years later, his closest neighbor, aside from a caretaker, was
the ashes of the famous English author. Roth was not inclined to
indulge in Laurentian rhapsodies, but he too was affected by the vast
vistas and warm winters in the Land of Enchantment. After twenty-
two lean years in Maine, he and Muriel settled in the state notable for
attracting Billy the Kid and Georgia O'Keeffe—as well as Lawrence—
among its adopted residents. But there is a personal poetry to Roth's
choice of final habitation; he was ending his days where Eda Lou Walton began hers.

Lawrence and his wife, Frieda, came to New Mexico at the invitation of Mabel Dodge Luhan, the wealthy socialite and patron of the

arts. Lawrence detested the assiduously, ostentatiously benevolent Luhan, calling her "a big white crow, a cooing raven of ill omen, a white buffalo."[3] And though Lawrence liked to think of himself as the scourge of bourgeois values, she in turn called him "a typical lower middle class, puritanical conventional Englishman."[4] Nevertheless, Luhan offered to be his benefactor, and he accepted, living for several months in a cabin on a tract of land she owned atop Lobo Mountain. Luhan eventually deeded the 160-acre property, 20 miles north of Taos, to Frieda. Five years after Lawrence died in Vence, in Southern France, in 1930, Frieda disinterred his body, cremated it, and brought the ashes back to rest in a cement altar near their cabin in New Mexico. In 1955, eight months before her own death, Frieda donated the estate to the University of New Mexico. It became known as the D. H. Lawrence Ranch.

To make appropriate use of the property, the university created a D. H. Lawrence Fellowship, each year inviting a writer to spend the summer in a cabin set back in the woods, a few hundred yards from the path of Lawrence's pilgrims. The entire property is accessible only by a dirt road that winds through the mountains above Taos. By the late 1960s, David Greenhood, Roth's old New York friend, and his wife, Billy, were living in Santa Fe. They urged Dudley Wynn, who was director of the General Honors Program at the University of New Mexico and responsible for the Lawrence Fellowship, to extend an invitation to Roth, who had read very little of Lawrence's work. From June 10 to September 1, 1968, the Roths were paid $700 to live amid the spectacular setting that had inspired Lawrence to write *St. Mawr*. Describing the landscape around the ranch, Lawrence was rhapsodic: "Ah! It was beauty, beauty absolute, at any hour of the day: whether the perfect clarity of morning, or the mountains beyond the simmering desert at noon, or the purpose lumping of northern mounds under a red sun at night."[5]

If Luhan had not already decamped for New Mexico in 1923, Roth might have met her in New York through Eda Lou Walton. She died in 1962, before the Roths arrived in 1968. A high school classmate of Ruth Benedict, in Buffalo, New York (where she was known as Mabel

Ganson), she became the monarch of America's bohemia as Mabel Dodge, using the surname of the second of her four husbands. Almost every modern artist and radical thinker in New York eventually showed up for one of Dodge's evenings in the posh Village apartment at Fifth Avenue and Ninth Street she moved into in 1912. After marrying Antonio Luhan, a Tiwa from New Mexico, Mabel Dodge transferred her operations to Taos, where her guest list included, among others, Ansel Adams, Willa Cather, Edna Ferber, Paul Horgan, Robinson Jeffers, John Marin, Georgia O'Keeffe, Jean Stafford, Leopold Stokowski, Thornton Wilder, and Thomas Wolfe. But it was D. H. Lawrence who stayed the longest and left the strongest mark.

In the summer of 1968, Roth wrote in one letter, "The place is almost too ideal for me."[6] Though the site spurred Lawrence's creativity, Roth's own fiction was still blocked; but, prompted by his embrace of Jewishness, ideas had begun to germinate. Yet another artists' colony would, like MacDowell and Yaddo, change Roth's life.

Energized by their stay on Lobo Mountain, the Roths decided to remain in New Mexico. Both Jeremy and Hugh were now on their own, and summer in the Southwest had spoiled the couple for another long winter in Maine. Officials at the university helped the Roths find a place to live in Albuquerque, where its main campus is located. Founded by the Spanish in the early eighteenth century, Albuquerque, whose population in the 1960s numbered 250,000, is the largest city in New Mexico. A destination for the mass migration of people and capital from the rust belt of the industrial North to the newly air-conditioned Sunbelt, Albuquerque's population would almost double by the time of Roth's death three decades later. However, in contrast to the fashionable tourist destinations of Taos and Santa Fe, Albuquerque is a working-class town, about 35 percent Latino, whose median family income when the Roths arrived was slightly more than $8,000. Living there might at first have reminded Roth more of Brownsville or Harlem than Greenwich Village.

James Weaver, a prominent orthopedic surgeon, his wife Norma, and their three children occupied a twenty-acre hacienda in Albuquerque's affluent North Valley. The Roths rented from them a stable that had been converted into living quarters. Dr. Weaver maintained an aviary and was delighted that Roth, an experienced waterfowl farmer and former high school marksman, could help tend and kill the birds.

"He was an excellent shot," recalled Weaver. "He'd get his .22 out and harvest the animals. He was very skilled at doing kosher slaughter."[7]

Roth did tell his landlord, the chairman of the Department of Orthopedics at the University of New Mexico Medical School, that he was a writer, but never showed him any work. Weaver knew Roth as a "wonderful" and "very humble" man. He remembered his tendency to disparage himself and to fall into depressions. Another doctor, David Bennahum, who first met Roth soon after his arrival in Albuquerque, maintained that Roth suffered from a lifelong depression, though it did not prevent him from flourishing in old age. "I'm a wretch," he announced to Bennahum.[8]

Bennahum, a specialist in rheumatology and gerontology, treated Roth for his worsening rheumatoid arthritis until he returned to full-time teaching in 1989. Despite a gap of thirty years in their ages, patient and physician became fast friends. "He had a real gift for young people," Bennahum observed.[9] Later on, in early 1981, experimenting with the vague idea of developing a book called *Poet and Patient*, Roth and Bennahum tape-recorded a series of rambling conversations in which depresssion figures as a central theme. On January 7, for example, Roth reports that he has just gotten over "a serious depression. Unaccountable, except I never do know, sometimes a word from Muriel can throw me into a hell of a mess." Asked whether he had only recently begun to experience these bouts of gloom, Roth replies:

> I seemed to have them for a good many years. I mean extreme depression, but lately they have got to a point where it would take a practical form well how are you going to end it, that kind of in what, well it is just existence, I mean. How do you do it, as the ad goes, without any fuss or muss and the rest of it.[10]

However, life in New Mexico offered a stark contrast to the bleak
years in Maine. It was pleasant to sit out on the patio until 1:00 a.m.
without fear of frost or insects. The Weaver estate seemed, to the awkward newcomers, a place of constant merriment. Parties were held
frequently beside the swimming pool. The Weavers' three children
grew up with priviliges denied the Roth boys, forced to help their
melancholy father slaughter ducks and geese. Roth grew increasingly
uncomfortable with the kind of life he encountered among the
Weavers and their friends. Though he marveled at an affable existence
devoted to tennis, horseback riding, and hunting, he found it sterile.

In February, 1973, Henry and Muriel Roth moved to Paradise
Acres Mobile Home Park in Albuquerque, paying $100 per month to
squat on Lot 17. The comfortable two-bedroom unit they purchased
was spacious—60 by 14 feet, large enough to hold Muriel's ebony
Baldwin grand. Out of a piano crate, Roth constructed a toolshed that
he dubbed "Steinway Hall." Beyond the fence bordering their lot they
could watch another man—a Rothian doppelgänger?—raising ducks.

Aside from its frugality and affirmation of working-class allegiance, life in a mobile home was testimony to impermanence, to the
imminence of moving on. Though portable in principle, mobile homes
are rarely mobilized. However, in 1981, when the Roths grew weary
of their surroundings, and particularly the raucous motorcycles of
unruly neighbors, they relocated to "the tightest, tidiest court in
town,"[11] a property called South's Mobile Villa. Though just a few
blocks from Old Town, Albuquerque's quaint quarter of Spanish colonial structures and tourist shops, Roth could feel almost at home at
his new address on New York Avenue. An enlarged photograph of the
Lower East Side hung over his desk. The family pet was now a dog
named Shiksa, which the neighbors pronounced "Trixie." Lenny Bruce
said that trailer parks are, like instant potatoes and lime Jell-O, quin-
tessentially goyish; but it was in a mobile home in Albuquerque that
Roth, embracing his fate as Jewish author, took on his final epic task.

Ever since the rediscovery of *Call It Sleep*, Roth had been tormented by the repeated question: "What have you written lately?" It
was no simple matter to write a second novel when your first was

published more than thirty years before. Having abandoned two projects, Roth was still searching for a theme as late as 1973, when he thought of joining forces with John Savage, a scientist at one of the laboratories in Los Alamos, New Mexico. They conceived the idea of traveling together to their respective ancestral homelands—Ireland and Israel—and collaborating on a book about their experiences. Circulating the proposal among New York publishers, they asked for a $50,000 advance. No one bit.

However, as early as September 25, 1968, Roth was writing Mario Materassi about autobiographical ramblings he called "a kind of continuum, about which much can be said, or very little. A landscape of the self; to epitomize its meaning for myself and others, I offer you the title, *Portrait of the Artist as an Old Fiasco*."[12] Such a "continuum" might conjure up the continuity that Roth felt missing from his life. Gradually, journal entries that he had been making since the late fifties evolved into a plan for a meandering autobiographical *roman fleuve*. In a May 6, 1969, letter to Robert Manning, editor of the *Atlantic Monthly*, Roth mentioned his current venture: "A rambling interminable multivolume opus is my present incubus from the provisional title *Portrait of the Artist as an Old Fiasco*."[13] By 1983, when Stanley Burnshaw suggested just such a project, Roth was already long at work on it. "Why don't you try to write your autobiography in some unconventional form?" asked Burnshaw. "From what you have added to what I had known, I think there is more than enough. And I know that thousands—scores of thousands, possibly—would hang on your words. Have you ever given the notion serious thought? Might you now?"[14]

If not now, when? In 1979, when Roth began composing what would be his final, immense opus, he was already seventy-three. Recent surgery for cataracts and his hip, as well as the increasingly painful and debilitating effects of rheumatoid arthritis, concentrated the mind on ineluctable mortality. So did the death of Herman Roth, at age eighty-nine, in New York in October 1971.

Father and son never did reconcile, nor had there ever been conciliation in the first place. "This was a relationship that could not be resolved—and will not be resolved in my lifetime," Roth observed. "And that's all there is to it."[15] Any grief Roth might have felt over the loss of his father was tempered when he read the old man's will. Herman Roth bequeathed his only son the munificent sum of one dollar and an additional dollar each to Jeremy and Hugh. Rose Broder inherited the bulk of her father's modest estate; ever the loyal sister, she gave half of it—$1,458—to Henry.

In a letter to Rose in 1964, Roth called their father *"verdreit"* (twisted) and, with a venom that might have been directed to the hulking Albert Schearl, expressed regret over not having stood up to him: "I can only mourn the martyred existence of my dead mother; I can only wish that I was, say, 16, 18, had the manly courage somebody that age should have had, and separated her from that screwball."[16] Roth continued to resent Herman for his treatment of Leah: "Obviously I identified with Mom, whom I came to regard as a martyr in her marriage to this infantile, rash, irascible spouse (read: screwball). The only consolation I derive from my detestation of him is that practically all who had anything to do with him came to more or less the same conclusion I did."[17]

Despite "the essential and irreconcilable animosity that existed between us,"[18] Roth had gone on inviting Herman to spend summers in Maine, and even had his Augusta neighbors look in on his father while he and Muriel were in Taos. Furthermore, among the papers found after Henry Roth's death were documents suggesting that Herman was not exactly an uncouth brute and that enmity was not the entirety of his relationship to Henry. Roth preserved the manuscript of *Der Zind Fun Get* (*The Sin of Divorce*), a three-act play in Yiddish that Herman had written in 1939–40, during Henry's own fallow period. He also preserved a translation of the play that he himself made in 1989, while struggling with his own work and health. With no prospect for production or publication, the translation from his loathed late father's Yiddish could only have been a labor of love.

Herman Roth did receive recognition from Local 6 of the Hotel, Motel, and Club Employees Union. Their newsletter, *Hotel and Club Voice*, concluded: "He is a good waiter as he had been a good printer and milkman and husband and father." The article noted that Herman Roth's son wrote *Call It Sleep* and quoted his reaction to the father in that novel: "I was a little stern, but not like the book."[19]

Despite occasional bouts of depression, the move to Albuquerque reinvigorated Roth and made him more gregarious than he was in Maine. Doing his best to pass for native, he was often seen in southwestern garb, sporting a bolo string tie, bandana, and chimayo vest over his flannel shirt. Interviewing him for *Commentary* in 1977, John S. Friedman found a striking resemblance between the New Mexico Roth and David Ben-Gurion, the Israeli prime minister who spent his final years on a kibbutz, Sde-Boker, in the torrid, arid Negev.[20]

Roth's thoughts and hopes turned increasingly toward the Middle East. Back in 1972, he and Muriel had made their first visit to Israel, virtually incognito. Roth turned down an invitation from the Israeli consulate to visit as a distinguished guest. Rather than be received as illustrious American Jewish novelist and his wife, the Roths arrived by chartered plane as paying sightseers, on a standard tour arranged by Hadassah, the Zionist women's organization. "I wanted no sense of being obligated in the least because I felt it might inhibit me, especially if I thought the place was impossible,"[21] Roth told an interviewer later. He even declined an offer to talk at the University of Haifa during his two-week stay. Five years after the Six-Day War brought many venerated sites under Israeli control, and a year before the costly, sobering victory of Yom Kippur, it was still an exhilarating novelty for a Jew to be able to wander through the ancient alleys of Jerusalem's Old City and ascend to the peak of the Maccabean mountain fortress, Masada. Back in Albuquerque, the Roths studied Hebrew, subscribed by mail to the daily *Jerusalem Post*, and pondered a return to Zion.

In the American Negev, the arid Southwest, many of Roth's social and political activities took on a Jewish inflection that would have been unlikely in the sullen waterfowl farmer of Maine. He joined the Friendship Club of Albuquerque, which, he explained in a postcard to an old friend, Boris Gamzue, a professor of drama at NYU, was "sort of displaced Jewish retirees and refugees from metropoli, two or three with socialist radical pasts like mine."[22] He was active in the Israel committee of the Albuquerque Jewish Community Center, and he sent donations to the American Israel Public Affairs Committee, a powerful Washington lobbying group. Roth was intensely concerned about the plight of Soviet Jews, who faced persecution at home but were stymied in their attempts to emigrate to either Israel or the United States. "Refuseniks," those who declared their intention to leave the Soviet Union, were denied permission to do so and, after being fired from their jobs, were frequently prosecuted as economic parasites. Because Senator Henry "Scoop" Jackson of Washington State sponsored a law that tied American trade concessions to Soviet policies on Jewish emigration, and because he was a staunch champion of the State of Israel, Roth supported Jackson's unsuccessful campaign for his party's presidential nomination in 1976. A conservative Democrat who led the party's right flank in a field that included Hubert Humphrey, Frank Church, Jerry Brown, Lloyd Bentsen, Morris Udall, and the eventual winner, Jimmy Carter, Jackson was a very different sort of politician from the Communists and Socialists who had earned Roth's allegiance forty years before.

Roth corresponded frequently with government officials, most often about matters of moment to Jews. He wrote to New Mexico Senator Pete Domenici urging him to support asylum in America for Soviet Jews and to oppose the sale of weapons to Jordan, which still denied diplomatic recognition to its embattled neighbor, Israel. Concerned about the danger to Israel, Roth wrote his Congressman, Manuel Lujan, opposing the sale of AWACS, a sophisticated military surveillance system, to Saudi Arabia. He sent a letter to Israeli president Chaim Herzog expressing his dismay over the commercial boycott of Israel by the Arab nations. And he wrote to President Jimmy Carter in January 1978 to warn him against duplicity by Anwar Sadat, the Egyptian president who was promising peace with Israel, and again on March 11, to recommend regulation of media coverage, lest lurid reports of Arab terrorism encourage its proliferation.

During Roth's Albuquerque years, the historic national alliance between Jews and blacks in support of a variety of progressive causes and candidates was splintering. One crucial issue over which the two ethnic minorities diverged was Israel: whereas American Jews maintained a strong emotional bond with the fledgling Jewish state, some prominent blacks questioned its fundamental legitimacy. Agreeing with the controversial UN Resolution 3379—the "Zionism is racism" proclamation adopted by the General Assembly on November 10, 1975—many African Americans identified with the Palestinian Arabs as kindred people of color who were victims of Israeli oppression. Eldridge Cleaver, leader of the militant Black Panthers, did not. In fact, though he became infamous for advocating and engaging in armed struggle against the racist American power structure, Cleaver, now a born-again Christian, had become a vehement champion of Israel. For that reason, he earned Roth's respect, as did the Black Americans to Support Israel Committee, an organization headed by the civil rights leader Bayard Rustin to which Roth mailed a ten-dollar donation.

On February 1, 1976, Roth sent words of encouragement to Cleaver while he was incarcerated, on charges of attempted murder, in the Alameda County Jail in Oakland. "Any substantial voice among the Blacks that speaks out in defense of Israel and speaks out against the infamous racist equation promulgated in the U.N.," he wrote, "that voice ought not to be pent up in prison, but given full range to transmit its message."[23] On August 8, Roth sent a letter to Judge Lionel Wilson urging a reduction in Cleaver's bail, "as a practical contribution to humanism and to individual liberty—and to Israel's survival."[24] It is unlikely that Wilson was more concerned about Israel's survival than the gravity of the charges against a defendant who had fled the United States following a shoot-out with Oakland police in 1968. Cleaver was freed on $100,000 bail on August 13, eventually given a suspended sentence, and required to perform community service.

In May 1977, Roth received an invitation from Teddy Kollek, the popular, ebullient mayor of Jerusalem, to spend two months with Muriel as distinguished guests of the non-profit Jerusalem Foundation. They would be housed in Mishkenot Sha'anim, a compound

occupying a choice piece of Jerusalem real estate with spectacular vistas, elegant gardens, and a signature windmill. Constructed in 1860
by the British philanthropist Sir Moses Montefiore as the first Jewish
building beyond the walls of the Old City, *Mishkenot Sha'ananim*—
Hebrew for "Dwellings of Serenity," derived from a phrase in Isaiah
32:18—was redesigned after the Israeli victory in the Six-Day War,
when the area between East and West Jerusalem ceased to be a bullet-
riddled no-man's-land. At the time of the Roths' visit, the site consisted
of nine palatial apartments placed at the disposal of distinguished visiting scholars and artists. It was, in essence, Yaddo-in-Zion.

By August 1977, when Roth and Muriel arrived, Mishkenot
Sha'ananim had already housed dozens of eminent guests from
throughout the world, including Isaiah Berlin, Heinrich Böll, Alexander Calder, Pablo Casals, Marc Chagall, Iris Murdoch, Octavio Paz,
Mordecai Richler, Jean-Paul Sartre, and Isaac Stern. However, Roth
was particularly mindful of following in the footsteps of Saul Bellow,
who had stayed there the previous year and created an international
sensation by publishing his acerbic observations in a memoir called
To Jerusalem and Back. Nine years younger, but far more productive
than Roth, Bellow, recently awarded the Nobel Prize for Literature,
was the most celebrated American Jewish novelist. Roth was often
asked to comment on Bellow, and his response usually betrayed a
blend of resentment and envy. In 1978, Roth attacked what he saw,
in the transcript of a speech Bellow gave to the Anti-Defamation
League, as the younger author's complacency toward Jewish life in
the Diaspora. He faulted Bellow for denying the necessity and vitality
of Israel.

At a time when familiarity with *The Adventures of Augie March*,
Seize the Day, and *Herzog* was a virtual litmus test for passing as an
American Jew or an American intellectual, Roth was not embarrassed
to admit that he had never read any of Bellow's novels. In fact, after
moving to Maine, Roth effectively ceased to read any fiction, though
he continued to be a voracious consumer of newspapers and magazines. He acknowledged that his assessment of Bellow's literary
achievement was not based on personal acquaintance. "The reviews

themselves give me some guide as to what his novels are about—and what they're about hasn't interested me,"[25] Roth confided to his journal. On February 10, 1986, when Mario Materassi asked what he had against Bellow, Roth conceded that he still had not read any of the other man's books. Yet he offered several reasons for his disdain: "I suppose I've become offended by his intellectual arrogance? Or intellectuality that I don't possess myself . . . ? I don't know. But I suppose I demand of any person of any stature a degree of humility, and I guess I don't feel it in Bellow."[26] In 1993, the novelist and short story writer Leonard Michaels found the neglected author of *Call It Sleep* "ferociously resentful of Bellow's success in a decaying society."[27]

Roth affected similar indifference toward the other American Jewish novelist he was frequently asked about. He wrote a correspondent in New York that a younger literary Roth, Philip, simply did not interest him: "I dipped into P. Roth's *Portnoy's Complaint* once upon a time, and found it easy to shrug off—not superciliously, because the man is much cleverer than I could ever hope to be. His world doesn't mesh with mine, which is not his fault; his search isn't mine. So we're out of sync."[28] Yet Philip Roth only later read and admired the older novelist. (In his general editorship of the *Writers from the Other Europe* series published by Penguin and in his collection of essays entitled *Reading Myself and Others* (1975), Philip Roth showed a lively interest in his literary peers. And in 1998, he would tell Henry Roth's editor, Robert Weil, that he considered at least one of the volumes of *Mercy of a Rude Stream* a masterpiece.)[29]

Roth arrived at Mishkenot Sha'ananim—"same place Bellow stayed in and came home with glittering chitchat"[30]—resolved that his experience "would prove polar opposite of Mr. Bellow."[31] He was determined to savor his time in Zion. A veteran of MacDowell, Yaddo, and Taos, Roth was still able to gush about "what a joy it is to live in this place, a joy to the senses and a joy to common sense."[32] During their Hadassah trip in 1972, the Roths had been mere tourists; now they established enduring links with Israelis and began to think of making *aliyah*—emigrating from the United States to the Jewish state. They were befriended by Shirley Kaufman, an American poet who had moved to Israel in 1973, and her husband, Bill Daleski, a professor of English at Hebrew University who left his native South Africa to fight in the 1948 War of Independence. With the two transplanted Jerusalemites as enthusiastic guides, the Roths reveled in the land of Israel. The four spent a day visiting the poet Abba Kovner at Kibbutz Ein HaHoresh, a staunchly leftist collective farm located about midway between Tel-Aviv and Haifa. "If we'd only known about the communist idealism of the kibbutz in Israel before we left New York to go duck farming," said Muriel, "we would have come here."[33] Henry hoped that they could still make *aliyah*. "I could be perfectly happy in Albuquerque, but the logic of my literary development seems to require that I live in Israel," he told a reporter for the *Jerusalem Post Magazine*, before returning home to New Mexico.[34]

On February 10, 1978, Roth came back to Israel, alone, to scout out a place where he and Muriel might settle. But instead of ancient, enchanting Jerusalem, Roth focused on Tel-Aviv, a homely metropolis that was less than a century old. At first, he sought out modest lodgings—the Hotel Star on Trumpeldor Street, a couple of blocks from the beach—but then he economized further by renting a room in a private apartment. Roth explained that Tel-Aviv was "the one city in Israel where he could still discern the vestiges of his boyhood. It was the one city that paralleled and evoked the East Side. For him, the keyword was not *roots*; the keyword was *continuity*."[35] But Tel-Aviv was hardly New York; the visitor did not speak its language, and it did not speak to him. Fending for himself without the woman he had been inseparable from for thirty-nine years, Roth felt lost and lonely in this strange Middle Eastern city. He flew back to Albuquerque and Muriel on March 14.

A decade later, he would offer this diagnosis of his failure at *aliyah*:

I felt, essentially, like a foreigner. I mean, here's the land I espoused, here's the land I identified with, here's the people and so forth—but, as an individual, as a person, I'm a *foreigner* here. It's not merely the language. It's the landscape, you know? And I realized that if I were to make this transition—*aliya*, as it's called—I would have to go through a thorough process of acclimatizing myself to a new land, even though it is the land of the Jews. It is not the land, it is not the culture, for that matter, quite apart from the language, it is not that profound, that wonderful, deep culture that the English language, that English literature has given me.[36]

Shirley Kaufman had already been living in Jerusalem for about five years, yet her command of Hebrew remained rudimentary, and she continued using English as the medium of her poetry. Roth realized that his personal identity was tied to his writing, and he could not imagine resuming his fictional project in Hebrew. Nor could he imagine writing vibrant prose in English while perched in Tel-Aviv, removed from the habitat of the living language. It would make as much sense as composing fiction in the Latin he used to tutor in Maine.

In 1979, Roth made one final attempt to visit Israel. Though a sojourn at Mishkenot Sha'ananim is an honor bestowed unsolicited, Roth wrote to inquire whether the Jerusalem Foundation might extend him a second invitation. On October 7, Ruth Bach, the director of Mishkenot Sha'ananim, replied that he was welcome to come again, but this time he would have to pay forty dollars a day. On November 11, Roth wrote back that he had to postpone his trip for reasons of health. Reasons of economy likely also played a part in keeping Roth from ever going back to Israel. Recognizing that Israel would never be for him the "Jewish mini-state" he fantasized was the Lower East Side of his early childhood, Roth found the only way to reintegrate himself into the Jewish community—through the sumptuous English language he would have had to abandon in Tel-Aviv. Forced to make peace with his fate as a Diaspora Jew, he was now ready to return to his writing. "The long detachment seemingly at end, and what next?" Roth asked in a postcard to Boris Gamzue in New York.[37] The answer to his Talmudic question would come in the second wind that attained gale force during the author's final years.

Chapter 15

THE LION IN ALBUQUERQUE

What I have in mind is to portray the
evolution of the insufferably self-centered,
immature, in many ways parasitic and
contemptible autodidactic literary youth
into approximate adulthood, approximate
regeneration, his reconciliation with self
and with the necessity of change.

—HENRY ROTH[1]

IN JUNE 1981, when Mary Power, a specialist in James Joyce at the University of New Mexico, organized a Bloomsday symposium on the Irish master, it seemed natural to invite Henry Roth as an honored guest. Roth had written an important novel notably influenced by Joyce, he lived nearby, and he was on record as revering the author of *Ulysses*. He had first read Joyce's masterpiece in the powder blue–covered copy that Eda Lou Walton smuggled back from France, when it was still banned in the United States and the edition published by Shakespeare & Company in Paris was the only one available, as contraband. Judge Woolsey's landmark decision absolving the book of obscenity did not come until December 6, 1933, after most of *Call It Sleep* had already been written under Joyce's hypnotic spell. *Ulysses* taught Roth that he did not have to look beyond his own lackluster life in order to find the stuff of art: "You didn't need to go to the South Sea Isles, didn't need to float down the Mississippi on a raft, or flounder through the snow of the Yukon. It was all here, right here. It was the language that made the difference, that transmuted meanness into literature."[2]

Roth's own goal of transforming the quotidian into literature, his project of painting the portrait of an artist as a very young man, and his use of stream of consciousness were clearly indebted to Joyce, a fact Roth freely acknowledged after the rediscovery of *Call It Sleep*. "Joyce and Eliot are my favorites," he told Jane Howard in 1964 when *Life* sent her to Maine to interview him.[3] He claimed that he never read William Faulkner or Virginia Woolf before 1934. So, to the scholars converging on the Bloomsday symposium in Albuquerque, putting Roth on the program must have seemed like inviting General William Westmoreland, American commander in Vietnam, to a conference of World War II historians. They could expect a respite from academic discourse and pungent personal testimony to the importance of their hallowed subject.

Instead, the audience was both astounded and offended. Roth did not come to praise Joyce but to bury him beneath a barrage of complaints. He assailed Joyce with all the fury of an apostate repudiating the church in which he used to worship. It was as if, during the special session on Henry Roth held six months earlier in Houston at the annual convention of the Modern Language Association, a scholar had stood up and maligned *Call It Sleep*. Though he had once revered Eliot and Joyce as the twin deities of literary modernism, Roth could no longer abide the poet's casual anti-Semitism, and he even found fault with how Joyce contrived to make Leopold Bloom a Jew without, to Roth's thinking, giving him an authentic Jewish soul ("What the hell kind of Jew is that?" Roth asked David Bennahum).[4]

Roth would continue to recognize *Ulysses* as "the greatest seminal work of English literature of the twentieth century,"[5] but he now denounced its insidious influence. In January, he had told Bennahum that he regretted having become "kind of a junior Jewish analogue of Joyce."[6] Roth used the Bloomsday symposium at the University of New Mexico to wrestle with the causes of his own writer's block, which he now attributed in part to the Mandarinism he identified with Joyce. In the still embryonic new book that, echoing Joyce even as he condemned him, he was calling *Portrait of the Artist as an Old Fiasco*, Roth would describe his "crescendo of loathing"[7] for the author of *Ulysses*.

While conceding Joyce's technical virtuosity, Roth came to deplore the fact that it was acquired at the cost of alienation from his people: "*Ulysses* had become to him an evasion of history; its author *resolved* to perceive nothing of the continuing evolution of Ireland, refusing to discover anything latent within the seeming inane of a day in 1904. History may have been a nightmare, but the ones who could have awakened him were the very ones he eschewed: his folk."[8] The estrangement from community that Roth found in Joyce was to him a willful version of his own catastrophic removal from a Jewish environment. Each guaranteed creative paralysis and the personal discontinuity that Roth was now struggling to overcome. "Detach the writer from the milieu where he has experienced his greatest sense of belonging," Roth would tell an Italian audience in 1987, "and you have created a discontinuity within his personality, a short circuit in his identity. The result is his originality, his creativity comes to an end. He becomes the one-book novelist or the one-trilogy writer."[9]

Roth's unexpected tirade might be attributed in part to the onset of rheumatoid arthritis and a heavy dose of Percocet, which he had just taken for the first time; but an extensive, long-term transformation in attitudes was a more convincing cause. In any case, his outburst did not convert the assembled Joyceans, but it crystallized Roth's own readiness to undertake the last, vast labor of his literary career. Through communion with the ghosts of Jewish Spain and commitment to the fate of Israel, Roth had begun the final act of reconnecting with his people. From now on, his fiction would affirm his continuity with the immigrant boy on the Lower East Side. Like Joyce, Roth would use his gift for language to transform contingent dross into enduring gold, but he was determined to make his writing an act of immersion, not detachment. After rejecting abstract Marxist formulas, he was now repudiating the aloof aestheticism he found in Joyce. Henceforth, Roth would pursue art for the sake of situating himself back within the course of Jewish history. Whereas Joyce celebrated the proud artist's detached autonomy, Roth was attempting to create a personal and collective continuum. He longed for redemption, not evasion.

An autobiographical impulse, slighted in the aborted Dan Loem and Marrano projects, was the basis of Roth's strongest work. To continue where he had left off in 1934, with a frightened eight-year-old tucked into bed, Roth would have to reawaken monsters from his own adolescence. Early in the proceedings, he recognized that creating continuity between the old man in Albuquerque and young David Schearl would be very troubling not only to the author but also to those around him. Anxious not to hurt Muriel, he never showed her any of his work-in-progress, and he determined not to permit publication before her death, which he felt would surely come after his. Roth was too old and too spooked by false starts to be anything but honest now, yet he knew that honesty demanded secrecy to protect his beloved wife. Like Chateaubriand with his *Mémoires d'outre-tombe*, he would be writing as if from beyond the grave. "But the candor of it is such I'm almost certain the work is destined to be posthumous, or if I allowed it to be wrung from me, barely pre-posthumous," he concluded while still at the Lawrence Ranch.[10]

Both Henry and Muriel Roth endured serious health problems during the Albuquerque years. Muriel suffered from recurrent myelitis, but Roth had been able to count on her, the principal breadwinner during most of their time in Maine, to be the mainstay of the family. According to Bennahum, "She was the Astarte of his life,"[11] a Gentile goddess who, following Roth's frustration with Walton and his writing, granted him a fresh start. And he was certain that Muriel deserved to and would survive him. In 1976 and again in 1980, Roth was operated on for cataracts. He underwent surgery on his hip in 1979, and in 1985 was hospitalized four days for treatment of a hernia. His hospital roommate was, he complained, "the Average American," always watching TV and talking "pap, such pitiful, endless palaver."[12] (All through his childhood, Hugh had resented his father's refusal to bring a television set into the house, and even now the only broadcasts that interested Roth were of baseball games and opera.)

The demon of depression that had haunted Roth throughout his life was establishing a stronghold in physical infirmity. By 1978, he was measuring out his life in anodynes—Indocin, Bufferin, Dalmane, Ecotrin. "Praise God for Percodan."[13] Roth's rheumatoid arthritis had become so severe that it became agony for the writer, his hands bloated and reddened, even to manipulate a pencil. In 1985, when typing on his Olivetti portable electric, which had only recently replaced a manual model, induced unbearable pain, Roth wandered into a computer store. On the advice of a twenty-two-year-old salesman named Brian Errett, he bought one of the newly developed personal word processors that had just begun to transform the culture of literacy. An IBM PC Junior enabled Roth to continue to write by pressing lightly on an electronic keyboard.

Errett taught Roth to use the computer program, and for help with manuscripts recommended his girlfriend, Felicia Jean Steele. Though he claimed she was an English major, the seventeen-year-old Steele was in truth still in high school and had not even heard of Henry Roth. But she could type seventy-five words a minute and seemed responsive to training. Roth hired her, initially to spend a few hours every Saturday working as the novelist's factotum. "Dear, versatile, acute, indispensable,"[14] Steele would for five years serve as Roth's secretary, editor, and even, at least for a few paragraphs, ghostwriter.

A full decade earlier, in 1975, Muriel had undergone a mastectomy of the left breast. In 1976, she was treated for tendonitis in her right arm, a condition that for a while kept her away from her Baldwin piano. When Betty Parker Miller died, in 1983, Muriel composed a memorial to her sister out of poems by Yvor Winters, T. S. Eliot, Galway Kinnell, Howard Moss, and others that she set to music as *Songs of Separation*. Muriel Parker had once shown such musical promise that Nadia Boulanger chided other pupils for not performing to her standard. In the 1930s, it was as rare to find a woman composing as running a major corporation. Yet during her residence at Yaddo and her apprenticeship to Roger Sessions, Parker seemed on the verge of a successful career as a pianist and a composer. However, despite an auspicious debut at Town Hall, she abandoned music in order to be a wife and mother. "I had one year with Sessions," she recalled. "Then I changed to Henry Roth."[15]

Exceptionally strong-willed, except in asserting her own artistic talent, Muriel Roth struck most who saw her in company as self-effacing, attentive entirely and solely to the words of her husband. Throughout the arduous years in Maine, she gave music lessons in order to supplement the family's meager income. But by 1983, her sons were living far away, and her husband, reimmersed in writing, seemed less needy. "It was then, at age 75," Muriel told Bob Groves, a music critic for the *Albuquerque Journal*, "that I thought I better do something with music. I gave myself until I was 85. I doubt that I'll make it that far, but I'll try."[16]

Muriel's return to music, in the final decade of her life, is almost as remarkable as her husband's literary resurgence. Once a week throughout her last twenty years, she visited the violinist Jean Coulthurst at her home in Rancho Rio, where the two would spend much of the day performing duets. "I thought Muriel was as great a pianist as Henry was an author," recalled Coulthurst. Though she never entirely gave up playing or teaching, Muriel did not return to composing until seven years before her death. "If she had continued her musical path she would have become a composer of fame. She had great gifts," insisted Rosalie Heller, a pianist and cultural impresario who was born in New York but had been living in Los Alamos since 1956.[17]

Muriel became a member of the New Mexico Women Composers Guild. At one of their meetings she met Scott Wilkinson, who taught composition at the University of New Mexico, and who persuaded her to enroll as a non-degree student. Paying the senior citizen tuition of five dollars, she ended up taking one course with him every semester. After assigning her an elementary exercise, the professor soon realized that his student was no novice. One of the first pieces she wrote under Wilkinson's tutelage was a musical setting for a Yiddish poem by the Soviet author Shike Driz (1908–1971). *Babi Yar: For Soprano, Violin or Viola, Cello, and Piano* tells the story of a woman whose children were among the 35,000 Jews slaughtered by the Nazis at the infamous Ukrainian killing field. Performed in 1986 in Albuquerque, Santa Fe, and Los Alamos, the piece drew strong reactions. "The singer really threw herself into it and gave us all the shivers," recalled Maya Hoffman, who played the piano for the Santa Fe recital. "People began to cry and at the end they were stomping and yelling."[18]

Encouraging her to expand her repertoire beyond song settings, Wilkinson suggested a work for cello, an instrument Muriel was partial to because of her son Hugh's efforts to master it. The cellist Joanna de Keyser worked closely with the composer on the challenges and possibilities unique to her instrument, convincing Muriel to discard some notes as unplayable or simply not right for the timbre of the cello. The result, *Rhapsody for Cello*, impressed the performer: "She's kept up with the times. I like it because it has so many moods: It's dramatic, playful, fiery; it has humor. I'd say the most difficult thing about it is to make sense of where the phrases begin and end. It leaps around a lot in the high register. It's very improvisatory. It's often a matter of rubato and when to play the next note."[19]

The program notes that Muriel wrote for *Vagaries*—a chamber work for piano, flute, bassoon, and marimba—might also have served as a prospectus to the long autobiographical novel that her husband was toiling over at the same time: "During my 80 years, I have wandered down many different roads, all interesting, some exciting, some happy, some sad, some very rough, some more rewarding than others. You also have undoubtedly tried different paths through life. In *Vagaries* I invite the listener to wander briefly down some of mine."

When Rosalie Heller obtained a "Meet the Composer" grant encouraging interaction between composer and audience, she commissioned Muriel to write a chamber piece for the reopening of the renovated Fuller Lodge in Los Alamos. Based on the diaries in Peggy Ponder Church's *The House at Otowi Bridge*, *Los Alamos Diary* is a three-part composition for soprano, violin, clarinet, cello, and piano. "Henry and Muriel came to Los Alamos and stayed with us for several days while she gave talks around town at the Laboratory, at University of NM–Los Alamos, at the senior center and finally at the performance before a large audience," Heller recalled. "She was elated and considered this a high point in her life. I believe it was the first time that the attention was centered upon her work and not Henry's. He was quite passive and seemed not to know how to handle her success. She recognized this and so when she was not involved in concert preparations she gave him every bit of attention and drew him out of himself, listening closely to everything he said. She treated him with incredible courtesy and love, and obviously found his conversation fascinating."[20]

It was a novelty for Muriel to be perceived as the principal creative force in the Roth family. But attention remained centered upon Henry's work most of the time. In 1985, Mario Materassi—Roth's "*figlio*"—came to Albuquerque for a filial visit. Materassi had become one of Italy's leading authorities on American literature, with particular interest in William Faulkner and Jewish and black authors. He had translated Faulkner, Ford Madox Ford, James Baldwin, and Cynthia Ozick, and his translation of *Call It Sleep*—as *Chiamalo sonno*—was so successful that Roth was admired more in Italy than in any other country in Europe.

Materassi could also claim priority over American critics in promoting Roth's reputation. When he arrived in Albuquerque in 1985, Materassi had just finished putting together *Rothiana: Henry Roth nella critica italiana*, a collection of essays by Italian scholars and critics. The editor also included his own Italian translation of something by Roth that had not yet been published in English—an excerpt from the journal Roth kept in June 1967 while living in Guadalajara and reacting to the Six-Day War in Israel. Nothing like *Rothiana* existed yet in any other language. Even in English, only one book was devoted entirely to Roth, and it was by a young academic named Bonnie Lyons, whose *Henry Roth: The Man and His Work*, published in 1976 by Chafetz and Solomon's Cooper Square Editions, was a version of the doctoral dissertation she wrote at Tulane University. The fact that a compilation of Roth criticism appeared in Florence before New York, London, Paris, Berlin, or Tel-Aviv was a tribute to the energy, talent, and dedication of Mario Materassi.

He had also found the time to translate Norman Mailer's *Advertisements for Myself* (*Pubblicita per me stesso*). Accompanied by his third wife, a South Korean named Millicent who was fifteen years his junior, Materassi had now come to New Mexico in order to persuade his American "father" to endorse a project similar to Mailer's—a kind of autobiography through excerpts. He proposed to gather as many of Roth's miscellaneous writings as he could track down. He would arrange them in chronological order and insert connective commentary in the form of extracts from Roth's letters and interviews.

Though initially resistant, Roth was won over by the idea of beginning with his early, City College piece, "Impressions of a Plumber," and by Materassi's ambition to organize the disparate fragments of his life into an integral text. That was precisely Roth's own goal in the long new fiction he was currently struggling with. In a brief Foreword that he wrote to *Shifting Landscape: A Composite, 1925–1987*, Roth pinpoints Materassi's purpose as being "nothing less really than to exhibit the continuity within the desolating discontinuity of the frustrated writer's existence—and to show the development that had taken place over all those barren years." Roth looks to Materassi, his devoted editor/friend/disciple, to ". . . accomplish something that I had not been able to accomplish, because I had been disabled by that very same discontinuity."[21] *Shifting Landscape* provided Roth with a model for integrating his identity and an inspiration for his culminating work of autobiographical fiction.

It took strenuous scavenging for Materassi to track down copies of "Impressions of a Plumber," "If We Had Bacon," and "Equipment for Pennies" in their obscure sources—ancient issues of CCNY's *Lavender, Signatures: Works in Progress*, and *The Magazine for Ducks and Geese*, respectively. However, who touches *Shifting Landscape* touches a man, one who could no longer be known merely as the author of *Call It Sleep*. While lamenting the slightness of the individual parts, which nevertheless "exhibit the flickerings of an enormous talent," Robert Alter in *The New Republic* hailed the collection as providing "the outlines of a spiritual autobiography."[22] Roth's own judgment of the new book was also a verdict on his own life: "It impressed me quite objectively with the rather tragic thread—a trace went through it, I don't know whether it's frustration, a block, or what have you. It's a man fighting or serving his destiny. It had that overtone of a person too obdurate to give up."[23]

In his Foreword, Roth maintained that "The book is primarily

Mario's, not mine."[24] Though dedicated "To my wife Muriel Roth," *Shifting Landscape* credited Mario Materassi as its editor. Roth was at first as nonchalant about sharing revenues with Materassi as he had earlier been with Ribalow. Though Materassi later persuaded him to reduce the commission to a more seemly 10 percent, Roth initially offered his *figlio* one third of any royalties from *Shifting Landscape*. Without the younger man's initiative and persistent effort, the book would not have existed at all. And besides, it was itself the kind of "continuum" that Roth was hoping to create in the massive fiction he was laboring on. Two years earlier, he had appealed to Materassi for assistance. "Think of Pound's services to one T. S. Eliot," he wrote, recalling how Eliot acknowledged Pound as "*il miglior fabbro*" in the creation of *The Waste Land*. But Roth assured Materassi, "Nothing will change my affection for you, however you greet all this."[25] Fifty years before, he had pledged eternal love to Eda Lou Walton, and there would be more hope than truth to this pledge as well.

By January 30, 1987, Materassi had not quite finished putting together *Shifting Landscape* when the Roths showed up in the northeastern Italian town of Percoto, in the Friuli-Venezia Giulia region. Through Materassi's efforts, Henry Roth had been selected for the Premio Internazionale Nonino, a prestigious annual award whose previous recipients had been Jorge Amado, Léopold Sédar Senghor, and Claude Lévi-Strauss; V. S. Naipaul, Chinua Achebe, and Ngugi wa Thiong'o, among others, would receive the prize in later years. In 1987, Roth was still only a one-book author—if we disregard a four-page volume printed privately in 1979 by William Targ under his own special imprint, Targ Editions, in a limited run of 350 signed copies. Dedicated "to Bill Targ for the vision and faith to begin anew," *Nature's First Green* is a short autobiographical sketch nurtured by Targ's insistence that Roth return to writing fiction. But Roth's one true book, in Materassi's translation, was revered in Italy. As a result of the Nonino Prize, *Chiamalo sonno*, in its third edition, returned to the country's best-seller lists. In addition to a trip to Italy, the prize's sponsors, Giannola and Benito Nonino, gave Roth $7,000, part of which he used to purchase a new computer.

The ceremony was witnessed by an audience of more than five hundred, and it was widely covered in the Italian media. Despite his fondness for Italian arias, Roth delivered his acceptance speech in English; it appeared as the concluding text of *Shifting Landscape* when the book was finally published a few months later. Roth reviewed his stunted literary career, again blaming the discontinuities in his life on his having been wrested at a tender age from "the Jewish mini-state on the East Side to Harlem among the Irish and Italians." But he credited Israel for a renewed sense of belonging and a recovery of his creative powers. "May the phenomenon of the one-book writer, of which I and many other of my contemporaries in America, and perhaps elsewhere, are unhappy examples, be ended forever. May all people feel at home. May all people feel they belong, and may their sense of identity never be impaired."[26]

Roth recognized that as a retired machinist, hospital attendant, and waterfowl farmer, he was an unconventional choice for an international literary prize. Though he felt a bit of an impostor in Percoto, he was exhilarated by "that giddy whirl known as Premio Nonino."[27] At least for the moment, Percoto was more effective medicine than Percodan. Claiming as his address a mobile home in Albuquerque, Roth felt about as much at home in Italy as anywhere else. His identification with the strong working-class traditions of Italian politics had led him to speak Italian while trying to radicalize New York dockworkers in the 1930s. In 1987 in Percoto, when he proclaimed, "I am the eternal plebeian,"[28] Roth must have been especially gratified that the book American Marxists had faulted for insufficient attention to oppression of the working class was now the toast of Italy.

Back in 1977, Roth and Muriel had stopped off in Florence on their way back to Albuquerque from Mishkenot Sha'ananim. When Roth saw a swarm of workers marching in the street below, he hurried down to join them. Materassi, whom Roth was visiting in Italy, concludes his Preface to the second edition of *Chiamalo sonno* with a vivid recollection of the white-haired old New York leftist "in the midst of the red mass of demonstrators . . . singing at the top of his voice 'Bella Ciao' at the windows of the Italian Social Movement

Party (a party of the extreme right). There glows the image (renewed, he would say) of a man who is impervious to any classification, and has rediscovered himself and at the same time his brothers."[29]

ALL MEN ARE naturally brothers, proclaims Friedrich von Schiller in *An die Freude* ("Ode to Joy"). Fatherhood is another matter. Herman Roth was anything but a paragon of paternity, and his son extended the family tradition. Hugh continued to fault his father for favoring Jeremy, and for the unnecessary hardships he had endured in Maine. An urban man's romantic gesture in living off the land condemned his sons to a grim childhood of rural poverty. In and out of schools, jobs, and his parents' lives, Hugh never seemed able to please his father. His conversion to Orthodox Judaism exacerbated the tension, as did his marriage to Carole. "To me they were in-laws, and very distant," she recalled. "They neglected their grandchildren—out of sight, out of mind. They paid no attention to birthdays and never sent them gifts."[30] Roth himself concurred about his deficiencies as a family man. He admitted to beating his sons, as his father had beaten him. "I was not a good father," he said in a documentary made in the final months of his life.[31]

Though Roth took pride in his firstborn son's academic accomplishments, he and Jeremy began to grow apart. Occasional postcards from Burundi, Peru, and India testified to the global range of the geologist's professional assignments, and mirrored the increasing distance between father and son. Long after breaking up with Jeremy, a former girlfriend continued to write and call Roth frequently and at voluminous length (one letter filled forty-one pages). But Jeremy himself severed all contact with his father for several years. Joy Williams maintained affectionate relations with her former in-laws, while her former husband distanced himself from his father and most of the rest of the family, including Hugh. Roth noted that the qualities his older son ("barbed, contrary, caviling, ready to shift blame, and impatient—and wrong, often wrong")[32] shared with him were also the qualities creating a rift between them. In the manuscript of his final narrative, he would write that the fictional older son "had a hair-line crack in him."[33]

Yet Roth had forged strong bonds with other men, including Frank Hussey, Lester Winter, and Bill Targ. Now he was attracting filial devotion from several men young enough to be children or even grandchildren. Though fiercely attached to Roth, these "Sons of Henry" were wary or hostile toward one another. Using a somewhat affectionate Yiddish term to soften the harshness, David Bennahum called Mario Materassi "a bit of a schnorrer." Yet Bennahum, the physician who became Roth's trusted friend, conceded that "Henry was a little harsh on Mario." In long, intimate conversations with Roth, Bennahum discussed how he had coped with the death of his own biological father, who, like Roth's, was a Jew born in Europe. Materassi was born in 1935 (a year after the publication of *Call It Sleep*), Bennahum in 1936. Though he recognized the author's flaws ("He was a very rough guy"), Bennahum revered the seasoned octogenarian for his intelligence and courage. And he marveled at the ailing man's determination to revive his writing career: "I will admire it for my whole life."[34]

On January 15, 1988, after Nonino and after *Shifting Landscape*, another son of Henry suddenly came knocking at his door in South's Mobile Villa. A stranger from New York, his name was Larry Fox, and he was at the time a named partner in a spin-off from two major old-line law firms in New York. A specialist in anti-trust and intellectual property litigation, Fox, who had worked in a used-book store in Virginia while studying law at Georgetown University, was an avid book collector who had been chief counsel to the Antiquarian Booksellers' Association of America for eight years when *Shifting Landscape* appeared. He had also represented one of the nation's largest art galleries in a year-long jury trial involving the work of Salvador Dalí. In addition, he represented a national beverage company in a First Amendment case when Native American activists contested its use of the name Crazy Horse for a malt liquor product.

Fox had championed *Call It Sleep* while still in high school and, likening himself to a kind of literary Johnny Appleseed, later planted copies of the novel in the hands of any acquaintance unfamiliar with it. Though he revered Roth, he dared not disturb his seclusion in Maine. When *Shifting Landscape* was published, Fox was excited both because of the contents and because he thought there might at last be a chance to meet the author. He called the publishers, the Jewish Publication Society, to find out whether Roth might be visiting New York to promote *Shifting Landscape*. Beryl Rosenstock, Roth's editor, informed Fox that his call was just a tad late. Only a few days before, Roth had put in an appearance at the Harmonie Club in New York. The news left Fox crestfallen; the Harmonie Club happened to be just a few blocks from his office, and he was distressed to think that he had come so close to meeting the contemporary writer he most admired. Sympathetic, Rosenstock promised that if he wrote Roth a letter, she would ensure that the novelist received it. She did, and Roth was impressed. He invited Fox to visit him in New Mexico.[35]

Fox prepped for his visit the way he might have for a case before the Supreme Court. In order to be worthy of the time Roth allotted him, Fox reviewed all of Roth's short stories and published interviews. He arrived at the door bearing flowers. "It must be my wedding day," said Muriel. "No, it's mine," replied Fox. Roth himself was gracious toward his new suitor, forty-three years younger, and the two men connected immediately. "It was," Fox recalled, "like meeting an incredibly intelligent, self-deprecating yet solicitous grandfather."[36] Impressed by his energy and ambition, Roth described Fox as the son he had always wanted. In a 1991 interview, he characterized their sudden friendship as something that "usually happens over the course of a lifetime."[37]

Though he cherished the novelist's gift of friendship, Fox, like Bennahum and others, was struck by Roth's parsimony, what the lawyer called his "poverty mentality."[38] "If you wanted a glass of whiskey, you had to bring it." Roth's doctor observed that his patient knew nothing about food, and when he once invited Bennahum and his wife out to dinner, "It was the worst restaurant I had ever been to."[39]

Fox, a prosperous attorney born a decade after the Great Depression ended, was bemused by Roth's habit of buying day-old bread (three loaves for a dollar) at Pastian's bakery on Second Street, a favorite Roth pastime later mentioned in a *Vanity Fair* profile by Jonathan Rosen. Pastian's was then the only source of rye in Albuquerque, and Roth went there to stock up on stale bread that he would freeze. He loved dark German *Kommissbrot* toasted beyond recognition, and he included bread in every meal, although in later years he relished the price more than the product and would in fact merely gnaw at it. According to Brian Errett, who was now serving as Roth's gardener as well as computer technician and often ate with him, his elderly employer had had enough of cold comforts in Maine: "He could never have his food hot enough—if it didn't burn your tongue (temperature) he didn't want it. Always complained about that."[40] Prednisone, the corticosteroid medication that Roth took orally to treat his arthritis, caused trouble with his gums, making him less sensitive to heat.

During his initial visit, Fox observed none of the gruffness that others found in Roth. Nor was his host as abstemious with him as he was with other guests. He served Fox whiskey, though concerned about impairing his ability to drive. Fox took Roth to tour a local flea market and to shop at Home Depot. They laughed throughout their time together. When Fox joked about Roth's address on New York Avenue, Roth noted that the next block over was Manhattan Street and that it was a dead end. "He was the most authentic person I have ever met," said Fox. Fox had assembled an extensive collection of first editions, manuscripts, and other materials on nineteenth- and twentieth-century authors, including Poe, Melville, Hawthorne, Kafka, and Joyce, but he prized his Rothiana more than any other material. He acquired Roth as a cherished friend, displacing other sons of Henry, biological and metaphorical. He visited Roth often and spoke to the author by phone at least once a week for the rest of Roth's life.

Though literature was what drew Fox to Albuquerque, Roth also called on him for advice about his will. But, wary of creating any confusion between friendship and professional service, Fox referred him to a colleague. Wills were not one of Fox's specialties anyway, though McDermott, Will & Emery, where he was now a partner, maintained the largest estate planning practice in the United States. Steve Chiles, a partner in the firm, took over the responsibility for revising Roth's will. Roth asked Chiles to appoint Fox his literary executor.[41] Through honored by the request, Fox, convinced there were others more qualified, hesitated. When Roth insisted, he accepted.

Rudolfo Anaya, a year younger than Materassi, never became close enough to Roth to count as one of the sons of Henry, but he was emphatically an admirer. Though he recognized that "Henry could be a tough old bastard," Anaya added that "men like Henry are giants who really affect our lives, crawl under our skins. I was lucky to have shared time with him, to share ideas." *Bless Me, Ultima* (1972), the story of seven-year-old Antonio Márez y Luna's coming of age in New Mexico in 1943, is Anaya's best known work. It echoes David Schearl's experiences in New York forty years before, even down to the parallel of an apocalyptic flash, although instead of a sudden, shocking glow from the live rail of a New York streetcar, here it is an atomic explosion at White Sands, New Mexico. Anaya occupies roughly the same position in Chicano literature as Roth does in American Jewish literature. And both men lived in Albuquerque during the last three decades of the twentieth century. "What brought us together, aside from both being writers," Anaya recalled, "was our particular ethnic identity: he Jewish, me Chicano."

Anaya and his wife traded visits with the Roths and encountered them at occasional parties around town. While Anaya remained deeply anchored in the Latino culture of the American Southwest, Roth had rejected his Jewish legacy for the lure of Marxist universalism. "I felt he wished he had not given up his roots for the socialist world ideal," Anaya recalled. "Henry and I were drawn to each other, usually winding up sitting together and talking literature, and always returning to the same theme, his disappointment and how it contrasted with my staying in my place, within my culture." Anaya was unmoved by Roth's later fiction, but he remained in awe of *Call It Sleep*. "Perhaps that's why I loved Henry," he explained. "We weren't really that far apart. In age, yes, but he gave us the anima of his New York, working-class Jewish culture of the time, as I try to give something of my time and place."[42]

On January 1, 1988, Anaya invited Roth to contribute to an anthology that he was editing, *The Best Stories of New Mexico*. By 1988, Roth had been living in New Mexico for twenty years, sixteen years longer than his interlude on the Lower East Side and six years longer than his stay in Harlem. But it was only his postal address that defined Roth as a New Mexican writer. He spent his days in the mobile home on Albuquerque's New York Avenue struggling to put into words a young Jew's experiences in Manhattan seventy years before. Roth declined to contribute to *The Best Stories of New Mexico*, as he declined numerous other requests—to talk to a class at Harvard, to speak at the 92nd Street Y, to write blurbs for books, to appear at conferences. (He wrote only one blurb, for Thane Rosenbaum's short story collection *Elijah Visible*, in his entire life; he commented: "Anyone concerned with the decay of Diaspora Judaism should read these stories"). Roth tried to answer, sometimes at considerable length, most of the fan mail he continued to receive, from awestruck high school students as well as seasoned professional scholars. For terser responses, he wrote back on items from his collection of picture postcards. One correspondent sent Roth a handful of wine labels, with a request that he autograph them.

At least one fan of *Call It Sleep* remained immune to the charms of its author. Sam Girgus, a professor of American Studies at the University of New Mexico and later Vanderbilt University, often presented copies of the novel to his graduating students as parting gifts. But he was deeply disappointed by its creator in person. Particularly distressing to him was Roth's "lack of engagement with ideas." Girgus maintained: "I don't think that there was a memorable thing that he said that had any intellectual content." During numerous social encounters, Girgus found Roth to be a monologist. "You couldn't really argue with him."[43]

In 1979, Irving Howe lectured at the University of New Mexico, and Girgus held a reception at his house to honor the visiting intellectual celebrity. He invited the Roths, as well as many other members of Albuquerque's small literary community. Anyone familiar with the history of *Call It Sleep* must have relished the prospect of an encounter between famous novelist and famous critic, the one whose *New York Times* review had been responsible for the novelist's fame. According to Girgus, however, the meeting was remarkably unremarkable. Roth and Howe nodded to each other from across the room and spent the evening talking to others. Howe would later tell Robert Weil that he was disappointed in *Mercy of a Rude Stream*, because it was not *Call It Sleep*.[44]

In October 1989, Brian Errett and Felicia Steele helped Henry and Muriel celebrate their fiftieth wedding anniversary by driving them out to the Sandia Mountains for a picnic. "That's what she wanted to do," claimed Roth, "and she had a wonderful time."[45] "Henry wanted a fire," Steele recalled, "and Brian couldn't get one going, woodsman that he was, so Henry wanted to use Muriel's oxygen tank to 'fan the flames.' She looked on with frustration, but such love. And thank god we convinced the two fools not to do it."[46]

Much had changed since Yaddo, but Roth was more attached to his wife than ever. To spare her any pain, he made plans to have his new work published five years after his death—sufficient time for Muriel to have died as well or to be able to absorb whatever shocks the book might cause. Roth created one exception to this strategy: he decided to allow Mario Materassi to publish the opening section of the new book exclusively in Italian, a language Muriel could not read. In 1990, his Milanese publisher Garzanti brought out *Alla mercé di una brutale corrente*, a 114-page volume translated by Materassi. Four years before the American public, Italian readers were offered a peek at what would become *Mercy of a Rude Stream*.

Observers often felt that Henry was all the society that Muriel needed. Yet she kept in touch by telephone with a circle of friends and musical collaborators. Muriel observed an etiquette all her own. When she sensed that a conversation had run its course, instead of saying good-bye, she would simply hang up.[47] It was harder to leave life so abruptly. By the end of 1989, Muriel's health was failing, but she bitterly resisted the realization that *Free Flight*, the piece for solo marimba that she was composing for percussionist Chris Schultis, would have to be her musical farewell. "So much left to learn, so much still to do, and now no time left to do it," she protested to Scott Wilkinson on December 17, as she struggled to complete the work.[48] In early January of the new decade, Muriel was taken by ambulance to St. Joseph's Hospital, diagnosed with pneumonia. After two weeks, she was released—prematurely, Bennahum contended,[49] because of the economies of managed care. Because of his own infirmities, Roth depended on a tricycle walker to get about and a housekeeper—Stella Romero, who lived nearby, in the same trailer court—to get by, and he was in no position to care for a convalescent. So Muriel was transferred to the Horizon Nursing Home. She survived another two weeks, emaciated and incontinent. On February 9 at 8:30 a.m., Roth, whose telephone blocked out calls that came through after midnight, heard a ring and picked up the receiver. It was the head nurse at Horizon. "We've been trying to get you since five this morning," she said, according to the account Roth wrote a few years later. "I'm sorry to tell you, Mr. Roth, your wife passed away at about 4:30 a.m. She passed away very peacefully."[50] It was the day after her husband's eighty-fourth birthday.

The cause of death was listed as congestive heart failure. A childhood bout with scarlet fever was said to have weakened Muriel's heart, but if so, that heart had been stout enough to keep beating seven more decades. During more than fifty years of marriage, Roth had become utterly dependent on Muriel, even for preparing his taxes, and, certain that his death would precede hers, he could not imagine surviving his beloved. "The loss of the dearest and most precious person in my life, the one who made mine possible, the one who regenerated mine,"[51] was a blow from which he could not—and did not want to—recover. "She was the very soul of decency, kindness, and sociability," said Roth.[52]

Chris Schultis had given Muriel an audiotape of *Free Flight* to listen to in the hospital. He performed the piece publicly for the first time on February 18 at a concert of the New Mexico Women Composers Guild at Central United Methodist Church in Albuquerque. The premiere was dedicated to the composer's memory. No formal funeral service marked Muriel's passing. In compliance with her wishes, her body was donated to the medical school of the University of New Mexico. What could not be used for science was cremated and kept by Roth in a cardboard box in a closet. He sold the Baldwin piano and used the proceeds to help fund the Muriel Roth Memorial

Music Scholarship for seniors and graduate students at UNM and a music prize in Muriel's name at Hebrew University in Jerusalem. Her music manuscripts were donated to the UNM library.

Felicia Steele, who was living near the UNM campus, helped Roth with his own manuscript in the afternoons and in mornings on weekends. In the summer of 1992, after he had moved out of his trailer court, she moved in with Roth as a full-time assistant. Though he continued to work daily, compulsively, the literary project often seemed pointless and impossible without Muriel. "*Oh, difficile est longum subito amorem deponere!*" he quoted Virgil—how painful is the sudden loss of a longtime companion.[53] Depression, an occasional tenant throughout Roth's life, now lodged tenaciously and would not be evicted. "I thought everything I'd done in my life a vast mistake," he later told Jonathan Rosen. The former sharpshooter of DeWitt Clinton High School still possessed a rifle and thought about pulling the trigger. "I own a gun and would have used it had it been higher-caliber," he confessed. "This one's only .25. Had it been a .38 I'm sure it would have been big enough to blow my brains out."[54]

Roth spent six months of 1991 in Charter Hospital under treatment for suicidal depression. One of his medications, Wellbutrin, made his balance shaky, causing him to fall and crack several vertebrae. He was also shaken by the realization that childhood sexual trauma was at the root of much depression, even in the geriatric ward where he was being treated. Many of his fellow patients were suffering the long-term effects of abuse and incest.[55] Roth had of course himself been accosted by a stranger he met in Mt. Morris Park and tormented throughout his childhood by his own father. Perhaps what, drawing on his store of Latin, he was fond of calling *tedium vitae* was not simply generic despondency, a depletion of *élan vital*, but rather a lingering consequence of the psychological damage inflicted on him seven decades earlier.

Released from the hospital, Roth reconciled himself to leaving the mobile home he had shared with Muriel. With help from Steele and others, he sold the trailer and, in late 1991, moved into Las Colinas, an assisted living facility for elderly residents located in Albuquerque's

North Valley. The two-room unit into which Roth tried to cram the couple's old furniture reminded one visitor of a warehouse.

Almost immediately, Roth realized that consigning himself to Las Colinas was a mistake—"an altogether lonesome and barren experience." He followed news of the aborted Kremlin coup to overthrow Mikhail Gorbachev and end the Soviet movement toward democracy, and he mourned his own loss of freedom. Roth was not yet—or ever—ready to relinquish the illusion of independence, and he saw nothing in common with the ancients occupying the other 127 units in Las Colinas. "I found not the least interest or diversion in the interests and diversions of my fellow residents," he wrote.[56] Steele came over daily to help him with the enormous task of revising and editing the manuscripts, but he longed to be out again on his own.

The next step after assisted living is usually a nursing home, a hospital, or a cemetery. However, after eleven months at Las Colinas, Roth managed to engineer an escape. A woman who worked at the facility helped him scout out properties and obtain a mortgage for $84,498. In December 1991 Roth bought a ramshackle white stucco house, complete with red tile roof and cupola, located several blocks from the Rio Grande. Roth was particularly impressed by the hand-carved front door. At 300 Hendrix Road NW, Roth's new home stood secluded behind a cinder-block wall on a dead-end street half a block from a commercial thoroughfare.

According to Felicia Steele, Roth was a bit smitten with the woman who had helped him find the house. But, though he expected her to stay with him, she soon left the state. Instead, Steele and Brian Errett took up residence at Hendrix Road, and with their support Roth again took up his final project. In that house, designed in the 1930s as a funeral parlor, the former Latin teacher struggled to complete a fictional sequence, *Mercy of a Rude Stream*, whose acronym, MORS, means death. After the death of his beloved wife, Roth's only goal was to confront the end having completed his last great literary task. The aging author had the Cumaean Sibyl's pronouncement, "*Apothanein Thelo* (I wish to die)," inscribed and hung in his study. Only after the work was done could the wish be granted.

Chapter 16

STRONG WILL AND
LAST TESTAMENT

One of my main virtues is tenaciousness;
I will not give up a problem.
—HENRY ROTH[1]

AFTER AVON relinquished the rights to *Call It Sleep*, Roslyn Targ
resold the novel to Farrar, Straus & Giroux (FSG), which reissued it in both hardcover and trade paperback in 1991 under its
Noonday Press imprint. The new publisher chose the famous tenement photo from the Avon edition for a revised cover. But the Afterword by Walter Allen was dropped and substituted was an essay by
Alfred Kazin that began: "*Call It Sleep* is the most profound novel of
Jewish life that I have ever read by an American."[2]

In the summer of 1991, Bill Daleski, Roth's friend at the Hebrew
University in Jerusalem, sent him a copy of another essay, "Between
Mother Tongue and Native Language," by a younger academic
named Hana Wirth-Nesher who was raised in the United States but
had moved to Israel. The work, which examines the complex play of
languages within *Call It Sleep*, impressed Roth enough to write its

author that: "The analysis is not only an [sic] superb piece of work, but lives its own life as a moving piece of prose."[3] The new edition of *Call It Sleep* was about to go to press, but Roth halted production, insisting that Wirth-Nesher's essay be used instead of Kazin's as the Introduction. However, FSG had already paid Kazin and was contractually obligated to publish his piece. So the Noonday paperback included two essays: Kazin's as Introduction and Wirth-Nesher's as Afterword.

Roth urged Wirth-Nesher to visit him, stressing she should do so without delay since his age and infirmity might before long make it impossible. She had teaching responsibilities at Tel-Aviv University, but as soon as the academic term ended, in February 1992, she flew to Albuquerque and spent two memorable days with Roth. Wirth-Nesher told him she had signed a contract with Cambridge University Press to edit a collection of essays on *Call It Sleep*, part of a series called *New Essays on the American Novel*. Informed that other authors covered in the series included Melville, Hemingway, James, and Faulkner, Roth replied: "Oy, the company I keep!"[4] But he was particularly impressed by Wirth-Nesher, saying that he felt a special bond between the two of them. Mario Materassi was his spiritual son, he said, and he now had a spiritual daughter. When it came time for Steele to drive Wirth-Nesher back to the airport, Roth came along. As a parting gesture, he handed his visitor a copy of the manuscript of Volume 1 of *Mercy of a Rude Stream*. (She would later discover that, by written order of the author, its posthumous translation into Hebrew required her approval.)

William Targ had been excited by early drafts of Roth's new work, and he urged his friend to keep to the task. "The trouble with the publishing business," Targ once quipped, "is that too many people who have half a mind to write a book do so."[5] In Roth, the veteran publisher animated an author whose full, keen mind and failing body became intent on creating a final, redemptive book. "I was simmering, simmering, simmering. Emerson brought me to a boil,"[6] said Walt Whitman, acknowledging the older poet's decisive role in germinating *Leaves of Grass*. After decades of aimless brooding, Targ got Roth boiling, though Roth preferred a chemical metaphor. He told an interviewer in 1983: "There's such a thing as a supersaturated solution which needs only one crystal to cause the whole to crystallize. The crystal was Bill Targ, who got me started."[7]

His rheumatoid arthritis and other physical ailments kept Roth dependent on a steady stream of housekeepers, caregivers, nurses, and aides in the house on Hendrix Road. But the affliction that most ruled Roth during his late eighties was diagnosed by Juvenal as *cacoethes scribendi*; an insatiable urge to fill his computer screen with more and more words was the last infirmity of a restless mind. Each sentence meant exquisite torture to gnarled fingers and tormented soul. But as Roth accumulated dozens, hundreds, thousands of pages, he came closer to release.

Bill Targ, who was now eighty-five, had retired from an active role at Putnam in 1978 and, his own health failing, could not help to put Roth's new work into print. But Roslyn Targ, as Roth's literary agent, began sounding out other New York editors. Though it would have been logical for FSG to publish Roth's second novel as well as his first, an editor rejected the first volume of the manuscript that Roslyn Targ sent them, explaining: "This is not like *Call It Sleep*."[8]

A publisher who insisted that all acquisitions be like *Call It Sleep* could count on a very slim catalogue. But in November 1992, Robert Weil, a senior editor at St. Martin's Press who was working with Targ on another project, jumped at the chance to publish a new Roth manuscript. Ever since joining St. Martin's in 1988, he had been quizzing Targ regularly about Roth's work-in-progress and offering to fly down to Albuquerque to look at it. She kept putting him off, noting that Farrar, Straus & Giroux had first dibs on the book. When FSG turned it down, Weil saw his chance. The 400 or so pages of manuscript that he was shown would require substantial editing, but Weil relished the challenge of reorganizing the material and whipping it into shape. However, he had to fight stubborn opposition from his colleagues at St. Martin's, who were skeptical about the work's literary merits and commercial prospects. One senior editor even begged

Weil to reject the manuscript in order not to tarnish Roth's distinguished literary reputation.

But Weil persisted and became so adamant that Thomas McCormack, the firm's chairman and editorial director, finally relented. Impressed by Weil's passionate advocacy, McCormack gave him $10,000 to purchase the manuscript of *Mercy of a Rude Stream*. In Catholic iconography, the cloak of St. Martin, the fourth-century bishop of Tours, is a symbol of heroic charity, and eleemosynary editing is exactly what acquisition of Roth's shapeless manuscript must have seemed like to the publishing board of St. Martin's. In 1992, $10,000 was equivalent to not much more than the mingy $2,500 that Avon had given Peter Mayer to reissue *Call It Sleep* in 1964. But Targ took a deep sigh on the phone and accepted the offer. In January 1993, Weil flew down to Albuquerque to meet Henry Roth.

Indian summer is what Americans call autumnal brilliance before the winter's desolation. The equivalent British term might serve best to describe an octogenarian author's final burst of creativity—St. Martin's summer. Weil, whose German-born father was seven months older than Roth, hit it off with Roth immediately and became another of the sons of Henry, a devoted admirer and friend. "He was the greatest author I ever worked with,"[9] Weil said; he also found Roth to be among the most congenial. "We never had a disagreement about editorial matters. We got along so well. We both loved words; we both loved vocabulary. There were very few words he didn't know!"[10]

In 1935, when Roth signed a contract with Maxwell Perkins, Perkins had become the most famous book editor in America in part because of his success at transforming Thomas Wolfe's fervid verbal clutter into *Look Homeward, Angel*. Because he never received a final manuscript from Roth, Perkins never had a chance to do for him what he had done for Wolfe. Forty-six years after Perkins's death, Robert Weil took on an editorial task as daunting as anything the Scribners magician confronted. When he agreed to edit a new book by Roth, Weil had seen only Volume 1. He had no idea that he would soon be wrestling with more than 5,000 pages of unruly text.

In Albuquerque, Weil insisted that the book, which he had been handed as one undifferentiated block of print, needed chapters and sections. Roth concurred. He also accepted Weil's suggestion that two separate typefaces be used to distinguish the voice of the elderly author in the present tense from the retrospective narrative that is the bulk of the book. Roth did request that no italic type be used since it was too hard to read. In addition, Weil persuaded Roth to eliminate extended observations on personal matters, such as his medications, that would be of little interest to most readers.

"I also said that certain characters I find are a little too much," Weil recalled, "and the one I particularly had trouble with is a character named Jane. The sections concerning her were kind of obsessive; they never went anywhere. It reflected his obsessions of the moment. He agreed immediately, so she was cut from the book."[11] A distraught woman who is forever contacting the narrator even after breaking with his son, Jane occupies hundreds of pages in the original manuscript; her elimination tightened up the narrative considerably.

Also discarded was a man who had assumed he would be the work's virtual co-author. Materassi had accepted Roth's request to help him turn the meandering "continuum" into publishable form. Roth's *figlio* had been successful in assembling and constructing *Shifting Landscape*, and he had already translated the opening section of *Mercy of a Rude Stream* into Italian. So he was under no illusion about how much more difficult it would be to turn the entire output into a coherent series of novels. It was more than a matter of a little typing and proofreading. The full manuscript—most of which Weil had not yet seen and some of which Roth was still writing—was a discordant mass that caused Roth himself to compare it to the quirky work of the composer Charles Ives: "Both sought to compose a vast pastiche, incorporating whatever they chose, guided only by an elemental sense of the rightness of the whole."[12] To make the work accessible, Materassi would need to perform extensive literary surgery over the course of several years. He saw it as a labor of love for an author he adored as if he were his father, but the professor also expected fair compensation. In return for his services on *Mercy of a Rude Stream*, Materassi asked for $40,000–$50,000—a sum of money that would not be unreasonable compensation for five years of editorial work—plus a decent percentage of the royalties.

Roth was aghast, and felt that this demand, even from Materassi, was going too far. The old fear of being exploited that surfaced during his association with Harold Ribalow reasserted itself. His mistrust intensified when Materassi brought in a lawyer and presented Roth with a lengthy document stipulating the rights and responsibilities of each party in the project. Fox met with Materassi and pleaded with him not to let business overshadow art, and he urged Roth not to allow this disagreement to poison his friendship with Materassi. But pushed into a corner, Roth had become intractable, and he refused to work with Materassi any more under any conditions. In January 1993, not long after Weil flew back to New York from Albuquerque, Fox sent a formal letter to Materassi notifying him that Henry Roth was no longer interested in committing to an editing contract with him. Chiles revised Roth's will so that Materassi would no longer be his literary executor or heir to any part of his estate.[13]

The blow hurt and baffled Materassi. Seeking an explanation, he wrote to his old friend. In a letter dated February 2, 1993, Materassi tried to justify the financial terms on which he had suggested they work together. He noted the immensity of the task, and pointed out that if he had been intent on manipulating Roth for personal profit he would not have talked him out of sharing a third of the royalties of *Shifting Landscape*, asking for only 10 percent instead.[14] Roth was stubborn and silent. Another letter from Materassi accused Roth of betraying their friendship and proclaimed in the voice of injured innocence his conviction that thirty years of loyalty and affection had earned him the right to some sort of explanation.[15] When Roth still did not respond, Materassi flew to Albuquerque in hopes of patching up their differences and salvaging the friendship. Hugh Roth was visiting at the time, and he recalled that his father had nothing to say to his Italian caller and refused to let him past the door. Materassi returned to Europe wounded and embittered, a favored son of Henry banished from the fold.

During an earlier visit, Materassi had treated Felicia Jean Steele,

Roth's young live-in assistant, curtly, as a servant. But Steele, now an undergraduate at the University of New Mexico, was playing a vital role in the production of Roth's new book. She also handled some of his voluminous correspondence. While Roth struggled to add new sentences to his vast autobiographical cycle, Steele retyped early pages and, following suggestions from both Roth and Weil, helped to rearrange them. When pounding on the computer keyboard simply became too agonizing for Roth, Steele took dictation.

Drawing on a powerful eidetic memory, the author summoned up in precise detail a city that he had not lived in for fifty years. Weil, who called Roth "the best chronicler of New York in this century,"[16] was astonished at the accuracy of a description of a statue in Columbus Circle that he, living and working in Manhattan, walked past almost every day but that Roth had not seen in decades. Roth sprinkled his text with colorful phrases appropriate to immigrant Jewish characters from his faded native language, Yiddish, but Weil was apprehensive that the exotic vocabulary might baffle readers. He proposed a Yiddish glossary for the back of the book, and Steele set about compiling a list of about 150 terms and idioms with their English translations. Steele's glossary ranged from the relatively obvious *blintzes* ("rolled up pancake with filling"), *goy* ("gentile"), and *shlemiel* ("an ill-fated person; a bungler") to such esoterica as *d'rirstikh vie a klutz* ("you move like a log"), *shrotchkee* ("diarrhea"), and *verfollen zoll er vie e likt* ("may he rot where he lies").[17]

Though energized by the prospect of returning to print, Roth remained lonely, frail, and anguished. His urge to write competed with the longing to expire. "I've lived too long," he told Leonard Michaels, who found the author looking "as if he were lingering in someone's house at the end of a party."[18] (During the early 1990s, Michaels began conducting research into Roth's life. Like Roth, Michaels grew up on the Lower East Side; but depressed by his subject and convinced that, finally, he was not a biographer, he eventually abandoned the project.) Roth's wispy hair was white, his skin badly discolored, his eyesight dependent upon dense bifocal lenses. His left foot, minus an amputated toe, had swollen to almost twice its normal size. The arthritis medication he was taking was causing problems with his adrenal glands. Now nearly eighty-eight, he was able to get through the day and progress with his epic project only with the help of numerous pills, potions, and assistants. A red plastic whistle hung around his neck enabled him to summon help. "He really looked ghastly," recalled Dr. Noah Harris, who took over as Roth's primary physician. "But he perked up over the next few months, especially as the royalty checks came in."[19]

After graduating with honors in English from the University of New Mexico in 1993, Steele left the house in June. She would soon be attending graduate school at the University of Texas at Austin; but, though reluctant to abandon Roth, she felt an urgent need to extricate herself from her relationship with Brian Errett, and so flew off to Europe. Roth had come to Eda Lou Walton as an uncouth young Jewish immigrant. Steele was an unsophisticated high school student who had never even heard of *Call It Sleep* when she went to work for its author. "There's more than a little bit of symmetry between his relationship with Eda Lou and mine with him (apart from the lack of sexual connection)," she observed later. "He was my mentor, a surrogate father before and after my own father's death, the greatest teacher I ever had. But I had to go on."[20] The house on Hendrix Road began to undergo a changing of the guard.

Avery Cheser provided some companionship for Roth after Steele's departure. A part-time student at the University of New Mexico, he came by to assist with the computer and enjoyed long conversations with Roth about philosophy, mathematics, and religion. "I watched him go from being vibrant to being immobile," Cheser recalled.[21] After Roth's longtime housekeeper Stella Romero got married, her sister, Helen Mitchener, replaced her in the household. For a while, until she took over as principal caretaker, Mitchener worked a night shift while a woman named Margaret Trujillo handled days. Trujillo's son, Leroy, helped out on weekends. Mitchener recalled what a pitiful figure Roth presented when she and Trujillo started work: "I didn't think he was going to last a week." However, the two women helped revive the shriveled man whom Mitchener called "a little genius." "He was very depressed," Mitchener noted, but she and Trujillo tried to reduce his dependency on a basketful of medications. Mitchener cut and groomed Roth's shoulder-length, matted hair. "By the time he died," she claimed, "he looked twenty-five years younger."

Roth tried to get by on a diet of bread and jelly, with a portion of oatmeal for dinner. "He was very, very cheap," Mitchener said, remembering how he instructed her to economize on groceries. But Mitchener bought what she thought Roth needed nutritionally and cooked balanced meals for him. She admired the old author's fortitude —"He never gave up." Yet she was also proud of her role in resuscitating a prodigy: "We brought that man back to life."[22]

A PUBLIC REMINDER that the man who published *Call It Sleep* in 1934 was still alive and writing surfaced in January 1994, when copies of Volume 1 of *Mercy of a Rude Stream* went on sale. (Roth had discarded two other working titles—*Portrait of the Artist as an Old Fiasco* and *Advanced English for Foreigners*.) The 290-page book was entitled *A Star Shines Over Mt. Morris Park*. An epigraph from Shakespeare's *Henry VIII* (III, ii, 363–64)—a self-pitying soliloquy in which Cardinal Wolsey describes himself as left "Weary and old with service, to the mercy / Of a rude stream that must for ever hide me"—announces the theme: senescence. This would be just the first installment of *Mercy of a Rude Stream*. Though Materassi had hoped to have a hand in the new novel, the dedication, to newcomer Larry Fox, reads: "So here's a hand my trusty friend." Roth was no longer inclined to sing *Auld Lang Syne* in Italian.

The book that broke the longest writer's block in American literary history takes up where *Call It Sleep* left off. It is August 1914, twelve months after the first novel ends, and the immigrant protagonist, an eight-year-old named Ira Stigman (stained, suggests Roth, with a psychic stigma), is on the brink of puberty, the world on the verge of World War I. A very slightly older version of David Schearl, Stigman—who in earlier manuscripts is called Michael Sorg and then Kestril—becomes a man who bears the stigma of Henry Roth's own overwhelming woe. Distinctions between autobiography and fiction are confounded by the reproduction of an actual Roth family photograph, from the second decade of the century, on the endpapers. Roth and his sister Rose are in the picture, and the man in his World War I army uniform is Uncle Morris. At Weil's suggestion, the book has a two-page genealogy at the front, which is remarkably similar to the actual Roth and Farb family trees (see front matter p. xii). Some but not all of the names are changed. Roth's cousins Sylvia and Pauline become Stella and Pola, respectively, but Stigman's parents, like Roth's, are named Leah and Chaim. (Pola, abruptly, without explanation, becomes Hannah in the second volume and remains Hannah for the rest of the series.) Mr. Danroe, Roth's pederastic high school Spanish teacher, is renamed Mr. Lennard, though the proofreaders at St. Martin's Press failed to catch one instance in which the original name, Danroe, made it into print.[23] Events in the novel bear a striking resemblance to events in Roth's life.

When the parents of Ira Stigman's mother arrive in New York from Galicia, Ira, Chaim, and Leah Stigman move from the Lower East Side to live near the newcomers in a Jewish section of Harlem. However, because Leah is unhappy with their rear apartment, the Stigmans soon move again, to a cold-water flat in a largely Irish area of Harlem. Ira is tormented by local anti-Semitic bullies, but when he visits his old neighborhood on the Lower East Side the boy realizes that he no longer belongs there either. He also feels estranged from his newly arrived relatives, who speak Yiddish and do not adapt to American ways.

Rambling and anecdotal, *A Star Shines Over Mt. Morris Park* introduces members of Ira's extended family, including its patriarch, his grandfather, Ben Zion Farb. After being drafted into the army, Uncle Moe returns as a local hero from combat in Europe. Louie, the socialist postman who, though Ira calls him "Uncle," is really his father's nephew, impresses the boy as "a real American, a Yankee."[24] But Uncle Louie does not impress Leah Stigman enough to reciprocate his romantic attentions while her husband is away in St. Louis looking for a job. Ira's truculent father, Chaim, avoids the war by finding brief employment in what is classified as essential work, as a streetcar conductor, before taking a position as a waiter. As ineffectual a provider as he is a father, Chaim Stigman, is—like Albert Schearl and Herman (Chaim) Roth—a moody, menacing figure to his young son, who finds he must make his way in an ominous world alone.

Because of their move out of a Jewish neighborhood and because of the family's limited means, Ira does not attend Hebrew school. Although he does, at thirteen, undergo bar mitzvah, the ritual initiation into the community of Jewish men, Ira feels no meaningful connection to it. He is convinced that Jewishness is an oppressive category he can and must escape. In the eighth grade, when he gets a job as a stockboy at Park & Tilford, gourmet grocers, he feels liberated by exposure to non-kosher foods. Delivering expensive baskets to wealthy customers, Ira is also initiated into the intricacies of American social stratification.

A Star Shines Over Mt. Morris Park follows Ira into the early 1920s, but it alternates between the experiences of its young protagonist and miscellaneous commentary, in a different and more modern typeface, by a weary, older Ira. Looking back on his life, the octogenarian Ira Stigman, who, like Roth himself, suffers from rheumatoid arthritis and lives in Albuquerque, addresses his computer directly, personifying it and naming it "Ecclesias." It is a pioneering instance of an author's incorporating the new electronic technology into the fabric of his fiction. However, except for the metafictional interpolations in which Stigman the author talks to Ecclesias about the book he is writing, as well as about history, literature, and current events, the novel stylistically might have been written during the period it covers. It is a time capsule from early in the twentieth century devised and unveiled at its end. In deliberate contrast to the lyrical effusion of *Call It Sleep*, which Roth wanted to put behind him once and for all, *A Star Shines Over Mt. Morris Park* is written in serviceable, naturalistic prose. It is as if James Joyce has been dislodged by James T. Farrell. The book is of compelling interest to any reader curious about Roth's life and New York City during and after World War I. Yet, before subsequent volumes appeared, it seemed to be shapeless, a mere recitation of incidents from long ago.

Roth was in no condition to travel to New York to celebrate the birth of his book, but some of New York came to New Mexico for the purpose. On February 6, two days before his eighty-eighth birthday, an audience of more than 150 assembled in the sanctuary of Congregation Albert, one of Albuquerque's three synagogues, to honor the aging author of a new novel. Roth sat beaming in his wheelchair as Fox, Targ, Weil, and others praised him in public. Two actors read from his novel, and the Sage String Quartet performed. Roth himself spoke briefly, insisting again that he felt distanced from "that arrogant young whippersnapper" who wrote *Call It Sleep* sixty years earlier. Describing this new work as the product of hard-won maturity, of learning at last to be a mensch, "this old codger of eighty-eight" as he called himself, suggested that *Mercy of a Rude Stream* was finally bringing its troubled author redemption and the right to be at rest: "I've earned, I hope, an eternal truce with aches and itches, with medications and their side effects, a truce with the agonizing choices the thoughtful individual has to make in an era of social turbulence and political change when humanity seems on the road to chaos and perhaps extinction."[25] When the book editor of the *Albuquerque Journal* tried to draw Roth out on his future plans for remaining volumes, the response was a tease. "Volume two is scandalous," warned the author. "How? You'll have to read it."[26]

A Star Shines Over Mt. Morris Park was a Book-of-the-Month-Club alternate and a selection of the Quality Paperback Club. *Library Journal* announced that Roth's first novel in sixty years was "proof that his earlier effort was no fluke," and Donna Seaman in *Booklist* described it as "fiction of exquisite specificity, lyricism, and humor." It was, for the *Chicago Sun-Times*, "a marvelously poetic chronicle," and, for Jonathan Rosen, writing in *Vanity Fair*, "the literary comeback of the century." Leonard Michaels, who despaired of his intention to write Roth's biography, remarked that the arrival of a new Roth novel was as astounding as would be news that the reclusive J. D. Salinger was preparing a sequel to *A Catcher in the Rye*.[27]

In a private letter greeting Roth as "*estimado maestro*," Rudolfo Anaya announced: "I have just finished reading *Mercy of a Rude Stream* and want to write to congratulate you. It is an engrossing masterpiece! You have not only written a chronicle of your life (through Ira's life, of course) but a history of your community. In many ways, a history of what this country is about."[28] Later, after Roth's death, the Chicano author would confess that "I read the new novel he had worked on for so long, but I wasn't moved."[29]

Despite a few raves, Roth's startling return was an embarrassment to many of the critics who reviewed his novel when it appeared in 1994. As in Samuel Johnson's infamous comparison between a woman's preaching and a dog's standing on its hind legs, they were astonished not by how well the book was written but that it got to be written at all. "If prizes for writers came in the same categories as those for athletes," exclaimed Lee Lescaze in the *Wall Street Journal*, "Henry Roth would win Comeback Novelist of the Year hands down. Maybe of the century."[30] Some belligerent reviewers seem forever eager to draw blood out of ink, but most approached Roth with reverence for *Call It Sleep*. It was painful for many to have to report that the old man had lost his touch.

The authorial commentary in the new work was faulted as superfluous and tendentious. In *The New York Review of Books*, Robert Towers called the Ecclesias passages "slackly written, self-obsessed, and coy."[31] While marveling over Roth's unexpected, belated return to book-length fiction, many reviewers were disappointed by what seemed an artistic chasm between *Call It Sleep* and *A Star Shines Over Mt. Morris Park*. Noting that Ira Stigman lacked "the depth and dynamism of a fully realized fictional character," Robert Alter in *The New York Times Book Review* found an even more fundamental deficiency: "What the book lacks is novelistic tension."[32] Written in a straightforward style that now eschewed Joycean flourishes, the new work appeared episodic and inconclusive. It was, wrote Paul Gray in *Time* magazine, "a pretty grim, no-frills narrative," one that "displays documentary rather than novelistic ambitions." Before the publication of the remainder of *Mercy of a Rude Stream*, it was difficult to discern the shape and the achievement in this first installment of Roth's autobiographical cycle. The competing narrative voices, the tension between the perspectives of Ira Stigman young and old, had not yet become pronounced. Dislocation of identity across time would make the entire sequence into an elaborate psychomachia, an arena in which Roth worked out his private struggles with himself. "For now," concluded Gray, "the book may strike all too many expectant Roth fans as an invitation to fall asleep."[33]

Roth did not have the luxury to pause over praise or reproach. Time was running out on his torturous effort to complete his great work. A bout with pneumonia brought a fresh reminder of mortality. "I'm dying," he announced, when a journalist called in hopes of flying down from New York to interview him. "If you want to talk to me, you'd better come quick. It's my time."[34] Tapping out the string of words that would finally bring redemption was more painful and more urgent than ever.

Yet, on May 14, Roth took a break from his writing regimen to attend graduation ceremonies at the University of New Mexico. The institution had decided to award the novelist, an undistinguished undergraduate at City College many years before, an honorary Doctor of Letters degree. The tribute was initiated by Digby Wolfe, a recent addition to UNM's Department of Theater, who was elated to discover that he now lived in the same town as the author of *Call It Sleep*. However, to obtain approval for the honorary degree, Wolfe had to overcome faculty objections that, though he had been living in New Mexico for more than twenty-five years, Roth was not a local writer.

The convocation was held outdoors, on the campus. Planks were laid across the grass to make it easier to push Roth's wheelchair up to the dais. The speaker who preceded him was a Latina who antagonized much of the largely non-Hispanic audience with proclamations of ethnic pride. "*Mi casa no es su casa!*" she announced, in a taunt not likely to bring down the house. But the first, self-deprecating words out of Roth's mouth immediately won over the crowd. "What I really need at this moment isn't a doctorate," he declared. "It's a commode."[35] In his unpretentious acceptance speech, Dr. Roth

referred to himself as "a tottering, doddering old fiasco," but, offering "your honored guest, who took sixty years before he got himself
together sufficiently to complete a second novel which a publisher
would see fit to publish," as an example of adversity overcome, he
exhorted his student audience not to abandon hope. "So don't let
yourself become hopeless or demoralized," he who had himself been
demoralized so often insisted. "Too much depends on your constancy,
your staying powers: Not only your loved ones, and your own future
but the future of all of humanity depends on your grit and staunch-
ness to extricate them and you from the unspeakable mess you're in.
Why, any day now you may snap out of what seems to me purpose-
less lethargy; any day now you may emerge from that murk of opportunism, so many now are milling about in, emerge into the daylight of
constructive purpose and worthwhile achievement."[36]

Roth was also invited to Cincinnati, to receive an honorary doctorate from Hebrew Union College. He asked Noah Harris whether traveling to Ohio would be advisable. The physician replied that the
journey would drain him of energy, but asked: "What are you saving
it for?" Roth made the trip, and Harris was convinced that all the
attention his patient was receiving, from academics, journalists, and
unknown readers, gave him a fresh burst of energy. "The stimulation
kept him going."[37]

While composing the gerontological ruminations that fortify the
later volumes of *Mercy*, Roth contributed a brief essay on aging to a
book of photographs by Harvey Wang and text by David Isay called
Holding On. "While I'm alive I feel an obligation to exercise the long-
dormant (or repressed) talent I have—in my case, writing," he wrote.
"To me it's an exercise in decency and humanity. It probably does me
good too, gives me an incentive, a goal, mitigates the misery inherent
in these pitiless eighties and nineties."[38]

Roth's temper flared at his longtime agent Roslyn Targ when she
tried to get him to cooperate with a couple of Dutch filmmakers, Peter
and Petra Lataster, who came to Albuquerque in July 1995 to make a
documentary about the legendary American novelist. They finally
won him over, with veneration and a $5,000 payment. Their elegiac

sixty-minute film, *Call It Sleep*, shows a feeble old man in a hospital gown at home, urinating into a plastic container. "I never had any trust in what I was doing," admits Roth, reviewing his career. Propped up beside a computer, he types haltingly, as if every letter is an excruciating victory over oblivion. "Call this picture 'The Last Days of the Dying Author,'" he says.[39] Weil, too, recalled seeing Roth at work on *Mercy* while urine trickled down his leg.

James Thomson, who had been spelling Helen Mitchener, is visible on camera feeding Roth, wheeling him about, and emptying his chamberpot. Not shown is Felicia Steele, who was off in graduate school in Austin. She played an even more important part in preparing the second volume of *Mercy* than the first, and she flew back from Texas to help out on the third; but her place as daily literary aide was taken by Eleana Zamora, a UNM undergraduate who was Avery Cheser's companion.

St. Martin's Press brought out the first volume of *Mercy of a Rude Stream* before Robert Weil had a chance to read the second. As he pored over Roth's text preparing the next installment for publication, Weil discovered something bizarre. An only child in *A Star Shines Over Mt. Morris Park*, Ira Stigman has suddenly acquired a sister, two years younger. Called Ruth in the original manuscript, her name would be changed to Minnie in an attempt to satisfy legal concerns by distancing her from Roth's own sister, Rose. Minnie had been missing from the Stigman family tree planted at the entrance to the previous book, and there is no mention of her in the text there. Yet, by about a third of the way through the new work, Ira and Minnie have become partners in furtive, incestuous sex. Ira had also begun sneaking off for illicit trysts with his first cousin, named Stella.

Roth's own first cousin, Sylvia, had died at fifty-seven, decades earlier; but his sister, Rose Broder, was still alive, in Brooklyn. Weil urged Roth to alert her that he was about to publish an autobiographical novel featuring sibling incest. In response to a short note from Roth, Rose wrote back in utter anguish. Roth's sister, who typed *Called It Sleep* and facilitated its rediscovery, had always been his steadfast, ardent supporter. When Herman Roth left his son one dollar, Rose

voluntarily split the full inheritance with her older brother. Her correspondence with Henry over the years expresses pride in his accomplishments and unfeigned love. But the letter that she sent on July 7,
1994, signed with uncharacteristic frostiness "Sincerely," is the outcry
of an old woman who is perplexed, angry, and crushed. Why taint
their few remaining years with public exposure of a base relationship
that concluded more than sixty years before? Did Henry suppose that
titillation from shameful sex would sell more copies of his book? Why
provide salacious proof to confirm anti-Semitic stereotypes?

Helen Mitchener was present when the letter arrived at Hendrix
Road. "I just don't want to open it," said Roth. He refused to reach
for the switchblade brought back by Steele from a trip to Germany
that he used as a letter opener. Mitchener slit open the envelope and
read the letter to him.[40]

Rose wrote that she was more than mystified by her brother's
motives in making these revelations, which she called foul and unworthy of his artistry. Inclusion of the sleazy incest story would not only
discredit the author in the eyes of his readers, she warned. It would
humiliate her, parading her before the world as a whore. She pleaded
with Roth, asking how, despite all the loving support she had always
provided him over the yeas, he could now behave this way toward her.

If Rose Broder could not dissuade her brother from this reckless,
hurtful plan by appealing to his fraternal sympathies, perhaps she
could scare him into silence. She acknowledged that neither of them
had much longer to live, but she warned that she had no intention of
allowing her memory to be defiled by the actions of "you or your
cohorts," sensing, inaccurately, that her brother was put up to this
desperate, disgraceful measure by his publisher or his lawyer. Her letter concluded by threatening that if Roth published his book without
removing the objectionable material, she would sue him and his publisher, St. Martin's Press. She added that she would also speak out to
the press, exposing his lies and revealing her feeble old brother for
what he was, a "sensationalist—grabbing for the gold."[41]

Hugh Roth's wife, Carole, also thought that little good could be
gained from publishing *Mercy of a Rude Stream*. In this exploitation

of an old man's urge to write she saw the handiwork of Larry Fox, whom she resented as a usurper. "Henry was not a good judge of character," she said. "Anyone who loved him could win him over."[42] According to Roth's daughter-in-law, Fox had insinuated himself into the author's life, displacing both Materassi and his own two sons. Publishing the last books was another blunder.

Only Muriel could have stopped the presses. Intent on shielding at least his loving wife from shame, Roth had not shown Muriel any of his work-in-progress and had determined to delay publication until after her death. But she was gone now, and nothing, not even a frantic plea from his distraught sister, could stop Roth from baring and bruising his soul. In the final months of a tormented life, Roth wrote only to tell the truth—and the truth, he was convinced, is lacerating. Intent on redemption through excruciating confession, he even exaggerated his burden of guilt, magnifying the horror of his own incest with Rose by rendering it graphically and frequently between Ira and Minnie Stigman—more frequently than it in fact occurred between Henry and Rose.

On October 28, 1994, in order to protect St. Martin's Press against possible liability, Weil flew down to Albuquerque to record Roth's testimony on the biographical foundation of his fiction. During a two-hour interview, which was preserved on videotape, Roth explained that he did indeed maintain a sexual relationship with Rose, starting when she was ten and ending when she was twenty. He pointed out that the acts of incest were less frequent than portrayed in his novel, and that, although Ira Stigman coaxes Minnie into bed with dollar bills, bribery was never a factor in his own encounters with Rose.[43]

FOR DECADES, Roth had been pursued by a single haunting question: Why the silence after *Call It Sleep*? To hundreds of strangers who posed the question, and to himself, he alternated between two answers. The seductive abstractions of socialist realism had lured him from the human basis of his art. And alienation from the Jewish community severed his ties with the muse. However, at the age of eighty-eight, Roth offered Weil another, more compelling reason for his legendary writer's block: the paralyzing guilt of covert incest. It would also explain the dark secret he often alluded to and why he discouraged both Harold Ribalow and Leonard Michaels from writing his biography. It might in addition explain his curt dismissal of Mario Materassi after translating the first volume of *Mercy of a Rude Stream*. Having revered Roth for thirty years, the Italian had been on the verge of discovering what the author considered his depravity.

If Roth, whose fictional inspiration was almost always his own life, were to continue beyond *Call It Sleep*, he would have to take his protagonist through adolescence. And if he were to be true to his experience, he would be obliged to confront his own shameful behavior with his sister and his cousin. Roth was not prepared to do that until—in his eighties and embracing his own extinction—most of the people who could be hurt by his shocking revelations were gone, and wounding himself might bring redemption. As early as 1979, he had begun typing out raw drafts of what would evolve into *Mercy*, but the writing acquired momentum only after Ira Stigman's sister suddenly materialized. Roth had lived in anguish for most of a miserable century, and his new work would make long shrift of it. No longer afraid to face his past, Roth told Weil: "We're all headed for oblivion. It's all vanity. We all share the same kind of obliteration."[44] To Steele, back from Texas for a month-long working visit in May, he vowed that, if still alive at ninety, he would end it all himself.

Volume 2 of *Mercy of a Rude Stream*—whose dedication, to Felicia Jean Steele, is followed by "profound acknowledgment for the work of my devoted agent, Roslyn Targ, and Robert Weil, editor supreme"—was published in February 1995. Roth had originally thought to call the book *Mind-forg'd Manacles*, a phrase from William Blake's "London" that forms the epigraph. Instead, he accepted Weil's suggestion to title it *A Diving Rock on the Hudson*, derived from the scene in which young Ira Stigman, caught stealing fountain pens at school, is tempted to drown himself in the river. Like *A Star Shines Over Mt. Morris Park*, *A Diving Rock* alternates between the aged, ailing Ira's comments to his computer, Ecclesias, and episodes from his youth more than seventy years earlier. Like the first volume, it contains a Yiddish glossary compiled by Steele, and it also begins with facing pages of Ira's paternal and maternal family trees. At the outset of the story, the year is 1921, and the protagonist is just entering Peter Stuyvesant High School. In the final pages, the year is 1925, and, though he receives a D in his college English class, Ira, a student at City College, is encouraged to continue writing when an essay he produces on assignment, "Impressions of a Plumber," is published in the literary magazine *Lavender*. The novel begins with a callow, cowed high school freshman and concludes with the first intimations of a literary vocation.

Like much of the rest of *Mercy, A Diving Rock on the Hudson* is a document of self-loathing, a narrative whose aging narrator finds many reasons to despise his awkward, erring younger self and who welcomes his own imminent demise. Ira, the author, provides graphic, extensive accounts of his guilty encounters with his sister, Minnie, and his cousin, Stella, though he confides to Ecclesias that he tried to omit them from an earlier draft. But he regrets that the work did not ring true and that he would not have been able to continue writing if he had expunged all trace of incest from the story.

The younger Ira becomes convinced that his father's contempt for him is justified and that he is an unworthy companion to Farley Hewin, a celebrated track star who was his loyal friend until Ira, disgraced, stopped seeing him. Nor does his friendship with Billy Green, an energetic Protestant boy who seems to lack Ira's Jewish neuroses and with whom he enjoys boating and camping, survive their high school graduation. Likening himself to Charles Baudelaire's Albatross, Ira feels he is an ungainly outsider whose strengths make him unfit for normal company. A relationship with Larry Gordon lasts a bit longer and exposes Ira, a blue-collar immigrant who spends his summers hawking soft drinks at the Polo Grounds and Yankee Stadium, to the way that a stable, middle-class family lives. When Ira is a student at City College, Larry, who is enrolled at New York University, introduces his friend to his teacher and lover, Edith Welles. And that is just the beginning of more torment.

"This is a work of fiction," announces the copyright page of *A Diving Rock*. "Although some characters were inspired by people whom the author knew, the narrative is not intended in any way to be a depiction of any real events. This novel is certainly *not* an autobiography, nor should it be taken as such." Volume 1 lacked any such disclaimer.

Like *The First Man*, a bildungsroman by Albert Camus that was also published in 1995, fifteen years after the French Algerian author's death, Roth's near-posthumous offering was transparently not fiction. Though some details are changed, it is difficult not to equate the character called M, a musician whom the widowed Ira Stigman had been married to for fifty years, with Henry Roth's own Muriel, or two sons named Jess and Hershel with Jeremy and Hugh, respectively. Stigman publishes a piece called "Impressions of a Plumber" in the City College magazine *Lavender*, which happens to be exactly what Roth himself did. The endpaper even offers a 1924 photograph, tracked down by a staff member at St. Martin's, of young Roth's actual rifle team at DeWitt Clinton High School. Because *A Diving Rock* seems so patently derived directly from Henry Roth's life, the apparent disclosure by its venerable, elderly, "fictional" author of sexual transgressions during his adolescence immediately brought the actual author more attention than he had received for anything else since 1964.

David Mehegan, in an otherwise glowing review in the *Boston Globe* in which he called *A Diving Rock on the Hudson* "one of the most poignant, strangest and most strangely disturbing projects in American literature," described the shocking new book as "tawdry, repugnant, and also a bit puzzling."[45] Stefan Kanfer, in the *Los Angeles Times Book Review*, called it "as provocative as anything in the chapters of St. Augustine or Rousseau." As a literary theme, sibling incest has an ancient lineage, including stories of Osiris and Isis, Uranus and Rhea, Zeus and Hera, and Abraham and his half sister Sarah. Among moderns, it surfaces in works by William Faulkner, Thomas Mann, Tennessee Williams, Vladimir Nabokov, and Iris Murdoch. As the portrait of an era through the escapades of one wayward young man, James T. Farrell's Studs Lonigan trilogy bears comparison to Henry Roth's *Mercy*, and in the first volume, *Young Lonigan* (1932), Studs suffers guilt for lusting after his sister Frances.

But the most dramatic instance of incest in a work by Roth's contemporaries occurs early in a novel by Ralph Ellison, who, until the posthumous publication of the incomplete *Juneteenth* in 1999, shared Roth's notoriety as a blocked one-book author. In the second chapter of his one great book, *Invisible Man* (1952), Ellison introduces Jim Trueblood, a black sharecropper who has impregnated both his wife and his daughter. Horrified by his behavior, respectable Negroes in the area ostracize Trueblood, though whites, pleased to find a confirmation of their racial stereotypes, treat him well. In Ellison as in Roth, incest is a particular horror for members of a minority aspiring to assimilate. Violation of a fundamental sexual taboo confirms the larger society in its bigotry toward blacks and Jews. But for Trueblood, as for Ira Stigman, incest is a defense mechanism, a turning inward by a man not especially welcome in mainstream America. By embracing, illicitly, his own clan, Stigman reinforces views of Jews as clannish, and compounds his own guilt.

Roth stands in roughly the same relationship to the canon of American Jewish fiction as Ellison does to that of African American fiction. It took several decades for each to publish a second, culminating novel. Yet, though their lives overlapped and their deaths occurred within eighteen months of each other, the two men apparently never met or corresponded. Though Roth was well aware of Ellison as another one-book author, there is no evidence that he ever read the other man's book.

No one reacted to revelations of incest in Roth's new book with greater revulsion than his own sister. In a brief, curt letter sent on March 5, 1995, Rose Broder demanded compensation for the damage that publication of *A Diving Rock on the Hudson*, defying her prior warning, had done to her. Roth was not opposed to toning down the remaining volumes of *Mercy*, but the man who had subsisted in dire poverty in Maine and was still buying day-old bread in New Mexico choked at the reparation that his sister sought to extort from him— $10,000. However, Larry Fox persuaded Roth, his friend and a client of his firm, to part with the money in order to get on with the work. In the general release agreement dated May 24, 1995, that Fox drew up, Roth affirmed that "in future volumes of the fictional work entitled *Mercy of a Rude Stream* by Henry Roth, the character of Minnie Stigman, who is identified as the sister of Ira Stigman, will no longer be portrayed as having any further sexual relationship with her brother, Ira Stigman."[46] Rose Broder signed the agreement after receiving her check for $10,000. It was the same sum that the skeptical head of St. Martin's had used to buy peace with Robert Weil by purchasing Henry Roth's problematic novel. To encourage readers to buy his latest novel, Roth spent the evening of April 2 at a Borders bookstore in Albuquerque signing copies of *A Diving Rock*.

Aside from wonder, shock, or dismay over salacious prose from an old man, the reaction to Volume 2 was muted. It was as if the extraordinary story of Roth the literary revenant had already been covered by reviews of the first volume; although reception of Volume 2 was generally favorable, many publications did not bother to write anything about it at all. In her *New York Times* review, the novelist Mary Gordon, struggling to rationalize garrulity and narcissism as assets, offered the condescending praise of a Gulliver who has discovered an exotic tribe of elders: "Part of the fascination of *A Diving Rock on the Hudson* is that it is a deliberately unflattering self-portrait of the garrulity and narcissism of old age. This is something we haven't seen before in literature, and if for no other reason, it is valuable as the speech of a tribe until now silenced."[47]

A Star Shines Over Mt. Morris Park is the weakest of the four volumes that would comprise *Mercy of a Rude Stream*, and it lowered expectations for *A Diving Rock* and subsequent offerings from Roth. Though Weil had not yet read Volume 2 when he published Volume 1, he became convinced that he had erred in publishing the first volume by itself, without the rest of the cycle to provide context. "I think one of the big mistakes I made—but I hadn't seen the second volume—was that I didn't have the ability to combine volume one and volume two," he told Alan Gibbs, an Englishman writing his doctoral dissertation on Roth. "I've always felt that if volume two could be attached to volume one it would've been a scandal and a sensation. But it wasn't, and that's history. I always recommend to people, when they begin to read them, that they start with volume three or two. I think if they start with volume one it's very daunting. I've had people start with volume three and just get totally hooked."[48]

In preparing Volume 2, Weil had edited out as superfluous some of the more graphic accounts of Ira copulating with Minnie. Though intent on emphasizing his character's degradation, Roth had consented to the cuts. Now, while continuing to rearrange the text to give it dramatic shape, Weil and Steele set out to eliminate all incest between Ira and his sister from volumes 3 and 4. Ira's shocking behavior with his cousin Stella continued. Weil believed that the deletions improved the writing: "As Henry would say, it almost was an editorial gift that we got this restraint, because I felt the final works are far more balanced and they read better." He recalled that "Henry was very happy with the changes. His major unhappiness with the agreement was the $10,000."[49]

Roth was growing weaker, yet his temper remained robust. He quarreled regularly with Helen Mitchener about domestic details, and he fired several workers, including a bothersome aide who ate nothing but sausages, hired to help her out. Mitchener alerted the police to a couple of assistants who took drugs. Exasperated with her sick, irascible employer, the housekeeper kept threatening to quit.

In June, Pageant Books, which had established the Cooper Square imprint in 1960 in order to bring *Call It Sleep* back into print, moved from its location on East Ninth Street in Manhattan. Moving to the Internet, it would cease to be a bricks-and-mortar enterprise in 1999. But Arion, a specialty press, was now offering a collector's edition of *Call It Sleep* that included forty-eight photographs of New York City taken between 1907 and 1913. Signed by the author, and limited to a print run of 300, it sold for $700 a copy, a far different fate from that of the 1934 edition that Robert Ballou struggled to market for $2.50 a copy.

In late September, a heartening letter arrived from Meir Ribalow, who remained grateful to Roth not only for *Call It Sleep* but also for his education at Phillips Exeter. When Meir's father died in 1982, the

Harold U. Ribalow Award was established in his memory. Administered by *Hadassah* magazine, the prize was given annually to an author "deserving of recognition." Harold Ribalow had helped lift Roth out of legendary obscurity, and it now seemed appropriate to honor the author with a Ribalow Award designed ordinarily to recognize unsung talents. "Since you yourself are rightly regarded as a giant of American literature," wrote Meir Ribalow, "you of course do not qualify as an author struggling for recognition. But the Ribalow family thought it uniquely appropriate to honor your new book, especially since the life of Harold Ribalow, and the concept of a Ribalow Prize for emerging authors, has such a singular relationship to *Call It Sleep* and to your own subsequent career. So we would like to honor *Mercy of a Rude Stream*, and its justly celebrated author, with a special Harold U. Ribalow Award in this, the Bar-Mitzvah year of the Ribalow Prize."[50]

Roth wrote back: "Thanks for the encomia. Things like that keep me alive, I'm sure: what little is left me capable of feeling swells with pride like the staves of an old barrel when filled." But very little was left alive.

Early in October, Helen Mitchener, whose sister had been stricken with cancer, was under more stress than usual. On Friday, October 6, she informed Roth, who had developed a rash in addition to his other problems, that she was taking a leave of absence. The news upset Roth—who would take care of him? James Thomson was still putting in his hours, and Mitchener arranged to have an agency provide temporary assistants. On Saturday, Thomson received word from Lovelace Hospital that Roth, depleted and depressed, had been admitted there.

David Bennahum visited him at Lovelace, not as a physician but as the patient's friend. He refused Roth's request for medication to end his life. During much of the past year, Roth had also asked Noah Harris for assistance in euthanasia.[51] But while Roth had often discussed suicide, he never actively pursued it. He was hospitalized, though, with a "do not resuscitate" order that barred the use of extraordinary measures to sustain his waning life.

Robert Weil, about to fly off to California to attend his own father's deathbed, spoke by phone from New York on Monday. "Continue the good work," Roth urged.[52] He was testy with the nurses attending him, but he concluded a melancholy call from Joy Walker, his ex-daughter-in-law, in Brooklyn by crooning an Irish lullabye. Jeremy arrived during the week, and he stepped outside the room while his father took the call from Joy, as well as one from Hugh. On Friday morning, October 13, Steele phoned from Austin. She was flying to Albuquerque the next day, but Roth, in the faux-tough tones she knew so well, asked why the hell she wasn't with him for the end. In the late afternoon, Helen Mitchener stopped by Lovelace to visit. "I'm going to die," he told her. An hour later, just after sundown, Henry Roth's tired heart failed.

Throughout the final days, Jeremy, the prodigal son back from Toronto, left his father's bedside only for brief breaks to visit the hospital coffeeshop or the men's room. On Friday, he had not abandoned his post for more than ten minutes when he returned to find that the patient had died. "It was just like my father to do that," Jeremy complained.[53]

It was not only Friday the 13th but also the conclusion of Sukkot, the holiday of mobile homes in which, to commemorate the wanderings of the Israelites after leaving Egypt, Jews spend time in temporary, makeshift habitations. Jeremy was at first unable to reach Hugh with news of their father's death; the Jewish holy day of Shemini Atzeret had begun, and his newly pious younger brother was not answering the telephone.

Roth passed away ninety-one years to the day after Sigmund Freud, another child of Tysmenitz, published *The Interpretation of Dreams*. Both Henry and his father, Herman, died at the age of eighty-nine. Like Muriel, Roth had stipulated that his body be donated to the medical school of the University of New Mexico. However, by the time he died, the corpse was so wasted that none of the organs served any scientific purpose. Roth's body was cremated directly, the ashes deposited in a cardboard box that Thomson placed in the closet above the box containing Muriel's remains.

Chapter 17

REQUIEM FOR HENRY

Human life is but a series of footnotes to a vast
obscure unfinished masterpiece.
—VLADIMIR NABOKOV[1]

FELICIA STEELE ARRIVED back in Albuquerque twelve hours
too late to see Henry Roth alive but still in time to attend a small
memorial service. About two dozen mourners participated in the simple ceremony, conducted by a Reconstructionist woman rabbi named
Lynn Gottlieb. An obituary in *The New York Times*, written by the
critic Richard Nicholls, hailed Roth for having created "one of the
most exact portraits in modern American literature of the immigrant
experience."[2] It also noted that the arc of his eighty-nine years represented "perhaps the most mysterious career in modern American letters." February 29 occupies a rare spot on the calendar, but in leap
year 1996 it was made even more remarkable when, at the Museum
of the City of New York, Manhattan Borough President Ruth
Messinger officially proclaimed it "Henry Roth Day." Though Roth
was born in Europe and spent most of his adult life in Maine and New

Mexico, he had earned recognition as the laureate of New York City. No one ever wrote so vividly about the ordeals of greenhorns on the Lower East Side, yet he was also the chronicler of uptown immigrant life less familiar to succeeding generations. Reviewing the French translation of *Mercy of a Rude Stream*, the novelist J. M. G. Le Clézio, who lived part of the year in New Mexico, proclaimed that Henry Roth's Harlem would, like Dublin, Combray, and Yoknapatawpha County, enter "the magic inventory of eternal places."[3]

Roth's will bequeathed $2,500 to Steele and $500 to Stella Romero. Jeremy, one of two principal heirs, abruptly returned to Toronto. The errant older son who sat beside his father during the final days remained aloof from public conversation about the famous author. In New York, Hugh accepted the Ribalow Award on behalf of his late father. Yet he claimed no interest in reading the books: "I don't read his stuff, because I internalize it."[4] He demonstrated his devotion by assembling family photographs and testimonials to both his parents. In the last months, Hugh had reconciled with his prickly sire, and Larry Fox, visiting, was touched to see the younger Roth tidy up the old man's kitchen. Hugh put together a 32-page memorial that included commentary on Muriel's music and a list of the arcane words (e.g., *basiate*, *hispid*, *nubilous*, *scut*) that Henry loved to scrawl in the margins of a battered dictionary. The booklet also contained a poem by Hugh, "Advice in the 17th Year," in which he imagines how his parents might describe their estrangement from their younger son:

We see each other across an unbridgeable space,
While dancing the dance of recrimination and regret,
Fitting poorly into the complex jigsaw of family, you fade,
Like a bright light before the thermonuclear sun of day.[5]

The 250 copies of the pamphlet, printed by Hugh at his own expense, only increased the discord with his wife, Carole. To her mind, the project was a sentimental gesture that the couple could ill afford.

Meanwhile, the task of completing Henry Roth's final fiction continued without Henry Roth, who had fulfilled his sly desire "to die with one's books on."[6] He had lived long enough to approve the shaping and cutting—including expurgation of further sex between Ira and Minnie—done to Volume 3 of *Mercy of a Rude Stream*. Though Weil devised the title, *From Bondage*, Roth approved, and he lived to give his blessing to the title that Steele thought up for Volume 4: *Requiem for Harlem*. Roth had had a chance to map out Volume 4 with Steele and the premed student Eleana Zamora, but much additional cobbling remained to be done, particularly of the ending. Using bits and pieces of Roth's sentences and their own intimate mastery of his style, Steele and Weil together wrote the cycle's parting words. "Felicia and I," Weil recalled, "agonized over that final paragraph, and we would bounce off each other exactly what Henry would have said."[7]

By the time the dedication to Volume 3, "To the memory of Leah, my mother," appeared in print, her son was but a memory, too. Published posthumously, in July 1996, *From Bondage* acknowledged "the sustaining help of my agent, Roslyn Targ, my editor, Robert Weil, my assistant, Felicia Jean Steele, and my attorney, Larry Fox." Like the previous volume, the new installment provided a family tree, a glossary, and an advisory that the book be read as fiction. The novel begins and ends with allusions to Samuel Taylor Coleridge, under the sign of the Ancient Mariner; an initial epigraph is lifted from the famous poem about an aging, obsessive storyteller, and exegesis of the line "He prayeth best, who loveth best" is worked into the book's conclusion. Like Coleridge's Wedding Guest, readers are spellbound by ancient Ira's evocations of assignations, conversations, and job assignments seventy years earlier. The novel was a bid by Roth to free himself from the personal albatross hanging about his stiff neck for most of the century.

The brief Prologue to *From Bondage*, first published in the *New York Times Magazine* on December 31, 1995, depicts Ira Stigman, an eighty-nine-year-old widower, confronting his own mortality with the aid of a word processor. The opening scene recalls an exhilarating summer that Ira spent sharing a cottage in Woodstock, New York, with Edith and Larry. Ira covets his buddy's lover, though he fears that domestic lechery has rendered him unworthy of the older, more sophisticated Gentile woman. Ira envies Larry's glibness, as well as his assimilation into middle-class America. "Larry could relate his adventures; they slipped easily through regular channels. His didn't, his were deformed, fitted no channel, could never be told."[8] They are of course told, many years later, in *From Bondage*, a novel very much like the one that Ira, dying, struggles over in his agonizing, solitary sessions with Ecclesias. It is a book that, more than Larry's conventional writing, overpowers with the force of delayed revelation and the hope of ultimate but earthly redemption.

Edith serves as the uncouth young Jew's mentor, initiating him into the mysteries of Joyce and Eliot, whose esoteric texts he at first admires and later despises. Ira concludes that the modernist masters abandoned the common people from whom art derives its power. Like Ira's literary forebears, his feckless father, Chaim Stigman, a failed milkman turned waiter, also deserted his community. Ira resents him for having forced the family to move away from the Lower East Side. Rejecting Marxist abstractions, the older Ira understands that he can overcome his creative aridity only by returning to the kindred ordinary Jews whom he sought to transcend, the kind of people he sexually abused. Late in life, he realizes that incest is a symptom of the arrested development that enabled him to devise a child's-eye masterpiece but obstructed other writing. *From Bondage* diagnoses the emotional captivity from which Ira learned to liberate himself only much later—and through his writing.

Like Roth himself, Ira puzzles over the "grave and disabling discontinuity" following the publication of his ambitious first novel. At last, staring at the computer screen and his own imminent demise, Roth began to tap out the answers to enigmas that had burdened his life, each key delivering a blow of truth as well as a jolt of pain to his arthritic fingers. Both the author and his fictional alter ego had for decades been trying to explain to others and themselves why they failed to follow up on an early masterpiece. Now, with his precious Muriel gone and no one, Roth thought, who could be hurt but himself, the words came unclogged, page after page, day after day, in the former funeral home on Hendrix Road. Ira spends much of *From*

Bondage attempting to justify *this* shocking, shameful book. He asks himself: "why was he doing this, demeaning himself—and perhaps jews, the multitude of jews who had transformed one previous novel into a shrine, a child's shrine at that—to the extent he was?"[9] Can literature this lacerating be good for the Jews?

Ira initially yearns to transcend his origins as the child of poor, uneducated Eastern European immigrants. But he eventually learns that the only way to attain the universal is through embrace of the parochial. He credits the creative renewal in his eighties to his belated identification with the Jewish people, particularly with the revived Jewish state. From a proudly self-reliant aesthete, Ira sees himself transformed into a voice for his people, and it is by discovering and cultivating that voice that he is able to overcome his obstructions, to write a novel very like the one that Roth constructs about him. While composing *From Bondage*—the volume of the tetralogy that is richest in incident, character, and theme—a weak and weary old man was lifted out of himself into creative ecstasy. Roth now lived to write, and the writing sustained a fading life.

From Bondage immerses its reader in the struggles of an earnest young man who aspires to move beyond the meager cold-water tenement of his unschooled, working-class parents into the enchanted intellectual bohemia that he imagines Edith inhabiting. In one of the most memorable sequences, Ira accompanies Edith to the pier in Hoboken to see her lover, Lewlyn, off to England, where he intends to join another woman. While Ira pines for Edith, Edith, apparently oblivious to the hold she has on her young chaperon, longs for the inconstant Lewlyn. After his ship departs for Europe, Ira accompanies the distraught Edith back to the Village and, solicitous about her state of mind, spends the night, chastely, beside Edith in her bed.

Roth was particularly proud of a tense nocturnal scene in Aunt Mamie's apartment, claiming that it could stand alone as the finest novella he had ever written.[10] About three quarters of the way into the book, Ira pays a visit to his relatives in the nearby Harlem apartment that his grandfather, Zaida (Ben Zion Farb), shares with Mamie, her husband, and her two daughters. During a private audience with Ira,

Zaida, like Reb Yidel Pankower, the *cheder* teacher in *Call It Sleep*, describes himself as besieged by barbarians. Deploring the erosion of religious observance, he declares: "I tell you we live in botched times. Botched, ruined. Fit for burial, no more." Eager to die before the inevitable slaughter, Zaida is convinced that the world is filled with bigots determined to do violence to Jews: "Immeasurable the menace that hangs over them, the woe in store for them." He acknowledges that Jews are tolerated in America, but only at the price of abandoning their piety.[11]

The aging Zaida's premonition of a global holocaust—recounted by an aging Ira after Auschwitz—adds to the dramatic tension of a scene in which Ira proceeds to commit a flagrant sin within a few feet of his devout grandfather. As everyone retires for the night, Ira leaves the apartment, goes to a drugstore to purchase a condom, and slips back in for a sexual tryst with his cousin Stella, whose bedroom is within earshot of her grandfather's. Zaida is indeed an observant Jew, and Roth constructs suspense and ambiguity over the old man's powers of observation, over whether he is wise to the abomination that his two grandchildren are committing confident that no one else in the darkened apartment notices.

Throughout the work, Roth constructs a counterpoint between Stella, Ira's incestuous sexual partner, and Edith, the older, sophisticated woman he does not dare to imagine as his partner, even as that prospect takes hold of his overwrought imagination. Elsewhere in *From Bondage*, Ira's menial jobs as a clerk in a fancy candy shop and as a grease monkey on a repair crew of the New York subway system are vividly rendered. So is the old man's frank desire for death. Yet suffusing and exalting all is Ira's literary mission and his love for M, the musician he met at Yaddo so long ago, from whom he has been widowed for five years, and who is the object of the adoration expressed in the novel's final words: "the passionate homage he now so keenly felt."[12]

David Mehegan, in the *Boston Globe*, hailed *From Bondage* as "a landmark of the American literary century."[13] And, inevitably, comparing the new volume to *Call It Sleep*, Frank Kermode in *The New*

York Times Book Review proclaimed that Roth's autumnal offering "enhances its brilliant youthful original by casting upon it the calmer, contemplative light of old age."[14] *From Bondage* did not arouse the widespread curiosity of Volume 1, which offered the novelty of a notorious writer's block broken, or of Volume 2, which offered the frisson of an old man's blunt account of incest. It was received respectfully, even enthusiastically. A finalist for the National Book Critics Circle prize in fiction, it was the only one of the four volumes to be a contender for a leading national literary award. But in a culture of reduced attention spans, Henry Roth seemed to be making excessive demands. How much more of an unblocked elder's final effusions could readers be expected to absorb? Most of Coleridge's wedding guests brush right past the garrulous Ancient Mariner, though the haunting *Rime* endures.

Published in March 1998, *Requiem for Harlem* concluded the four-volume künstlerroman that serves as Roth's scathing portrait of the artist as young wretch, narrated by "an old fiasco." Volume 4 is dedicated to "Roz and Bill Targ, Paragons of Loyalty." Even more than the previous three installments of *Mercy of a Rude Stream*, *Requiem for Harlem* both recounts and enacts its protagonist's humiliation, and he is the literary voodoo doll for his tormented author, Roth. Though Rose Broder had died the year before, the copyright page includes another disingenuous declaration that the story that follows is fiction. In an affecting Editor's Afterword, Robert Weil recounts how he personally lost "two giants, both men atavistic in wholly different ways,"[15] within sixteen days of each other. Henry Roth and Weil's German-born father asked about each other while each lay dying, one in New Mexico and one in California, in October 1995. In his final instructions to his editor, Roth urged Weil "to soldier on and continue the work, my friend."[16] *Requiem for Harlem* is proof that he did so.

Roth's novel begins in gluttony and dyspepsia, wallows in revulsion, and concludes with the prospect of redemption. Yet its title suggests nostalgia for a troubled adolescence in the lowly uptown neighborhood on which the final pages close the book. It is an elegy for anguished youth. The year is 1927, and Ira Stigman, now twenty-one, is attending his senior year at City College. The opening pages recount Ira's arduous journey, with weary feet and—after gorging himself on pasta—a bloated stomach, from Harlem all the way downtown to the Village, where Edith Welles is occupied with another man. In the final pages of *Requiem for Harlem*, Ira again makes his way down to Edith's house, to stay. In the novel's parting, plangent words (devised by Steele and Weil and quoted by several reviewers), Ira, brooding on infernal guilt, takes a screeching subway train "downtown and the hell out of Harlem." Change of address does not necessarily mean a change of fortune. Though Ira manages to get the hell out of Harlem, perhaps, like Milton's Satan, he carries hell with him wherever he goes.

A college exam on *Paradise Lost* forces the immigrant scholar to ponder the vile connections between Satan and his daughter Sin. Yet Ira, who has ended sexual intimacy with his younger sister Minnie, continues his own incestuous relationship with his sixteen-year-old cousin, Stella, even as his sentimental apprenticeship to Edith, who is older and more accomplished, deepens into something resembling mature love. After one last brazen act of self-degradation, Ira moves out of his family's Harlem flat and into a Village apartment with Edith.

Requiem for Harlem reads more rapidly than the other three volumes. Present-tense interpolations and metafictional apostrophes to Ecclesias the computer have almost disappeared. With a narrower palette of character and incident than the earlier volumes, *Requiem for Harlem* offers an excruciating focus on Ira's guilty desperation after learning that Stella might be pregnant. Anxiety and shame cause him to break, rudely, with Larry Gordon, by spurning his invitation to Thanksgiving dinner. And, during Ira's parting conversation with his parents, the novel also provides revelations about further foulness within the Stigman family. Chaim Stigman admits that he too had sexually abused Stella, though, belligerent as always, he denies any guilt. "A pretty young plaything yields to a man's caresses," he explains. "He toys with her, and such a little toy. Does he merit the gibbet for that?"[17] It is of course a tautology that incest runs in families; but despite Chaim's rationalizations, Ira abhors incest as the particular curse of the Stigman/Farb clan.

Though they are fewer and shorter than in the previous three volumes, occasional interludes describe an elderly Ira, struggling, like Roth himself, to record his lacerating memories on his word processor. But *Requiem for Harlem* acquires intensity from its searing concentration on Ira's dreadful burden and its confinement to a single week in November 1927. Pounding out these pages in a final burst of inspiration, Roth forgot about Ecclesias and its dying interlocutor; he was again the young man on the verge of leaving Harlem. In the days preceding Thanksgiving, Ira—a helpless witness to ferocious squabbles between his mother and father—consolidates his energies to free himself from the toxic snares of family. Like Albert Schearl in *Call It Sleep*, Chaim Stigman is a violent bundle of festering resentments, a man possessed of a permanent sense of personal offense. Ira cannot understand why his long-suffering mother did not leave her abusive husband many years before.

It is easier for him to guess why Zaida, his maternal grandfather, moves away from Aunt Mamie's apartment in Manhattan in order to live with other relatives in Queens. Ambiguous statements lead Ira to infer that the pious old man knew exactly what was going on between his two adolescent grandchildren and was too horrified to remain within the polluted household. Ira begins to panic at the possibility that the entire family will learn of his depravity. But his most immediate concern is over the fact that Stella, a pudgy girl who does not even appeal to him either physically or intellectually, is four days late with her menstrual period. During the course of several days, Ira remains frantic over the possibility that Stella is pregnant and that, because of a broken condom, he might be the ignominious sire of a genetic monster. While Ira, sick with dread, scurries about to arrange, with the help of Edith, for an abortion, the unruffled Stella neglects to tell him that her scare was a false alarm.

Yet even after dodging the dire consequences, Ira still cannot keep his hands off Stella. In an excruciating scene that Roth charges with the intense disgust that Ira—and he—felt for themselves, Ira takes

Stella into the balcony of a movie theater near her secretarial school downtown. It is the middle of the day, and the dark theater is otherwise empty as Ira begins to initiate another sexual encounter. But soon three black youths, like avenging angels, harass the illicit couple, forcing them to flee out into the daylight.

Like Zaida's decision to move out of Mamie's apartment, Ira's departure from the Stigman household in Harlem is, however belated, an assertion of will, the feckless young man's emergence *from bondage*. Ira's continuing servitude to family—his mother and his cousin—has infantilized him, and his departure marks a coming of age. Under the tutelage of Edith, a mature Gentile woman and a writer, he can look forward to advancing outside the constrictive circle of Jewish immigrants and to developing the literary talents latent in his college compositions. The elder Ira looks back on a successful first novel that sounds very much like *Call It Sleep*, even as he struggles to write the cathartic new book whose awful secrets kept him for sixty years from extending his literary career and whose successful completion will provide him with "the Promethean catalytic exercising of his consciousness."[18] In the final pages of the cycle's final published book, Ira bids farewell to his damaged, debilitating family and his loathsome sexual compulsions. The apprentice artist is ready at last to write a novel very much like *Call It Sleep*. And, having disburdened himself of excruciating secrets, sixty-four years after David Schearl was put to bed, the eighty-nine-year-old Roth was finished writing and prepared at last to call it sleep.

"What happens to a dream deferred?" asks Langston Hughes in the poem he called "Harlem." Readers of *Requiem for Harlem* could finally learn what happens to a young Jewish immigrant whose dreams of literary achievement dried up for six decades, like a raisin in the sun.

Almost 2,000 pages remained unpublished. A manuscript that Roth called only "Batch 2" continues his story after Harlem, through the years with Walton in the Village. "A Maine Sampler," which was bequeathed to Felicia Steele, recounts the author's retreat to rural New England. Roth and Steele began editing "Batch 2" even before

"Batch 1," which is what *Mercy of a Rude Stream* originated as, but they put it aside to work with Weil on what became Volume 1 of *Mercy of a Rude Stream*. "Batch 2" and "A Maine Sampler" contain fascinating biographical material and splendid passages of vintage Roth prose. Amorphous clumps of anecdote and reflection, they await the labor of a dedicated editor to knead into dramatic form. For the moment, they are available only in the Roth Archives assembled after the author's death at the American Jewish Historical Society in New York.

Mercy of a Rude Stream is a document of the second and third decades of the twentieth century that happens to have been written seventy years later, in a style, by turns supple and wooden, that recalls both Yiddish melodrama and the audacity of the post–World War I avant-garde. The narrative adopts the form by which the elder Ira imagines life itself: "full of chaotic fragments, discreet [*sic*], in the mathematical sense, disparate, often dull and banal, but often fiercely engrossing, disparate but often desperate. And as often unexpected and unforeseen."[19] Donna Seaman in *The Booklist* hailed the final installment, *Requiem for Harlem*, as "the most clarion and metaphysical of the four novels."[20]

Meanwhile, first the *New York Observer* and then the *New York Times* published stories revealing that Roth had paid his sister $10,000 in an agreement following the publication of *A Diving Rock on the Hudson*.[21] After reading the article in the *Times*, Philip Roth, through Jeffrey Posternak, then an assistant to his agent, Andrew Wylie, contacted Weil. Twenty-seven years younger than Henry Roth, Philip Roth had published his first book of fiction, the short story collection *Goodbye, Columbus*, in 1959, and produced more than a dozen additional works during the remaining years of the older author's silence. He considered at least two of the volumes in *Mercy* "masterpieces," and he interviewed their editor with the thought of writing a novel that would draw on the background of Henry Roth's incest. But Philip Roth, who had published a book called *The Ghost Writer* twenty years before, ended up abandoning his plans to fictionalize the life of Henry Roth.[22]

Reviewers cited and quoted the last paragraph of *Requiem for*

Harlem as a powerful culmination of Roth's prose. "His final burst of bravado says it all," wrote Sanford Pinsker in the *Washington Post Book World*.[23] What none of the book's first critics could have known is how much of the bravado was editorial rather than authorial. Felicia Steele and Robert Weil dared to supply an ending where Roth had not. Left to shape a great work's conclusion, the two continued the process of pruning and rearranging that they had begun with Volume 1, except that Roth was now no longer available to render his approval. Uncertain how to draw the entire sequence to a conclusion, they actually put words into their author's mouth—albeit a single, final paragraph.

Was ghost-writing the finale of a novelist who had himself given up the ghost as scandalous—and vandalistic—as concocting a conclusion to Samuel Taylor Coleridge's inspired fragment *Kubla Khan*? The fact that Giacomo Puccini never finished *Turandot* or Jacques Offenbach *Tales of Hoffmann* has not stopped opera companies from staging productions of either, in versions completed by various hands. During the final decades of the twentieth century, posthumous publication of unfinished novels—including Jane Austen's *Sanditon*, Charlotte Brontë's *Emma*, Edith Wharton's *The Buccaneers*, Ernest Hemingway's *Islands in the Stream*, Truman Capote's *Answered Prayers*, and Vladimir Nabokov's *The Enchanter*—raised questions about an editor's responsibility to the intentions and integrity of a dead author. It is one thing to match one's wits against Charles Dickens, as several literary tinkers have done, by inventing an outcome for *The Mystery of Edwin Drood*. But it is quite another for musicologist Semyon Bogatyriev to have conjured out of scattered hints in Peter Ilyich Tchaikovsky's papers the entirety of a phantom Symphony No. 7 in E flat. When Steele and Weil came up with a concluding paragraph to *Requiem for Harlem*, their inventiveness was far more modest than Alexandra Ripley's when, under license from the Margaret Mitchell estate, she devised an extension to *Gone With the Wind* published as *Scarlett*.

When Ralph Ellison, Roth's darker doppelgänger, died in 1994, he too left behind the makings of a long-anticipated second novel. But

Juneteenth was much further from completion than *Mercy of a Rude Stream*. Gathering the notes, typescripts, computer files, and printouts that Ellison had generated over a period of forty years, his executor, John F. Callahan, struggled to put together "a single, coherent, continuous work" out of "multifarious, multifaceted, multifocused, multivoiced, multitoned" material that its author had not been ready yet to publish.[24] To do so, Callahan exercised his own judgment about what to prune, how to organize the sections, and where to place chapter breaks. The rough-edged sketch that he published as *Juneteenth*, whose title page credits Ellison as author and himself as editor, is a tantalizing hint of what might have been. But *Mercy of a Rude Stream* is Roth's *Turandot*, ready for public presentation except for its final duet. On April 25, 1926, a year and a half after Puccini's death, Arturo Toscanini conducted the premiere of *Turandot* at La Scala; when he reached the last note written by the composer, he abruptly put down his baton, turned to the audience, and announced: "*Qui finisce l'opera, perchè a questo punto il Maestro è morto* (The opera ends here, because at this point the Maestro died)."[25] According to a few accounts, the conductor added something that sounded like "*La morte era pi forte dell'arte* (Death was stronger than art)."[26]

Steele and Weil were not so reticent. They composed the final song to conclude their master's work and allow his art to triumph even over death. They might have been miffed by what Callahan had to say when, a year after *Requiem for Harlem* appeared, he made a point of noting that everything in *Juneteenth* was Ellison's: "Now, the editor of a posthumously published novel should not use his own words to finish what the author left unfinished or unsaid."[27] Steele and Weil used their own words only in the final paragraph of Roth's four volumes, and those words are faithful to Roth's spirit as they knew and cherished it. Presentation of *Requiem for Harlem* as a finished work was a skillful act of literary ventriloquism.

Publishing the individual volumes of *Mercy of a Rude Stream* serially, as installments, discouraged readers from seeing the work as a literary continuum, one that gathers momentum as the pages multiply. A publisher would be wise to decide that *Mercy of a Rude Stream* is best experienced as a single volume. It may seem odd to describe a massive *roman fleuve* as minimalist, but, like Samuel Beckett's trilogy (*Malone, Malone Dies*, and *The Unnamable*), Roth's tetralogy is a pared twilight encounter with elemental truths about Eros and Thanatos. Gone are the rhapsodic riffs and other stylistic flourishes that made Roth seem like the Keats of East Ninth Street. Though *Mercy of a Rude Stream* derives its title from *Henry VIII*, it is another Shakespeare play, *King Lear*, whose spirit Roth evokes in his final cycle. A foolish, fond old man approaches wisdom by plumbing folly.

Altersstil is a term that, conceding majesty to seniority (and authority to German), art historians have applied to the style of aging masters. The monumental *Water Lilies* that the arthritic Claude Monet executed months before his death at eighty-six are among the glories of modern painting. Frank Lloyd Wright was ninety-two and designing the Guggenheim Museum when he died. Donatello continued to create extraordinary work until his death at eighty, as did Titian until eighty-eight, Michelangelo until eighty-nine, Frans Hals until eighty-six, Henri Matisse until eighty-five, Georgia O'Keeffe until ninety-nine, Rufino Tamayo until ninety-one. Like *Falstaff*, composed when Verdi was eighty, and *Faust*, completed by Goethe when he was eighty-one, *Mercy of a Rude Stream* is a triumph of *Altersstil* and endurance.

"You are not required to finish," declares the Talmudic dictum that Roth, wracked by rheumatoid arthritis as he tapped out every word, adapted as epigraph even as he denied it. The authorization for insufficiency from Mishnah Abot 2:16 appears at the outset of *Requiem for Harlem*. But after six decades of silence, exile, and brooding, the octogenarian author, afflicted with "that unique, unutterable afflatus of creativity,"[28] became a veritable Niagara of narrative, pouring out 5,000 manuscript pages that recount an anguished life much like his own.

Roth finished his career, with a posthumous adieu, as dramatically as he began it. "Hello, I must be going," sang Groucho Marx in *Animal Crackers*. But it is Roth who is at once salutatorian and valedictorian of modern America. Imagine D. W. Griffith, the inventor of

American narrative cinema, abjuring his rough magic shortly after *Birth of a Nation* and then, on the verge of ninety and extinction, reemerging to create four extraordinary films to send out the century. Roth is a cohort of Don DeLillo and Thomas Pynchon as well as James Joyce and Virginia Woolf.

In one final, mighty torrent of language, Roth put to rest the monsters that had tormented him for eight decades: the fatherless infant uprooted from his rural homeland and hauled to a distant, raucous metropolis; the runty son in dread of his raging, brutal papa; the chubby young Jew skulking through the streets to dodge bigoted neighborhood bullies; the disgraced schoolboy compelled to return purloined fountain pens; the self-loathing adolescent impelled toward furtive, incestuous sex; the coddled young writer distressed over social injustices he cannot remedy; the old man's disgust for a blighted life that might have been different. *Palingenesis*—rebirth—is one of the recondite words that Roth avidly collected, and painfully reenacted. Roth was dead, but his books survived, the weight of their pages a victory over frailty and mortality. Roth opened eyes to terrible shared truths about being human. If readers nod, it is not because they call it sleep. One might as well call it redemption.

⁞▯ NOTES ▯⁞

Introduction

1   Victor Hernandez Cruz, "The lower east side of Manhattan," *Massachusetts Review* 36:4 (Winter 1995): 602.

2   Interview with Al Bierce, July 2, 2001.

3   Letter to HR from David Remnick, April 12, 1985, Henry Roth Papers, Box 7, American Jewish Historical Society.

4   Eugene Walter, "Federico Fellini," *Atlantic Monthly* 216:6 (December 1965): 62.

5   Letter to the author from Robert Weil, August 24, 2004.

6   Gabriel García Márquez and Plinio Apuleyo Mendoza, *El olor de la guayaba: Conversaciones con Plinio Apuleyo Mendoza* (Barcelona: Bruguera, 1982), p. 50.

7   James Boswell, *Life of Johnson*, Vol. 1, p. 166.

8   Henry Roth, *From Bondage* (New York: St. Martin's Press, 1996), p. 28.

9   Harold U. Ribalow, "The History of Henry Roth and *Call It Sleep*," in *Call It Sleep* (New York: Cooper Square Editions, 1970), p. xix.

Part I
Chapter 1

1   Hebrew notebook, Henry Roth Papers, Box 11, American Jewish Historical Society.

2   Joseph Roth, *The Wandering Jews*, trans. Michael Hofmann (New York: W. W. Norton, 2000), pp. 5, 6.

3   Quoted in Ann Douglas, *Terrible Honesty: Mongrel Manhattan in the 1920s* (New York: Farrar, Straus & Giroux, 1995), p. 4.

4   Henry Roth, *Call It Sleep* (New York: Noonday, 1991), p. 11; future references to *Call It Sleep* are from this edition unless otherwise stated.

5   Gerald Sorin, "Immigration, Russian," in Jack Fischel and Sanford Pinsker, eds., *Jewish-American History and Culture: An Encyclopedia* (New York: Garland, 1992), p. 270.

6   Gerald Sorin, *A Time for Building: The Third Migration 1880–1920* (Baltimore: Johns Hopkins University Press, 1992), p. 58.

7   Neil Baldwin, *Henry Ford and the Jews: The Mass Production of Hate* (New York: Public Affairs, 2001), p. 137.

8   Henry James, *The American Scene* (Bloomington: Indiana University Press, 1968), pp. 131, 139, 135.

9   Joseph Telushkin, *The Golden Land: The Story of Jewish Immigration to America* (New York: Harmony, 2002), p. 9.

10   Sorin, *A Time for Building*, p. 96.

11   Jonathan Rosen, "The 60-Year Itch," *Vanity Fair* (February 1994): 39.

12   Alfred Kazin, *A Lifetime Burning in Every Moment: From the Journals of Alfred Kazin* (New York: HarperCollins, 1996), p. 336.

13   Ibid.

14   *Call It Sleep*, p. 21.

15   Leonard Dinnerstein, *Uneasy at Home: Antisemitism and the American Jewish Experience* (New York: Columbia University Press, 1987), p. 19.

16   Peter Derrick, *Tunneling to the Future: The Story of the Great Subway Expansion That Saved New York* (New York: New York University Press, 2001).

17   Hasia R. Diner, *Lower East Side Memories: A Jewish Place in America* (Princeton, NJ: Princeton University Press, 2000), p. 37.

18   Henry Roth, *Shifting Landscape: A Composite, 1925–1987*, intro. and ed. Mario Materassi (Philadelphia: Jewish Publication Society, 1987), p. 230.

19   Quoted in Bernard G. Richards, Introduction, in Abraham Cahan, *Yekl and the Imported Bridegroom and Other Stories of Yiddish New York* (New York: Dover, 1970), pp. vii–viii.

20   *Harper's Magazine* CXXX (May 1915): 957–58.

21   Irving Howe, "Life Never Let Up," *The New York Times Book Review*, October 25, 1964, p. 1.

22   *Shifting Landscape*, p. xiii.

23   Márquez and Mendoza, *El olor de la guayaba*.

24   Jeffrey S. Gurock, *When Harlem Was Jewish* (New York: Columbia University Press, 1979).

25   Quoted in Irving Howe, *The World of Our Fathers* (New York: Simon & Schuster, 1976), p. 131.

26   Henry Roth, *A Star Shines Over Mt. Morris Park* (New York: St. Martin's Press, 1994), p. 75.

Chapter 2

1   Claude McKay, "Harlem Shadows," in *Complete Poems*, ed. William J. Maxwell (Urbana, IL: University of Illinois Press, 2004), p. 162.

2   *Call It Sleep*, p. 374.

3   *From Bondage*, p. 305.

4   *A Star Shines Over Mt. Morris Park*, p. 161.

5   Reprinted in *Shifting Landscape*, p. 168.

6   Paul Johnson, *A History of the American People* (New York: HarperCollins, 1997), p. 579.

7   *Shifting Landscape*, p. 230.

8   *From Bondage*, p. 188.

9   Bonnie Lyons, taped interview with HR, 1972, #2 (cited hereafter as Bonnie Lyons tapes).

10   Henry Roth, unpublished known as "Batch 2"—Henry Roth Papers, American Jewish Historical Society, New York (cited hereafter as Batch 2), p. 967.

11   *A Star Shines Over Mt. Morris Park*, p. 25.

12   *Shifting Landscape*, p. 66.

13   Batch 2, p. 495.

14   *Shifting Landscape*, p. 256.

15   Ibid., p. 298.

16   John Sanford, *The View from Mt. Morris: A Harlem Boyhood* (New York: Barricade, 1994), p. 4.

17   *A Star Shines Over Mt. Morris Park*, p. 151.

18   *Call It Sleep*, film directed by Peter Lataster and Petra Lataster-Czisch (1996).

19   Rosen, "The 60-Year Itch," p. 39.

20   HR, letter to Byron Franzen, November 14, 1968, Henry Roth Papers, Correspondence, Franzen file, American Jewish Historical Society.

21   Henry Roth Papers, Box 41, American Jewish Historical Society.

22   David Bronsen, "A Conversation with Henry Roth," *Partisan Review* 36:2 (1969): 269.

23   *Shifting Landscape*, p. 96.

24   Office of War Records, American Jewish Committee.

25   Henry L. Feingold, *The Jewish People in America*, Vol. 4: *A Time for Searching: Entering the Mainstream 1920–1945* (Baltimore: Johns Hopkins University Press, 1992), p. 27.

26   *From Bondage*, p. 281.

27   Ibid., p. 238.

28   *Shifting Landscape*, p. 252.

29   Quoted in Morris U. Schapps, ed., *A Documentary History of Jews in the United States, 1654–1875* (New York: Schocken Books, 1950, 1971), pp. 1–2.

30   Henry Roth, *A Diving Rock on the Hudson* (New York: St Martin's Press, 1995), p. 34.

31   Ibid., p. 20.

32   Robert Weil, interview with HR in Albuquerque, videotaped for St. Martin's Press, October 28, 1994 (cited hereafter as videotaped interview with HR).

33   *A Diving Rock on the Hudson*, p. 32.

34   Sanford, *The View from Mt. Morris,* p. 168.

35   *A Diving Rock on the Hudson*, p. 163.

36   Interview with Morris Dickstein, March 12, 2002.

37   Bonnie Lyons, *Henry Roth: The Man and His Work* (New York: Cooper Square Publishers, 1976), p. 160.

38   *A Diving Rock on the Hudson*, p. 334.

39   Ibid., p. 140.

40   Ibid., p. 143.

41   Batch 2, p. 208.

42   Robert Weil, videotaped interview with HR, October 28, 1994.

43   Interview with Hugh Roth, May 22, 2000.

44   *A Star Shines Over Mt. Morris Park*, p. 104.

45   Taped conversation between Henry Roth and David Bennahum, January 14, 1981.

46   Interview with Robert Weil, August 24, 2004.

47   *A Star Shines Over Mt. Morris Park*, p. 106.

48   Interview with Felicia Steele, September 16, 2000.

49   Vernon R. Wiehe, *Perilous Rivalry: When Siblings Become Abusive* (Lexington, MA: Lexington Books, 1991).

50   *A Diving Rock on the Hudson*, p. 334.

51   Henry Roth, *Requiem for Harlem* (New York: St. Martin's Press, 1998), p. 72.

52   *From Bondage*, p. 168.

53   Lyons, *Henry Roth*, p. 162.

Chapter 3

1   Ruth Benedict, *Patterns of Culture* (1934; Boston: Houghton Mifflin, 1959), p. 254.

2   July 1, 1971, diary entry, Henry Roth Papers, American Jewish Historical Society.

3   *A Diving Rock on the Hudson*, p. 251.

4   *Requiem for Harlem*, p. 45.

5   *A Diving Rock on the Hudson*, p. 252.

6   Stephen Steinberg, *The Academic Melting Pot: Catholics and Jews in American Higher Education* (New York: McGraw-Hill, 1974), p. 9.

7   William Barrett, *The Truants: Adventures Among the Intellectuals* (Garden City, NY: Anchor, 1982), pp. 23, 22.

8   Henry Roth Papers, Box 45, American Jewish Historical Society.

9   Ross Wetzsteon, *Republic of Dreams: Greenwich Village: The American Bohemia, 1910–1960* (New York: Simon & Schuster, 2002), p. 1.

10 Sam Hunter, *Modern American Painting and Sculpture* (New York: Dell, 1959), p. 68.

11 Ibid., p. 71.

12 Wetzsteon, *Republic of Dreams*, p. ix.

13 Feingold, *A Time for Searching*, p. 15.

14 *Saturday Review*, June 29, 1963.

15 *A Diving Rock on the Hudson*, p. 347.

16 Lyons, *Henry Roth*, p. 160.

17 Eda Lou Walton, untitled poem in *WB in California: A Tribute* (Berkeley: privately printed, 1919).

18 *From Bondage*, p. 23.

19 Ibid., p. 168.

20 Batch 2, p. 1426.

21 Lyons, *Henry Roth*, p. 168.

22 *From Bondage*, p. 75.

23 Ibid., p. 144.

24 Eda Lou Walton, ed., *The City Day: An Anthology of Recent American Poetry* (New York: Ronald Press, 1929), p. vii.

25 *Shifting Landscape*, p. 191.

26 Lois W. Banner, *Intertwined Lives: Margaret Mead, Ruth Benedict, and Their Circle* (New York: Alfred A. Knopf, 2003), p. 218.

27 *Shifting Landscape*, p. 20.

28 *Requiem for Harlem*, p. 46.

Chapter 4

1   Pat Conroy, "Stories," in Will Blythe, ed., *Why I Write* (Boston: Little, Brown, 1998), p. 52.

2   "Last Respects," Henry Roth Papers, Box 23, American Jewish Historical Society.

3   George K. Anderson and Eda Lou Walton, eds., *This Generation: A Selection of British and American Literature From 1914 to the Present with Historical and Critical Essays*. Revised ed. (Chicago: Scott, Foresman, 1949), p. 169.

4   *Shifting Landscape*, p. 295.

5   HR, letter to Eda Lou Walton, August 1932, Berg Collection, New York Public Library.

6   *Shifting Landscape*, p. 295.

7   Interview with Ben Belitt, July 22, 2000.

8   Ben Belitt, "From the Bookless World: A Memoir," *Contemporary Authors Autobiography Series*, Vol. 4, ed. Adele Sarkissian (Detroit: Gale Research, 1986), p. 60.

9   Ibid.

10   *A Diving Rock on the Hudson*, p. 237.

11   *Requiem for Harlem*, p. 22.

12   Belitt, "From the Bookless World," p. 60.

13   Eda Lou Walton, letter to HR, June 24, 1930, Berg Collection, New York Public Library.

14   Belitt, "From the Bookless World," p. 61.

15   Quoted in ibid.

16   Letter to the author from Robert Weil, August 24, 2004.

17   P. Andrew Spahr, *Community of Creativity: A Century of MacDowell Colony Artists* (Manchester, NH: Currier Gallery of Art, 1996), p. 10.

18   *From Bondage*, p. 216.

19   *Shifting Landscape*, pp. 19, 18.

20   Irit Manskleid-Makowsky, "The 'Jewishness' of Jewish American Literature: The Examples of Ludwig Lewisohn and Henry Roth," M.A. thesis, John F. Kennedy-Institut, Freie Universität Berlin, 1978, p. 114. Quoted in Werner Sollors, "'A world somewhere, somewhere else': Language, Nostalgic Mournfulness, and Urban Immigrant Family Romance in *Call It Sleep*," in Hana Wirth-Nesher, ed., *New Essays on Call It Sleep* (New York: Cambridge University Press, 1996), p. 158.

21   Lyons, *Henry Roth*, pp. 159–60.

22   HR, letter to Eda Lou Walton, August 1932, Berg Collection, New York Public Library.

23   Batch 2, p. 555.

24   Letter to the author from Stanley Burnshaw, July 24, 2002.

25   Batch 2, p. 363.

26   Lyons, *Henry Roth*, p. 162, 176.

27   Louise Bogan, letter to Morton D. Zabel, December 3, 1935, quoted in Ruth

Limmer, ed., *What the Woman Lived: Selected Letters of Louise Bogan 1920–1970* (New York: Harcourt Brace Jovanovich, 1973), p. 120.

28   Interview with Ben Belitt, July 22, 2000.

29   The account that follows is based on an interview with Stanley Burnshaw, March 11, 2000.

30   Bonnie Lyons tapes, 1972, #4.

31   HR, letter to Eda Lou Walton, August 1932, Berg Collection, New York Public Library.

32   John S. Friedman, "On Being Blocked and Other Literary Matters: An Interview," *Commentary* 64 (1977): 28–38.

33   HR, letter to Eda Lou Walton, March 11, 1933, Berg Collection, New York Public Library.

34   HR, letter to Eda Lou Walton, Monday, March 1933, Berg Collection, New York Public Library.

35   Henry Roth Papers, Box 45, American Jewish Historical Society.

36   HR, letter to Eda Lou Walton, June 3, 1933, Berg Collection, New York Public Library.

37   HR, letter to Eda Lou Walton, June 1933, Berg Collection, New York Public Library.

38   Roth journal, Berg Collection, New York Public Library.

39   HR, letter to Eda Lou Walton, June 3, 1933, Berg Collection, New York Public Library.

40   HR, letter to Eda Lou Walton, June 5, 1933, Berg Collection, New York Public Library.

41   HR, letter to Eda Lou Walton, June 23, 1933, Berg Collection, New York Public Library.

42   "Robert O. Ballou" in *Dictionary of Literary Biography*. Vol. 46: *American Literary Publishing Houses, 1900–1980*, ed. Peter Dzwonkoski (Detroit: Gale Research, 1986), p. 33.

43   Walter B. Rideout, *The Radical Novel in the United States 1900–1954: Some Interrelations of Literature and Society* (Cambridge, MA: Harvard University Press, 1956), p. 141.

44   "Draft Manifesto of John Reed Clubs," *The New Masses* 7 (June 1932): 3–4.

45   William Freedman, "A Conversation with Henry Roth," *Literary Review* 18:2 (Winter 1975): 154.

46   Lyons, *Henry Roth*, p. 162.

47   Interview with Ben Belitt, July 22, 2000.

48   Harvey Klehr, *The Heyday of American Communism: The Depression Decade* (New York: Basic Books, 1984), p. 360.

49   Reprinted in *Shifting Landscape*, pp. 48–50.

50   HR, letter to Eda Lou Walton, June 23, 1933, Berg Collection, New York Public Library.

51   Alan Wald, "Jewish American Writers on the Left," in Michael P. Kramer and Hana Wirth-Nesher, eds., *The Cambridge Companion to Jewish American Literature* (New York: Cambridge University Press, 2003), p. 171.

52   HR, letter to Eda Lou Walton, July 1934, Berg Collection, New York Public Library.

53   HR, letter to Eda Lou Walton, August 9, 1934, Berg Collection, New York Public Library.

54   HR, letters to Eda Lou Walton, August 20, August 17, and August 23, 1934, Berg Collection, New York Public Library.

55   HR, letter to Eda Lou Walton, September 3, 1934. Berg Collection, New York Public Library.

Chapter 5

1   "Accepting Nobel Prize," *Newsweek*, December 24, 1962.

2   Freedman, "A Conversation with Henry Roth," p. 156.

3   Quoted in Wetzsteon, *Republic of Dreams: Greenwich Village: The American Bohemia, 1910–1960*, p. 22.

4   Jane Howard, "The Belated Success of Henry Roth," *Life*, January 8, 1965, p. 76.

5   Roth, *Call It Sleep*, p. 85.

6   Theodore Roethke, "My Father's Waltz," *Collected Poems* (Garden City, NY: Doubleday, 1966), p. 45.

7   Wirth-Nesher, ed., Introduction, *New Essays on Call It Sleep*, p. 5.

8   HR, letter to Hana Wirth-Nesher, August 8, 1991, Henry Roth Papers, Correspondence, Wirth-Nesher folder, American Jewish Historical Society.

9   Walter Allen, Afterword, in Roth, *Call It Sleep* (New York: Avon, 1964), p. 445.

10   Wirth-Nesher, Afterword, in Roth, *Call It Sleep* (Noonday, 1991), p. 447.

11   *Call It Sleep*, 153.

12   Ibid., p. 441.

13   Julie Eastlack Hopson, *The Literary Reputations of Henry Roth*, Unpublished M.A. thesis, Harvard University, June 1990, p. 4.

14   Fred T. Marsh, "A Great Novel About Manhattan Boyhood," *New York Herald Tribune Books*, February 17, 1935, p. 6.

15   Horace Gregory, "East Side World," *The Nation* 140 (February 27, 1935): 255.

16   Alfred Hayes, *Daily Worker*, March 5, 1935.

17   Joseph Gollomb, *Saturday Review of Literature*, March 16, 1935.

18   H. W. Boynton, *The New York Times*, February 17, 1935, p. 7.

19   Hayes, *Daily Worker*, March 5, 1935.

20   "Brief Review," *The New Masses* 14 (February 12, 1935): 27.

21   David Greenhood, "Another View of *Call It Sleep*," *The New Masses*, 14 (February 19, 1935): 21.

22 Edwin Seaver, "Caesar or Nothing," *The New Masses* 14 (March 5, 1935): 20.

23 *Call It Sleep*, film directed by Peter Lataster and Petra Lataster-Czisch (1996).

24 Gregory, "East Side World," p. 255.

25 Michael Harrington, Afterword, in Michael Gold, *Jews Without Money* (New York: Avon, 1965), p. 233.

26 Kenneth Ledbetter, "Henry Roth's *Call It Sleep*: The Revival of a Proletarian Novel," *Twentieth Century Literature* 12 (1966): 123.

27 Arthur Miller, *Echoes Down the Corridor: Collected Essays 1944–2000* (New York: Viking, 2000), pp. ix–x.

28 HR, letter to Byron Franzen, November 4, 1968, Henry Roth Papers, Correspondence, Franzen folder, American Jewish Historical Society.

29 *A Diving Rock on the Hudson*, p. 107.

30 Marsh, "A Great Novel About Manhattan Boyhood," p. 6.

31 Rideout, *The Radical Novel in the United States 1900–1954*, p. 186.

32 Lyons, *Henry Roth*, p. 173.

33 Granville Hicks, *The Great Tradition: An Interpretation of American Literature Since the Civil War* (New York: Macmillan, 1933), p. 290.

34 1977 interview with John S. Friedman, reprinted in *Shifting Landscape*, p. 23.

35 A. Scott Berg, *Max Perkins: Editor of Genius* (New York: Pocket Books, 1979), p. 352.

Chapter 6

1   John Fowles, *The Magus* (New York: Dell, 1968), p. 92.

2   Herman Melville, *Moby-Dick; or, The Whale* (Berkeley: University of California Press, 1981), p. 3.

3   *Shifting Landscape*, pp. 46, 298.

4   Bonnie Lyons tapes, 1972, #1.

5   David Mandel, Memorandum of October 27, 1964, Henry Roth Papers, Box 5, folder 4, American Jewish Historical Society.

6   Transcript of conversation between HR and David Bennahum, January 14, 1981, p. 4.

7   Ibid.

8   HR, interview with Margie Goldsmith, July 2 and 5, 1983, in *Shifting Landscape*, p. 44.

9   "If We Had Bacon," *Shifting Landscape*, pp. 39–40.

10 Lyons, *Henry Roth*, p. 162.

11 Eda Lou Walton, letters to HR, August 14, 1935, and June 1936, Box 9, American Jewish Historical Society.

12 Eda Lou Walton, letter to HR, 1938, Henry Roth Papers, Box 9, American Jewish Historical Society.

Chapter 7

1 Jonathan Franzen, "Perchance to Dream: In the Age of Images, A Reason to Write Novels," *Harper's* 292 (April 1996): 35.

2 Yaddo Web site—http://yaddo.org/yaddo/history.shtml.

3 Eda Lou Walton, letter to Elizabeth Ames, February 3, 1938, Yaddo Papers, New York Public Library, Rare Books and Manuscripts Division.

4 HR, letter to Richard Parker, February 19, 1977, Henry Roth Papers, Correspondence, Parker folder, American Jewish Historical Society.

5 HR, letter to Richard Parker, February 19, 1977, www.lhup.edu/~rparker/yaddoames.htm

6 Sales figures provided by Daniel Fuchs in the Preface to reissue of *The Williamsburg Trilogy* (New York: Berkley, 1965), p. 7.

7 Batch 2, p. 312.

8 Quoted by Felicia Jean Steele in the memorial pamphlet for his parents published privately by Hugh Roth (1999, cited hereafter as Memorial pamphlet), p. 5.

9 *Shifting Landscape*, p. 100.

10 Lyons, *Henry Roth*, p. 162.

11 Interview with Hugh Roth, May 22, 2000.

12 *Shifting Landscape*, p. 105.

13 Belitt, "From the Bookless World," pp. 60–61.

14 Batch 2, p. 53.

15 Ben Hecht, *A Child of the Century* (New York: Simon & Schuster, 1954), p. 466.

16 Batch 2, pp. 77–78.

17 *From Bondage*, p. 272.

18 Batch 2, p. 79.

Part II
Chapter 8

1 Jack London, "What Life Means to Me," in *The Portable Jack London*, ed. Earle Labor (New York: Penguin, 1994), pp. 481–82.

2 Batch 2, p. 411.

3 Ibid., p. 412.

4 Ibid., p. 688.

5 Neal Gabler, *An Empire of Their Own: How the Jews Invented Hollywood* (New York: Crown, 1988), p. 290.

6 Batch 2, p. 445.

7 Eda Lou Walton, letter to HR, November 20, 1938, Henry Roth Papers, Correspondence, Walton folder, American Jewish Historical Society.

8   Eda Lou Walton, letter to HR, Henry Roth Papers, November 21, 1938, Correspondence, Walton folder, American Jewish Historical Society.

9   Ibid.

10   Batch 2, pp. 1330–31.

11   Paul Jacobs, *Is Curly Jewish?* (New York: Atheneum, 1965), p. 15, quoted in Peter Novick, *The Holocaust in American Life* (Boston: Houghton Mifflin, 1999), pp. 40–41.

12   Max Frankel, *The Times of My Life and My Life with The Times* (New York: Random House, 1999), p. 48.

13   Susan E. Tifft and Alex S. Jones, *The Trust: The Private and Powerful Family Behind The New York Times* (Boston: Little, Brown, 1999), p. 217.

14   www.pbs.org/wbgh/amex/lindbergh/filmmore/reference/primary/desmoines speech.html.

15   Batch 2, p. 1335.

Chapter 9

1   Herman Melville, letter to Nathaniel Hawthorne [June 1?], 1851, in Lynn Horth, ed., Herman Melville, *Correspondence* (Evanston: Northwestern University Press, 1993), p. 191.

2   Batch 2, p. 1434.

3   *Shifting Landscape*, p. 54.

4   Bonnie Lyons, "Interview with Henry Roth, March 1977," *Studies in American Jewish Literature* 5 (Spring 1979): 51.

5   *Shifting Landscape*, pp. 59–60.

6   HR, letter to William Maxwell, June 6, 1943, *New Yorker* Archives, Manuscript Collection, New York Public Library.

7   William Maxwell, letter to HR, September 13, 1956, *New Yorker* Archives, Manuscript Collection, New York Public Library.

8   Letter from Robert Hemenway to Roslyn Targ, November 17, 1967, *New Yorker* Archives, Manuscript Collection, New York Public Library.

9   HR, letter to William Maxwell, January 14, 1957, *New Yorker* Archives, Manuscript Collection, New York Public Library.

10   Batch 2, p. 1490.

11   Ibid., p. 955.

12   Ibid., pp. 1849–50, 818–19.

13   Ibid., p. 27.

14   Ibid., p. 29.

Chapter 10

1 Leo Rosten, *Leo Rosten's Treasury of Jewish Quotations* (New York: Bantam, 1977), p. 106.
2 Batch 2, p. 495.
3 Howard, "The Belated Success of Henry Roth," p. 75.
4 Batch 2, pp. 1855, 1861.
5 Ibid., p. 1862.
6 HR, letter to William Maxwell, November 12, 1952, *New Yorker* Archives, Manuscript Collection, New York Public Library.
7 Batch 2, pp. 1487–89.
8 Bonnie Lyons tapes, 1972, #3.

Part III
Chapter 11

1 *Ethics of the Fathers*, 2:5.
2 Hamilton Wright Mabie, *Backgrounds of Literature* (1904; Freeport, NY: Books for Libraries, 1970), p. 74.
3 Robert Weil, videotaped interview with HR, October 28, 1994.
4 E-mail from Hugh Roth to the author, January 6, 2003.
5 FBI report 100-17564, filed in Boston, May 3, 1951, pp. 3–4.
6 Teletype message, labeled "very urgent," from Agent Thornton in Boston to Inspector A. H. Belmont in Washington, February 9, 1951, p. 1.
7 Office Memorandum on Henry Roth, from SAC, Boston (100-17564), to Director, FBI (100-345488), October 30, 1953, p. 1.
8 Robert Weil, videotaped interview with HR, October 28, 1994.
9 Interview with Joy Walker, June 18, 2000.
10 Quoted in Hugh Roth, Memorial pamphlet (1999), p. 3.
11 Interview with Joy Walker, June 18, 2000.
12 E-mail to the author from Penny Markey, December 4, 2001.
13 *A Diving Rock on the Hudson*, p. 161.
14 Letter to the author from Robert Weil, August 24, 2004.
15 Batch 2, p. 1715.
16 Interview with Mario Materassi, February 8, 1986, in *Shifting Landscape*, p. 81.
17 Interview with Mario Materassi, April 24, 1985, in *Shifting Landscape*, p. 78.
18 HR, letter to Diane Levenberg, June 16, 1987, in *Shifting Landscape*, p. 83.
19 Howard, "The Belated Success of Henry Roth," p. 75.
20 Interview with Carole Roth, February 3, 2002.
21 Interview with Hugh Roth, June 22, 2000.
22 Interview with Vicky Elsberg, February 28, 2001.
23 Batch 2, pp. 1668–69.

24   "Assassins and Soldiers: Sundry Epistles from *The Era of Nam*," *Shifting Landscape*, pp. 124–25.

25   *From Bondage*, p. 239.

26   E-mail to the author from Hugh Roth, August 15, 2004.

27   *Requiem for Harlem*, pp. 249, 44.

28   Batch 2, p. 1673.

29   Friedman, "On Being Blocked and Other Literary Matters: An Interview," p. 32.

30   *A Diving Rock on the Hudson*, p. 401.

31   Interview with Pauline Nadler, October 19, 2002.

32   Interview with Joy Walker, June 18, 2000.

33   Vicky Elsberg, letter to HR, February 16, 1994, Henry Roth Papers, Correspondence, Elsberg folder, American Jewish Historical Society.

34   Interview with Ruth and Ted Bookey, March 21, 2001.

35   Wallace Stevens, "The Snow Man," in *The Palm at the End of the Mind: Selected Poems and a Play*, ed. Holly Stevens (New York: Vintage, 1972), p. 54.

Chapter 12

1   Harold U. Ribalow, "The History of Henry Roth and *Call It Sleep*," in *Call It Sleep* (Cooper Square, 1960), p. xx.

2   James T. Farrell, "The End of a Literary Decade," *American Mercury* 48 (December 1939): 412.

3   Marie Syrkin, "The Cultural Scene: Literary Expression," in Oscar I. Janowsky, ed., *The American Jew: A Composite Portrait* (New York: Harper & Brothers, 1942), p. 102.

4   *The Radical Novel in the United States 1900–1954*, p. 186.

5   Alfred Kazin, "Neglected Books," *The American Scholar* 25 (Autumn 1956): 486.

6   Leslie Fiedler, "Neglected Books," *The American Scholar* 25 (Autumn 1956): 478.

7   Interview with Meir Ribalow, March 15, 2002.

8   Ibid.

9   Harold U. Ribalow, letter to HR, December 10, 1959. Henry Roth Papers, Box 7, American Jewish Historical Society.

10   Dorothy Parker, *Esquire* (March 1961).

11   Quotations and information about how Avon came to publish *Call It Sleep* come from an interview with Peter Mayer, September 21, 2001, and an e-mail from him, February 11, 2005.

12   Kenneth C. Davis, *Two-Bit Culture: The Paperbacking of America* (Boston: Houghton Mifflin, 1984), p. 356.

13   Walter Allen, Afterword, in *Call It Sleep* (Avon, 1964), p. 447.

14   The account of how Irving Howe came to review *Call It Sleep* on the front page of *The New York Times Book Review* was provided by Stanley Burnshaw in an interview on March 11, 2000.

15   Irving Howe, "Life Never Let Up," *The New York Times Book Review*, October 25, 1964, p. 61, 1.

16   Norman Zierold, *The Moguls* (New York: Avon, 1972), p. 197.

17   Rose Broder, letter to HR, November 12, 1964, Box 1, Henry Roth Papers, American Jewish Historical Society.

18   Interview with Gerald Vizenor, April 21, 2004.

19   Gerald Vizenor, *Interior Landscapes: Autobiographical Myths and Metaphors* (Minneapolis: University of Minnesota Press, 1990), p. 158.

20   Belitt, "From the Bookless World," p. 62.

21   Bonnie Lyons tapes, 1972, #4.

22   Ben Belitt, "The Cremation: New Mexico," in *Possessions: New and Selected Poems (1938–1985)* (Boston: David R. Godine, 1986), p. 100.

23   Hilary Lapsley, *Margaret Mead and Ruth Benedict: The Kinship of Women* (Amherst, MA: University of Massachusetts Press, 1999), pp. 176, 351.

24   Witter Bynner, "On Teaching the Young Laurel to Shoot," *The New Republic* 37 (December 5, 1923): 5.

25   *A Diving Rock on the Hudson*, p. 270.

26   *Requiem for Harlem*, pp. 272, 267.

27   Ted Bookey, letter to HR, October 25, 1964, Correspondence, Bookey folder, American Jewish Historical Society.

28   Brian M. Sietsema, letter to HR, February 3, 1994, Box 3, Henry Roth Papers, American Jewish Historical Society.

29   Howard, "The Belated Success of Henry Roth," p. 75.

30   Martha MacGregor, "The Week in Books," *New York Post*, November 8, 1964, p. 47.

31   Frank Sleeper, "Augusta Man's First Novel Scores . . . After 30 Years," *Portland Sunday Telegram*, December 6, 1964, p. 11A.

32   Interview with Ruth and Ted Bookey, March 21, 2001.

33   David Bronsen, "A Conversation with Henry Roth," *Partisan Review* 36:2 (1969): 278.

34   HR, letter to Stephen Adams, August 9, 1987, Henry Roth Papers, Box 1, American Jewish Historical Society.

35   Norman Mailer, *The Spooky Art: Some Thoughts on Writing* (New York: Random House, 2003), p. 23.

36   Howard, "The Belated Success of Henry Roth," p. 76.

37   *Boston Globe*, March 23, 1965, in Henry Roth Papers, Box 47, American Jewish Historical Society.

38   Allen, Afterword, *Call It Sleep* (Avon, 1964), p. 447.

39   Rosen, "The 60-Year Itch," p. 45.

Chapter 13

1   Margaret Mead, *Culture and Commitment: The New Relationships Between the Generations in the 1970s* (New York: Columbia University Press, 1978), p. 63.

2   Kazin, *A Lifetime Burning in Every Moment*, p. 223.

3   Henry Roth Papers, Box 6, American Jewish Historical Society.

4   HR, letter to National Institute of Arts and Letters, May 19, 1965, Henry Roth Papers, Box 45, American Jewish Historical Society.

5   HR, letter to Iven Hurlingen, Winter 1965, in *Shifting Landscape*, p. 248.

6   Interview with Philip Levine, February 27, 2003.

7   Interview with John A. Williams, March 3, 2003.

8   HR, letter to John A. Williams, July 25, 1966, John A. Williams Papers, Rush Rhees Library, University of Rochester.

9   HR, letter to Jeremy Roth, December 17, 1965, Henry Roth Papers, Box 8, American Jewish Historical Society.

10   Robert Weil, videotaped interview with HR, October 28, 1994.

11   HR, letter to Iven Hurlinger, Winter 1965, in *Shifting Landscape*, pp. 247–48.

12   *A Star Shines Over Mt. Morris Park*, p. 161.

13   *From Bondage*, p. 188.

14   Henry Roth, "The Meaning of *Galut* in America Today." *Midstream* 9:1 (March 1963): 33.

15   William Targ, *Indecent Pleasures: The Life and Colorful Times of William Targ* (New York: Macmillan, 1975), p. 88.

16   Ibid., p. 359.

17   HR, letter to Harold Ribalow, October 19, 1964, Henry Roth Papers, Correspondence, Ribalow folder, American Jewish Historical Society.

18   Harold Ribalow, letter to HR, October 21, 1964, Henry Roth Papers, Correspondence, Ribalow folder, American Jewish Historical Society.

19   HR letter to Harold Ribalow, October 25, 1964, Henry Roth Papers, Correspondence, Ribalow folder, American Jewish Historical Society.

20   E-mail to the author from Roslyn Targ, January 30, 2003.

21   HR, letter to Harold Ribalow, January 31, 1965, Henry Roth Papers, Correspondence, Ribalow folder, American Jewish Historical Society.

22   Morris Dickstein, "Call It an Awakening," *New York Times Book Review*, November 29, 1987, p. 1.

23   Henry Roth Papers, Box 11, American Jewish Historical Society.

24   HR, letter to Mario Materassi, July 25, 1966, Henry Roth Papers, Correspondence, Materassi folder, American Jewish Historical Society.

25   Interview with Ruth and Ted Bookey, March 21, 2001.

26   Friedman, "On Being Blocked and Other Literary Matters: An Interview," p. 38.

27   Bronsen, "A Conversation with Henry Roth," p. 278.

28 Henry Roth, "Kaddish," *Midstream* 23:1 (January 1977): 54–55.

29 Ibid., p. 55.

30 Henry Roth, "Segments," *Studies in American Jewish Literature* 5 (Spring 1979): 58.

31 David Mandel, letter to HR, April 18, 1971, Henry Roth Papers, Correspondence, Mandel folder, American Jewish Historical Society.

32 *From Bondage*, p. 215.

33 Ibid., p. 70.

34 *Shifting Landscape*, p. 300.

35 Interview with Joy Walker, June 18, 2000.

36 Batch 2, pp. 1868–69.

37 Interview with Carole Roth, February 3, 2002.

38 Letter to the author from Robert Weil, September 26, 2004.

39 Interview with Carole Roth, February 3, 2002.

40 Interview with Vicky Elsberg, February 28, 2001.

Part IV
Chapter 14

1 Abbey, Edward, *Fire on the Mountain* (Albuquerque: University of New Mexico Press).

2 Harry T. Moore, *The Priest of Love: A Life of D. H. Lawrence* (New York: Farrar, Straus & Giroux, 1974), p. 357.

3 Ibid., p. 354.

4 Rosemary Lévy Zumwalt, *Wealth and Rebellion: Elsie Clews Parson, Anthropologist and Folklorist* (Urbana: University of Illinois Press, 1992), pp. 239–40.

5 D. H. Lawrence, "St. Mawr," in Frank Kermode and John Hollander, eds., *The Oxford Anthology of English Literature*, Vol. 2 (New York: Oxford University Press, 1973), p. 1933.

6 HR, letter to David Bronsen, June 23, 1968, Henry Roth Papers, Correspondence, Bronsen folder, American Jewish Historical Society.

7 Interview with James Weaver, August 23, 2002.

8 Interview with David Bennahum, June 29, 2001.

9 Interview with David Bennahum, April 22, 2001.

10 Transcript of taped conversations between David Bennahum and HR, January 7, 1981, pp. 1, 5.

11 HR, letter to Roslyn Targ, November 15, 1981, Henry Roth Papers, Box 9, American Jewish Historical Society.

12 HR, letter to Mario Materassi, September 25, 1968, in *Shifting Landscape*, p. 179.

13 HR, letter to Robert Manning, May 6, 1969, Henry Roth Papers, Box 1, American Jewish Historical Society.

14 Stanley Burnshaw, letter to HR, February 13, 1983, Stanley Burnshaw Papers, Harry Ransom Humanities Research Center, Austin, Texas.

15 Lyons, *Henry Roth*, p. 175.

16 HR, letter to Rose Broder, June 4, 1964 Henry Roth Papers, Box 1, American Jewish Historical Society.

17 HR, letter to Harold S_____, October 5, 1994, Henry Roth Papers, Box 8, American Jewish Historical Society.

18 Friedman, "On Being Blocked and Other Literary Matters: An Interview," p. 32.

19 Profile of Herman Roth, *Hotel and Club Voice* (April, 1966): 19.

20 Friedman, "On Being Blocked and Other Literary Matters: An Interview," p. 27.

21 William Freedman, "Henry Roth in Jerusalem," *Literary Review* 23:1 (Fall 1979): 6.

22 HR, postcard to Boris Gamzue, August 10, 1975, Henry Roth Papers, Correspondence, Gamzue folder, American Jewish Historical Society.

23 HR, letter to Eldridge Cleaver, February 1, 1976, Henry Roth Papers, Correspondence, Cleaver folder, American Jewish Historical Society.

24 HR, letter to Judge Wilson, August 6, 1976, Henry Roth Papers, Correspondence, Wilson folder, American Jewish Historical Society.

25 "Segments," in *Shifting Landscape*, p. 232.

26 Interview with Mario Materassi, February 10, 1986, in *Shifting Landscape*, p. 236.

27 Leonard Michaels, *Time Out of Mind: The Diaries of Leonard Michaels 1961–1995* (New York: Riverhead, 1999), p. 188.

28 HR, letter to Joan Baum, November 24, 1988. Henry Roth Papers, Correspondence, Baum folder, American Jewish Historical Society.

29 Letter to the author from Robert Weil, September 26, 2004.

30 HR, letter to Mario Materassi, May 24, 1977, in *Shifting Landscape*, p. 221.

31 HR, letter to Mario Materassi, July 6, 1977, in *Shifting Landscape*, p. 222.

32 "Report from Miskenot Sha'ananim," in *Shifting Landscape*, p. 223.

33 E-mail to the author from Shirley Kaufman, August 24, 2003.

34 Marsha Pomerantz, "A Long Sleep," *Jerusalem Post Magazine*, September 23, 1977, p. 8, quoted in *Shifting Landscape*, p. 225.

35 "Vale Atque Ave," in *Shifting Landscape*, p. 227.

36 Interview with Mario Materassi, February 10, 1986, in *Shifting Landscape*, p. 229.

37 HR, postcard to Boris Gamzue, August 10, 1975, Henry Roth Papers, Box 3, American Jewish Historical Society.

Chapter 15

1 HR, letter to Mario Materassi, April 21, 1981, in *Shifting Landscape*, p. 260.

2 *Shifting Landscape*, pp. 198–99.

3   Howard, "The Belated Success of Henry Roth," p. 75.

4   Transcript of taped conversations between HR and David Bennahum, January 7, 1981.

5   *From Bondage*, p. 68.

6   Transcript of taped conversations between HR and David Bennahum, January 7, 1981, p. 1.

7   *From Bondage*, p. 68.

8   Ibid.

9   *Shifting Landscape*, p. 299.

10   HR, letter to David Bronsen, June 23, 1968, Henry Roth Papers, Correspondence, Bronsen folder, American Jewish Historical Society.

11   Interview with David Bennahum, April 22, 2001.

12   HR, letter to Boris Gamzue, June 1, 1985, Henry Roth Papers, Correspondence, Gamzue folder, American Jewish Historical Society.

13   *Shifting Landscape*, p. 234.

14   Batch 2, p. 295.

15   Hugh Roth, Memorial pamphlet (1999), p. 9.

16   Bob Groves, "Going Back to School Later, Much Later," *Albuquerque Journal*, undated, p. D1.

17   Hugh Roth, Memorial pamphlet (1999), p. 5.

18   David Steinberg, "Composer Excelled Late in Life," *Albuquerque Journal*, February 16, 1990, p. D1.

19   Hugh Roth, Memorial pamphlet (1999), p. 10.

20   Rosalie Heller, letter to the author, March 7, 2001.

21   *Shifting Landscape*, pp. xiii–xiv.

22   Robert Alter, *The New Republic* 198 (January 25, 1988): 33.

23   Morris Dickstein, "Call It an Awakening," *New York Times Book Review*, November 29, 1987, p. 1.

24   *Shifting Landscape*, p. xiv.

25   HR, letter to Mario Materassi, January 17, 1983, Henry Roth Papers, Correspondence, Materassi folder, American Jewish Historical Society.

26   *Shifting Landscape*, pp. 299–300.

27   HR, letter to Mario Materassi, February 22, 1987, in *Shifting Landscape*, p. 301.

28   *Shifting Landscape*, p. 298.

29   Mario Materassi, "The Return of Henry Roth: An Inside View," trans. William Boelhower and Mario Togni, *In Their Own Words* (Venice: Libreria Editrice Cafoscarina, 1983) p. 55.

30   Interview with Carole Roth, February 3, 2002.

31   *Call It Sleep*, film by Peter Lataster and Petra Lataster-Czisch (1996).

32   *Shifting Landscape*, p. 125.

33   Batch 2, p. 640.

34   Interview with David Bennahum, April 22, 2001.

35   Interview with Larry Fox, May 23, 2000.

36   Interview with Larry Fox, April 22, 2000.

37   *Firsts* I (July 1991): 11.

38   Interview with David Bennahum, April 22, 2001.

39   Interview with David Bennahum, April 22, 2001.

40   E-mail to the author from Brian Errett, June 13, 2001.

41   Interview with Larry Fox, August 18, 2004.

42   Letter to the author from Rudolfo Anaya, May 8, 2001.

43   Interview with Sam Girgus, September 1, 2001.

44   Letter to the author from Robert Weil, September 13, 2004.

45   Quoted in Steinberg, "Composer Excelled Late in Life," p. D1.

46   E-mail to the author from Felicia Jean Steele, April 6, 2004.

47   Interview with Leslie Schultis, September 25, 2001.

48   Muriel Roth, letter to Scott Wilkinson, December 17, 1989.

49   Interview with David Bennahum, June 29, 2001.

50   Batch 2, p. 1922.

51   Ibid., 1906.

52   Robert Weil, videotaped interview with HR, October 28, 1994.

53   Box 6, Henry Roth Papers, American Jewish Historical Society.

54   Rosen, "The 60-Year Itch," p. 38.

55   E-mail to the author from Felicia Steele, April 6, 2004.

56   Batch 2, p. 1906.

Chapter 16

1   Lyons, *Henry Roth*, p. 162.

2   Kazin, Introduction, *Call It Sleep* (Noonday Press, 1991), p. ix.

3   HR, letter to Hana Wirth-Nesher, August 8, 1991.

4   E-mail to the author from Hana Wirth-Nesher, March 16, 2004.

5   Quoted in William R. Cole, "No Author Is a Man of Genius to His Publisher," *New York Times Book Review*, September 3, 1989.

6   John Townsend Trowbridge, *My Own Story, with Recollections of Noted Persons* (Boston: Houghton Mifflin, 1903), p. 367.

7   *Shifting Landscape*, p. 257.

8   Alan Gibbs, "Conversation with Robert Weil, March 2002." *Studies in American Jewish Literature* 22 (2003): 154.

9   Interview with Robert Weil, February 4, 2002.

10   Gibbs, "Conversation with Robert Weil," p. 155.

11   Ibid.

12   Henry Roth Papers, Box 37, American Jewish Historical Society.

13   Mario Materassi, letter to HR, February 2, 1993, Henry Roth Papers, American Jewish Historical Society.

14   Interview with Larry Fox, August 18, 2004.

15   Mario Materassi, letter to HR, June 10, 1993, Henry Roth Papers, Correspondence, Materassi folder, American Jewish Historical Society.

16   David Mehegan, "Call It Writer's Block," *Boston Globe*, February 1, 1994, p. 52.

17   *A Star Shines Over Mt. Morris Park*, pp. 286–88.

18   Michaels, *Time Out of Mind*, p. 188.

19   Interview with Noah Harris, July 11, 2003.

20   E-mail to the author from Felicia Jean Steele, April 6, 2004.

21   Interview with Avery Cheser, January 30, 2000.

22   Interview with Helen Mitchener, November 17, 2001.

23   Gibbs, "Conversation with Robert Weil," p. 158.

24   *A Star Shines Over Mt. Morris Park*, p. 94.

25   Text of HR's comments at Congregation Albert on February 6, 1994.

26   David Steinberg, "Word Dam Broke After Nearly 60 Years," *Albuquerque Journal*, February 6, 1994, p. 1F.

27   See Richard E. Nicholls, "Henry Roth, 89, Who Wrote of an Immigrant Child's Life in 'Call It Sleep,' Is Dead," *New York Times*, October 15, 1995, p. 41.

28   Rudolfo Anaya, letter to HR, April 26, 1994, Henry Roth Papers, Correspondence, Anaya folder, American Jewish Historical Society.

29   Rodolfo Anaya, letter to the author, May 8, 2001.

30   Lee Lescaze, *Wall Street Journal*, January 21, 1994, A12.

31   Robert Towers, *New York Review of Books* 4 (March 3, 1994): 24.

32   Robert Alter, *New York Times Book Review*, January 16, 1994, p. 3.

33   Paul Gray, "Ending a 60-Year Silence," *Time*, January 31, 1994.

34   Rosen, "The 60-Year Itch," p. 36.

35   E-mail to the author from Digby Wolfe, July 7, 2001.

36   Speech delivered at the University of New Mexico, May 13, 1994, Henry Roth Papers, American Jewish Historical Society.

37   Interview with Noah Harris, July 11, 2003.

38   Henry Roth, Foreword, in David Isay, *Holding On*, photographs by Harvey Wang (New York: W. W. Norton, 1996), p. 9.

39   *Call It Sleep*, film directed by Peter Lataster and Petra Lataster-Czisch (1996).

40   Interview with Helen Mitchener, November 17, 2001.

41   Rose Broder, letter to HR, July 3, 1994, Henry Roth Papers, Correspondence, Broder folder, American Jewish Historical Society.

42   Interview with Carole Roth, February 3, 2002.

43   Robert Weil, videotaped interview with HR, October 28, 1994.

44   Ibid.

45   Mehegan, "Henry Roth: No Mercy from a 60-Year-Old Memory," p. B38.

46   Elizabeth Manus, "A Sister's Angry Letter Unravels Roth Incest Tale," *New York Observer*, May 18, 1998, p. 30.

47   Mary Gordon, *New York Times Book Review*, February 26, 1995, p. 5.

48   Robert Weil, interview with Alan Gibbs, March 2002, p. 2.

49   Manus, "A Sister's Angry Letter," p. 30.

50   Letter from Meir Ribalow to HR, September 26, 1995, made available to the author by Meir Ribalow.

51   Interview with Noah Harris, July 11, 2003.

52   Letter to the author from Robert Weil, September 13, 2004.

53   E-mail to the author from Dr. Grace Davis, August 11, 2003.

Chapter 17

1   Vladimir Nabokov, *Pale Fire* (New York: Vintage, 1989), p. 272.

2   Nicholls, "Henry Roth, 89, Who Wrote of an Immigrant Child's Life in 'Call It Sleep,' Is Dead," *The New York Times*, October 15, 1995, p. 41.

3   J. M. G. Le Clézio, "La mémoire magique," *Le Nouvel Observateur*, August 25, 1994, p. 55 (translation by Kellman).

4   Interview with Hugh Roth, February 13, 2000.

5   Hugh Roth, Memorial pamphlet (1999), p. 27.

6   HR, letter to Mario Materassi, February 25, 1987, in *Shifting Landscape*, p. 301.

7   Gibbs, "Conversation with Robert Weil, March 2002," p. 159.

8   *From Bondage*, p. 341.

9   Ibid., pp. 28, 116.

10   Letter to the author from Robert Weil, September 27, 2004.

11   *From Bondage*, p. 301.

12   Ibid., p. 388.

13   David Mehegan, *Boston Globe*, July 14, 1996, p. B33.

14   Frank Kermode, *New York Times Book Review*, July 14, 1996, p. 6.

15   *Requiem for Harlem*, p. 275.

16   Letter to the author from Robert Weil, September 27, 2004.

17   *Requiem for Harlem*, p. 272, 269.

18   Ibid., p. 244.

19   Ibid., p. 168.

20   Donna Seaman, *The Booklist* 94:9/10 (January 1–15, 1998): 744.

21   Manus, "A Sister's Angry Letter," *New York Observer*, May 18, 1998, p. 30. Robin Pogrebin, "A Deep Silence of 60 Years, and an Even Older Secret," *New York Times*, May 16, 1998, p. B9.

22   Letter to the author from Robert Weil, September 27, 2004.

23   Sanford Pinsker, "Against the Current," *Washington Post Book World*, March 15, 1998, p. 15.

24   John F. Callahan, Afterword: A Note to Scholars, in Ralph Ellison, *Juneteenth*, ed. John F. Callahan (New York: Random House, 1999), p. 365, and Introduction, p. xxi.

25   William Ashbrook and Harold Powers, *Puccini's Turandot: The End of the Great Tradition* (Princeton, NJ: Princeton University Press, 1991), p. 152.

26   William Weaver, *The Golden Century of Italian Opera from Rossini to Puccini* (New York: Thames & Hudson, 1980), p. 242.

27   Callahan, Afterword, *Juneteenth*, p. 366.

28   *Requiem for Harlem*, p. 64.

:▊ C H R O N O L O G Y ▊:

1882	Chaim/Herman Roth born in Tysmenitz, Galicia
1897–1900	Herman Roth travels to the United States and is naturalized in St. Louis
1902	Herman leaves St. Louis for New York
1903	Herman returns to Tysmenitz
1905	January 10: Herman Roth and Leah Farb marry
1906	February 8: Herschel (Henry) Roth (HR) born in Tysmenitz
	Herman returns to America
1907	August: Leah and Henry emigrate in steerage, settling with Herman in Brownsville, New York
1908	Rose Roth born
1910	Move to Ninth St. and Avenue D, Lower East Side
1914	Move to Harlem—first the Jewish section, 114th St., then to non-Jewish 108 East 119th St.
1918	Uncle Morris goes off to World War I
1920	HR takes a summer job in vaudeville theater
1921	Caught stealing pens, HR withdraws from Stuyvesant High School

1924	June: HR graduates from DeWitt Clinton High School
	Autumn: Enrolls at College of the City of New York
1925	HR meets Eda Lou Walton. Summer in cottage at Woodstock, NY. Autumn: job at Loft's candy shop
1927	HR works at the IRT repair barn
1928	HR moves into Walton's 61 Morton St. apartment
	September: Graduates, B.S., from College of the City of New York
1930	HR at Peterborough Inn while Eda Lou Walton is at MacDowell Colony HR begins *Call It Sleep*
1932	June: HR drives to Maine. Stays in the Burnshaws' cottage, Norridgewock
1934	HR joins Communist Party of the United States (CPUSA)
	Summer: To California with Iven Hurlinger
	December: Robert Ballou publishes *Call It Sleep*
1935	May: HR beaten up visiting dockworkers; burns MSS
1938	Walton moves to third-floor apartment, Waverly Place
	Summer: HR at Yaddo Artists Colony; meets Muriel Parker, breaks with Walton. Drives to Los Angeles with Bill Clay
1939	February: HR hitchhikes and rides freights, then bus back to New York, arriving March 1
	Summer: Boardinghouse, 351 East 51st St., WPA job digging ditches in Queens
	September: Moves with Muriel to 17th-floor penthouse on 23rd St., shared with John and Betty Miller
	October 7: HR and Muriel Parker are married in Manhattan
1939–40	HR becomes a substitute teacher at Theodore Roosevelt High School, Fordham Rd., Bronx; the couple live at at 220 East 23rd St.
1940–44	HR registers with American Labor Party
1941	September–May 1942: HR works at Clix Zipper Co., NYC
	December 23: Jeremy Roth born
1942	May–December: HR at Master Tool and Die Co., NYC
1943	January–December: HR at Federal Machine Tool Company, NYC
	September 8: Hugh Roth born
	December–May 1945: HR at Gussack Machine Co., Long Island City
1945	June: The Roths move to the Boston area
	May–June: HR works at Federal Products Co., Providence, RI
1945–46	July 1945–August 1946: HR works at Keystone Manufacturing Co., Boston
	Family moves to 24 Hayes Street, Cambridge
1946	HR is appointed President, Industrial 1-A (Metal) Branch, CPUSA, District 1, Boston
	September: HR buys 110 acres in Montville, ME; works at Singer Sewing

Machine Co. in Dover-Foxcroft

October: Burns MSS; murders puppy

1947–48   HR teaches in a one-room schoolhouse at Montville

1949   Autumn: Buys house on 3.5 acres at Church Hill Road, north of Augusta

1949–53   HR works in the Augusta State Hospital

1950   Muriel contracts Guillain-Barré syndrome

1953–63   HR leaves Augusta State Hospital and starts "Roth's Waterfowl"

1956–65   HR tutors in math and Latin

1956   *Call It Sleep* is mentioned twice in "The Most Neglected Books of the Past Twenty-Five Years"—*The American Scholar*

1958   Charles Angoff lectures in Queens; Rose Broder tells him that her brother is alive

1959   Jeremy graduates from Phillips Exeter Academy

Summer: Harold Ribalow visits HR on his farm

1960   March 23: Leah Roth dies

September: Cooper Square Editions publishes *Call It Sleep*

November 30: NBC *Eternal Light* broadcasts a half-hour radio adaptation of *Call It Sleep*

1961   HR tutors in English, algebra, geometry, trigonometry, Latin

December: Mario Materassi requests permission to translate *Call It Sleep* into Italian; Eda Lou Walton dies in Oakland

1963   November 7: Hugh Roth joins U.S. Army

1964   Avon issues paperback edition of *Call It Sleep*

October 25: Irving Howe review in *New York Times Book Review*

1965   January: Roslyn Targ becomes Roth's literary agent

May 19: HR receives a grant in Literature, National Institute of Arts and Letters

October 1: Accepts Townsend Harris Medal for outstanding achievement by CCNY alumnus

1965–66   October 1965–January 1996: The Roths visit Seville and Morocco

1967   May: Roths travel to San Miguel de Allende and Guadalajara

June: HR becomes a Zionist

September 15: Joy Walker and Jeremy marry

1968   HR accepts D. H. Lawrence Fellowship at University of New Mexico, residence in Lawrence cottage north of Taos

1968–70   The Roths live on James and Norma Weaver's hacienda

1970   April: Herman Roth dies

1972   The Roths' first visit to Israel, on Hadassah tour

1973   February: The Roths move into Lot 17, Paradise Acres Mobile Home Park, Albuquerque

1975   Hugh marries Carole Nobel

Muriel has a mastectomy of the left breast

1976	January: HR has cataract removed from left eye
1977	August–September: The Roths are invited to Mishkenot Sha'ananim, Jerusalem
1978	February 10–March 14: HR returns, alone, to Tel-Aviv
1979	*Nature's First Green* published
	HR's hip operation
	HR begins writing the first volume of *Mercy of a Rude Stream*
1980	HR has a second cataract operation
1981	Mobile home moved to New York Avenue
	June 11–16: HR, as guest of honor at Bloomsday symposium, UNM, rails against Joyce
1985	HR's hernia operation
	Mario Materassi visits to persuade HR to publish collection of shorter pieces
1987	January 30: HR receives the Premio Internazionale Nonino—Percoto, northern Italy
	Shifting Landscape published
1988	January 15: Larry Fox meets HR
1989	February: Felicia Steele begins working for HR
1990	February 9: Muriel dies
	June: HR establishes Muriel Roth Memorial Music Scholarship at UNM
	HR spends six months in the Charter Hospital
1991	HR moves to the Las Colinas Retirement Center
	December: HR buys house at 300 Hendrix Road NW, Albuquerque
1992	February: Hana Wirth-Nesher visits HR
1993	January: Robert Weil meets HR
1994	May 14: HR awarded Honorary Doctor of Letters, UNM, and an honorary doctorate from Hebrew Union College, Cincinnati
	A Star Shines Over Mt. Morris Park published
1995	*A Diving Rock on the Hudson* published
	October 13: HR dies at Lovelace Hospital, Albuquerque
	November: Hugh Roth accepts posthumous Ribalow Award from *Hadassah* magazine
1996	February 29 declared "Henry Roth Day" in New York
	Holding On published
	From Bondage published
1998	*Requiem for Harlem* published

▌ HENRY ROTH: WORKS ▐

"Impressions of a Plumber," *Lavender* 3 no. 3 (May 1925): 5–9.

"Lynn Riggs and the Individual," in B. A. Botkin, ed., *Folk-say: A Regional Miscellany.* Norman, OK: University of Oklahoma Press, 1930, pp. 386–95.

Call It Sleep. New York: Robert O. Ballou, 1934.

"If We Had Bacon," *Signatures: Works in Progress* 1 no. 2 (1936): 139–58.

"Where My Sympathy Lies," *The New Masses* 22 (March 2, 1937): 9.

"Broker," *The New Yorker*, November 18, 1939, pp. 45–48.

"Somebody Always Grabs the Purple," *The New Yorker*, March 23, 1940, pp. 37–40.

"Many Mansions," *Coronet* (September 1940): 134–38.

"Equipment for Pennies," *The Magazine for Ducks and Geese* (Autumn 1954): 15–16.

"Petey and Yotsee and Mario," *The New Yorker*, July 14, 1956, pp. 66–70.

"At Times in Flight: A Parable," *Commentary* 28 (July 1959): 51–54.

"The Dun Dakotas," *Commentary* 30 (August 1960): 107–9.

Call It Sleep. New York: Cooper Square Editions, 1960.

"The Meaning of *Galut* in America Today," *Midsream* 9 no. 1 (March 1963): 32–33.

Call It Sleep. London: Michael Joseph, 1963.

Call It Sleep. New York: Avon, 1964.

"The Surveyor," *The New Yorker*, August 6, 1966, pp. 22–30.

"Final Dwarf," *The Atlantic* 224 (July 1969): 57–61.

"Henry Roth: No Longer at Home," *The New York Times*, Op-Ed, April 15, 1971, p. 43.

"Prolog in Himmel," *Shenandoah* 25 (Fall 1973): 44–47.

"Statement of Purpose," in Bonnie Lyons, *Henry Roth: The Man and His Work* (New York: Cooper Square Publishers, 1976).

"Kaddish," *Midstream* 23 no. 1 (January 1977): 53–55.

"Itinerant Ithacan," *New America* 3 (Summer–Fall 1977): 76–85.

"Report from Mishkenot Sha'ananim" and "Squib," *Albuquerque Jewish Community LINK* 6 (October 1977): 9.

"Vale Atque Ave," *Jerusalem Post Magazine*, October 14, 1977, p. 8.

"Segments," *Studies in American Jewish Literature* 5 (Spring 1979): 58–62.

Nature's First Green. New York: William Targ, 1979.

"Weekends in New York: A Memoir," *Commentary* 78 (September 1984): 47–56.

Shifting Landscape: A Composite, 1925–1987, intro and ed. Mario Materassi. Philadelphia: Jewish Publication Society, 1987.

Call It Sleep. New York: Noonday, 1991.

A Star Shines Over Mt. Morris Park. New York: St. Martin's Press, 1994.

A Diving Rock on the Hudson. New York: St. Martin's Press, 1995.

From Bondage. New York: St. Martin's Press, 1996.

Foreword to *Holding On*, ed. David Isay, photographs by Harvey Wang. New York: W. W. Norton, 1996. pp. 9–10.

Requiem for Harlem. New York: St. Martin's Press, 1998.

"Antica Fiamma." *Princeton University Library Chronicle*, LXIII 1–2 (Autumn 2001–Winter 2002): 282–91.

"Excerpt from Journal" *Princeton University Library Chronicle* LXIII 1–2 (Autumn 2001–Winter 2002): 292–300.

⫸ INDEX ⫷

ABOUT THE AUTHOR

Steven G. Kellman is the author of *The Translingual Imagination* (2000), The Plague: *Fiction and Resistance* (1993), *Loving Reading: Erotics of the Text* (1985), and *The Self-Begetting Novel* (1980). He is editor or coeditor of *Switching Languages: Translingual Writers Reflect on Their Craft* (2003), *UnderWords: Perspectives on Don DeLillo's* Underworld (2002), *Torpid Smoke: The Stories of Vladimir Nabokov* (2000), *Leslie Fiedler and American Culture* (1999), *Into* The Tunnel: *Readings of Gass's Novel* (1998), and *Perspectives on* Raging Bull (1994).

A contributing writer for the *Texas Observer*, Kellman received the 1986 H. L. Menken Award for his column in the daily *San Antonio Light*. His essays and reviews have appeared in *The American Scholar, Atlantic Monthly, Michigan Quarterly Review, New York Times Book Review, Georgia Review, The Nation, San Francisco Chronicle, Los Angeles Times, Chicago Tribune, Atlanta Journal-Constitution, Forward*, and *Virginia Quarterly Review*. He served two terms as a director of the National Book Critics Circle and was founding president of the literary center Gemini Ink. He has taught at universities in Minnesota, California, Israel, and Bulgaria and is currently a professor of Comparative Literature at the University of Texas at San Antonio.